GAMES AND DANCES

A SELECTED COLLECTION OF
GAMES, SONG-GAMES AND DANCES
SUITABLE FOR SCHOOLS, PLAY-
GROUNDS, GYMNASTIC ASSOCIA-
TIONS, BOYS' & GIRLS' CLUBS, ETC.

By

WILLIAM A. STECHER, M. P. E.

DIRECTOR, PHYSICAL EDUCATION PUBLIC SCHOOLS OF PHILADELPHIA, PA.
SECRETARY, COMMITTEE ON PHYSICAL TRAINING, AMERICAN GYMNASTIC UNION
EDITOR OF "MIND AND BODY"

Fourth Edition—Revised and Enlarged

PUBLISHED BY

JOHN JOSEPH McVEY

PHILADELPHIA, PA.

PREFACE

INCREASED attention to the physical welfare of children and adults, also the greatly increased number of playgrounds, has created a demand for a separate and enlarged edition of those activities of the Philadelphia "Handbooks of Lessons in Physical Training and Games," found under the headings of Games, Song-Plays, Dances and Roundels.

The plan followed in the other books is also adhered to here, namely, the games and dances suitable for children or adults of each particular school-grade or age-group are printed together. This procedure places into the hands of a teacher a graded selection of tried and effective games and dances. The games and dances are arranged in nine progressive grades. Games marked (R) can be played in a room as well as in a playground. In an appendix a limited selection of "quiet games" and "problems" for hot weather is presented. This is followed by a list of track and field events which may be undertaken on the average playground, and by the records which the ordinary boy and girl should make. Then come seven compositions suited for mass drills on play days or field days. Lastly comes much valuable information relating to the space necessary for different kinds of play, to play-courts, to the preparation playground teachers should have, to programs, salaries, etc., etc.

Games and plays may be classified into (a) play activities upon stationary apparatus of various kinds, and (b) into play without stationary apparatus. Into the first group fall the playful activities upon the swinging and traveling rings, giant strides, swings, low horizontal bars, ladders, poles, teeter boards, and like forms of suitable play apparatus for children and adults. These are all forms of appliances upon which any one without gymnastic training and without the aid of a teacher of gymnastics or of play may amuse himself to his heart's content. Quite a number of easy "stunts" may be performed upon such apparatus.

Into the second group, namely, play without stationary apparatus, fall all the play activities we know under the name of games. Guts Muths, in his classic book, "Games for Practice and Recreation," divides all games into two classes—motion games and quiet games.   In playground work we are interested mainly in games of motion, and in such forms of these as are found in the sub-division of "games which train observation and sense-judgment." These latter games may again be divided into so-called "teasing games" and "team games."   The team games may again be sub-divided into games of low and of high organization.   In games of low organization all participants play practically all parts of the game.   In games of high organization the team is divided into distinct groups, the members of each group performing some strictly defined part of the play.

Teachers often make the mistake of thinking that teasing games, like "Jacob, Where Are You?" "The Beetle Is Out," "Cat and Mouse," "Pussy Wants a Corner," "Spin the Plate," or games of imitation, like "Railroad," "Steamboat," etc., do not appeal to children over 8 years of age.   They do; even adults like to play such games.   But the interest in them lasts only a short period.   All players, even young children, soon tire of them.

What, then, makes some games appeal to players seemingly at all times? When such universally popular games, like most ball games, are analyzed, we find that their activities consist of chasing, throwing, striking, catching and like fundamental movements.   Now, while each separate one of these activities interests us, it is only as the difficulty of the execution of each separate activity is increased, or as several of these activities are combined into a game, that our interest also increases.   And if we study and inquire into the reason for this increased difficulty in games we find that it is principally the mental requirements which make games more difficult.   Very often the physical requirements are not increased at all in games that are of great interest to older children and to adults.   Note the following gradations of games where the physical activities are practically unchanged, but where, on account of the added, unforeseen incidents, a simple game for young children becomes a game for adults—e. g.:

A.   (1) Plain Tag, (2) Cross Tag, (3) Last Pair Run, (4) Three Deep, (5) Rabbits, (6) Prisoner's Base; or

B.   (1) Toss a Ball to a Player, (2) End Ball, (3) Corner Ball, (4) Center Ball, (5) Captain Ball; or

C.   (1) Toss a Ball Into a Box on the Ground, (2) Toss a Ball Into a Suspended Basket, (3) Chase Ball, (4) Basket Ball.

Every teacher should know these facts, as without them he is prone to lose his bearings. A fact never to be lost sight of is, that as more intricate psychic elements enter into the composition of a game such game will appeal more strongly to older players. If this is once understood it can readily be seen why even such fundamental activities as running, jumping, vaulting, climbing, swimming, etc., do not hold the interest of participants for any great length of time. As soon, however, as the element of competition (a mere psychic addition) is introduced the interest increases. This competition may be against other players, or it may be in the form of striving for a standard which every boy or girl of a certain age or of a specified school-grade should reach (exemplified by the "Efficiency Tests" or 'Button Tests" found in many cities, see pages 384-390. If, eventually, a number of players are formed into a team and are pitted against another team, the welfare of the group, of the school, of the community, is another added psychic element. When used for team competition one finds that the fundamental activities spoken of above, which in their simple form do not hold the interest of the participants for any length of time, are indulged in for much longer periods and with greater zest. The best types of games offer to the players both physical and mental difficulties. Games that afford a wise combination of physical and mental requirements are, therefore, an admirable means for physical, mental and moral training.

Instruction in plays and games should embrace a presentation of the central idea of the game or exercise to be learned; a statement of the physical, mental and moral effects (couched in language the player can understand) ; an explanation of the advantages and dangers of the game, and an outline of the rules with the reasons for the same.

Experience has shown that even in cold weather it is advisable for boys and girls to play in light-weight clothing. Hats and caps, except in very cold weather, should not be worn. Shoes without heels, but with broad soles, should be worn whenever possible. Girls should be encouraged to wear bloomers; unless they wear bloomers they should be forbidden to indulge in forms of exercise upon play-apparatus which cause their skirts to fly upward. The wearing of corsets should be discouraged continuously.

The natural expressions of joy or happiness caused by play should not be suppressed nor discouraged. Games and plays should give to the players opportunities to indulge in running, catching, dodging, throwing, etc., to their heart's content.   The laughing and shouting engendered by play are excellent forms of training for the respiratory organs, and as nerve-tonics they hold a high place.   The emotions aroused by play should, however, find a natural expression.   They must not be allowed to degenerate into roughness and rudeness.   Order and harmony must prevail on all playgrounds if play is to be of the greatest benefit to the players.   Play, therefore, demands supervision. This supervision must be sympathetic.   It should consist mainly of the organization of activities suitable to each particular playground, to each group of players and to the time of the year.   It should give all players an equal chance, and it must never degenerate into a "schoolmastering" of the players.

A liberal supply of good drinking water is a necessity on a playground. The players should be cautioned not to drink hastily, and not to drink too much water at a time.   Toilet facilities, also, are a great necessity.   The toilets should be placed so that they can easily be overseen.

Games, as a rule, should be played in the open air.   During the hottest part of the summer-days, also on days with excessive humidity, teachers should select games that do not demand much running.   On cold winter days games must be chosen that continuously keep all players in vigorous action. Experience has shown that there are very few days during the year when suitable games cannot be played.

While this book presents a rather large number of games for each grade and age, it would be a mistake to try and teach all of them.   A large selection is presented, so that teachers may find a sufficient number of good, lively games from which they may select those suited to their needs or conditions.   A few new games should be taught during each school-year, so that at the end of its school-life every child will thoroughly understand and play a goodly number of real gymnastic games.   What children—and adults—need is not an infinite number of games and dances, etc., but sufficient time and space to indulge in games and other physical activities suited to their age and to the season.

There is another mistake often made by inexperienced teachers.   This is the tendency continually to change standard games.   All true games are a natural growth.   They have sprung into existence because there was a demand for the organized activity which resulted in a game.   It is wise, therefore, not to depart from the fundamental forms of the best games. Variations, naturally, will suggest themselves. Temperature, space, equipment, the number of players, etc., will at times make it necessary and proper to vary games, but the true teacher will soon feel that players instinctively prefer the fundamental forms "as a regular diet."

Many games printed in this book were published in "Mind and Body," Milwaukee, Wis. The "Spring Song" and "Summer Breezes, by Arthur Richards; "The Wind" and "See-Saw," by W. B. Olds, from "Songs and Games for the Schoolroom," are from Novello's "Series of School Songs," and are printed by permission of the publishers, Novello, Ewer & Co., New York, N. Y. "In the Barn," by Charles Lindsay, and "Eros" by George Dudley Martin, are printed by permission of the publishers, Theo. Presser Company, Philadelphia, Pa.

"The Dorothy," by J. Bodewalt Lampe, is printed by permission of the publishers, Jerome H. Remick & Co., New York and Detroit. "Cupid and Butterfly" is printed by permission of the publisher, Carl Fischer, New York.

Permission to use songs or games was kindly given by the Milton Bradley Company, Springfield, Mass., for "Have You Ever Seen a Lassie," "Drop the Handkerchief," "Circles," and "Let Us Chase the Squirrel," by Miss Mari Ruef Hofer, for "How D'ye Do, My Partner," and "Needle's Eye," and by Mr. Jakob Bolin for "The Carrousel" and "I See you."

My thanks are further due to Mr. Emil Rath, dean of the Normal College, Indianapolis, Ind., for the contribution of numerous dances; to Miss Elizabeth O'Neill, supervisor of playgrounds, Philadelphia, for the plays and song-games for young children, and, finally, to Mr. Enoch W. Pearson, director of music, public schools, Philadelphia, for the arrangement of the music for many dances.

WILLIAM A. STECHER.

PREFACE TO SECOND EDITION

The many letters of appreciation received from practically all parts of the globe show that the arrangement of games and dances by age-groups and by grades has helped many teachers in their playground and school work. Although the present edition is enlarged considerably, the idea underlying the original book of presenting a limited number rather than many games and dances is still adhered to. After a new teacher has found himself in playground work, and he thoroughly knows most of the games and dances in this book applying to his particular problem, then he can use the larger games and dance books with much more profit.

My thanks are due to many teachers of physical training who by their suggestions have helped to increase the value of GAMES AND DANCES.

WILLIAM A. STECHER.

May, 1916.

PREFACE TO THIRD EDITION

The great war, naturally, has affected all forms of education and training. The changes in physical training work that have been suggested by the war are to be found in a simplification of the physical training material used, in a greater stress upon fundamental activities, and in a stronger emphasis upon mass athletic competition.

In this edition there have been added, therefore, besides many new games and dances, a very simple course in physical training, a chapter on the most usable forms of mass athletics and a teacher's guide for the coaching of the more common forms of athletic events. The course of study in physical training is based upon a few fundamental track and field events, and a carefully selected set of games for each school grade. Where the conditions are favorable these activities should be augmented by folk dances for each school grade.

Recent years have seen a great increase in the use of dances for physical development. The chief value of folk dances in physical education is that with a minimum of equipment they provide vigorous, enjoyable exercise in a comparatively small area. The dances selected for the course of study spoken of were chosen on account of their vigor, simplicity of steps and provision for limited or large numbers. They have been used in mixed classes, and have proved equally enjoyable to boys and girls. Heretofore there has apparently been no definite custom as to the direction in which the circular dances move. In these descriptions all dances which progress in the line of march have been directed counter-clockwise. They are thus made to harmonize with the general direction of ballroom dancing and of gymnastic marching.

The basis of the more spectacular parts of all pageants, plays and festivals is to be found in the marches, drills and dances as exemplified in the more advanced physical training work. Under the direction of Mrs. Bertha Fisher Welling and Miss Janet Walter the members of the physical training department of the Philadelphia Public Schools wrote and produced a pageant entitled: The Revival of the Play Spirit in America. There have been so many requests for copies of this elaborate production that the complete composition is included in this edition.

WILLIAM A. STECHER.

PREFACE TO FOURTH EDITION

GAMES AND DANCES has become the official games book for hundreds of cities. It is the result of much co-operation on the part of many teachers.

Teachers from all parts of the country are continually sending to us new games that they have devised, asking that these be added in a new edition. At other times, they advocate changes in standard games and dances. In the course of time these new games, and also the suggested changes, are tried out under the exacting conditions of a large school system with hundreds of playgrounds and gymnasiums. Teachers with years of experience apply rigid tests to all new suggestions. Sometimes it is found that a little change is needed to put life into a listless game; then, again, a game that is suggested for younger children may be changed into a good team game for older children or adults; and often it is found that new games hold the interest of the players for only a short period and then are no longer popular.

A new game, therefore, or a variation of a standard game must prove its usefulness for a long period and under different conditions before it is taken up in GAMES AND DANCES. This has resulted in making the book what it now is.

A book of games must have exceptional merit if there is such a continued demand for it that each succeeding edition is much larger than the preceding one. This has been the case with GAMES AND DANCES. From a book of one hundred sixty-five pages it has grown to one of four hundred twenty-four pages. In order not to increase the bulk of the book, thirty-two pages devoted in the former editions to organization and administration have been omitted in this fourth edition. As a result of this omission, and because of the inclusion of much new material in the form of song-plays for young children and of new games for older children and adults, the book has increased in value.

GAMES AND DANCES is a text-book for classroom teachers and for playground teachers. Teachers in recreation centers will find it indispensable. Normal schools and teachers' colleges will find that it is a valuable book to be placed in the hands of their pupils. And, lastly, parents have found the book of value in stimulating play among the members of the household.

Thanks for new material are due to so many teachers of physical education that it is impossible to mention them individually.

Philadelphia, June, 1926.   WILLIAM A. STECHER.

TABLE OF CONTENTS

PAGE

SONG-GAMES FOR CHILDREN UNDER NINE YEARS........................ 1

We All Stand Here, 1; Drop the Handkerchief, 2; Let Us Chase the Squirrel, 3; Did You Ever See a Lassie? 4; How D'ye Do, My Partner, 5; The Needle's Eye, 6; Oats, Peas, Beans and Barley, 7; The Muffin Man, 9; One by One, 10; Jolly Is the Miller, 12; The Farmer in the Dell, 13; Off for a Ride, 14; The Butterflies, 15; Pretty Birdie, 17; Snow Frolic, 18; Rig-a-Jig-Jig, 20.

GAMES AND SONG-GAMES FOR CHILDREN OF SIX TO NINE YEARS. FIRST
    SCHOOL-GRADE 23

Cat and Mouse (Cat and Rat), 23; What Are You Doing in My Garden? 23; Long Jumping Rope, 24; Running Races, 24; Hand Tag, 25; Squat Tag, 25; Skip Tag, 25; Follow the Leader, 25; Ball Games, 25; Catching the Beanbag, 26; Bound Ball, 26; Running Race, 27; Little Sister, Come With Me, 27; Chimes of Dunkirk, 29; Our Little Girls, 30; Dance of Greeting, 32.

GAMES AND SONG-GAMES FOR CHILDREN OF SEVEN TO TEN YEARS.
    SECOND SCHOOL-GRADE 35

Cat and Mouse (more difficult), 35; Change Tag, 35; Spin the Plate, 36; Hoop Toss With Peg Board, 36; Catch the Wand, 37; Jacob, Where Are You? 37; Jump Over, 37; Long Jumping Rope, 37; Racing, 37; Ball Games, 38; Bag Board, 38; Bag in the Ring, 38; Stand Dodgeball, 38; Catch Me, 38; Long Jumping Rope, 39; I See You, 39; My Brother, 41; The Carrousel, 44; Children's Polka, 45; The First of May, 46.

GAMES, SONG-GAMES AND DANCES FOR CHILDREN OF EIGHT TO TWELVE
    YEARS. THIRD TO FOURTH SCHOOL-GRADES............. 49

Running and Hopping Races, 49; Third Tag and Run, 49; Pussy Wants a Corner, 49; Animal Blind Man's Buff, 50; The Beetle Is Out, 50; Puss in the Circle, 51; Change Seats, Change, 51; Bag Relay, 52; Ball Games, 52; Duckstone, 52; Guess Who, 53; Fox and Chickens, 53; Potato Race, 53; Dayball, 54; Water Sprite, 54; Come, Little Partner, 54; Will You Dance With Me? 56; Spring Song, 58; The Fairies, 60; Shoemaker's Dance, 62; Annie Goes to the Cabbage Field, 63; Gustaf's Greeting, 64; Mountain March, 66.

GAMES AND DANCES FOR CHILDREN OF NINE TO FOURTEEN YEARS.
    FOURTH TO SIXTH SCHOOL-GRADES..................... 69

Black Man, 69; Lame Goose, 69; Break Through, 69; Catch the Wand, 69; Long Jumping Rope, 70; Leap Frog, 70; Wrestle for the Wand, 70; Hand-Pulling Contest, 70; Hand-Pushing Contest, 71; Shoulder-Pushing Contest, 71; Pushing Between Two Wands, 71; Pull-Over, 72; Foot in the Ring, 72; Ball Games, 72; Toss Up, 72; Day or Night, 73; Last Pair Run, 73; Circle Tag, 73; Red Rover,

PAGE

74; Chicken Market, 74; Trades, 75; Advancing Statues, 75; O'Leary, 76; "The Wind," 78; Children's Quickstep, 79; "See Saw," 81; The Elf's Frolic, 82; "Summer Breezes," 83; Playground Roundel, 83; Bleking, 86; Hop, Mother Annika, 86; Clap Dance, 87; Tantoli, 88.

GAMES AND DANCES FOR PLAYERS OF TEN TO FIFTEEN YEARS. FIFTH TO EIGHTH SCHOOL-GRADES....................................... 91

Relay Race, 91; Human Burden Race, 91; Poison, 92; Hopping Contests, 92; Ring Toss, 93; Quoits, 93; Hoop Toss, 93; Long Jumping Rope, 94; Ball Relay, 94; Bag Relay, 95; Chase Ball, 96; Medicine Ball, 96; Three Deep, 97; Jumping Circle, 98; Promotion Ball, 98; Stand Ball, 99; Volleyball (Form I), 100; Baseball as Playground Ball, 101; Corner Ball, 102; Endball (Form I), 104; Endball (Form II), 106; Wild Man's Field, 110; Broncho Tag, 110; Three Broad, 111; Number Race, 111; "In the Barn," 113; The Jolly Crowd (Form I), 116; The Jolly Crowd (Form II), 117; Ace of Diamonds, 119; Sweet Kate, 119; Come, Let Us Be Joyful, 121; Three Dance, 122.

GAMES AND DANCES FOR PLAYERS OF TWELVE TO SIXTEEN YEARS. SIXTH TO TENTH SCHOOL-GRADES..................... 125

Rabbits, 125; Hand Wrestling, 126; Wrist Wrestling, 126; Stick-I-Spy, 126; Overtake, 127; Pass Ball, 127; Pass Ball Variation, 128; Pass Ball With Encircling, 128; Wall Ball, 129; Basketball Far Throw, 129; Hurlball Far Throw, 129; Goal Throw, 130; Tower Ball, 130; Relievo, 131; Hop Scotch, 131; Rob and Run, 133; Foot and a Half, 134; Hat on Back, 135; Hat Ball, 135; Dodgeball (In a Circle), 136; Double Dodgeball, 140; Base Dodgeball, 141; Soccer Football (Form I), 141; Safety Tag, 143; Basket Endball, 143; Hand Tennis, 145; Block Baseball, 147; "Eros," 149; Butterfly Dance, 153; "Santiago," 155; A Spanish Couple Dance, 156; Crested Hen, 157; The Black Nag, 158; Czebogar, 159; Virginia Reel, 160.

GAMES AND DANCES FOR PLAYERS OF THIRTEEN YEARS AND OVER. SEVENTH TO TWELFTH SCHOOL-GRADES................ 163

Prisoner's Base, 163; Punch Ball, 164; Progressive Dodgeball, 164; Dodgeball in Three Fields, 167; Run Dodgeball, 167; Circle Pins, 168; Warball, 169; Volleyball (Form II), 170; Captainball, 171; Human Hurdle Race, 178; Soccer Football (Form II), 178; Shuttle Ball Relay, 181; Fox and Chickens Dodgeball, 182; May Day, 182; "Larkspur," 184; Normal School Mazurka, 187; Cupid and Butterfly, 189; Gathering Peascods, 196; Bluff King Hal, A May-Pole Dance, 198; Irish Lilt, 200; Reap the Flax, 201; Variations of Standard Games and Events, 203.

GAMES AND DANCES FOR PLAYERS OF FOURTEEN YEARS AND OVER. EIGHTH TO TWELFTH SCHOOL-GRADES................... 207

Rider Ball, 207; Battle Ball, 207; Handball, 208; Tether Ball, 208; Field Ball, 209; Captain Dodgeball, 211; Kick Ball in a Circle, 212; Wall Baseball, 213;

PAGE

Three Pins, 214; Jumping Circle Race, 214; Circle Relay Race, 215; Human Hurdle Circle Relay Race, 215; Jumping Circle Relay Race, 216; Combination Volleyball, 216; Tag Football, 216; Goal Ball, 220; Pinball, 222; Foot Baseball, 222; Wicket Ball, 223; Volleyball (Form III), 227; Soccer Football (Form III), 234; Frolic of the Brownies (Form I), 239; Frolic of the Brownies (Form II), 241; "Venus-Reigen," 244; Venus-Reigen (Dance, Form I), 247; Venus-Reigen (Form II), 248; "The Dorothy," Alumni Three-Step, 249, 253; Highland Schottische, 256; Oxdansen, 257; Rufty Tufty, 259; Ritka, 261.

APPENDIX I.   A SELECTION OF DRILLS AND DANCES SUITABLE FOR EXHIBITIONS, PLAY-DAYS, FIELD DAYS, PAGEANTS, ETC......... 263

Group I (Free Exercise Drills), No. 1, to the music of "Old Faithful," 263; No. 2, to the music of "In the Arena," 266; No. 3, to the music of "National Emblem March," 271; No. 4, to the music of "Here, There and Everywhere," 275; No. 5, to the music of "Officer of the Day March," 279; No. 6, to the music of "Sari," 281.
Group II (Free Exercises, with Dance Steps or Hopping), No. 7, to the music of "Teddy Bears' Picnic," 283; No. 8, to the music of "In Lilac Time," 287; No. 9, to the music of "Our Director March," 291.
Group III (Free Exercises and Marching), No. 10, to the music of "Keeping Step with the Union," 293; No. 11, to the music of "Marcia Militaire," 296; No. 12, to the music of "The Jolly General," 298; No. 13, to the music of "The Thunderer," 302.
Group IV (Free Exercises and Athletic Events), No. 14, to the music of "Moon Winks," 306; No. 15, to the music of "Hindustan," 310; No. 16, A Stunt Drill for Boys, 311.
Group V (Dances), No. 17, The Playful Sprites, to the music of "The Parade of the Wooden Soldiers," 315; a Dance for Girls, to the music of "Entr' Acte Gavotte," 317; No. 19, an Aesthetic Dance for Girls, to the music of "Marsovia Waltz," 320; No. 20, an Aesthetic Dance, to the music of "April Smiles," 322; No. 21, "The Nymphs," an Aesthetic Dance, to the music of "The Waltz Is Made for Love," 324.

APPENDIX II.   THE REVIVAL OF THE PLAY SPIRIT IN AMERICA—A PAGEANT 329

The Program, 329; Action of the Pageant, 332; Characters and PProperties, 337; Costumes, 339; Description of the Dances, 344-363.

APPENDIX III.   SUGGESTIONS FOR COACHING..................... 365

Sprinting, 365; Shuttle Relay Race, 366; Pursuit Relay Race, 367; Standing Broad Jump, 368; Running Broad Jump, 369; Hop, Step and Jump, 369; Running High Jump, 370; Basketball Overhead Far Throw, 372; Knee Raising, 372; Chinning, 372; Potato Race, 373; Tug of War, 373; Hurdling, 374.

PAGE

APPENDIX IV. COMPETITIVE MASS ATHLETICS.................... 377

Track Events, 377; Field Events, 378; Combative Events, 380; Team Games of
Low Organization, 380; Handicap and Combination Races, 381; Stunts, 382.

APPENDIX V. ADDITIONAL PLAYGROUND ACTIVITIES................ 383

Charts Showing Aims in Track and Field Events, for Elementary Schools,
384, 385; for High Schools, 386, 387, 388; Events and Standards for Athletic
Ability Tests, 389.

APPENDIX VI. QUIET GAMES, EXPERIMENTS, PROBLEMS, ETC., FOR
WARM DAYS 393

Simon Says Thumbs Up, 393; Bird Catcher, 393; Arms, Legs and Trunks, 393;
Fly Away, 394; Buzz, 394; Save Yourself If You Can, 394; Tossing the Cap, 395;
Advancing Statues, 395; How Many Angles, 395; Floating Feather, 395; Button,
Button, Who's Got the Button? 395; What Am I Thinking Of? 396; Rope and
Ring, 396; Earth, Air and Water, 396; A Talk-Fest, 397; Hit or Miss, 397;
Charades, 397; Simple Experiments, 398.

GAMES AND DANCES

SONG-GAMES
FOR CHILDREN UNDER NINE YEARS

Many games and dances described for the lower grades in this book
may with perfect propriety be selected for older children and adults.

We All Stand Here.

We all stand here in this nice ring And as we stand we gai - ly sing, Now

clap your hands for this is fun, The one I touch shall quick - ly run.

The children stand in a ring, joining hands. One child is chosen to
be the runner, who leaves the ring and walks around the outside until the
words of the song, with the accompanying action, indicate the time the pursuer
must leave the ring to give chase. If the runner is not caught before he reaches
his place in the ring the children clap hands and the game proceeds as before.

1

Drop the Handkerchief.

By a Wheelock Graduate, '01,

Round the ring {she he} goes. Drop the handkerchief, Drop the handkerchief,

Where {she'll he'll} drop it no-bod-y knows, Tra la, tra la, tra la!

Copyright by Milton Bradley Co., Springfield, Mass.

This is a melody first published in the *Kindergarten Review*, and sung while playing a game similar to "The Beetle Is Out," described among the games for the third grade. The players, standing closely together, are formed in a ring facing toward the center. One player, with a handkerchief in his hands, walks around the outside. During the singing, "Where He'll Drop It, Nobody Knows," he drops the handkerchief behind a player standing in the ring. This player must pick it up, pursue the one who dropped it and try to tag him before he reaches his place in the ring.

Let Us Chase the Squirrel.*

Words and Music by Annie L. Preston.

Lively.

1. Let us chase the squir - rel, Up the hick - o - ry, down the hick - o - ry,
2. If you want to catch me, Up the hick - o - ry, down the hick - o - ry,

Let us chase the squir - rel, Up the hick - o - ry tree.
If you want to catch me, Learn to climb a tree.

Copyright by Milton Bradley Co., Springfield, Mass.

A game of pursuit, in which there is an obstruction, necessitating more alertness and cunning (dodging) on the part of the one pursued.

The children stand apart, in concentric circles or in straight rows, representing trees. Two children are chosen, one to be the runner and the other to be pursuer.

Care must be taken that the spaces between the trees will permit freedom in running between and dodging in and out and around in any direction until the end of the song, when the successful evader is vigorously applauded. Each child ought to know his position in the game, and at the end of each game each child chooses one to take his place, saying: "You are to be the squirrel"; or "You are to *chase* the squirrel."

GAMES AND DANCES
Did You Ever See a Lassie?

E. S.

Allegro.

Did you ev - er see a las - sie, a las - sie, a las - sie, Did you

ev - er see a las - sie do this way and that? Do

this way and that way? Do this way and that way? Did you

ev - er see a las - sie do this way and that?

The children are formed in a ring, facing inward. A lassie (or a laddie) is chosen, and takes her place in the center. All sing. When singing "Do this way and that," the player in the center shows a movement that may be performed by all players. Upon seeing the chosen movement, all players imitate it while singing the rest of the song. The movement chosen should admit of being performed in the rhythm of the song. This game gives a fine opportunity for creative activity. The teacher should give as much opportunity for freedom of choice as the game may suggest.

How D'ye Do My Partner?

Swedish.

How-d'ye do my part - ner, How dy'e do to - day?

Will you dance in the cir - cle? I will show you the way.

Repeat, skipping with a chorus of tra-la-la during the skip.

This may be played as a very simple skipping game for very little children. The children stand in a circle, one child steps in and chooses a partner, as the words indicate, then two, or more, children choose, etc. The children in the circle clap in time to tra-la-la.

For older children the game may be played in the form of a folk dance.

Count off 1, 2, around the circle. The odd number steps into the circle and faces the child to the left, thus forming a double circle.

When singing, "How d'ye do, my partner," the partners bow to each other; "How d'ye do to-day," the partners shake hands.

"Will you dance in the circle?" }
"I will show you the way." } Cross arms, grasping hands, and face to the head of the circle, taking a position for skipping.

During the chorus of "Tra-la-la," skip around the circle until arriving at one's place; the children on the outer side of the circle remain in place, those on the inside move forward to the next partner. Then repeat the whole play as often as desired.

The Needle's Eye.

American.

The need-le's eye that doth sup-ply The thread that runs so tru-ly,

There's many a lass that I've let pass Be-cause I want-ed you;

Be-cause I want-ed you, Be-cause I want-ed you;

There's many a lass that I've let pass Be-cause I want-ed you.

This is a song-game, similar to "London Bridge." Two children grasp hands, and by raising their arms form an arch. While singing, the other players continue to pass through the arch. When "Because I wanted you" is sung the last time the two leaders drop their arms around the child just passing under the arch. The question is then put to this one (so that the other players do not hear it), "Do you choose pins or needles?" After making a choice the child takes its place behind the one whose side was chosen. The play continues until all are caught. The players then catch a good hold of the one in front of them and a tug-of-war ensues.

Oats, Peas, Beans and Barley.

English.

Oats, peas, beans and barley grow, Oats, peas, beans and barley grow, Can you or I or

an - y-one know How oats, peas, beans and barley grow? Thus the farmer sows his seed,

Thus he stands and takes his ease, Stamps his foot and claps his hands And

Oats, Peas, Beans and Barley.—Concluded.

3.

turns around and views the land. Waiting for a part-ner, Waiting for a part-ner,

O-pen the ring and choose one in, While we all gai-ly dance and sing.

1. Front circle formation, neighbors' hands grasped. One player stands in the center and is the "farmer." The other players walk in a circle left and sing the first stanza.

2. During the second stanza the players in the circle stand still, release grasp and go through the motions of the "farmer," who does as the song says. For instance, during the singing of the first line they imitate a farmer scattering seed, during the singing of the second line all stand in a stride position, arms folded, as though they were taking life easy. During the singing of the third and fourth lines they stamp their left foot, clap their hands and turn around (to the left or right) as though viewing the land.

3. All during the third stanza the players march in a circle left. During the singing of the first two lines the "farmer" walks up to one of the players, and as the third is sung this player steps into the circle. As the fourth is sung both skip around inside the circle, moving in opposite directions to the circle.

The one chosen into the center now becomes the "farmer," and all is repeated.

The Muffin Man.

American.

Oh, do you know the muf - fin man, The muf - fin man, the
muf- fin man, Oh, do you know the muf-fin man, That lives in Dru - ry Lane?

The class is in a front circle formation, neighbors' hands grasped.

One of the pupils enters the circle and, while singing the following words, takes four skipping steps (or walking steps) forward and four backward in front of one of the players:

1. "Oh, do you know the muffin-man,
    The muffin-man, the muffin-man?
    Oh, do you know the muffin-man
    That lives in Drury Lane?"

2. The other players answer while jumping in place, with hands on hips:

    "Oh, yes, I know the muffin-man," etc.

The one addressed and the one in the center then take hands, and while skipping around the inside of the circle, sing:

    "Now, two of us know the muffin-man," etc.

Those in the circle clap hands and jump in place.

The play is then continued by these two players repeating 1 in front of two others.

Then the four sing while skipping around in the center:

"Now, four of us know the muffin-man," etc.

When all the players have partners, they skip in a circle and sing:

"Now, all of us know the muffin-man,
The muffin-man, the muffin-man;
Now, all of us know the muffin-man
That lives in Drury Lane."

One By One.*

B. E. Hailmann.

1. One by one, one by one, One by one, here we go! With

mer - ry hearts and cheer - ful song, As we march in a sin - gle row With

mer - ry hearts, and cheer - ful song, As we march in a sin - gle row.

* Copyright by B. E. Hailmann.

FIRST STANZA.

The children stand in a circle, which has been divided into two parts, each part having a leader. When beginning to sing, they face their leaders, following them through the center and then outward to their original position.

Repeat these movements and stand until the song ends. (See Diagram I.)

SECOND STANZA.

Two by two, two by two,
    Two by two, here we go!
Now we arch the way, in long array;
    We will creep thro' the double row.
Now we arch the way, in long array;
    We will creep thro' the double row.

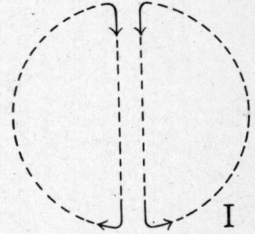

Again march through the center, joining hands. When arriving at the opposite side of the circle march to the left (by twos), to the starting point. (See Diagram II.) Then again march through the center; halt and face partner, raising the grasped hands to form an arch. The leaders march through the arch, the others following. One leader then marches to the left and the other to the right around the circle. (See Diagram III.)

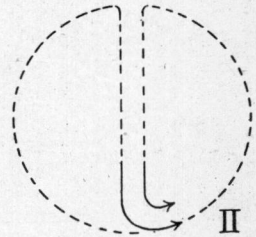

THIRD STANZA.

Hand in hand, hand in hand,
    Hand in hand, here we go!
Now we make the ring, and gaily sing,
    With a ho, ho, ho, ho, ho;
Now we make the ring, and gaily sing,
    With a ho ho, ho, ho ho!

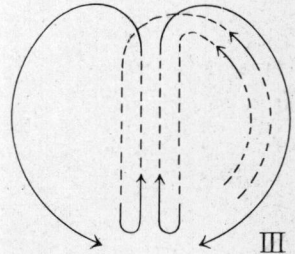

The partners join hands and dance around the circle, as the words indicate, clapping hands when singing "With a ho, ho, ho, ho, ho!"

Repeat as often as desired. When singing the first stanza the leaders march through the center as indicated in Diagram I.

Jolly is the Miller.

English.

Jol - ly   is   the   mil - ler   who   lives   by   the   mill,   The

wheel goes 'round with   a   right good   will;   One hand   in   the hop - per and the

oth - er   in   the sack,   The   right   steps   for-ward and the   left   steps back.

This song-game may be played by adults and children. The players form a circle composed of couples. When teaching the game to children, play at first without the miller (the player who has no partner and who is in the center). Starting the game, the players sing and march in the circle. At the words, "The right steps forward and the left steps back," the children do as indicated. As soon as this changing of partners is well understood add the miller. Now, as change of partners takes place, the miller tries to get a partner. If he succeeds, the player left without a partner becomes miller.

The Farmer in the Dell.

The far - mer in the dell, The far - mer in the dell,

Heigh - ho, the Der - ry oh, The far - mer in the dell.

Formation: The children stand in a single circle, facing inward, hands grasped. In the circle stand four children, personifying the farmer, the sun, the rain and the wind.

First verse: All sing: "The farmer in the dell, the farmer in the dell, heigh-ho, the Derry oh, the farmer in the dell." During the singing the children in the circle, without releasing hands, face right and march around in a circle.

Second verse: All sing: "The Farmer sows his seed," etc. The child personifying the Farmer rounds his left arm as if it were a basket. Walking around in the inside of the circle, he sows the seed with a large, sweeping motion of his right hand. The players forming the circle stoop as the farmer passes by.

Third verse: All sing: "The Sun begins to shine," etc. The child personifying the Sun, raising her arms in a circle overhead, skips around the inside of the circle, shining on all the Seeds. The Seeds, while stooping, wiggle from side to side.

Fourth verse: All sing: "The Rain begins to fall," etc. The Rain runs around the circle, arms raised high and moving the fingers in imitation of falling raindrops. The Seeds raise their heads.

Fifth verse: All sing: "The Seeds begin to grow," etc. During the singing the children in the circle rise slowly and gradually stretch their arms upward.

Sixth verse: All sing: "The Wind begins to blow," etc. The Wind runs around in the circle, waving her arms from side to side. During the singing the Wheat sways gently from side to side.

Seventh verse: All sing: "The Farmer cuts his Wheat," etc. The Farmer, walking around the circle, with a wide movement of his right arm cuts the wheat. The players in the circle drop their (upraised) arms to the side as the Farmer passes them.

Eighth verse: All sing: "He binds them into sheaves," etc. The Farmer, running around, forms groups of three or four pupils into sheaves. Each group of pupils forming a "bundle" of wheat joins hands.

Ninth verse: All sing: "The Sheaves begin to dance," etc. Each bundle or sheaf of wheat skips around in its own little circle. Repeating the last verse, the players dance in the opposite direction.

Off for a Ride.

1. { I would like to go to Shet-land, Come and take a trip with me ;
I would like to ride a po-ny— I can do it, you shall see. }

CHORUS.

Gee up, come a-long, Gee up, come a-long, Gee up, come along, Whoa! Back! Whoa!

2. I would like to go to Lapland,
    Come and take a trip with me;
  I would like to drive a reindeer—
    I can do it, you shall see.

3. I would like to go to Highland,
    Come and take a trip with me;
  I would like to drive a big goat—
    I can do it, you shall see.

Formation: The players are standing in a front circle. They then count off by twos, forming horse and rider. All face to the right, march forward (in single file) and sing the first verse. At the chorus number one holds his hands out behind him, and number two grasps them. All gallop forward, arranged in couples. They stop when singing, "Whoa," step backward at "Back," and stand still at "Whoa."

The Butterflies.

Words and Action by W. A. Oakes.

German Folk Song.

We are but-ter-flies flit-ting And we dip here and there, We are aft-er the hon-ey from the blos-soms so fair. Pret-ty flow-er where have you All the sweet-ness I crave? Oh, I thank you most kind-ly For the hon-ey you gave.

Formation: The players are arranged in couples standing in a large circle, the partners (a boy and a girl) facing each other. The boys, on the inner side of the circle, represent flowers. The girls, on the outer side, represent butterflies. The boys kneel on one knee.

SONG.

I.

1. We are butterflies flitting,
   And we dip here and there;
   We are after the honey
   From the blossoms so fair.

2. Pretty flower, where have you
   all the sweetness I crave?

3. Oh, I thank you most kindly

4. For the honey you gave.

II.

1. We are butterflies flitting,

2. And we dip here and there,

3. For we're after the honey

4. From the blossoms so fair.

ACTIVITY.

I.

1. Girls run around the circle to the left, arms fluttering to imitate butterflies. Nod to each flower in passing.

2. Girls stop in front of boys and, with arms sideward, step curtsy in line of march. Step curtsy in opposite direction.

3. Girls, with arms raised to a circle overhead, turn about to the right on toes (running steps in place).

4. Girls, with arms sideward, bend forward.

II.

1. Girls run to center of circle, 6 counts, passing to left of partner.

2. Boys begin to grow. Girls turn right-about in 6 counts.

3. Girls run out to former place, 6 counts.

4. Boys bow, girls extend arms sideward, bend forward.

5. Pretty flower, where have you all the sweetness I crave?

5. Boys and girls join hands, extend arms sideward, step and curtsy in line of march. Step and curtsy in opposite direction.

6. Oh, I thank you most kindly

6. Both raise arms to a circle overhead and turn about on toes.

7. For the honey you gave.

7. Both bow.

PRETTY BIRDIE.

Same song as "The Butterflies." Song game for young children. Formation: The children are formed in a single front circle, arranged in couples.

SONG.

1. Pretty Birdie, who are you,
2. Flying 'round in the air?

3. Are your little ones hiding
4. In the tree tops up there?
5. You fly and you chatter,
6. You turn and you peep;

7. Are your little ones hiding
8. In the tree tops up there?

Little Birdies are grown now,
Flutter early and late,
And they soon find a partner
Whom they like as a mate.
You hold them, you scold them,
Want to keep them at home,
But they soon find a partner
Whom they like as a mate.

ACTION.

1, 2. While singing, each child describes a small circle left, waving arms as if flying.

3, 4. Stand and point up in the air.

5, 6. With small steps, run in the line of march, wave arms and turn about once.

7, 8. Stand and point up in the air.

1, 2. Each child describes a small circle left, waving arms.

3-8. Partners join hands. Step forward in the line of march.

Snow Frolic.

1. Ho! Ho! Ho! So! So! So! Read-y for frol-ic and fun,
We'll pick up snow and roll it so, In-to a snow-ball round;
Here's one for you, and one for you, And one for you and you.

Formation: The pupils are arranged in a single front circle, hands grasped. One player has been selected by the teacher to act as the snowman.

SONG.	ACTIVITY.
I.	I.

Ho! Ho! Ho!
So! So! So!　　　　} Swing arms forward and backward.
Ready for frolic and fun;

We'll pick up snow
And roll it so
Into a snowball round;

> Stoop, pick up snow and make snowballs.

Here's one for you
And one for you
And one for you and you.

> Throw balls at each other across the circle.

II.

Big snowman,
You must go;
We will knock you down;

> The snowman slowly walks to center of circle, with arms raised sideward. The other children point at him.

Your right arm first,

> Snowman drops right arm.

Your left arm next,

> Snowman drops left arm.

> The other children throw balls at him.

And *pop!* there goes your head!

> Snowman drops head.

> Children clap hands on *pop*.

Your body falls,

> Snowman bends trunk forward.

Your great legs, too;

> Falls to ground.

> Continue throwing.

I think you must be dead.

> Children point at the fallen snowman.

NOTE—At the end of the second verse the snowman rejoins the circle of players.

III.

Ho! Ho! Ho!
Fingers cold;
Feet are frozen, too;

> The players stand still, arms raised forward, shake hands and fingers. Stamp feet.

Then slap, slap, slap!
And clap, clap, clap,
As scamp'ring home we go!

{ Cross arms over chest and slap shoulders three times.
Clap hands in front of chest three times.
Grasp hands, face right and run forward in tiny steps.

Then slap, slap, slap!
And clap, clap, clap,
As scamp'ring home we go!

{ Cross arms over chest and slap shoulders three times.
Clap hands in front of chest three times.
Grasp hands, face right and run forward in tiny steps.

Rig-a-jig-jig.

As I was walk-ing down the street, Heigh-o, heigh-o, heigh-o, heigh-o, A
Said I to her "Will you skip with me? Heigh-o, heigh-o, heigh-o, heigh-o," Said

pret - ty girl I chanced to meet, Heigh - o, heigh - o,...... heigh - o.
she to me, "With a one, two, three, Heigh - o, and a - way we go."

Rig-a-jig-jig — Concluded.

CHORUS.

Rig- a - jig-jig and a-way we go, A-way we go, a-way we go;

Rig- a - jig-jig and a-way we go, Heigh-o, heigh-o, heigh-o. Heigh-

o, heigh-o, heigh-o, heigh-o, Heigh-o, heigh-o, heigh-o, heigh-o;

Rig- a - jig-jig and a-way we go, Heigh-o, heigh-o, heigh-o.

Front circle formation, hands grasped, one player in the center. During the verse the players in the ring walk in a circle left. The player in the center walks to the right and, during the words, "A pretty girl I chanced to meet," chooses a partner from the ring. Joining hands, they walk on together.

During the chorus the players forming the ring stand in place and clap. Those in the center skip (or polka) to the right during the first half of the chorus and to the left during the second half.

Players in the center separate at the end of the chorus and repeat the actions, choosing new partners at the proper time. The game is repeated until all players have partners.

GAMES AND SONG-GAMES
FOR CHILDREN OF SIX TO NINE YEARS

First School-Grade.

CAT AND MOUSE.   (Cat and Rat.)

The players stand in a circle facing inward, grasping hands.   The teacher chooses one child as the cat, who stands outside, and another child as the mouse, who stands inside the circle.   The cat tries to catch the mouse, who runs in and out of the circle.   When the mouse is caught, or when the teacher finds the two have run enough, they return to their places, and the next two players standing to the right become the cat and mouse.

As the children become more proficient, or when the cat is very active, the players try to prevent the cat from catching the mouse by suddenly lowering their arms after the mouse has slipped through the circle.

WHAT ARE YOU DOING IN MY GARDEN?   (Garden Scamp,

Fox and Gardener.   Cat and Mouse Variation.)

The players stand in a circle with hands grasped.   One player, without the circle, is the gardener, and another within is the thief.   The following dialogue then ensues:

Gardener: "What are you doing in my garden?"

Thief: "I am eating apples" (or any other fruit).

Gardener: "Who gave you permission?"

Thief: "Nobody."

Gardener: "Then escape if you can."

The thief now runs out of the circle underneath the arms of two of the players, then runs anywhere, in and out, till he finally re-enters the circle by the opening through which he first passed out.   The gardener all the while pursues him, following him in all the turns he makes, and tries to touch him before he can re-enter the circle through the right opening.   If successful, the

23

gardener chooses a new thief, the caught one taking his place in the circle, and the play goes on as before. If the gardener does not catch the thief, or makes a mistake in following in his path, he forfeits his part; the thief now becomes gardener, chooses a new thief, and the former gardener returns to the circle.

LONG JUMPING ROPE.

Form the children in a column of twos. Tie one end of the rope to a post, or let a pupil hold it. Swing the rope in a circle toward the class, and at first let them run through at will. Later let them run through at every second swing. After that let them catch hands by twos and run through at every second swing.

After the running is accomplished fairly well, take up the jumping over the rope. The rope must be held so lightly that if any child in jumping touches it, the rope will fall. Insist that all jumping is done on the balls of the feet.

Lastly, take up the jumping "in the rope." Let a child run in, jump twice, or three times, and then run out. Later have this done by twos.

JUMPING ROPE. (R.)

A pupil holds one end of the rope and the teacher the other. The rope must be held so lightly that if any one touches it, it will fall to the floor.

The first row rises and passes to the front. Now swing the rope in a circle toward the class. Let each one run through the rope. (See that the children run on the balls of their feet.) Then let the second row rise, face to the rear and follow in the course of the first, etc.

Variations: As described in the preceding game.

RUNNING RACES.

Arrange your class in ranks of six or eight. Put a chalk-mark on the floor where the first rank stands and another one about twenty to thirty feet away. At the commands "Get ready" and "Go," the ones in the first rank run toward the goal. They re-form a few steps back of the goal line, while the second rank steps up to the starting line, etc.

Races over a short distance may also be had by allowing the contestants to hop on one foot instead of running.

In a clear yard or on grass, little boys also enjoy a short race on "all fours." Upon command they get down on hands and feet (not knees) and race.

HAND TAG. (R.   May also be played in the yard.)

Arrange the class in an oval in the space in front of the seats.   All pupils raise their arms forward, palms up.   One of the class passes along the inside of the oval and tries to tag the hand of a pupil.   As soon as the tagger tries to slap a hand, it should suddenly be lowered.   Who is tagged three times is out of the game.   Change the tagger frequently; or play the game so that he who is tagged takes the place of the tagger.   In crowded rooms the seats may be raised and the pupils stand between the desks, the tagger walking up and down the aisles.   In the yard this game is played in a circle.

SQUAT TAG.   (R.)

The children move about; any one may be tagged who does not quickly bend his knees and "squat" when the tagger approaches.   The one tagged when not squatting is "it."

SKIP TAG.   (R.   May also be played in the yard.)

Arrange the class in a half circle in front of the seats.   One of the class skips along the front, tagging a comrade.   The tagged one skips after the tagger, trying to catch him.   The tagger skips around the outside of the room (where the aisles are usually wide, so that no one can stumble) until he reaches his place.   Now the second pupil is tagger, and so on.   Insist on skipping on the balls of the feet and allow no running, and this will be a safe room game.

In the yard this game is played in a circle, the children facing inward, the tagger being on the outside.

FOLLOW THE LEADER.   (R.)

One player is chosen as leader, and at the head of a line of players leads them around, in and out, over obstacles, running, hopping, and doing various evolutions, each player following the movements of the leader as exactly as possible.   The teacher should at times change the leader.

A variation of this is to have the leader stand facing the line of players and do various movements of any part of the body, the others following as rapidly and accurately as possible.

BALL GAMES.

In the lowest grades beanbags (about 5 x 6 inches) are used.   Each pupil should have a beanbag.   Arrange your class in a circle facing inward.

(a) First let the children toss the bags upward, catching them with both hands.

(b) Let them toss up and catch with one hand.

(c) Arrange your class by twos, facing each other, one bag for the two players. Upon command let them toss from one to the other. Increase the difficulty by having the children catch with one hand, by having them toss high, or by increasing the distance between the players.

(d) Teacher-ball. Arrange your class in front ranks of eight. The first one is the teacher (or leader). He stands about six or eight feet in front of his rank and begins the game by tossing the bag to the one now at the head of the rank; this one tosses it back, then the teacher tosses it to the second, who returns it, etc. Whoever misses goes to the foot of the rank. If the teacher misses he also goes to the foot, the player at the head of the rank taking his place.

CATCHING THE BEANBAG. (R. May also be played in the yard.)

The children are in their seats. The teacher has two or more beanbags. Saying, "John, catch this," she tosses it to John. If he catches it the boys count one. The next time she throws a bag to Mary, and if she catches it the girls score one. (If a bag is not caught no score is made.) See who wins after a specified number of tosses are made.

For older children, this may be varied by letting them count two, three, etc., for each catch, and by deducting a certain number for every miss.

If you have no beanbags, make a ball by rolling up a newspaper and tying a string around it.

With older children, a small gas ball, or tennis ball may be used (as this is more difficult to catch).

BOUND BALL. (R. May also be played in the yard.)

Apparatus: An inflated rubber ball about six inches in diameter (a gas ball) and a wastebasket. Arrange from four to six boys in the open space on one side of the room and the same number of girls on the other side. Put the wastebasket in the center of the free space between them. The first one of the boys will throw and bounce the ball on the floor, trying to make it bound into the basket. The first girl gets the ball and tries the same from her side. Every basket made counts one point for the side that made it.

If played in the yard a box may be used in place of a basket. A large, inflated ball (basket-ball, dodge-ball, volley-ball, etc.) may also be used.

RUNNING RACE.

Have the first four girls and four boys step to a chalk-mark on the ground, arm's length apart. Let them run to another chalk-mark, about twenty steps distant, and back again. Command, "Get ready. Run." Those who run step to the rear of their files, and the next eight get ready. After all have had a run, quickly re-form the class.

Little Sister Come With Me.

German.

Lit - tle sis - ter come with me, Both my hands I give to thee;

Come with me 'round the ring As we march and as we sing.

With our heads we nod, nod, nod, With our fin - gers shake, shake, shake,
With our feet we tap, tap, tap, With our hands we clap, clap, clap,

Then we dance, then we sing, Then we glad - ly dance and sing.

LITTLE SISTER COME WITH ME (German).

Steps: Marching, skipping.

Formation: Double circle of couples, boy on the left of girl, left sides toward center.

Music: Two parts of 8 measures each. The last 4 measures of Part I are repeated and all of Part II. Polka rhythm (2 counts to a measure).

PART I.

Little sister come with me;	Partners bow to each other.
Both my hands I give to thee.	Partners cross inner arms and grasp hands.
Come with me 'round the ring	While singing remainder of stanza all march around in a circle counter-clockwise.
As we march and as we sing,	
Come with me 'round the ring	
As we march and as we sing.	

PART II.

With our heads we nod, nod, nod;	Halt. Partners face and perform the movements named.
With our fingers shake, shake, shake;	Shake right forefinger three times.
Then we dance, then we sing;	Partners face in line of march, join hands and skip in circle counter-clockwise.
Then we gladly dance and sing.	

PART III.

With our feet we tap, tap, tap;	Same as Part II. (Stamping left, right, left.)
With our hands we clap, clap, clap;	
Then we dance, then we sing;	
Then we gladly dance and sing.	

NOTE—On the Victor Record there are 16 measures following Part I, which do not appear in the music on page 27. During those 16 measures the following action is used:

Partners join inside hands, and face.

Dance would I, if I knew how;	Step sideward in the line of march, and curtsy (place other foot in rear, and bend knees).
When to dance and how to bow.	Repeat to the other side.
Please tell me what I ought to do,	Join both hands, and in four running steps circle clockwise, finishing facing partner.
So I can dance the steps like you.	Four glides sideward in the line of march.
	Repeat the above 8 measures.

CHIMES OF DUNKIRK (French).

Victor Record 17,327 (Chord—Dance is played twice).

Steps: Running, marching.
Formation: Single circle of couples, facing center, boy on the left of girl.
Music: Two parts of 8 measures, first part repeated and played once after second part. Polka rhythm (2 counts to a measure).

PART I.

Measures:

2. Partners face. Beginning left, march three steps in place and pause (counts 1 to 4).

2. Clap hands three times and pause (counts 5 to 8).

4. Grasp partner's hands, arms sideward, and beginning left, run in a small circle clockwise, turning once and slightly turning body left (counts 9 to 16).

8. Repeat above 8 measures (counts 1 to 16).

PART II.

8. All face center, grasp hands and beginning left, with sixteen running steps circle clockwise (counts 1 to 16).

8. Repeat 8 measures of Part I (counts 1 to 16).

WORDS.

||:Come now mark time with me,
And clap your hands in glee,
And when the chimes so sweetly sound
Join hands and swing around.:||—*Fine.*

Step away with me,
Oh step away with me,
Oh step away with me
With a one, two, three.—*D. C.*

NOTE—Music may be found in "Folk Dances and Singing Games,"
E. Burchenal; "Children's Song Games," Mari Hofer.

OUR LITTLE GIRLS (Swedish).

Victor Record 17,510 (Introduction, chord—Dance is played three times).

Steps: Marching and skipping.

Formation: Single circle, all facing center, hands joined, several boys or
girls inside circle.

Music: Sixteen measures, repeated. Polka rhythm (2 counts to a
measure).

PART I.

Measures:

8. Dancers forming large circle, beginning with left foot, march in
a circle counter-clockwise, two steps to a measure, swinging joined hands
in and out, in time with music. At the same time dancers inside circle march
in opposite direction, keeping close to large circle (counts 1 to 16).

8. As they sing the words "And if" those within the circle choose
partners from circle. Those in circle close gaps and continue marching in
same direction, while couples continue the march inside (counts 17 to 32).

PART II.

Measures:

4. Those in circle skip in same direction, while couples in center join hands and skip around in place clockwise (counts 1 to 8).

4. All skip in opposite direction (counts 9 to 16).

8. As they sing the words "And if you will be," all march again in the same direction as before (counts 17 to 32).

At the end of the chorus there is a short pause during which those who were originally in the center quickly take places in the circle, leaving their partners inside.

WORDS.

Our little girls (or boys) we know,
When to dancing they go,
Would like a boy (or girl) to know,
With whom to dance just so.
And if you will be
A partner to me,
Just put your hand in mine,
And dance so merrily.

Then boom-fa-ra-la, boom-fa-ra-la, boom-fa-ra-la-la,
Yes, boom-fa-ra-la-la, yes, boom-fa-ra-la-la,
And if you will be
A partner to me,
Just put your hand in mine,
And dance so merrily.

NOTE—Music can be found in "Dances of the People," Burchenal.

Dance of Greeting.

(DANISH.)

Words by Eva E. Linn.

Clap, clap, partner, Clap, clap, neighbor, Stamp, stamp, turn yourself around, Clap, clap, part-ner, Clap, clap, neighbor, Stamp, stamp, turn yourself around, Danc-ing so mer-ri-ly, so mer-ri-ly we're danc-ing, Danc-ing so mer-ri-ly, so mer-ri-ly, heigh oh!

Victor Record 17,158 (Chord—Dance played five times).

Steps: Curtsy, running.

Formation: Single circle of couples, facing center, boy on the left of girl.

Music: Two parts of 8 measures. Polka rhythm (2 counts to a measure).

PART I—Greeting to all the dancers.

Clap, clap, partner,

1. Clap hands twice, face partner, and execute a curtsy (step backward with foot farthest from partner, pointing other foot and bending trunk forward).

Clap, clap, neighbor,

    2.   Clap hands twice, at the same time turn on the balls of both feet, face neighbor (away from partner) and execute a curtsy.

Stamp, stamp,

    3.   Face the center, stamp twice, first with the foot farthest from partner, then with the other foot.

Turn yourself around,

    4.   With three running steps execute a whole turn, beginning with facing away from partner.

Clap, clap, partner,
Clap, clap, neighbor,
Stamp, stamp, turn yourself around.

    5.   Repeat 1, 2, 3, 4.

PART II—Represents pleasure of all being together and should be rollicking and full of fun.

1. Dancing so merrily, so merrily we're dancing, Dancing so merrily, so merrily, heigh-oh!

    1.   All grasp hands, face left, and beginning left, 16 running steps forward (around the circle clockwise).

2. Dancing so merrily, so merrily we're dancing, Dancing so merrily, so merrily, heigh-oh!

    2.   Same, counter-clockwise.

GAMES AND SONG GAMES
FOR CHILDREN OF SEVEN TO TEN YEARS

Second School-Grade.

CAT AND MOUSE.

The cat and mouse game described in games of Grade I can be made more difficult for older pupils by

(a) Having two cats and one mouse. In this form the players must assist the escaping of the mouse by obstructing the way of the cats.

(b) Arranging your class in two concentric circles and having one cat and one mouse.

(c) The players may be divided into groups of four or five who form small circles by grasping hands. These groups stand five or six steps from each other. The mouse runs into and out of the circles, or it dodges about among them until caught by the cat, or until it is relieved by another player.

(d) The players are arranged as in (c), but there are two mice. If, now, one mouse runs into a circle (into a hole) the other must run out. This form of the game requires much skill on the part of the players. It therefore appeals also to older players.

CHANGE TAG. (Lane Tag.)

This is a form of tag in which the players are formed in front ranks of six or eight, with grasped hands, the ranks being two steps apart. Upon the command, "left face," the players release their holds, face left and immediately grasp hands with their new neighbors. This facing brings about new paths (lanes) between the ranks. The play itself is like plain tag. The teacher chooses two children, one of whom is "it." He tries to tag the other, who runs up and down the paths between the ranks. The teacher should frequently change the paths by commanding left or right face.

SPIN THE PLATE.

The players form a circle and are numbered 1, 2, 3, etc. The leader is inside the circle. He holds a disk or plate in his hand, and, setting it on edge on the floor, gives it a quick twist. While it is spinning he calls out some player by his number, who rushes forward to catch the plate before it settles flat. If successful he becomes leader, and the former leader takes his place in the circle. If unsuccessful he returns to his place, and the leader spins the plate again, calling another number.

Older players may also be required to clap their hands once or twice, in front or behind the body, hop, turn around, etc., before starting to catch the plate.

HOOP TOSS WITH PEG BOARD.

The apparatus consists of a board one foot square having on it five pegs three inches high. (See diagram.) The hoop is approximately ten inches in diameter. The object of the game is to toss the hoop so that it will fall over one or more pegs. Each peg encircled by the hoop counts one. If, therefore, the hoop encircles one peg this counts one, if two pegs are encircled it counts two, etc. The center peg, however, counts double. A corner peg and the center peg encircled by the hoop would count three points. If each peg were to count three, the encircling of one corner peg and the center peg would count nine points. As illustrated, a throw would count three points.

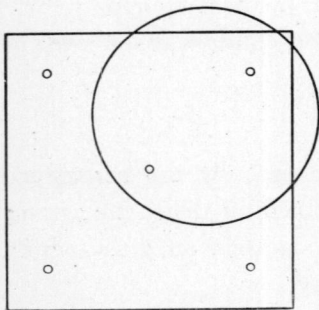

This game lends itself well to a lesson in arithmetic, having more interest to the child than the mere addition of 1 and 1, or 2 and 2. The fact that the center peg counts double adds another element of interest.

If used as an indoor game the players stand in line with the first desks, and the peg-boards are placed on the floor near the blackboard.

If played out of doors the distance between the throwers and the boards may be increased with the age and skill of the players.

With skillful players several hoops may be used with each board. In this case the hoops should be of different colors, so as to allow each player to distinguish his hoop easily.

CATCH THE WAND. (Variation of Spinning the Plate.)

The leader stands in the center of a circle, formed by the other players, holding a wand upright, his first finger resting on one end of the wand, the other end resting on the floor. At any moment, by raising his finger, he allows the wand to fall to the floor, at the same time calling the name of one of the players, who must quickly rush forward and catch the wand before it touches the floor. If he succeeds in doing so he becomes the leader; if not, the game continues with the same leader until some one catches the wand.

JACOB, WHERE ARE YOU? (R. Ruth and Jacob.)

Form your pupils in a circle, standing closely together with hands grasped. Two players are chosen by the teacher; one is Ruth, the other Jacob. Both are blindfolded. Ruth now calls, "Jacob, where are you?" Jacob answers, "Here," quickly and silently changing his place. Guided by the voice, Ruth tries to catch him. This procedure is repeated until Jacob is caught.

If the game is played in a schoolroom, form the children in an oval in the front part of the room.

JUMP OVER. (R.)

The pupils stand in the aisles, facing their seats. At the command, "One," they place their hands on their desk and the back of their seats, rising on their toes; on "Two," they jump over the seats, landing on their toes in the next aisle. Left about face and repeat a few times.

LONG JUMPING ROPE. (R.)

The exercises of the first grade may be made more difficult by having two, three or four pupils run through at the same time after a given number of swings. In the same manner have two (or more) run into the rope, jump four, three or two times, and then run out.

RACING.

The races of Grade I may be made more difficult by increasing the distance to be run or hopped. The winners of each rank should now be given a chance to run against each other.

BALL GAMES.　(R.)

Children of the second grade may still use the beanbags for tossing and catching, but the games of the first grade should be made more difficult by designating the hand that tosses and catches.　Hand-clapping before a bag is caught may also be required.

BAG BOARD.　(R.　Faba Baga.)

The bag board is about two by three feet in size, having in it three holes of unequal diameters.　It is placed slanting against a wall.　At a distance of about eight to ten feet each player is allowed to toss a number of bags, trying to toss them through the holes, the smallest giving a score of fifteen, the next ten and the largest five points.

BAG IN THE RING.　(R.　Bag-Toss.)

Three concentric circles are drawn, the largest about six feet in diameter. The players stand at a distance in accordance with their skill, and each throws a beanbag so that it will alight in the center circle, or as near it as possible. If it alights in the center one it counts fifteen points; in the next larger, ten, and in the largest, five.　If most of the bag is over a line it is counted as being in. that circle.　The player scoring the largest number of points in a given number of trials or a certain length of time wins the game.

STAND - DODGEBALL.　(R.)

Apparatus: A gas ball, or a small, light beanbag.　On the floor, at the front of the room, mark off a circle three feet in diameter.　A boy takes his place here with one foot in the circle.　From a mark about halfway across the room the pupils, one after another, get a chance to throw at the one in the circle.　He is allowed to dodge the missile, but must always keep one foot in the ring.　Frequently change the target.

If the game is played in the yard, place the circle near the wall or fence, so that the ball or bag does not go too far from the players.

CATCH ME.　(Come Along, Skip Away.)

Have the players form one or two circles.　Choose one child as the first tagger.　This child runs around the outside of the circle, tagging some one. The child tagged pursues the tagger, trying to catch him before he reaches the place vacated by the one tagged. The one tagged now becomes tagger and the game proceeds as before. Call for lively running and prompt tagging—and do not allow the "playing of partners," so that all get a chance to run. As a variation, have the runners run around or touch an object some distance from the circle before finishing. Another variation is to have the players skip instead of run. Still another is to have the players stand by twos or threes, who must all run when the last one is tagged. The one left over continues the game.

LONG JUMPING ROPE.

Arrange the children in ranks of two. Fasten one end of the rope to the fence. The teacher takes the other end and swings the rope toward the pupils. At every third swing the foremost pupils run through, around the teacher and form at the rear of the column. As the children become more proficient let them run through at every second (first) swing. Also let them run through by fours, sixes, eights. Later let them run in, jump twice, and run out as the next rank runs in.

I See You.*

(PEEK-A-BOO.)
Swedish.

I see you, I see you, Ti ral - la, ral - la, lal - la - la, I

see you, I see you, Ti ral - la, lal - la - la.

I See You.—Concluded.

2.

You see me and I see you, And you take me and I take you;

You see me and I see you, And you take me and I take you.

* Copyright, 1908, by Jakob Bolin.

Victor Record 17,158 (Chord—Dance is played nine times).

Step: Skipping.

Formation: The children are formed in two divisions, standing 10 feet apart, facing toward center. Each division is divided into couples, one in each couple standing behind the other. Those in front have hands on hips, those in rear have hands on shoulders of ones in front.

Music: Two parts of 8 measures each. Polka rhythm (2 counts to a measure).

PART I.

1. I see you, I see you,

    1. Those standing in rear alternately bend their heads once left and right.

2. Ti-ralla-ralla-lalla-la,

    2. The head is bent four times (thus playing "peek-a-boo" with opposites).

3. I see you, I see you,

    3. Repeat 1.

4. Ti-ralla-lalla-la.

    4. Repeat 2.

PART II.

5. You see me and I see you,

6. And you take me and I take you,

7. You see me and I see you,

8. And you take me and I take you.

5. On the first word all clap hands, then those in rear skip forward (passing left), and grasp both hands of those coming from the opposite division.

6. Skip around vigorously in place.

7 and 8. All clap hands, skip to partner, grasp both hands, skip around vigorously in place, finishing with the two divisions again formed, the partners having changed places.

MY BROTHER.   (Mein Brüderle.)

The pupils are formed in a circle, standing in pairs, facing the leaders. The inner hands are grasped shoulder-high.

My Brother.

Adapted from a German Students' Song.

1. I've not seen broth-er for some time, For some time, for some time;

So let's be mer-ry now And sing, sing, sing.

FINE.

My Brother.—Concluded.

O sing, dear broth-er, sing, dear broth-er, Sing, sing, sing;

D.C. al Fine.

O sing, dear broth-er, sing dear broth-er, Sing, sing, sing.

1. I've not seen brother for some time,
   For some time, for some time;
      So let's be merry now and sing,
         sing, sing.

   } The children sing while marching around in the circle.

   |: O sing, dear brother, sing, dear
         brother;
      Sing, sing, sing. :|

   } Skip forward.

   I've not seen brother for some time,
   For some time, for some time;
      So let's be merry now and sing,
         sing, sing;

   } The children sing while marching around in the circle.

2. I've not seen sister for some time,
   For some time, for some time;
      So let's be merry now and
         dance, dance, dance.

   } March forward as above.

   |: O hop, dear sister, hop, dear sister;
      Hop, hop, hop. : |

   } Partners face each other, grasping both hands and gallop sideward toward the leader.

I've not seen sister for some time,
For some time, for some time;
   So let's be merry now and
   dance, dance, dance.

March forward as above.

3. I've not seen teacher for some time,
For some time, for some time;
   So let's be merry now and fly,
   fly, fly.

March forward as above.

|: O fly, dear teacher, fly, dear
   teacher,
   Fly, fly, fly.: |

Skipping forward, the children wave their arms as if flying.

I've not seen teacher for some time,
For some time, for some time;
   So let's be merry now and fly,
   fly, fly.

March forward as above.

The Carrousel.

Swedish.

Pret - ty chil - dren, sweet and gay, Car - rous - el is run - ning.

It will run 'till eve - ning, Lit - tle ones a nick - el,

big ones a dime. Hur- ry up, get a mate, or you'll sure- ly be too late.

CHORUS.

Ha, ha, ha, hap- py are we, Car-rous-el is run-ning, running so mer-ri - ly;

Victor Record 17,086 (Introduction, chord—Dance is played four times).

(This dance represents the merry-go-round with horses and riders.)

Steps: Gallop, closing step.

Formation: Two concentric circles, facing the center. Those in the inner circle grasp hands, while those in the outer circle place their hands on the shoulders of the ones in front.

Music: Two parts. Part I, 7 measures. Part II, 4 measures. Repeated. Polka rhythm (2 counts to a measure).

PART I (Carrousel just starting).

Pretty children, sweet and gay, Carrousel is running. It will run till evening, Little ones a nickel, big ones a dime. Hurry up, get your mate, or you'll surely be too late.	While singing, both circles move left sideward with closing steps (step sideward left and bring heels together).

PART II (In full swing).

Ha, ha, ha, happy are we, Carrousel is running, running so merrily, Ha, ha, ha, happy are we, Carrousel is running, running so merrily.	The players gallop left sideward during the first two lines, and gallop right sideward during the third and fourth lines.

At the end of the song the players change places and the dance is repeated.

For older players a suitable variation consists of letting the inner players face about after the first rendition. Still another variation consists of letting each circle gallop in opposite directions while singing "Ha, ha, ha," etc.

CHILDREN'S POLKA (German).

Victor Record 17,327 (Dance is played four times).

Steps: Glide, three-step.

Formation: Single circle of couples, facing center, boy on the left of girl.

Music: Two parts of 8 measures each. Polka rhythm (2 counts to a measure).

PART I.

Measures:

2. Partners face, join hands, arms sideward. Two glides toward center and a three-step (three running steps in place) (counts 1 to 4).

2. Repeat, moving outward (counts 5 to 8).

4. Repeat above 4 measures (counts 9 to 16).

PART II.

2.   Clap thighs, 1; clap own hands, 2; clap partner's hands three times, 3 and 4 (counts 1 to 4).

2.   Repeat above 2 measures (counts 5 to 8).

1.   With a hop on left foot, place right foot forward, and shake right forefinger threateningly three times at partner (back of left hand supporting right elbow) (counts 9 and 10).

1.   Repeat left (counts 11 and 12).

1.   Beginning left, whole turn left in three running steps (counts 13 and 14).

1.   Stamp right, left, right (counts 15 and 16).

THE FIRST OF MAY (Swedish).

Victor Record 17,761 (Introduction, chord—Dance is played three times).

Steps: Polka (or change step), skip.

Change step, left: Step left forward, 1; bring the right foot to the left heel and put the weight on it, "and," step left forward, 2 "and."

Polka left: Same as change step, hopping on the right foot on the "and" preceding the first count.

Formation: Double circle of couples, boy on the left of the girl, left sides toward the center.   Inner hands grasped.

Music: One part of 8 measures, repeated.   Polka rhythm (2 counts to a measure).

Measures:

PART I.

8.   Eight polkas (or change steps) forward, beginning with the outer foot, facing toward and away from partner, with arm swinging backward and forward (lightly and joyously) (counts 1 to 16).

PART II.

2.   Partners face, shake hands three times and pause (counts 1 to 4).

6.   All make a quarter turn right and, beginning left, skip forward in a circle with a clap and a stamp on the first skip step, until each passes first partner and meets dancer who is next (counts 5 to 16).

The outer circle moves in the same direction as in Part I, the inner circle in the opposite direction.

WORDS.

To-day's the first of May,
To-day's the first of May, May, May,
To-day's the first of May,
To-day's the first of May.

Good-bye, good-bye, dear friend,
We'll meet again some day, some day,
We'll meet again some day,
Before the first of May.

NOTE—The dance may be repeated as many times as desired, each time with a new partner. It may be used for a great variety of occasions, the names of which may be substituted for "The First of May."

The music can be found in "Folk Dances and Singing Games," Burchenal, and "Second Folk Dance Book," Crampton.

GAMES, SONG-GAMES AND DANCES
FOR CHILDREN OF EIGHT TO TWELVE YEARS

Third to Fourth School-Grades.

RUNNING AND HOPPING RACES.

Always have the class arranged so that from four to eight can run or hop at the same time. Increase the difficulty of the races (a) by running greater distances; (b) by having two pupils cross arms and run without releasing their hold; (c) by running around or over obstacles; (d) by hopping on one foot; (e) by hopping on one foot, holding the ankle of the other.

THIRD TAG AND RUN. (Third Slap.)

The class is divided into two divisions, standing ten to twenty steps apart. One player from one side crosses over to his opponents to give the three tags. Their hands must be held forward to receive his tag, of which three are given to the same or to different persons. As soon as the third tag is given the one giving it turns and runs to a goal behind him (previously decided upon—usually his own line) while the one receiving the third tag pursues him. If caught before reaching the goal, the runner is out of the game. The teacher then chooses the next tagger.

This game may also be played with sides, as follows: Two divisions line up, the hands being held as before. The leader of one side advances to the other and gives three tags, then turns and runs back to his side, pursued by the one receiving the third tag. If caught before reaching his own side he is a prisoner of the side that tagged him.

The other side then sends out a tagger, the two sides continually alternating in sending out the tagger. The side having the largest number of prisoners at the close wins the game.

PUSSY WANTS A CORNER.

Each player chooses a place, a corner of a house, an apparatus, a mark on the ground, etc. All, with the exception of one, have places. The places

49

being decided on, all go to the middle of a circle, and at a signal run for these places. The one who fails to get a place begins the play. He goes from place to place and says, "Pussy wants a corner." Meanwhile the players exchange places at will. The seeker for a place endeavors to secure one by outwitting some one who is exchanging places with another and by getting into the place first. The one thus deprived of a place becomes the next seeker. If a seeker, after repeated efforts, fails to secure a place he may call "All change places," and all must exchange. In the confusion of this general exchange he tries to get a place.

ANIMAL BLIND MAN'S BUFF.

A circle of players is formed, and they dance around a blindfolded player, who has a stick in his hand. When he taps on the ground or floor or claps his hands three times the players come to a stop. He then points to some player, who must take hold of the end of the stick. The blind man then asks him to make the noise of some animal, say of a dog, cat, cow or horse. The one making this noise should try to disguise his voice as much as possible. The blind man tries to guess who makes the noise, and if right they exchange places. In either case the circling about goes on as before. Players may disguise their height by bending their knees, standing on tip-toe, or in other ways.

THE BEETLE IS OUT. (The Twisted Kerchief, Plump Sack, Drop the Handkerchief.)

The players form a closed circle, shoulder to shoulder, facing inward and having their hands, with palms open, behind their backs. One of the pupils is outside the circle. He carries a handkerchief with a knot tied in one end of it (or a stuffed bag). Running around the outside of the circle, he puts the handkerchief into the hand of one of the players (if possible, without being noticed by the others). When the leader calls "The beetle is out," the one having the handkerchief turns and strikes his right-hand neighbor on the back with the knot, the neighbor seeking to avoid the blows by running around the circle until he regains his former place. The pursuer now starts around the circle, placing the handkerchief (the beetle) into some one's else hand, and the game continues as before.

PUSS IN THE CIRCLE.

A large circle is marked on the ground. One player, who is Puss, stands in the circle; the others stand outside of the circle. These players may be tagged by Puss whenever they have any part of their body inside of the circle. They will make opportunity for this by stepping in and out of the circle, teasing Puss in every possible way to tag them. Any one whom Puss touches fairly joins the first Puss in the circle and helps tag the others. The last one tagged is the winner of the game.

CHANGE SEATS—CHANGE—1-2-3-4-5-6-7-8-9-10.

This room game also is enjoyable and practical on a playground. As a means of developing good discipline it is splendid, teaching children to do a certain thing in a certain way at a certain time.

The teacher, or leader, commands "change seats"—"change," and then rapidly counts from one to ten. On the command "change" all children must change to a new seat (any seat in the room). On the tenth count they must be sitting in order with hands folded on top of the desk. The ten counts must follow the executive command immediately and must be given very quickly. Children are out of the game and pass to the front of the room in the following instances:

1. If two children are in the same seat they both are out.

2. Failure to be in a new seat and in order on count 10 is penalized by being out.

3. An attempt to move on the preparatory command "change seats" instead of waiting for the executive command "change" puts the offender out.

The success of this game depends entirely on the manner and voice in which commands are given. The pause between the preparatory and executive command should never be of the same duration. The accent should often be used in the preparatory part of command to catch the unattentive players.

As the number of children in the game decreases the number of counts allowed for the changing may be decreased to 8 or 5 counts.

The last player to remain in the game is the winner.

BAG RELAY. (R.)

(a) Place one bag (eraser, handkerchief) on each front desk. At a given signal the occupant of the front seat passes the bag to the pupil behind him, who passes it on to the next, and so on till it reaches the end of the row, when it is returned in the same way. The row which returns the bag to the front desk soonest, wins.

(b) Same as above, but bags are supplied to all members of one end row, and passed sideward and back again.

(c) Instead of passing one bag, pass several in immediate successsion. Bags should be passed from hand to hand and not thrown.

(d) Place on the front desk of each row as many beanbags as there are seats in that row. At a given signal the pupil in the front row rises, places one of the bags on the desk behind him, gets another, places it on the next desk, and so on, carrying one bag at a time until all are distributed. The pupils occupying the second seats in the different rows return the bags, one at a time, to the front desks. This is continued until each pupil in the row has had a chance. The row to finish first is the winner.

BALL GAMES.

The ball games of the preceding grades should now be made more difficult by using large gas balls, indoor baseballs, or basket-balls instead of beanbags. With increased accuracy the desire arises to test this. Throwing into a suspended basket, or through a suspended hoop, offers this chance. A pleasing variation is to allow the children to throw at a bell which hangs in the center of a suspended hoop.

DUCKSTONE.   (R. Duck on the Rock. Ducks and Drakes. Duck on Davy.)

Apparatus: An eraser and a beanbag (if possible, a set for each row), With chalk, mark off a circle one foot in diameter on the floor, about one foot from the front wall. Put an eraser in this. The first pupil in the row rises, takes the beanbag, steps back a few steps and throws at the eraser. If he knocks it out his row counts one. Every one in the row throws from the same mark. In order to save time the next thrower takes his place near the circle, to get the beanbag and, if necessary, to replace the eraser.

GUESS WHO? (R.)

Apparatus: An inflated seven-inch rubber ball (gas ball). A boy hides his head against the front wall. The teacher tosses the ball to some pupil, who throws it at the hider. The hider then guesses who threw the ball. If he guesses correctly the thrower takes his place. Several sections may play at the same time.

FOX AND CHICKENS.

Divide the players into ranks of sevens. Six, representing the chickens, stand behind one another, catching around each other's waists; the one in front with outspread arms (wings) shoos off the fox (the seventh pupil), who tries to tag the last one in the rank. When the last one in the rank is tagged, the one in front becomes fox. The former fox takes his place at the end of rank.

POTATO RACE. (Potato Planting and Picking.)

Divide the players into six ranks of equal numbers. Have twenty-four potatoes (erasers, stones, handkerchiefs, etc.) The members of each rank stand behind one another. With chalk draw a small circle in front of the first one of each rank. Into each of these six circles put four potatoes. About ten feet ahead of these circles draw six more, repeating this three times (so as to have five circles for each rank). See diagram. Upon command, the first pupil grasps one potato, runs and places it into a circle. He then returns, grasps another potato, runs and places this into another circle. This is repeated quickly until all are placed. The next six gather the potatoes, by reversing the above procedure—i. e., by running for the first potato and placing this into the circle in front of each rank, then running for the second, then for the third, etc., until all potatoes have been gathered and are in the first circle. The rank winning in each race gets one credit. A variation of this race is to let the pupils hop instead of running.

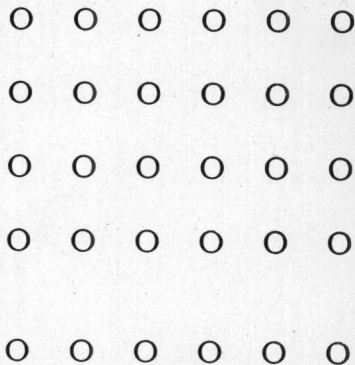

DAYBALL.   (Days of the Week.   Monday, Tuesday.)

This is a game for seven players.   Each one is given the name of a day in the week.   Sunday throws a tennis-ball, or another soft ball, against the side of a house, calling upon some other "day" to catch it.   If he catches it he throws the ball, calling upon some other player to catch it.   If he misses the ball, the first player again throws it.   Young, inexperienced players may be allowed to catch the ball on the first bounce.

If more players wish to join in the game, give each a number, and then call on a certain number instead of a day to catch the ball.

A variation of this game suitable for older children (stand-ball) is as follows: If the one called upon does not catch the ball the rest run away until this player has secured the ball and calls "Stand."   The runners now are not allowed to move from their places.   The ball-holder hereupon throws at a player, who may dodge, but not move his feet.   Who is hit three times is out of the game.

WATER SPRITE.   (Hill Dill, Cross Over.)

The players stand in two long lines, on opposite sides of the play field, the lines being twenty-five to thirty feet apart.   The open space between them represents a river.   The water sprite stands between the lines and calls on some one to cross over.   This player signals to a player on the opposite shore.   They then suddenly run across to exchange places.   If the water sprite tags either one he is "it" and exchanges places with the tagger.

When played as "Hill Dill" the tagger calls out, "Hill Dill, come over the hill," whereupon all players cross over.   The one tagged either takes the place of the tagger or helps him until all are caught.

Come, Little Partner.

Come, lit - tle part - ner, come a- long, Let's play and dance and sing   a song,

Come, Little Partner.—Continued.

Step this way now, and that way now, Then turn a-round and make a bow.

2.

Tra la, la, la, la, la, la, la, la, Tra la, la, la, la, la,

la, la, La, la, la, la, la, la, la, la, la, la, Tra la, la, la, la, la, la.

The players are arranged in couples, standing in a flank circle.

PART I.

1. Two steps forward, followed by three running steps forward.

2. Repeat 1, beginning with the right foot.

3. Step left sideward and curtsy (place right foot crossed behind left leg and bend both knees) ; repeat right sideward.

4. A complete turn right in eight running steps, making a slight bow during the last count.

5 to 8.   Repeat 1 to 4.

PART II.

The couples face inward (face to face) ; the grasped hands are raised sideward, the elbows slightly bent.

1. Two glides sideward and a change step sideward toward the head of the column.

2.   Repeat toward the foot of the column.

3.   The couples face toward the head of the column, inner hands shoulder-high, outer knuckles on hips; two glides forward and a change-step.

4.   Repeat 3.

5 to 8. Repeat 1 to 4.

Repeat Parts I and II as often as desired.

N. B.—When the dance is first learned the players, when performing Part I, may all begin with the left foot and execute the steps as written. After some proficiency has been attained, let the players standing on the right of each couple begin with the right foot. The step and curtsy will then be sideward, away from and toward the dancers.

Will You Dance With Me?

German.

Will   you   dance   with   me? Will   you   dance   with   me?

Will   you   dance   with   me? I'll   be   your part - ner   now.

Tra   la, la,   la,   la,   la, Tra   la, la,   la,   tra   la,   la,   la;

Will You Dance With Me?—Concluded.

Tra la, la, la, la, la, Tra la, la, la, la, la.

The players are arranged in a large front circle, facing inward. Two or more players are inside.

PART I.

The players forming the circle grasp hands and walk to the left. Those on the inside stand still. All sing:

"Will you dance with me? Will you dance with me?

Will you dance with me? I'll be your partner now."

While singing the last strain each player on the inside chooses a partner from the moving circle. Those chosen step into the circle. These couples grasp both hands.

PART II.

The players forming the circle now stand still, and, with clapping hands, sing:

"Tra la, la, la, la, la; tra la, la, la; tra la, la, la;
Tra la, la, la, la, la; tra la, la, la, la, la."

During this the couples on the inside execute glide steps sideward around in the circle. Those dancing do not sing. At the end of the song the players last chosen stay within the circle, the others resuming their places in the circle, and all immediately begin marching to the left, singing the first part.

The game is continued as long as desired.

Spring Song.*

(VOCAL SCHOTTISCHE.)

Words by W. Comery.   Composed by Arthur Richard.

Let us glad - ly sing Of re- turn-ing Spring, For as queen she comes to   reign ;

With   a   fai - ry wand, She awakes the land ; And the swallow comes in her   train.

Let us glad - ly sing Of re - turn-ing Spring, For as queen she comes to   reign ;

* Copyright, 1893, by Novello, Ewer & Co

Spring Song.

With a   fai - ry wand, She awakes the land; And the swallow comes in her train.

The cuckoo's note O'er the green doth float, For the cuckoo loves the Spring of the year;

And the flow'rs around, Know the joyful sound, And array'd to greet her they ap-pear.

THE FAIRIES. I.

Music: "Spring Song," by Arthur Richard.

NOTE—In their simplest forms the following roundels may be performed by the pupils arranged in single file, or by having them formed in a column of twos, threes, fours, etc., as may be made compulsory by the space at disposal. These roundels have a progressive forward movement; there must, therefore, be space enough to allow the pupils to move forward and to the left around the hall or room. If arranged in single file, pupils place their knuckles on the hips; if arranged in a column, the pupils grasp hands shoulder-high, the outer ones placing the knuckles of the free hand on the hips.

The dance begins with the first beat of the second measure.

PART I.   Metronome 80.

Measure:

1.   Beginning with the left foot, three quick steps forward and raise the right knee (the knee is raised slightly, the foot extended and near the left leg).

2.   Beginning with the right foot, three quick steps forward and raise the left knee.

3.   As 1.

4.   Beginning right, three quick steps backward and raise the left knee. (If, at the beginning, this backward movement is too difficult, change it to a forward movement.)

5 to 16.   Repeat the above four measures three times.

PART II.

1.   Place the left foot forward and backward.
2.   Change step left.
3.   Place the right foot forward and backward.
4.   Change step right.
5 to 16.   Repeat the above four measures three times.
These two parts may be repeated as often as wished.

THE FAIRIES. II.

NOTE—This roundel is arranged for older pupils standing in a column of twos. The theme is the same as in the Fairies I, the variations consisting of movements to the opposite side. The partners, designated as Nos. 1 and 2, stand side by side, their right and left hands grasped shoulder-high, so that either may easily cross over without releasing the hold. No. 1 is standing at the right.

PART I.

Measure:

1. Beginning with the left foot, three quick steps forward and raise the right knee.

2. Beginning right, three quick steps forward and raise the left knee.

3. As 1, but during the three steps No. 1 crosses over to the left.

4. Beginning right, three quick steps backward and raise the left knee. (If this backward movement is too difficult, change it to forward.)

5 to 8. Repeat the above, except that during the seventh measure No. 1 crosses over to the right. (The left foot, when the crossing-over takes place, begins by crossing obliquely forward to the right.)

9 to 16. Repeat the above eight measures.

PART II.

1. Place the left foot forward and backward.

2. Change step left, No. 1 at the same time crossing over to the left.

3. Place the right foot forward and backward.

4. Change step right, No. 1 crossing over.

5 to 8. Repeat the above.

9 to 16. Repeat the above eight measures.

These two parts may be repeated as often as wished.

SHOEMAKER'S DANCE (Danish).

Victor Record 17,084 (Chord—Dance is played ten times).

Steps: Polka (or change step) and skipping.

Formation: Double circle of couples, partners facing, boys on inside of circle.

Music: Two parts of 8 measures. Polka rhythm (2 counts to a measure).

PART I.

Measures:

1.   Raise fists in front of chest, elbows high, circle (forward) one hand with the other three times (counts 1 and 2).

1.   Reverse three times (winding the thread) (counts 3 and 4).

1.   Vigorously pull the elbows backward twice (pulling the thread) (counts 5 and 6).

1.   Strike the left fist with the right three times (driving the pegs) (counts 7 and 8).

4.   Repeat the above 4 measures (counts 9 to 16).

PART II.

Face in line of march to move counter-clockwise, inner hands grasped.

8.   *Beginning with outer foot, 8 polkas forward, facing toward and away from partner, with arm swinging backward and forward (counts 1 to 16).

*Change steps may be substituted for polkas.

Change step, left: Step left forward, 1; bring the right foot to the left heel and put the weight on it, "and," step left forward, 2 "and."

Polka left: Same as change step, hopping on the right foot on the "and" preceding the first count.

WORDS.

||Cobbler, cobbler, mend my shoe,
Have it done by half past two.||
||Stitch it up and stitch it down,
Make the finest shoe in town.||

NOTE—This is an industrial dance which may be traced to the guild system of Europe.

Annie Goes to the Cabbage Field.

An - nie goes to the cab - bage field, cab - bage field, cab - bage field,

Seek - ing there some fresh green leaves, to feed her rab - bits fine.

John - ny sees her, ha, ha, ha, Now I'll catch you, tra, la, la,

Nay, nay, nay, go a - way, I'll not dance with you to - day.

ANNIE GOES TO THE CABBAGE FIELD (Bohemian).

Step: Polka (or change step).

Change step, left: Step left forward, 1; bring right foot to left heel and put the weight on it, "and," step left forward, 2 "and."

Polka left: Same as change step, hopping on the right foot on the "and" preceding the first count.

Formation: Double circle of couples, boy on left of girl, left sides toward center, inner hands grasped.

Music: Two parts of 8 measures each, Part I played twice and Part II played once. Polka rhythm (2 counts to a measure).

PART I.

Measures:

16. Beginning with outer foot, 16 polkas forward, facing toward and away from partner, with arm swinging backward and forward (counts 1 to 32).

PART II.

Partners face:

1. Stand still (counts 1 and 2).
1. Stamp left, right, left (counts 3 and 4).
1. Stand still (counts 5 and 6).
1. Clap own hands three times (counts 7 and 8).
1. Shake right forefinger threateningly at partner three times (counts 9 and 10).
1. Repeat, shaking left forefinger (counts 11 and 12).
1. Partners clap right hands, make a whole turn, whirling on left foot (counts 13 and 14).
1. Stamp right, left, right vigorously (counts 15 and 16).

Look fiercely at each other and make movements vigorous and threatening.

GUSTAF'S GREETING (Swedish).

Victor Record 17,330 (Introduction, chord—Dance is played four times).

Steps: Skip step, curtsy.

Formation: Square set of four couples. (Head couples, the one facing the music and the opposite couple; side couples, the other two). Boy on the left of girl.

Music: Two parts of 8 measures each, repeated. Polka rhythm (2 counts to a measure).

PART I (Dignified and Stately).

Partners join inside hands.

Measures:

2. Beginning left, head couples advance toward each other three steps, close and bow. (Boy makes bow with feet together, girl touches right toe behind left heel, slightly bending knees, making a bob curtsy) (counts 1 to 4).

2. Beginning right, head couples take three steps backward and close (counts 5 to 8).

4. Side couples the same (counts 9 to 16).

8. Repeat above 8 measures (counts 1 to 16).

PART II (Light and Jolly).

2. With inside hands joined, beginning left, head couples take four skips toward each other (counts 1 to 4).

2. Release partner's hand and with a quarter turn outward, join inside hands with opposite and skip under the arches made by the raised joined hands of the side couples (counts 5 to 8).

2. After passing under the arch, they release hands and each skips to his own place (counts 9 to 12).

2. Clap hands on the thirteenth count, and joining both hands with partner, skip around vigorously in place, clockwise (counts 13 to 16).

8. Side couples the same (counts 1 to 16).

WORDS.

||Gustaf's skoal!
There is no better skoal than this!
Gustaf's skoal!
The best old skoal there is!||

||Ho fal de-rol jan,
Le-jan, li-jan,
Ho fal de-rol jan,
Le-jan, li-jan,
Ho fal de-rol jan,
Le-jan, li-jan.
Gustaf's skoal!||

Music can be found in "Dances of the People," Burchenal; "Swedish Folk Dances," Bergquist.

MOUNTAIN MARCH (Norwegian).

Victor Record 17,160 (Chord—Dance is played five times).
Steps: Running.
Formation: Groups of three, with the center one forward one step, hands joined, forming a triangle (handkerchiefs may be used in joining hands to make the dance more effective).
Music: Two parts of 16 measures each. Waltz rhythm (3 counts to a measure).

PART I.
Measures:
1. Moving in a circle counter-clockwise, beginning left, take three running steps obliquely-left forward and bend trunk in the same direction, stamping on the first count (counts 1 to 3).
1. Repeat, beginning right (counts 4 to 6).
14. Repeat the above 2 measures seven times (counts 7 to 48).

PART II.

2. No. 1, standing in front, bending forward, moves backward and passes under the joined hands of No. 2 and No. 3, with six small running steps, while No. 2 and No. 3 run in place (counts 1 to 6).
2. No. 2, at the left, moves across in front of No. 1, and turns right about under No. 1's right arm, in six small running steps, while No. 1 and No. 3 run in place (counts 7 to 12).

2. No. 3, at right, makes a whole turn left under own (both) arms in six small running steps, while No. 1 and No. 2 run in place (counts 13 to 18).

2. No. 1 makes a whole turn right under own right arm in six small running steps, while No. 2 and No. 3 run in place (counts 19 to 24).

8. Repeat the above 8 measures (counts 1 to 24).

PART III.

Repeat Part I (counts 1 to 48).

PART IV.

Repeat Part II (counts 1 to 48).

This dance represents two mountain climbers with their guide, who appears to be pulling them after him. He should glance back occasionally, first over one shoulder and then over the other, to see how they are advancing.

THE MOUNTAIN MARCH.

||:Up to the mountain top,
Up to the mountain top,
Up to the mountain top gaily we go.:||

||:Up on the mountain top,
Up on the mountain top,
Up on the mountain top play we just so.:||

||:Down from the mountain top,
Down from the mountain top,
Down from the mountain top steady and slow.:||

||:Down from the mountain top,
Down from the mountain top,
Down from the mountain top, homeward we go.:||

GAMES AND DANCES
FOR CHILDREN OF NINE TO FOURTEEN YEARS

Fourth to Sixth School-Grades.

BLACK MAN. (Black Tom; Bogey Man; Pom, Pom, Pull Away; Kings.)

A player, chosen as Black Man, stands at one end of the yard, the other players stand at the opposite end. The Bogey Man calls, "Are you afraid of the Black Man?" The others answer, "No," and run, trying to pass him and reach the opposite end of the yard. The Black Man tags one or two, and they go with him to his side of the yard, and play as Black Men. The play is repeated until all the runners are caught by the Black Man and his helpers. The last one caught begins a new game.

LAME GOOSE. (Fox in the Hole.)

The one playing the goose takes his place at one corner of the yard, called "home." After three running steps he must hop (on one foot) and tag one of the other players who are running about. When one is tagged, and so becomes goose, he is chased by the other players, who strike him with knotted handkerchiefs, until he is "home." Should the goose in his attempts to tag a player put both feet on the ground he also is chased home by the other players.

BREAK THROUGH. (Bear in the Ring, Bull Pen.)

A number of players join hands and form a circle, the bear-pit. One of their number, previously selected as the bear, wanders about on the inside, attempting to get out by testing the bars. The bear may break through the bars by placing his weight on the grasped hands, or jump over or crawl under the same. If he breaks through and escapes, the keepers give chase, the one catching him becoming bear.

CATCH THE WAND. (Spin the Plate.)

Increase the difficulty by having the one called clap hands once or a number of times before catching the wand. Catching may be made still more difficult by asking for a complete turn around before catching. (See games of second grade.)

69

LONG JUMPING ROPE.

The difficulties of this game may be increased by introducing quarter and half turns while jumping; also by having a new pupil run into the rope after every swing until six or eight are in, and have them run out in the same order; also by always keeping a stated number in the rope—when one runs out, the next in order runs in.

LEAP FROG.

This may be played by any number of boys, one of whom assumes a stooping posture with his hands resting on his knees. The others, who stand behind him, leap over him with legs straddled, resting their hands lightly on his shoulders. As each goes over he assumes the same stooping posture as the first, a foot or two in front of the preceding player. When the last has leaped over, the one who stooped first stands up and leaps over the line of stooping players. As soon as he has passed over the one in front of him, that one leaps over the next, and so on until all have done so.

This game may also be played by the boys when standing in open order after their calisthenics. Each file jumps for itself.

WRESTLE FOR THE WAND. (Stick Wrestling.)

Two boys, standing opposite each other, catch hold of a thirty-inch wand. The right hand takes undergrip, the left uppergrip (right hand on the outside). By pressing down with the left hand and pulling with the right, each boy tries to twist the wand from the hands of his opponent. Who lets go with one or both hands loses. The wrestlers must remain on their feet.

HAND - PULLING CONTEST.

Two players take positions opposite to one another grasping right hands. Upon command they begin to pull, each trying to pull the other across a line lying from 3 to 6 feet back of the starting place.

A more difficult variation of hand pulling is as follows: Two players take position opposite to one another, grasping the opponent's wrist with the right hand. The right feet touch each other. Upon command, each tries to pull his opponent over to his side. In this contest the right feet must not be moved. An opponent can be pulled over only by the display of much skill and ingenuity.

HAND - PUSHING CONTEST.

In this contest two players stand with the inner sides of their right feet touching. The left foot of each player is placed backward. The players grasp right hands shoulder-high, bending the arms at the elbow. Upon command they try by pushing, to force their opponent to move one of his feet and thereby win the bout. In this attempt to get one's opponent to move his feet, pushing and suddenly stopping the push is allowable, also the bending of the knees or the trunk.

SHOULDER - PUSHING CONTEST.

Two players stand opposite to one another, placing the left foot forward and placing their hands against the shoulders of their opponent. Upon command each tries to push his opponent over a line lying from 3 to 6 feet back of the starting place.

WAND - PUSHING CONTEST.

Two players face each other in such manner that the inner side of their left feet and the left shoulders nearly touch. The right feet are placed backward (the four feet of the two players being in a straight line). A long wand, approximately 1½ by 46 inches, is held between the players, the right hand grasping the rear end, the left hand the middle of the wand. Upon command each player by pushing tries to force his opponent over a line lying from 3 to 6 feet back of the starting place.

PUSHING BETWEEN TWO WANDS.

Two players stand opposite to one another, place the left foot forward, bend the left knee, and firmly grasp two wands with hands and upper arm, one wand being held under each arm. The ends of the wands should protrude slightly beyond the backs of the contestants. Upon command each tries to push his opponent over a line. The arms must be held tightly against the sides of the body so as to prevent the wands from slipping. A firm hold of this character also enables a contestant to raise his opponent slightly, and thus more easily push him backward.

PULL - OVER.

Two players are seated on the ground opposite each other, the soles of their feet touching. Their arms and legs are extended, and they grasp a strong stick, which is held horizontally between them, exactly over their feet. One player grasps the stick at the ends (on the outside), the other has both hands on the inner side. Upon command they both pull. The player succeeding in pulling over his opponent wins. If played as a team game, credit the winning side with one point for each pull-over.

Pull-over may also be played by having two players, who are standing, grasp right hands (or wrists). Upon command, both begin to pull. He who pulls his opponent over a predetermined mark, wins.

FOOT IN THE RING. (Rooster Fight, Chicken Fight.)

A circle about two feet in diameter is drawn. A boy places one foot in the ring, folding his arms. A second boy hops around the ring with arms folded, trying to push the first boy out of the circle by nudging or shoving him as he goes by. When the first boy is put out, the second takes his place, and a new boy is chosen to attack. If the attacker is put out by having both feet on the ground the next one takes his place. After the game is learned, several circles may be used at the same time. A very agile boy will be able to defend himself against two attackers.

BALL GAMES.

In this grade the pupils should be led to play the games of the preceding grades with a small, regulation-sized ball. They should learn to throw and catch a tennis or soft baseball. They also should be led to bat a soft ball with their hands, and, later, with a paddle or short bat.

TOSS UP. (Flower-Ball, Number-Ball, Catch-Ball.)

The players form a circle, one of the pupils, standing in the center, having a basket-ball (or a tennis-ball). He tosses the ball high up within the circle, at the same time calling one of the players by name. The one named must quickly run and catch the ball after the first bounce. If he catches the ball he tosses it up and calls upon some other player. If the ball is not caught the first player again tosses it up. To increase the difficulty of the game, ask that the ball be caught on a fly.

A variation of this game is to form two sides, numbering the players, the odd numbers forming one side, the even numbers the other. The odd numbers must call on the even, and *vice versâ*. Count one point for every ball caught, and see who wins after twenty tosses.

DAY OR NIGHT. (Black or White, North or South.)

Separate the class into two ranks. These face each other, at two steps distance. One party is named Day, the other Night. Take a coin or a flat piece of wood, designate one side of the coin or wood as Day, the other as Night. Toss it up. Immediately after it has fallen call out the side on top. Should this be Day, this party runs to its goal (about twenty-five feet off), pursued by Night. Whoever is tagged in this pursuit is a prisoner and out of the game. Continue until all of one side are caught.

LAST PAIR RUN. (Last Pair Out, Long Tag.)

Form the players into a column of twos, with a single pupil standing at the head of the column. This one claps his hands three times, at the same time calling out, "Last pair run." Upon this, the pair standing at the rear end of the column runs forward (one at each side) and tries (anywhere in the yard) to join hands before the caller has caught one. If one is caught he becomes caller, and the other two form a pair at the head of the column. The caller is not allowed to turn around to see who is running forward.

CIRCLE TAG.

For older pupils a variation of the game of "Catch Me" (described in the games of Grade II) is known as "Circle Tag," which is played as follows: Form the players in a large, front circle and let them count off by fours. The "ones" then take two steps backward and face to the right. Upon command, these pupils (the ones) run forward, each one trying to tag the one in front of him. After the "ones" have resumed their places, the "twos" (threes and fours) run in the same manner.

To increase the difficulty, let the runners run around the circle twice, three or four times and see who has tagged the greatest number during the run. As soon as some one is tagged he must step into the circle.

This game may further be varied as follows: When all pupils are in place the teacher suddenly calls the "ones." Upon hearing this, the "ones" quickly step out of the circle, run to the right and try to tag those running in front of them. Later the teacher calls another number.

RED ROVER.   (Red Lion, Catching Fish.)

One player, the Red Rover (Red Lion, Fisherman), stands in his den. The others tease him by calling—

> "Red Lion, Red Lion, come out of your den.
> You tag me, you catch me, and I'll help you then."

He folds both hands, runs out and tries to tag one. If he succeeds, they both return to the base, join hands and again venture forth, each player tagged joining the line (lengthening the net). Players may be tagged only by the ones at the end of the line. If the line (net) is broken either by those forming it, or by a player breaking through, those "it" must return to their base.

CHICKEN MARKET.   (Rotten Eggs.)

Two of the players are buyer and seller; the rest are chickens. The chickens stoop down in a row with hands clasped under the thighs. The buyer says to the seller, "Have you any chickens for sale?" The seller says, "Yes, plenty of them. Will you walk around and try them?" The buyer now tries different chickens by laying his clasped hands, palm downward, on the head, and pressing downward. He pretends to find fault with some of the chickens, saying, "This one is too old," "This one is too fat," "This one is too tough," etc. When a chicken is found that is satisfactory, the buyer and seller grasp his arms, one on each side, and swing him back and forth, the chicken still remaining in a stooping position with hands clasped under the thighs. If he stands this test, the buyer leads him away to a place selected as the coop. The sale goes on till all the chickens are sold. Any chicken that smiles or does not stand the swinging test is "no good," and is out of the game.

TRADES. (Botany Bay, Three Wise Men.)

Sides are chosen. Goals are marked off forty or more feet apart. One side chooses some trade which it is to represent in pantomime. The players of this side advance from their goal to the goal of the other side, and arriving there, they say:

"Here are some men from Botany Bay,
Got any work to give us to-day?"

The other players say, "What can you do?" The answer is given by going through some motions descriptive of the trade chosen. The opponents guess what trade is represented. If they guess correctly the actors run back to their goal, pursued by the guessers. Any one tagged must join the other side, who now become the "men from Botany Bay." The game continues till one side captures all the players of the other side.

ADVANCING STATUES.

Lay off a "base line" about twenty feet long, and parallel to it, at a distance of 50 to 80 feet, another line of equal length, called the "home line." On the base line place from ten to twenty players, distributed at equal intervals and facing toward the home line. About five feet beyond the middle of the home line stands a player, the leader, with his back turned toward the base line. This player counts aloud from one to six (or any other number agreed upon). As soon as he begins counting the other players move forward in straight lines perpendicular to the base line. While he is counting they may move forward as fast as they wish, but the moment he says six (or the number agreed upon) the player who is "it" turns around quickly, facing the contestants. Those who are found to be standing perfectly still are entitled to keep their positions, and to move forward from there during the next counting. Any whom the leader finds moving when he turns around are called by name and must go back to the base line. The aim is to reach the home line. The player reaching it first becomes leader for the next game.

The counting may be done slowly or fast, as the leader chooses, or the words may be spoken in groups with irregular intervals, thus:

One, two three, four, five, six;
One-two-three, four, five, six;
One, two-three-four, five-six.

The leader should turn sometimes to the right, sometimes to the left, for the players near the end of the line on the side toward which he turns are at a slight disadvantage. An umpire may be appointed to decide doubtful cases and to enforce fair play on the part of the leader. When this game is played in a classroom the players may line up against the back wall as a base line, one in each aisle, and the home line may be fixed a few feet from the opposite wall.

O'LEARY.

A game with a rubber ball. The game consists in batting a small rubber ball with the hand a certain number of times, and of performing a definitely outlined set of movements while reciting the following:

> 1, 2, 3, O'Leary,
> 4, 5, 6, O'Leary,
> 7, 8, 9, O'Leary,
> 10, O'Leary, postman.

In starting the game, the girl throws the ball against the ground, and then bats it against the ground twice while counting 1, 2, 3. On 3 the ball usually is given a stronger bat, so that it rebounds higher, and then, upon saying the word O'Leary, the player successively performs the following movements:

Exercise No. 1.

1, 2, 3, O'Leary, swing the right leg outward over the ball.

4, 5, 6, O'Leary, swing the right leg outward over the ball.

7, 8, 9, O'Leary, swing the right leg outward over the ball.

10, O'Leary, postman.

When saying the last line catch the ball, and after a short rest take up No. 2, then 3, etc.

No. 2. Swing left leg outward over ball.

No. 3. Swing right leg inward over ball.

No. 4. Swing left leg inward over ball.

No. 5.   Form a circle by grasping hands and make the ball pass through from below.

No. 6.   As 5, but have the ball pass through from above.

No. 7.   Grasp the edge of the skirt with the left hand, and upon O'Leary make the ball pass upward between the arm and skirt.

No. 8.   As 7, but have the ball pass through from above.

No. 9.   Catch the ball in the hollow formed by holding the left thumb and forefinger together.

No. 10.   As 9, but right.

No. 11.   Perform a complete turn left.

No. 12.   As 11, but turn right.

After performing the prescribed movement while reciting 1, 2, 3, O'Leary, the ball is caught and held for a moment before beginning to count 4, 5, 6.

Should the player miss at any one exercise she must again start from the beginning.   If several girls are in competition the next one begins upon the failure of the one performing.   In this case it is customary, upon the next trial, for the player to begin with the exercise she missed at the preceding trial.   Agile pupils will be able to add more difficult exercises.

The Wind.*

Words by Bertha E. Bush.   Composed by W. B. Olds.

There's some-one push-ing hard out-doors, I hear him whis-tle by; And yet I can-not see..... him How-ev-er hard I try. Oo,........ Hear him whis-tle round, 'Tis the wind, the jol-ly, jol-ly wind, How we love the sound.

CHILDREN'S QUICKSTEP. I.

Music: "The Wind," by W. B. Olds.

For young children. The class is arranged in a column composed of ranks of four, which, during the steps, moves to the left around the hall or corridor.

He holds the kites up in the sky,
He tosses Katie's curls,
He fills the aprons held for sails
By happy little girls.

Oo. . . ., hear him whistle round.
'Tis the wind, the jolly, jolly wind;
How we love the sound.

Oh, such a glorious comrade he;
He helps all plays along,
And when we hear him whistle,
We'll greet him with a song.

Oo. . . ., hear him whistle round.
'Tis the wind, the jolly, jolly wind;
How we love the sound.

I.

Measure:

1. Three steps obliquely left forward, and place the right foot forward.
2. Three steps obliquely right forward, and place the left foot forward.
3. Step obliquely left forward, swinging the right leg forward, and then repeat the movement to the other side.
4. Four steps backward.

II.

5. Four gallops obliquely left forward.
6. Four gallops obliquely right forward.
7. Three gallops left forward and place the right foot crossed in front.
8. Three gallops right backward and place the left foot crossed in front.

Repeat I and II as often as desired.

CHILDREN'S QUICKSTEP. II.

For older children arranged in a column of twos. The inner hands are grasped shoulder-high, the knuckles of the outer hands are placed on the hips.

I.

Measures 1 to 4 as above in Children's Quickstep I, except that the couples begin with the outer foot—*i. e.*, those standing on the left begin with the left foot, those on the right begin with the right foot. The movement then is slightly away and toward each other.

II.

5. Four gallops obliquely outward.
6. Four gallops obliquely inward.
7. With a quarter turn the couples face each other, grasping both hands shoulder-high, three gallops sideward toward the front and place the inner foot crossed in front.
8. Three gallops sideward toward the rear and place the outer foot crossed in front.

Repeat I and II as often as desired.

See-saw.*

Words by Bertha E. Bush.

Composed by W. B. Olds.

mp Gracefully.

See - saw, see - saw, Now we're down so low;......

See - saw, see - saw, Up so high we go;........

See - saw, see - saw, Hap - py play - ers we,........

All the ups and downs of life Greet with jol - li - ty.........

* Copyright, 1905, by Novello & Co., Lt.

THE ELFS' FROLIC.

Music: "See-Saw" by W. B. Olds.

This roundel is for older children, arranged in a column of twos.

The inner hands are grasped shoulder-high, the outer knuckles are placed on the hips. The movements begin with the outer foot. To simplify the description the movements of only the one standing at the left are given; the one standing at the right performs to the opposite side.

Measure:

1. Balance-step obliquely left and right forward, the opposite foot crossed in front.

2. As 1.

3. Face inward, both hands grasped shoulder-high, balance-step sideward toward the former front and rear, crossing the opposite foot in front.

4. As 3.

5. Face front, glide obliquely left forward and hop while swinging the right leg crossed in front (cross-swing hop); then repeat this movement right.

6. As 5.

7 and 8. Three slow steps backward, and, with a bow, draw the right foot to the left.

9 to 16. Repeat 1 to 8.

Repeat as often as desired.

Summer Breezes.*

Words by William Comery.

Composed by Arthur Richards.

Should be played very lively.

1. Hark! the sum - mer breez - es say, Child-hood is the time for
2. Come! and we will mer - ry be, Full of laugh - ter, full of

play; Come then chil - dren, come a - way! Join our mer - ry sports to -
glee; Child-hood days should ev - er be Giv'n to mirth and rev - el -

day. Hark! the sum - mer breez - es say, Child-hood is the time for
ry. Come! and we will mer - ry be, Full of laugh - ter, full of

* Copyright, 1894, by Novello, Ewer & Co.

Summer Breezes.

play; Come then chil-dren, come a-way! Join our
glee; Child-hood days should ev-er be Giv'n to

mer-ry sports to-day. 2. Skip-ping thro' the sun-ny
mirth and rev-el-ry.

hours,...... Skip-ping 'tween the pass-ing show'rs, Where the

sun-shine gilds the bow'rs, Floods the mead-ows, paints the flow'rs.

D.C. for 3d verse.

D C

PLAYGROUND ROUNDEL.

A roundel for older children, arranged in a column of twos. Those standing at the left begin with the left foot, the others with the right foot. The movements of the one at the left are described.

There is no movement on the "up beat," preceding the first full measure.

I.

Measure:

1. Three steps forward, then place the right foot crossed behind the left leg and slightly bend the knees (the heels raised from the floor).

2. As 1, beginning with the other foot, crossing left.

3. Step left, then place the right foot crossed behind the left leg, slightly bending the knees; then perform the movement to the opposite side.

4. Two change-steps.

5 to 8. Repeat 1 to 4.

II.

9. With three steps forward, perform a half turn right, then place the right foot backward.

10. As 9, but facing left and placing the left foot backward.

11. Place the left foot forward, backward and a change-step left.

12. Place the right foot forward, backward and a change-step right.

13 to 16. Repeat 9 to 12.

III.

Part III is a repetition of the movements of Part I.

Repeat I, II and III as often as desired.

BLEKING (Swedish).

Victor Record 17,085 (Dance is played six times).

Steps: Bleking, hop step.

Hop step: Step on right foot, 1; hop on right foot, "and"; step on left foot, 2; hop on left foot, "and."

Formation: Single circle of couples, facing center, boy on the left of girl.

Music: Two parts of 8 measures each. Polka rhythm (2 counts to a measure).

PART I.

Measures:

1. Partners face, grasp hands, shoulder high, arms slightly bent. Hop on the left foot and place right foot forward on heel and straighten right arm forward (1) (Bleking step); with a hop change position of feet and arms (2) (counts 1 and 2).

1. Change position of feet and arms three times (quickly) (counts 3 and 4).

2. Repeat, beginning left (counts 5 to 8).

4. Repeat above 4 measures (counts 9 to 16).

PART II.

4. Beginning left, 8 hop steps, with a sideward swaying of the trunk, boy moving forward and girl backward (counts 1 to 8).

4. Repeat above 4 measures, making a whole turn, clockwise, on the last 4 counts (counts 9 to 16).

HOP MOTHER ANNIKA (Swedish).

Victor Record 17,331 (Dance is played five times).

Steps: Polka, skipping.

Polka left: Hop on right foot "and," step left forward, 1; bring the right foot to the left heel and put the weight on it, "and," step left forward, 2.

Formation: Double circle of couples, boy on left of girl, left sides toward center, inner hands grasped.

Music: Introduction of 2 measures. Four parts of 8 measures. Polka rhythm (2 counts to a measure).

INTRODUCTION.

Measures:

2. Partners face and bow to each other, then face in the line of march (counts 1 to 4).

PART I.

8. Beginning with outer foot, 16 marching steps forward, with arm swinging forward and backward (counts 1 to 16).

PART II.

8. Sixteen skip steps forward, also with arm swinging. Finish facing partner (counts 1 to 16).

PART III.

1. Stamp right forward and clap partner's right hand; stamp right foot to left and clap own hands (counts 1 and 2).

1. Same left (counts 3 and 4).

6. Repeat above 2 measures three times (counts 5 to 16).

PART IV.

8. Face in line of march, inner hands grasped. Beginning with outer foot, 8 polkas forward, facing toward and away from partner, with arm swinging backward and forward (counts 1 to 16).

The dance may be made progressive by having the boy move forward to the next girl on the last polka.

CLAP DANCE (Swedish).

Victor Record 17,084 (Dance is played four times).

Steps: Polka, heel and toe polka.

Polka left: Hop on the right foot, "and," step left forward, 1; bring right foot to left heel and put the weight on it, "and," step left forward, 2.

Heel and toe polka left: Place the left foot forward, heel touching, 1; place the left foot backward, toe touching, 2; polka left forward, 3 and 4.

Formation: Double circle of couples, boy on left of girl; left sides toward center, inner hands grasped.

Music: Two parts of 8 measures, each repeated. Polka rhythm (2 counts to a measure).

PART I.

Measures:

8. Beginning with outer foot, 8 polka-hops forward, facing toward and away from partner, with arms swinging backward and forward (counts 1 to 16).

8. Four heel and toe polkas with same arm movements (counts 1 to 16).

PART II.

1. Partners face, boys bow, while girls curtsy (counts 1 and 2).
1. Both clap hands in front of chest three times (counts 3 and 4).
2. Repeat above 2 measures.
2. Partners clap right hands, 1; clap own hands in front of chest, 2; partners clap left hands, 3; clap own hands in front of chest, 4 (counts 9 to 12).
1. Partners clap right hands and beginning left make a whole turn left in four running steps (counts 13 and 14).
1. Three stamps in place (left, right, left) (counts 15 and 16).
4. Repeat first four measures of Part II (counts 1 to 8).
1. Shake right forefinger threateningly at partner (left hand supporting right elbow) (counts 9 and 10).
1. Repeat left (counts 11 and 12).
1. Partners clap right hands and beginning left make a whole turn left in four running steps (counts 13 and 14).
1. Three stamps in place (left, right, left) (counts 15 and 16).

The dance may be made progressive by boys moving to next partner instead of making turn second time.

TANTOLI (Swedish).

Victor Record 17,159 (Chord—Dance is played six times).

Step: Heel and toe polka, step hop.

Heel and toe polka left: Place the left foot forward, heel touching, 1 "and," place the left foot backward, toe touching, 2; hop on right foot, "and," step left forward, 1; bring the right foot to the left heel and put the weight on it, "and," step left forward, 2, "and."

Formation: Double circle of couples, boy on the left of girl, left sides toward center, inner hands grasped.

Music: Two parts of 8 measures each. Polka rhythm (2 counts to a measure).

Measures:

PART I.

8. Beginning with the outer foot, four heel and toe polkas forward, with stamping during the polka (counts 1 to 16).

PART II.

Partners face and join hands.

8. Sixteen step hops with trunk swaying sideward in a circle counter-clockwise, turning partner clockwise (counts 1 to 16).

Step hop left: Step left forward, 1; hop left, raising right foot back of left, 2.

Face in the line of march and stamp on retard of music.

GAMES AND DANCES
FOR PLAYERS OF TEN TO FIFTEEN YEARS

Fifth to Eighth School-Grades.

RELAY RACE.

In most playgrounds it is best to run this race "to and fro," as a shuttle race. Divide the players into teams of eight pupils each. Each team is so arranged that four stand at one end of the space to be covered and the other four at the other end:

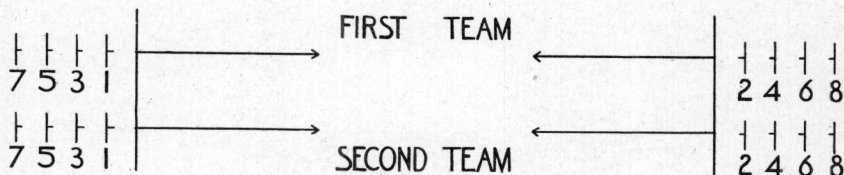

```
┝ ┝ ┝ ┝         FIRST   TEAM         ┥ ┥ ┥ ┥
7 5 3 1    ──────────────────►    ◄──        2 4 6 8

┝ ┝ ┝ ┝                                      ┥ ┥ ┥ ┥
7 5 3 1    ──────────────────►    ◄──        2 4 6 8
                SECOND TEAM
```

The first one of each half "toes the scratch." The commands for starting the race are: "Get on your marks;" "Get set;" "Go." Upon the command, "Go," No. 1, who has a flag (a handkerchief or a stick) in his hand, runs across the course and hands the flag to No. 2. No. 2 immediately runs across and hands the flag to No. 3 (who in the meantime has toed the scratch line), and so on, each member of the team running across the space once. The other teams of eight are doing likewise. The team getting its eighth runner across the line first wins.

HUMAN BURDEN RACE.

This is an amusing variation of the relay race. The halves of the team stand about twenty-five to thirty feet apart. Upon the command, "Go," No. 1 runs across the course, allows No. 2 to jump on his back, and immediately starts back to his original side. Arriving at the scratch line, No. 2 quickly dismounts. As soon as No. 3 has mounted on the back of No. 2 he races across to the other side. Here No. 4 mounts on No. 3, and so on until No. 8 has been carried across.

POISON.   (Poison Snake, Wrestling Circle.)

Divide the players into small circles of about eight pupils each.   In the center of each circle place an Indian club (a large, hollow ball, or a stick of cord-wood about fifteen inches high, or pile up a number of boys' hats or caps).   This object in the center of the circle is "poison."   The players grasp hands and, by pushing and pulling, try to make one of the players touch or overthrow the "poison."   The player doing so is poisoned and must leave the circle.   This continues until one is left.   This is a very strenuous game, and may be played during the coldest weather.

HOPPING CONTESTS.

(a) HOP AND PULL.

Divide the players into "ones" and "twos."   The twos march twelve steps forward and face left about.   Now let the first eight of each side step forward, and each pair of opponents grasp right hands.   Upon the command, "Go," they all hop (on one foot) and try to pull their opponents over to their side.   The side having pulled over the greatest number wins.   In case a player is forced to place both feet on the floor, the opponent wins.   Then take the next eight, and so on.

(b) HOP AND PUSH.

Proceed as above.   The opponents now grasp each other's shoulders, and while hopping try to push one another over into their territory.

(c) FOOT IN THE RING (Boys).

Divide the players into squads of about eight.   For each squad draw on the ground a circle of about two feet in diameter.   Boy No. 1 comes forward, places one foot in a ring, bending the knee and having the weight of his body over this foot.   He then folds his arms and awaits the attack of pupil No. 2, who, also having his arms folded, hops forward.   No. 2 hops around No. 1 (who keeps changing his front to where No. 2 is) until he finds a chance to attack No. 1 and, while hopping, push him out of the circle.   If he succeeds, he wins, and takes the circle, No. 3 coming forward to attack him, and so on.   If, however, during the contest No. 2 gets both feet on the floor, he loses, and No. 3 then comes forward to attack No. 1.   The player in the ring, so long as his foot is in the circle, may cause the attacker to fall by evading or dodging him. The arms always must remain folded, and the pushing must be done with the shoulders and never with the raised arms. For very skillful players, an exciting contest is had by putting two attackers against the one in the ring.

(d) FREE HOPPING. (Rooster Fight—Boys.)

Divide the players as above. This contest calls for the highest display of skill and endurance. Two players with folded arms hop about freely, each trying to force the other to place both feet on the ground, either by pushing or by dodging an attack. If in trying to avoid a fall a player touches the ground with his hand or any other part of his body except the foot he is hopping on, he is out. Players are not allowed to change feet during a "bout." The arms always must remain folded and held close to the chest.

RING TOSS.

This is a game of skill. Divide the players into as many squads as there are sets of rings. A ring-toss set consists of two bases and four rubber rings. The bases are placed from ten to fifteen feet apart. Each player gets two rings. Points are made by tossing the ring as close to the pin as possible.

A variation of this game is to draw three circles around the base, about one, two and three feet from the pin. Allow five points for a toss into the outer circle, ten points into the next, fifteen into the third, and twenty-five if a "ringer" is made. Horseshoes will answer where no rings can be had.

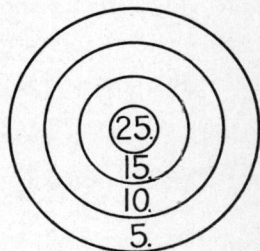

QUOITS.

The game of quoits is exactly like the game described above. You play for twenty-one points. As iron quoits are dangerous in most smaller playgrounds, rubber is advised. Buy only the best quality, as the cheap quoits will break in a few days.

HOOP TOSS. (Grace Hoops.)

This is a game of skill of the ring-toss order. It consists of tossing a large ring or hoop by means of a stick to another player, who catches the hoop with a stick. A hoop-toss set consists of two sticks and four hoops of about twelve inches in diameter. A pair of players stand from twenty to forty feet apart, each having a stick. No. 1, who has the four hoops, inserts the stick into one hoop and tosses this over to No. 2, who may run to catch it. The hoop must be tossed so that it flies through the air horizontally. The other three hoops are thrown similarly. Then No. 2 tosses the hoops. If used as a team game, have four players on each team and count the number of catches made by each side.

LONG JUMPING ROPE.

After the girls have learned to jump into the rope when it is swinging toward them, make the performance more difficult by having them jump into the rope as it recedes. (The rope is swung away from the jumper.) Perform quarter and half turns after each second jump, and run out after a definite number of jumps.

BALL RELAY.

(a) OVERHEAD.

Divide the players into three divisions, or as many divisions as there are basket-balls or round footballs to play with. Arrange them in three flank ranks, one pupil standing behind another, the one standing in front having a ball. Upon command, No. 1 passes the ball over his head into the hands of No. 2; he passes it to No. 3, and so on until the last one gets the ball.

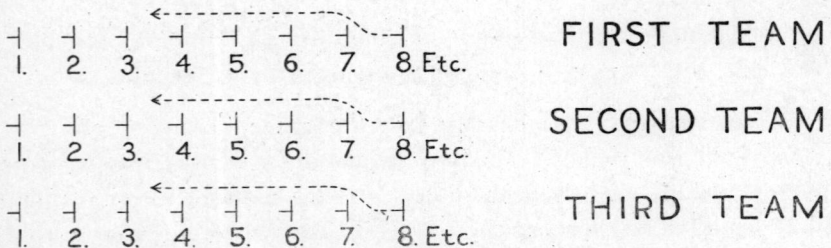

```
        <----------------
  ┤   ┤   ┤   ┤   ┤   ┤   ┤---┤            FIRST   TEAM
  1.  2.  3.  4.  5.  6.  7.  8. Etc.

        <----------------
  ┤   ┤   ┤   ┤   ┤   ┤   ┤---┤            SECOND  TEAM
  1.  2.  3.  4.  5.  6.  7.  8. Etc.

        <----------------
  ┤   ┤   ┤   ┤   ┤   ┤   ┤---┤            THIRD   TEAM
  1.  2.  3.  4.  5.  6.  7.  8. Etc.
```

As soon as he has it he races along the right side, places himself in front of his rank, and then the relay again takes place from the first to the last. The last one again runs to the head of his rank and starts the relay, and so on until every player in the rank has run to the front. The last runner will be the pupil who originally headed the rank.

N. B.—Dumb-bells, potatoes, handkerchiefs or any other articles may be used in place of balls.

(b) BETWEEN THE FEET.

A variation of the above game consists in having the players bend forward and stand with their feet apart. The play then consists of passing the ball backward between the feet. Every player must touch the ball as it is passed backward.

(c) OVER AND BACK.

Divide the players into as many divisions (or teams) as there are balls. Each team now counts off from right to left. The even numbers take four steps forward and face left about. Upon the command, "Go," No. 1 passes

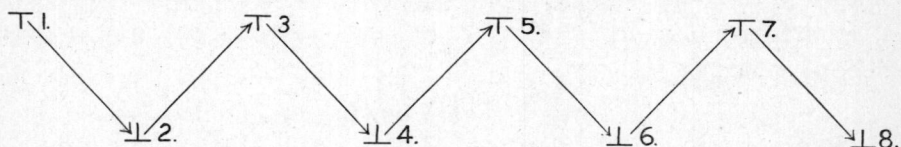

the ball over to No. 2, he to No. 3, he to No. 4, and so on. The team first getting the ball into the hands of its last member wins. The ball may also be relayed to the last member of the team and then back again into the hands of the first.

An interesting variation of the game is found by requesting each team member to bounce the ball on the floor once and catch it before throwing it over to the next player.

Bouncing may be replaced by tossing the ball up into the air, or by bouncing first, then tossing up before throwing over to the next.

BAG RELAY.

Teams for this Relay Race may be made up of any number of pupils. The players line up one behind the other, No. 1 standing on the "starting line." Sixty feet from the starting line there is a second line drawn parallel to the first called the "rear line." In front of the starting line a third line is drawn 30 feet away called the "front line." (See diagram.) The first player standing on the starting line holds a bean bag approximately eight inches in diameter, and weighing several pounds. (If no bag is convenient use a piece of wood, a ball, etc.)　Upon command the bag is passed backward overhead with both hands to player number 2, this one in turn passes the bag overhead to number

PLAYERS FACE THE "FRONT LINE"

3, and so on until the last player is reached.　This player turns about and runs to the rear line.　The player touches this line, quickly returns to the starting line and places himself at the head.　The bag is then immediately relayed overhead again from the first player to the last as described above. The successive members of the team thus run to the rear line, touch this, then along the right side of their team to the starting line until all have had a chance to run.　The last player, however, runs to the back line, and from this he runs at full speed to the front line, 30 feet from the starting line, and crossing this finishes the race.

CHASE BALL.

Divide the players into divisions of about twelve each.　Each division is again divided into two teams.　A basket-ball or football is given to one team, whose members throw the ball to one another.　The other team tries to intercept and catch the ball.　If they succeed, they try to keep the ball in their possession as long as possible.　The players run about within the territory allowed them.　The ball must never be taken out of a player's hands, and no tackling or rough play is allowed.　This is a splendid cold-weather game.

MEDICINE BALL.

A medicine ball is a stuffed ball, weighing from three to perhaps ten pounds, about the size of a basket-ball or a little larger.　As a rule, the weight determines the size of the ball.　It requires much more strength to throw the ball and, often, more skill to catch it.　Arrange the players in a circle.　Let one player after another come forward, grasp the ball with both hands, bend forward and toss the ball as high as possible. The next player steps into the circle when the ball is tossed and tries to catch it. If the players are numbered as "ones" and "twos," this simple game can be turned into a team game by keeping score of the number of catches of each side.

If the players are arranged in a front circle—*i. e.*, all facing the center—the ball may be passed rapidly from one player to the next. Pass ball with a medicine ball is quite a different game than when played with a basket-ball.

If the players are standing in a flank circle—*i. e.*, one behind the other—the ball may be thrown backward overhead from one player to the next, or it may be rolled backward by each player stooping and rolling it backward through his legs.

If the players are arranged in two teams facing each other and standing from 10 to 15 feet apart the ball may be thrown swiftly from one side to the other. For this throw the ball is held in the forearm and hand. With this hold strong players can throw a ball hard to catch. The game may be turned into a team competition by counting the number of catches made in a specified number of throws.

THREE DEEP. (Tag the Third.)

Arrange the players in a large circle, standing two deep (one behind the other). Now select one pair as a runner and a catcher. The runner runs around the outside of the circle and places himself in front of a pair, thereby forming a rank of three, "three deep." This must never be. The last one of these three, therefore, runs and places himself in front of some other pair, again forming three, etc. In the meantime the catcher is chasing the runner, trying to tag him before he places himself in front of a pair. As soon as the runner is tagged he becomes chaser, and the former catcher is the runner. The game then continues. In order to have a splendid game, note the following: Do not allow any running through the circle; insist that the players always run around the outside. Do not allow the playing of "partners," and encourage short runs outside, so as to get quick changes. If some players persist in running around the circle once or oftener, put them in the center of the circle to watch and learn how the game ought to be played. Do not allow the boys to indulge in hard slapping.

To make the game more difficult have the pairs in the circle face each other ⊤͟. The runner now must run between a pair and place himself in front of one of the players ⊤͞. This player now is "the third" and runs from the chaser.

To make the game easier, also when teaching it to young children, form a circle only "one deep." When the runner now places himself in front of some one they stand "two deep." The second one now runs as described above.

JUMPING CIRCLE. (Hopping Circle, Shotbag.)

Form the players in a circle. The pupils face inward and are about two steps apart. Get a rope, about twelve feet long, with a beanbag tied to the end of it. One of the players stands in the center and swings the rope around in a circle, keeping the bag close to the ground. As the rope approaches each player, he jumps upward and over the swinging bag. Whoever is struck by the bag or rope steps out of the circle. Insist that the bag be swung close to the ground, and, with timid players, that it is not swung too rapidly.

PROMOTION BALL.

Draw a circle of from 20 to 30 feet in diameter. On the periphery of this, place as many small circles, 2 feet in diameter, as there are players.

Number the small circles consecutively from 1 to whatever the last one may be. In the diagram the small circles are numbered from 1 to 16.

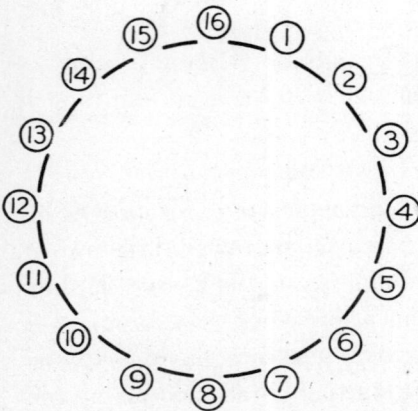

The game is begun by player number 1 tossing a basket-ball to any player. If this player catches it he in turn tosses the ball to another player. When catching the ball a player must have at least one foot in his circle. When a player misses the ball he must go after it. This opens the way for players standing lower down the line to advance—i. e., to be promoted. The player who missed the ball, therefore, when he comes back to the circle usually finds only the small circle with the highest number left for him. After taking his place he again starts the game by tossing the ball to any one. A ball, to be a "fair throw," must be thrown so that it is possible for the person for whom it is intended to have a chance to catch it. If it is a "foul" throw, the person throwing it must get the ball, thereby forfeiting his place.

STAND BALL.

Stand Ball may be called a development of Toss up, Flower Ball (see page 72). To the ball-catching of this game is added the throwing of the ball at an opponent.

Stand Ball is a game employing from 8 to 30 players. It is a simple game, giving much running to the players. To some degree it also develops skill, accuracy and quickness.

The players are arranged in a circle and are numbered from 1 upward, so that each player has a number. The leader steps to the starting mark in the centre of the circle (see diagram) and tosses a basket-ball upward. As it descends he calls a number. The player having this number runs into the circle and catches the ball. The rest of the players run away as fast as they can. As soon as the one called has the ball he cries "stand," remaining where he got the ball. Hereupon all players must stand where they are. The player with the ball now throws at any player, usually at the one standing nearest him. This person may bend or stoop to avoid being hit, but he is not allowed to move his feet.

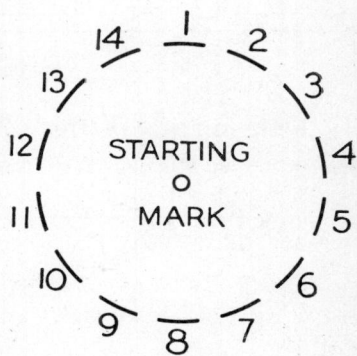

If he is hit he immediately runs to get the ball, crying "stand" as soon as he has it. (A player thrown at is not allowed to catch the ball when it is thrown at him.) The other players in the meantime have run away as fast as they can. The player now having the ball throws this at some one. In this manner the play proceeds until a player thrown at is missed. As soon as this happens any player may get the ball, run quickly to the starting mark and toss up the ball, calling out a number. The quicker this is done the better, as it helps to enliven the game. Calling the number of a player who is far from the starting mark adds to the merriment.

The game also may be played as a team game. In this form the ball is thrown from team-mate to team-mate until some one near an opponent gets the ball. The players during this passing of the ball may run at will until a player, after he has caught the ball, cries "stand." A miss-throw counts a point for the opposing team. Hitting a player counts a point for the throwing team. After a point has been made the ball goes to the side that scored the point.

VOLLEY BALL. (Form 1.)

Volley Ball is a game for older pupils and adults. It is, however, possible to get younger pupils to learn some of the rules of the game and to acquire some of the necessary skill. The form of game described below, for instance, appeals strongly to young boys and girls. In this game the ball is thrown over the rope (or net) instead of being batted over. Again, instead of the ball being batted back, the receiving player catches the ball. This makes a much simpler game, which is played, according to the following rules:

1. The game is played by two teams of nine (or more) players each.

2. The court is 40 x 20 feet, divided into two equal parts by a rope (or net) stretched 5 to 7 feet above the ground. (a) 5 feet for small players; (b) 7 feet for tall players.

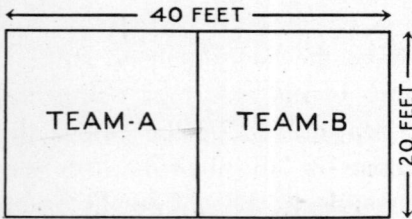

DIAGRAM OF COURT.

This division of the court makes each team's play-space 20 feet square.

3. The playing time shall be two halves of five minutes each.

4. Only one official is necessary. This is a referee. He calls all fouls, decides all questions about the ball, out of bounds, striking rope, etc.

5. An ordinary basket-ball or a medicine ball may be used for this game.

6. The object of Team A is to throw the ball in such a manner over the rope or net that it will strike the ground within Team B's territory before any member of this team can catch it. If the ball is caught Team B makes a return throw, and so on until the referee calls time. (In this lower form the

ball is caught and returned instead of being batted.) If the ball is not caught the throwing team scores a point.

7. Scoring. (a) A ball must be thrown fairly over the rope or net.

(b) If either team fails to catch a ball that is fairly thrown, and the ball strikes' the ground within their territory it counts a point for the opposing side.

(c) If the ball goes out of bounds, and any member of the opposing team catches it, the ball shall be put into play again. If he fails in an attempt to catch the ball going over the lines without having previously called "out of bounds," the opposing team scores one point.

BASEBALL AS PLAYGROUND BALL

Baseball is one of our great national games. It is so well known (especially to boys) that it needs no description. It cannot, however, be played on all playgrounds on account of the great space needed. Modifications of it, however, may be played on all playgrounds, be they ever so small or irregular in size. These modifications are here grouped under the head of playground ball.

The object of baseball is for the player at the home plate to strike a ball that has been pitched or thrown, and then to run to a base before the batted ball reaches there, or before he has been touched by the ball in the hands of an opposing player. In the old game of "townball," which was the forerunner of modern baseball, a batter could also be put out by being "thrown out"—that is, the ball was thrown between the runner and the base. He was also out if he was hit by a thrown ball before he reached his base (the thrown ball being soft). These various modes of putting a batter out may be used to good advantage in adapting the modern game of baseball to local conditions.

PLAYGROUND BALL—VARIATIONS BASED UPON THE NUMBER OF PLAYERS.

In its simplest form, baseball may be played by three players, a pitcher, a batter and a catcher (who stands behind the batter). The first base is placed some distance beyond the pitcher. The batter must reach this base and return to the home plate every time he hits the ball. If not, or if the ball he struck is caught on a fly, or if he is "thrown out," etc., he is out. The catcher then takes his place, the pitcher is made catcher and the former batter is made pitcher.

If there are four players, two of them are on the "ins"—*i. e.*, at bat— and two of them are on the "outs"—*i. e.*, out in the field. It now is not necessary for the batter to reach first base and return home in one stretch. If he reaches first base, he may wait until the second batter on the "ins" strikes the ball before attempting to reach the home base.

If there are five players, one of them is made first baseman. If there are six players, the additional player is made first fielder, etc. In this manner the game develops. Every time one of the batters is put out all the players on the "outs" advance to the next higher place, while the player that was put out takes the place of the last fielder.

Variations Based on Insufficient Space.

In playgrounds one often has enough players to play a regular game, but adequate space is lacking. This condition is met in several ways. First, there is the regular game played with a large, soft ball (a so-called indoor baseball, from fourteen to seventeen inches in circumference), and with a short, light bat. The bases, instead of being ninety feet, are now only thirty feet apart.

If the space is too small to allow this modification, the next step is to use a large, hollow ball (a basket-ball), and to bat this with the closed hand, with two hands or with the forearm. The bases may now be placed twenty feet apart. In this form, baseball may be played all winter.

The shape of the ground at one's disposal may make it advisable to lay out the field in a long diamond instead of a square, or to use only one base (long base)—a long distance from the home plate.

What teachers should understand is that the regular game of baseball may be modified to meet the conditions in any playground. It is a game every girl and boy should know and play.

CORNER BALL.

The field is an oblong, 30 feet by 40 feet, divided into two equal parts. (Any space may be used if this size is not available.) Each part contains two bases, placed in the far corners. A third may be added if desired. (See diagram.)

Any number may play. They are divided into two teams. Two players of each team are basemen and the others are guards. Their positions are shown in the diagram.

The bases are three (3) feet square.

The object of the game is to throw the ball from a guard to a baseman of the same team.

The game is played in halves of five (5) or more minutes each. Play is continuous during this time, the only stop being that made to call a foul.

A point is made whenever a baseman catches a ball (a basketball) from one of the guards of his own team. It must be a fair throw— that is, the ball must not touch the ground, wall, or ceiling before being caught by the baseman.

Rules—Guards are not allowed to cross the center line, nor to step into the bases, nor out of the field of play.

Basemen must always have both feet in their bases, but they are allowed to jump up to catch the ball.

The game is in charge of a referee, who calls all fouls. At the beginning of each half he tosses the ball up in the center of the field, between two opposing guards. In case of a foul he gives the ball to a guard of the other team.

There shall be a scorer, who is also timekeeper.

If in the course of play the ball rolls or is thrown off the field, it shall be brought back by a guard of the team whose line is crossed. He shall put

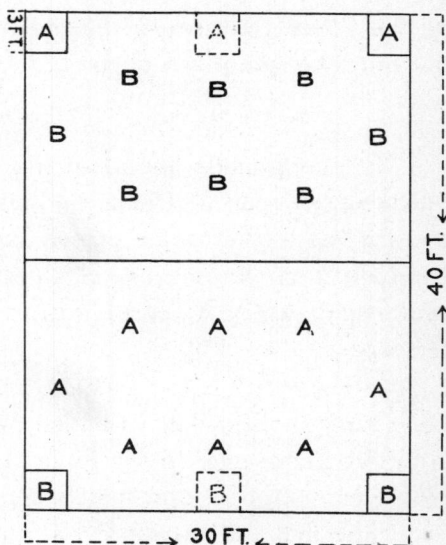

the ball in play by standing on the line, at the place where the ball left the field, and throw it to one of the guards of his own team.

Fouls are made as follows:

1. Carrying the ball (taking more than one step).

2. Striking or touching the ball when it is in the hands of a player.

3. Holding, pushing, striking, or tripping an opponent.

4. Stepping across the center line, or out of the field, with one or both feet.

ENDBALL. (Form I.)

1. *Equipment*—A rectangular space 40 by 50 feet, and a basket-ball.

2. *Teams*—Twelve members to a team, eight guards and four basemen.

3. *Object*—The object of the game is to pass or throw the ball from a guard to a baseman of the same team, the opposing guards trying to prevent this and pass the ball to their basemen.

4. *Length of Game* — (a) Two halves of 15 minutes or less.

(b) In case of a tie score, one or more extra periods of 5 minutes or less must be played through, until the tie is broken, at the end of one of these periods.

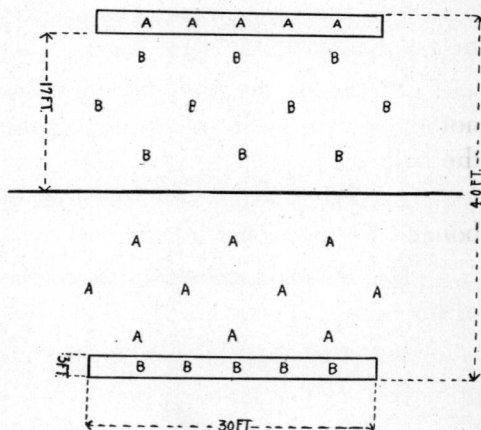

(c) At the end of the first half, and at the beginning of each extra period, teams change sides on the field.

(d) Time shall be taken out only by the referee for loss of ball, for change of player, accident, etc.

5. *Officials*—(a) The referee has entire charge of the game. He decides what points are scored and who shall possess the ball in case of disagreement, calls fouls, and awards penalties.

(b) The timekeeper shall keep time and score.

6. *Putting the Ball in Play*—At the beginning of each half and of

extra periods the referee tosses up the ball in the center between two opposing guards. As the ball is about to descend he blows the whistle. The ball must not be touched before the whistle is blown.

7. *Playing the Ball*—(a) When a guard and a baseman get possession of the ball at the same time, the referee shall give the ball to the guard.

(b) When two opposing guards get possession of the ball at the same time, the rcferee shall toss the ball up in the center.

(c) If the ball strikes some obstructions at the sides of the playing space, the ball is given at that place to the guard who would otherwise have obtained it.

(d) Baseman must always have both feet in the base (he may jump up and catch the ball).

8. *Scoring*—A point is scored when the ball is passed from a guard to a baseman of the same team.

NOTE—If the ball is touched or batted by an opposing guard, it does not prevent a score, unless that guard has unmistakably had possession of the ball.

9. *Fouls* are (a) To carry the ball more than one step or roll or bounce it and recover it at an advanced point.

(b) For a baseman to touch the ground outside his base with any part of his body.

(c) For any player to cross the center line.

(d) For a guard to step in a base.

(e) Purposely to push, strike or trip an opponent.

(f) Purposely to touch the ball while it is in the hands of an opponent.

(g) Jumping at center, to catch the ball or touch the ball a second time until it has been played by another player.

(h) To touch the ball while it is going up at center toss.

10. *Penalty for Fouls*—In case of a foul the ball is given to a guard on the opposing team.

11. *Substitutes*—Substitutions may be made at any time, but no player removed from the game may return to play during the half in which the removal occurs.

12. *Miscellaneous*—(a) Representatives shall not coach teams during play.

(b) A player may be removed from the game, after warning, for discourteous remarks to the referee.

ENDBALL. (Form II.)

THE GAME.

The game is played by two teams of 8 players each. The object of the game is to score as many points as possible by passing or throwing a ball from a guard to a baseman of the same team, the opposing guards trying to prevent this.

RULE I. EQUIPMENT.

SECTION 1. THE PLAYING COURT shall be a surface, 35 feet by 45 feet, free from all obstructions. There shall be no obstructions less than 15 feet above the playing surface.

SEC. 2. The court shall be divided into equal parts by a center line.

Four bases, 2 feet in diameter, shall be placed at each end of the court, parallel to the center line and 18 feet from it. The distance between the center of the bases shall be 9 feet.

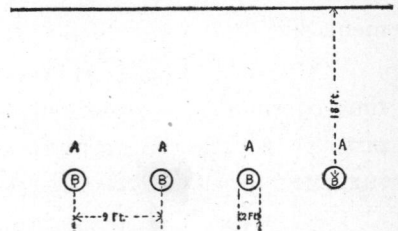

The center line and bases shall be marked by well-defined lines not less than 2 inches in width. The bases shall be at least 3 feet from any obstruction.

SEC. 3. The ball shall be round. It shall be made of a rubber bladder, covered with a leather case; it shall be not less than 26 nor more than 28 inches in circumference, and it shall weigh not less than 14 nor more than 17 ounces.

SEC. 4. The home team shall provide the ball.

SEC. 5. In case the visiting team refuses to accept the ball furnished, the Referee shall decide the ball to be used.

Rule II. Players and Substitutes.

Section 1. Each team shall consist of 8 players, one of whom shall be captain.

Sec. 2. The captain shall be the representative of his team and may address any official on matters of interpretation or to obtain essential information. Before the game he shall furnish the Scorers with the names and positions of the players.

Sec. 3. The players shall be divided into 4 basemen and 4 guards.

Sec. 4. A substitute may take the place of a player only when the ball has been declared dead. He shall first report to the referee.

Sec. 5. A player removed from the game may not re-enter the game during the same half, except to replace a disqualified player.

Rule III. Officials and Their Duties.

Section 1. The Officials shall be a Referee and two Timekeepers, who may also act as Scorers.

Sec. 2. The Referee shall be the superior official of the game. He shall put the ball in play, decide what points are scored, call fouls (designating the offender and the offense), decide who shall possess the ball in case of disagreement, and shall impose penalties for violations of rules.

Sec. 3. The Timekeepers shall note when the game starts; shall note time consumed by "time out" during the game; and shall indicate by gong, pistol or whistle the expiration of the actual playing time in each half. It is suggested the timekeepers use one watch.

Sec. 4. The Scorers shall record the points made. Their record shall constitute the official score of the game. They shall compare their scores after each point, and any discrepancy shall be referred at once to the Referee for decision.

Rule IV. Length of Game.

Section 1. The game shall consist of two halves of 10 minutes each, with an intermission of 5 minutes between halves. The teams shall change sides after the first half.

SEC. 2.   The sounding of the Timekeeper's signal shall terminate the game. If the ball is in the air when Timekeeper's signal sounds, the game shall continue until the ball comes into possession of a player.

RULE V.   CHOICE OF COURTS.

SECTION 1.   The captains shall toss for choice of courts.

SEC. 2.   At the end of the first half the teams shall change sides.

RULE VI.   PLAYING REGULATIONS.

SECTION 1.   The game shall be started by the Referee, who shall at center toss the ball up (at least 10 feet) between two opposing forwards. As the ball is about to descend, the Referee shall blow his whistle. The ball is then in play.

SEC. 2.   The ball shall be tossed up at center:

(a)   At the beginning of each half.

(b)   When two opposing guards or forwards get possession of the ball at the same time.

(c)   After each double foul.

SEC. 3.   When a guard and a baseman get possession of the ball at the same time, the Referee shall give the ball to the guard.

SEC. 4.   If the ball strikes some obstruction at the sides of the playing space, the ball shall be awarded to the guard nearest the obstruction.

SEC. 5.   A baseman must always have one foot in the base; he may jump up and catch the ball, in which case a foot must come down on the base first.

SEC. 6.   A scoring play consists of the passage of the ball from guard to baseman.

SEC. 7.   Fouls shall be called for:

(a)   Walking or running with the ball.

(b)   Dribbling.

(c)   Kicking the ball (it is permissible to block the ball with the feet).

(d)   Pushing, striking or tripping an opponent.

(e)   Touching the ball while it is in the possession of an opponent.

(f)   Stepping over the center line.

(g)   Guard entering base.

(h)   Catching the ball at toss-up or touching the ball a second time (before it has been played by another player or has touched the ground).

(i)   Forward touching ball on the toss-up as it ascends.

SEC. 8.   Penalties:

(a)   When a foul is committed against a baseman, which prevents a score, the ball shall be given to the baseman and one point awarded.

(b)   In all other cases the ball is given to an opposing guard.

SEC. 9.   Fouls committed during a scoring play shall not be penalized until the scoring play is completed.

RULE VII.   SCORING.

SECTION 1.   A point is scored when the ball is thrown, rolled or bounced from a forward to a baseman of the same team.

NOTE—If the ball is touched or batted by an opposing guard, it does not prevent a score, unless that guard has unmistakably had possession of the ball.

RULE VIII.   CONDUCT OF PLAYERS.

SECTION 1.   The Referee shall have power to disqualify for the remainder of the game any player making derogatory remarks to or about the officials or opponents.

SEC. 2.   A substitute shall take the place of a disqualified player.

RULE IX.   FORFEITED GAMES.

SECTION 1.   A team refusing to play after receiving instructions to do so from the Referee shall forfeit the game or match.

SEC. 2.   The score of a forfeited game shall be 1-0.

RULE X.   DECISIONS.

SECTION 1.   Decisions of the officials as to matters of fact are final.

SEC. 2.   Decisions pertaining to the interpretation of the rules may be called into question at once, but only by the captains of the contesting teams.

SEC. 3.   When a question pertaining to interpretation of the rules has not been settled conclusively, but is to be carried to higher authority for decision, the game shall proceed as before, the Referee making proper note of the protest.

RULE XI.   TIME OUT.

"Time Out" may be called by the Referee only, but the ball shall be in play until the whistle is blown by the Referee. He shall order "time out" at the request of a captain not more than 3 times for each team during the game.

RULE XII.   COACHING.

There shall be no coaching from the side lines during the game by any one officially connected with either team, nor shall any such person go on the court during the progress of the game, except with permission of the Referee. Penalty—Two free throws for the opponents.

WILD MAN'S FIELD.

A certain part of the yard is marked as the wild man's field.   This field should be an oblong of about 6 by 18 feet.   The object of the game is to run across this field without being tagged (or caught) by the wild man who roams about in it.   Who is caught takes the place of the wild man.   With skillful players it is advisable to have two or more wild men in the field.

When played as a team game half of the players are in the field, and the other half on the outside.   When three men have been tagged and made prisoners the sides change.

BRONCHO TAG.

This game is a variation of Three Deep.

The players have the same formation as in Three Deep and the game is played according to the same rules except the following:

As the person who is being chased tries to step in front of a line, No. 2 in line grasps No. 1 and turns this person, at the same time keeping in back of him, thus making it more difficult for the person being chased to step in front and form three in a line.   The person being chased does not need to have his back toward the couple, but can stand facing them. As soon as there are three in a line the third one must run.

THREE BROAD.

Formation: A body of front ranks of threes (or twos) in a circle formation with the left (or the right) side toward the center.

There are one runner and one catcher. The runner attempts to form at the side of one of the ranks (grasping the hand of the rank member) before the catcher is able to tag him. If he is successful the player on the opposite end of the rank becomes the runner and may be tagged by the catcher. Running always must be around the outside of the circle. If the runner is tagged by the catcher before he can form at the side of the rank he is "it" and must pursue the one who tagged him.

NUMBER RACE.

The pupils are standing in open order as during their calisthenics or setting up drill. Each rank of four is numbered from front to rear. See diagram. The places of the first and last players must be marked plainly. The object of the game is to have one player in each file or team run around his own file as rapidly as possible, and get back to his place sooner than the similar player from the other files. For example: The teacher calls " Number Three." Upon hearing the command the players standing in rank three face left about, run to the rear of their own file, around the last player, down the opposite side, around the first player and back into their places. In the diagram the path of only one player is shown.

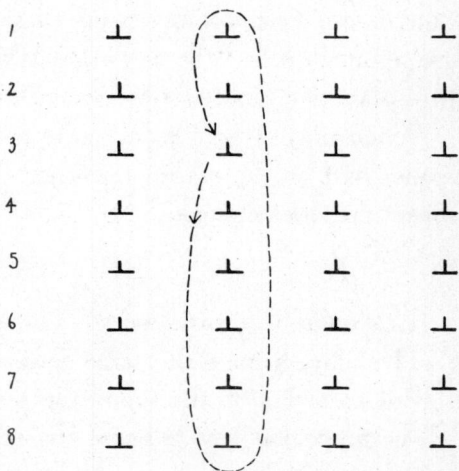

The file or team winning is credited with one point. This is a very lively game, creates much interest and can be played in a very short time.

With older players the teacher can have two members of a team run at the same time.

GAMES AND DANCES
In the Barn.*

Chas. Lindsay.

Moderato. M. M. ♩ = 84.

il basso marcato.

Poco animato.

GAMES AND DANCES
In the Barn.

GAMES AND DANCES
In the Barn.

THE JOLLY CROWD.　(Form I.)

Music: "In the Barn," by Chas. Lindsay.

The arrangement and the steps of this roundel are very simple.　Any number of children can take part.　The class is to be arranged in open order, the pupils being at arm's length apart.　Each measure of music has two counts. While there are seven parts to both music and roundel, Parts III, V, VI and VII are repetitions.

NOTE—The touch-step spoken of in the dance consists of quickly raising the leg forward (or in any other direction), then touching the extended foot lightly on the floor (like in a foot-placing), and again quickly raising it.

PART I.　(8 Measures, 16 Counts.)

1 to 2.　(Knuckles on hips)—Touch-step left forward and backward (counts 1 and 2), then change-step left (counts 3 and 4).　When touching the left foot forward, slightly bend the right knee, also, slightly bend the trunk forward; when touching the left foot backward turn the head right.

3 to 4.　The same exercise right, but while performing the change-step face left about (counts 5 to 8).

5 to 8.　Repeat measures 1 to 4 (counts 9 to 16).

PART II.　(16 Measures, 32 Counts.)

1 to 2.　With a quarter turn left, three steps forward, and touch-step right forward (counts 1 to 4).

3 to 4.　With a half turn right, repeat this movement in the opposite direction—i. e., to the right, and touch-step left forward (counts 5 to 8).

5 to 8.　Repeat measures 1 to 4 (counts 9 to 16).

9 to 16.　Repeat measures 1 to 8, but when executing the touch-step, bend the stationary leg and slightly bend the trunk forward, and at the same time swing the rounded arms sideward (counts 17 to 32).

PART III. (8 Measures—is like Part I.)

PART IV. (16 Measures, 32 Counts.)

1 to 2. Step and leap left sideward (counts 1 and 2), and touch-step right forward and backward (counts 3 and 4).

3 to 4. Repeat measures 1 to 2 to the opposite side (counts 5 to 8).

5 to 8. Repeat measures 1 to 4 (counts 9 to 16).

9 to 16. Raise the arms sideward and repeat measures 1 to 8. When performing the touch-step right forward and backward place the knuckles of the right hand on the hip and raise the left arm in a half circle overhead (*vice-versâ* when to the right), (counts 17 to 32).

PART V. (8 Measures—is like Part I.)

PART VI. (16 Measures—is like Part II.)

PART VII. (8 Measures—is like Part I.)

In performing the steps, follow the "swing" of the music to which this dance has been written.

THE JOLLY CROWD. (Form II.)

This dance, because of added arm movements, is more difficult than the preceding one.

MUSIC—"In the Barn"—Lindsay. Victor Record No. 17557.

Formation: The pupils are arranged in fours, the taller ones on the right. They march forward in closed ranks and, upon command, open ranks in 12 counts, raising the arms sideward on the last count.

PART I. (8 Measures.)

1. Place the left foot forward, left arm forward, right arm sideward; place left foot backward, left arm overhead, right arm sideward (1 measure); change step left forward, arms sideward (1 measure). When placing left foot forward, slightly bend trunk forward; when placing left foot backward, turn head right. 2 measures.

2. Repeat the above opposite, but while performing the change step, face left about and place knuckles on hips. 2 measures.

3 and 4. Repeat 1 and 2. 4 measures.

PART II. (16 Measures.)

1. Quarter turn left and beginning left, three steps forward and place the right foot forward. 2 measures.

With a half turn right, repeat opposite. 2 measures.

2. Repeat 1. 4 measures.

3 and 4. Repeat 1 and 2, but when placing the foot forward, bend the other knee, slightly bend the trunk forward and raise the arms sideward. 8 measures.

PART III. (8 Measures.)

Repeat Part I.

PART IV. (16 Measures.)

1. Step and leap left sideward (1 measure); place the right foot forward and backward (1 measure). 2 measures.

2. Repeat 1 opposite. 2 measures.

3 and 4. Repeat 1 and 2. 4 measures.

5. Step and leap left sideward, arms sideward (1 measure); place the right foot forward, right arm forward; place the right foot backward, right arm overhead (1 measure). 2 measures.

6. Repeat 5 opposite. 2 measures.

7 and 8. Repeat 5 and 6. 4 measures.

PART V. (8 Measures.)

Repeat Part I.

PART VI. (16 Measures.)

Repeat Part II.

PART VII. (8 Measures.)

Repeat Part I.

ACE OF DIAMONDS (Danish).

Victor Record 17,083 (Dance is played six times).

Steps: Polka step, swing hop, running step.

Swing hop left: Step left forward, 1; swing right leg forward and hop left, 2.

Polka left: Hop on the right foot, "and," step left forward, 1; bring the right foot to the left and put the weight on it, "and," step left forward, 2.

Formation: Double circle of couples, partners facing, boys on inside of circle.

Music: Three parts of 8 measures each. Polka rhythm (2 counts to each measure).

Measures:

PART I.

4. All clap hands, link right arms, and turn partner in eight running steps, boys beginning left, girls right (counts 1 to 8).

4. All clap hands and repeat, linking left arms (counts 1 to 8).

PART II.

4. Boys take four swing hops backward toward the center of circle, girls follow, taking four swing hops forward, boys beginning left, girls right (counts 1 to 8).

4. Repeat, returning to places, boys forward, girls backward (counts 1 to 8).

PART III.

Face in line of march, to move counter-clockwise, inner hands grasped.

8. Beginning with outer foot, eight polkas forward, facing toward and away from partner, with arm swinging backward and forward (counts 1 to 16).

SWEET KATE (English).

Victor Record 18,004 (No introduction—Dance is played once).

Steps: Running, swing hop.

Swing hop left: Step left sideward, 1; swing the right leg forward and hop on the left foot, 2.

Formation: Column of couples. (Boy on left of girl.)

Music: Two parts of 8 measures, A and B; B repeated, all played three times. Polka rhythm (2 counts to a measure).

Measures:

PART I.

A. 2. Right hands grasped. Beginning with outer foot, three small running steps forward and close (counts 1 to 4).

   2. Same backward (counts 5 to 8).

   4. Repeat above 4 measures (counts 9 to 16).

B. 1. Facing partner, swing hop left, striking right feet (counts 1 and 2).

   1. Same opposite (counts 3 and 4).

   2. Clap own hands, 5; right hands, 6; own hands, 7; left hands, 8 (counts 5 to 8).

   2. Raise hands, fists clenched in front of chest and circle forward one with the other as though winding wool, 9; hold up forefinger of right hand, 10. Repeat, holding up forefinger of left hand (counts 9 to 12).

   2. With four small running steps make a whole turn right (counts 13 to 16).

   8. Repeat above 8 measures (counts 1 to 16).

PART II.

A. 2. Beginning right, each takes four running steps forward, passing partner, left shoulder to left shoulder. Turn inward toward partner on third and fourth counts (counts 1 to 4).

   2. Repeat, passing right shoulder to right shoulder, returning to places (counts 5 to 8).

   4. Repeat above 4 measures (counts 9 to 16).

B. 16. Same as B of Part I (counts 1 to 32).

PART III.

A. 4. Beginning right, with running steps, partners linking right arms, make a whole turn and with running steps backward, return to places (counts 1 to 8).

   4. Repeat, linking left arms (counts 9 to 16).

B. 16. Same as B of Part I, finishing with a curtsy for the girls and a bow for the boys (counts 1 to 32).

COME, LET US BE JOYFUL (German).

Victor Record 17,761 (Introduction, chord—Dance is played three times).
Steps: Curtsy, skip step.

Formation: In circular formation, ranks of three, with sides toward center, every two ranks facing each other. Each rank consists of a boy and two girls, the boy in the middle.

Music: Three parts of 8 measures each, the third being a repetition of the first.

Measures:
PART I.

2.   Beginning left, march forward three steps, boys bow (heels together), girls curtsy (place right foot in rear and bend knees) (counts 1 to 4).

2.   Beginning right, march three steps backward and close (counts 5 to 8).

4.   Repeat above 4 measures (counts 9 to 16).

PART II.

2.   Boy and the girl on his right link arms, and beginning left, in four skip steps, turn in place, while girl on left circles left in four skip steps (counts 1 to 4).

2.   Same, with girl on left, linking left arms, while girl on right circles right in four skip steps (counts 5 to 8).

4.   Repeat above four measures (counts 9 to 16).

PART III.

2.   Beginning left, march forward three steps, girls curtsy, the boys grasp right hands and quickly change places (counts 1 to 4).

2.   Beginning right, march three steps backward and close (counts 5 to 8).

4.   Repeat above 4 measures with boys bowing instead of changing places (counts 9 to 16).

The dance may be made progressive by substituting the following for Part III.

2.   Beginning left, march forward three steps, boys bow, girls curtsy (counts 1 to 4).

2.   Beginning right, march three steps backward and close (counts 5 to 8).

4.   March four steps forward, release hands, and pass through opposite rank, passing right shoulder to right shoulder; three additional marching steps forward and close, meeting new rank (counts 9 to 16).

WORDS.

Come, let us be joyful,
While life is bright and gay
Gather its roses,
Ere they fade away.—*Fine.*
We're always making our lives so blue,
We look for thorns and find them, too,
And leave the violets quite unseen
That on our way do grow.—*D. C.*

THREE DANCE (Danish).

Victor Record 18,000 (Introduction, chord—Dance played four times with a finale of the first 8 measures played twice).

Steps: Step hop, balance step.

Formation: Square set of four couples.   Head couples, one facing music and opposite couple; side couples, the other two.   Boy on left of girl.

Music: Three parts.   First two parts, 8 measures, repeated; third part, 16 measures.   All repeated.   Polka rhythm (2 counts to a measure).

PART I.

Measures:

8.   All join hands, in circle, clockwise, execute eight step hops, beginning left (counts 1 to 16).

8.   Repeat same, moving in the opposite direction (counts 1 to 16).

Part II.

4.   Beginning left, with eight small running steps, head couples advance, passing each other, couple No. 2 separating, couple No. 1 passing between them (counts 1 to 8).

4.   Without turning, both couples run back to places with eight small running steps, this time couple No. 1 separating and couple No. 2 passing between them (counts 9 to 16).

8.   Side couples repeat same (counts 1 to 16).

Part III.

2.   Beginning left, head couples advance in two step hops, clapping on first three counts (counts 1 to 4).

3.   Opposite boy and girl link right arms and turn in three step hops (counts 5 to 10).

3.   Partners link left arms, turn in three step hops, finishing in original position (counts 11 to 16).

8.   Side couples repeat same (counts 1 to 16).

Step hop left: Step left forward, 1; raise the right foot back of left and hop on left foot, 2.

In repeating the dance, substitute the following figure for Part I:

4.   Partners join inside hands and, beginning with outer foot, execute four balance steps sideward (with foot placing forward) (counts 1 to 8).

4.   Partners join both hands, with four step hops, turning to the right twice, move around the circle counter-clockwise, to original position of opposite couple (counts 9 to 16).

8.   Repeat measures 1 to 8, completing circle (counts 1 to 16).

Balance step with foot placing forward: Step to the left, 1; place the right foot front of the left and rise on toes, "and," lower heels, 2, "and." Repeat opposite 1 and, 2 and.

GAMES AND DANCES
FOR PLAYERS OF TWELVE TO SIXTEEN YEARS

Sixth to Tenth School-Grades.

RABBITS.

The playfield is an oblong about thirty by ninety feet, divided into fourteen equally large parts. (See diagram.) The two playing teams each have nine men, one of whom is captain, the one team being guards (hunters), and the other runners (rabbits). The object of the game is for the rabbits to pass all the hunters, and, after having reached the other end, to return again to the starting place without being tagged. At the start the guards are stationed on their respective lines near the center of the field. During the game they must stay on their own cross lines, but are allowed to run from side to side; the captain, No. 9, can, however, run on any line (either lengthwise or across). After placing all his men, the captain calls "ready" or "rabbits." The game is then started by one or more of the rabbits quickly crossing over into one of the upper fields without being tagged by a guard. Then, as the opportunity offers itself, they cross over and move forward, evading the hunters (guards), who try to tag them. The others follow. Should a rabbit be tagged he is "dead," and takes a place away from the field of play. Five dead rabbits bring about a change of sides, those being rabbits becoming hunters, and *vice-versâ*. Should a rabbit succeed in getting across the eighth line he starts back, and now the hunters must watch the rabbits coming from both ends. If a rabbit succeeds in getting to the rear and back again to the starting point, he cries "Rabbit," which

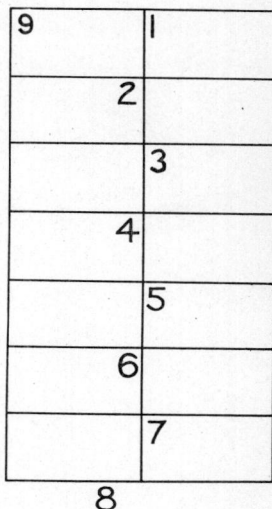

125

signifies a game won for his side, upon which all the runners again start a new game without changing sides.

When playing with a greater number of players add a few cross lines, and use less lines for fewer players. See that the "fields" are large enough that the hunters cannot tag a rabbit when one has safely entered the field. When played by children it is advisable to place two hunters at each cross line and to have no captain.

HAND WRESTLING.

Two players stand opposite to one another, the right foot placed forward, the left back, the outer part of the right feet touching. The right hands are grasped. The object of the game is by pressing sideward to make one's opponent move one of his feet.

WRIST WRESTLING.

This game is played as above, except that the inner part of the right feet touch, and that the opponents cross right arms at the wrists. The right hands are closed.

Both games may also be played by counting only the moving of the right foot as a failure.

STICK - I - SPY. (Kick-Can.)

Conditions at times are such that the well-known game of "I Spy" (Hide and Seek) may be played in playgrounds.

An interesting variation of this game 'suitable for older children consists in making the seeker run after a stick before having the right to spy any player. A certain spot is chosen as "home base," where all players assemble. A player takes the stick and throws it as far as he can. The player who is "it" runs after the stick and returns "home" as soon as he can, striking the base three times. In the meantime the rest of the players have hidden themselves. The seeker now looks for the others. If he spies one and returns home, getting the stick and striking the ground with it before the other player, this one is caught. The game continues until three players are caught. If, however, one of the hiders succeeds in getting home first he grasps the stick and throws it as far as he can. The player who is "it" must once more get the stick and strike the home base three times before he can again spy any one. If three players are out, the one caught first is "it" for a new game.

OVERTAKE. (Chase-Relay.)

The game of overtake belongs to the relay class, the object of the game being to relay a large hollow ball (a cap, a hat, a dumb-bell, a handkerchief filled with grass, etc.) from one point to another faster than the object moved by the rival team. The game may be played in various ways.

1. In its simplest form the players form a front circle, facing inward. Two balls are used, one being given to a player standing at one side, and the other to a player who stands at the opposite side of the circle. (See diagram.) Upon command, the ball is thrown to the player standing at the left. He throws it to his neighbor at the left, etc. Every player must catch the ball, no player to be passed. Who misses the ball must pick it up and throw it to his neighbor. The object of the game is to have one ball "overtake" the next. As a variation more balls may be used; also, balls of different weight and size.

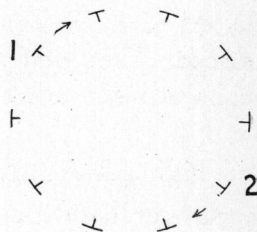

2. If played as a team game the players are numbered, the players with the odd numbers forming one team, the balance the other team. The game is started as described above, each team having one ball (which is thrown only to its own members). The side overtaking the other wins the game.

This game may also be played by giving the balls to two players standing next to each other. The balls should now be thrown twice (or three times) around the circle to see which team wins. This can readily be seen by having the first player raise his arms with the ball after this has completed its second (third) round. Placing the players far apart increases the difficulty of the game.

PASS BALL.

The players stand shoulder to shoulder in a front circle. The object of the game is to pass a large, hollow ball (a club, dumb-bell, stick, handkerchief, etc.) rapidly from one player to the next; no player may be skipped. One player is chosen, who is outside the circle, whose aim it is to tag the ball that is being passed along the inside. The player having the ball in hand

when it is tagged takes the place of the tagger. Should the ball be dropped
and then be tagged by the tagger the player in the circle who touched the
ball last is "it."

PASS - BALL VARIATION.

The following is a variation of pass ball, suited to few players. The
players, instead of standing closely together, stand in a
flank circle with a distance of from 3 to 6 feet between
the players. (See diagram.) Taking a side stride and
bending forward, the ball is passed either backward or
forward to the next player by being rolled between the
legs.

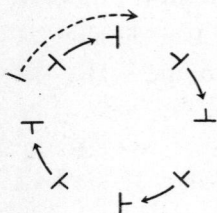

The chaser circles around the outside, trying to
intercept the ball. If the ball is touched by the chaser
with his hands the player who touched it last is "it."

PASS - BALL RELAY WITH ENCIRCLING.

The players are divided into teams, the members of each team standing
next to one another. Upon command a basket-ball (or any other suitable
object) is passed sideward from the first to the last player in each team. When
the last player receives the ball he turns and runs along the rear of his team,
then along the front, and then once
more along the rear, encircling the
team. (See diagram.) Arriving at

LAST   FIRST

the head he immediately passes the
ball to the next player. The ball
then is again passed along until it reaches the one who now is last. He, therefore, encircles the team as described above. This passing and encircling is
repeated until every member of the team has had his turn, and the team members again stand as at the start. When running around the ends it is permissible for the runner to hook his arm into that of the player at the end, as this
enables a quick turning of the ends.

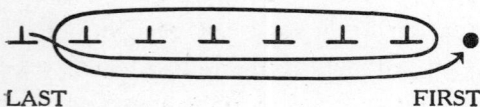

This game also may be played by having the players stand one behind
the other and passing the ball overhead (or underneath), from the first to the
last player. This last player then runs along the right side of his team, down

on the left side and up again on the right. The point to be observed in all styles of playing this game is that the runner must take his correct position at the head of the team before being allowed to pass the ball to the next player.

WALL BALL.

This game is of the same character as, but more difficult than, "Day Ball," described in the games of the Third Grade or "Toss-up," described in games of the Fourth Grade. Draw a line parallel with a high wall at a distance of about twelve feet. One player stands between the line and the wall; the rest of the players, who have received numbers, stand behind the line. The leader throws a tennis-ball (or a basket-ball, baseball, etc.) against the wall, at the same time calling up some number to catch the ball. If the ball is caught, the catcher continues the game, otherwise the first player again throws the ball.

If this game is to be used as a team game the players with the odd numbers call on the even-numbered ones to catch, and *vice-versâ*. The side having the greatest number of catches at the end of the five (or less) minutes wins the game.

BASKET - BALL FAR THROW.

The ball must weigh not less than eighteen nor more than twenty-one ounces. It shall be thrown from over the head from a stand behind a line, known as the scratch line. The feet may not be moved during the throw, nor until the ball falls to the ground. Raising the heels shall not be considered moving the feet. To be a fair throw, the ball must fall inside a lane, ten feet wide, running in the direction of the throw. Lines at right angles to the direction of the throw shall be drawn across the lane one foot apart. The distance of these lines from the scratch shall be distinctly marked to assist the judges in scoring. Credit will be given for whole feet only (no inches).

HURL - BALL FAR THROW.

Each contestant shall be allowed three throws. The hurl ball shall be a sphere, the circumference of which shall be not less than twenty-four (24) and not more than twenty-five (25) inches, with a handle so attached as to keep the backs of the fingers not more than one inch from the surface of the ball. Its weight shall be at least two pounds and not more than two and one-quarter pounds. The ball shall be thrown with one hand, from behind a scratch line, and with unlimited run. Crossing the line makes the throw without result. It shall, however, count as a try. The ball must fall between two lines, twenty-five (25) feet apart and parallel, drawn at right angles to the scratch line in the direction of the throw. Credit will be given for whole feet only (no inches).

GOAL THROW.

This is a team game of low organization that may be played in small yards. Two (or more) teams stand side by side and 15 feet from the baskets. The baskets are suspended from a wall, 10 feet above ground. The first player of each team has a basket-ball. The object of the game is to throw as many baskets as possible.

RULES: 1. The game is started simultaneously. The first player of each team steps to the throwing line and then tries to throw the ball into the basket.

2. Each player has three successive throws. If by that time he has not thrown the ball into the basket the ball is given to the next player in line. It is possible for one player to throw three goals.

3. Each basket (goal) made counts one point.

4. *The team having the most points* after finishing wins the game.

TOWER BALL.   (Hold the Fort.)

The players are formed into a rather large circle. In the center of the circle a tower is placed, made by tying together upper ends of three wands; (a number of clubs, hats, a basket-ball, etc., may also serve as a tower). One or two players are selected as guards, being stationed within the circle. The object of the game for the rest of the players is to destroy the tower by kicking a basket-ball against it. The ball must always be kicked close to the ground. If the tower is knocked down, the player who kicked the ball takes the place of the guard. If the guard upsets the tower, he is replaced by another player.

RELIEVO.

Divide the players into two teams. In one corner of the yard mark off a prison large enough to hold all the players of a team. The players are either taggers or runners. At the beginning of the game all taggers are close to the prison walls. After counting twenty-five the taggers (except a few prison guards) chase the runners. A runner who is tagged is a prisoner, and is put into the prison by his captor. No wrestling or trying to get away is allowed. If, after one or more prisoners have been made, one of the runners succeeds in getting into the prison (without being tagged), all prisoners are free. If the taggers capture all the runners the sides change places. A handkerchief tied around the arm, or other means, may be employed to mark the two teams.

HOP SCOTCH.

Hop Scotch is an interesting individual, hopping game, which can be played either in a very simple or in a very intricate form.

It is suited to a small number (4 to 8) of boys or girls, from 7 to 14 years of age. The simpler forms are used for young children.

Every player has a flat piece of flagstone or a wooden disc. For the simplest form of the game mark out a space 24 feet long by 4 feet wide, which is divided by five transverse lines into six equal 4-foot squares. Number the squares consecutively 1 to 6. (See Diagram 1.) This size is recommended so that the ordinary cement blocks or squares in the pavement may be used.

The games consist in kicking or pushing the disc with the hopping foot out of each square back to the starting point.

The first player stands in front of square No. 1, and tosses his disc into square No. 1. He then hops into square No. 1, kicks the disc back (with the hopping foot) and hops to the starting place without stepping on the line. He then tosses the disc into square No. 2, hops into square No. 1, then into 2. He then kicks the disc out in the same way through square No. 1 to the starting place, and so on to No. 6.

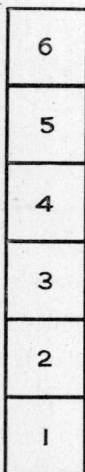

DIA-
GRAM 1

| 6 |
| 5 |
| 4 |
| 3 |
| 2 |
| 1 |

If a player fails to throw his disc wholly within the next square, or if in hopping he steps on any line, or if he kicks the disc on or out of the side lines he is out and the next player takes his turn.

DIA-
GRAM 2

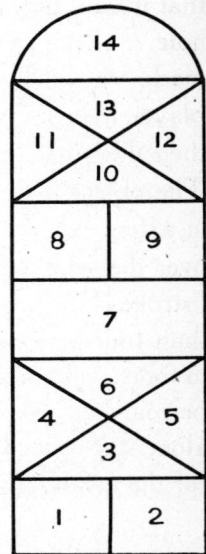

DIAGRAM 3

When each player has had a turn, the first player starts again by throwing the disc into the square in which he last failed. The one who completes the six squares first wins.

VARIETIES.

(a) After reaching the last square, a player, instead of winning the game, must work his way back to Square 1.

(b) After completing form (a) with left foot a player must repeat using the right foot.

(c) By making intricate designs. For instance, draw two diagonal lines in the second and one in fifth square, making each triangle equivalent to a square, making a total of 10 blocks. (See Diagram 2, or, still more intricate, see Diagram 3.) In the intricate designs the disc must be kicked out through each preceding number, exactly as in the simple design.

(d) The old-fashioned hop-scotch court, marked off in squares, on which a chip or block of wood is kicked until a foul is made, has been augmented by a newer style of hopping game known as hop-scotch golf, because the course resembles a miniature golf links.

Place eight or more "holes" in a circle about 25 feet in diameter (or use a promotion-ball court). The holes (about four inches in diameter) may be either drawn with chalk on the cement pavement (or may be made by sinking the lids of baking-powder cans or old pie tins in the turf of your back yard). Choose a particular spot, perhaps a post, or wall, for your starting point from which to kick off the chip.

Each circle is numbered, beginning with 1. The first player kicks his chip, hopping all the while, and with as few "strokes" as possible tries to put the chip into the first hole. After he has succeeded, the next player does likewise. Every player must keep track of the number of strokes that it took him to make the first hole. After all players have made the first hole, the first player tries for the second hole; then the others try in succession. The object is to make each hole in a few "strokes," and so to go over the whole course in as few "strokes" as possible. If more than four persons play, it is wise to open up another course. A person may even play the game alone, trying to break the record for the neighborhood.

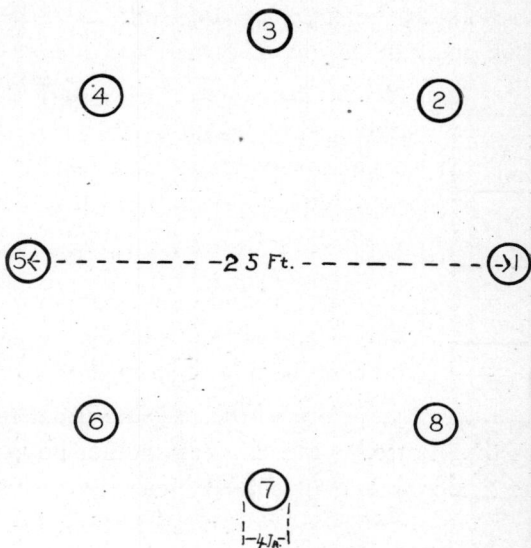

③

④   ②

⑤← - - - - - - -2 5 Ft. - - - - - - -→①

⑥   ⑧

⑦

ROB AND RUN.   (Catch the Robber.)

Divide the players into two teams, Nos. 1 and 2. The teams stand about sixty feet apart. Twenty-five feet from Team No. 1 place a box (or a chair, etc.), and upon this place a basket-ball (a hat, etc.). The object of the game is to have one player from each team run for the ball, get it, and return to his team before being tagged. Upon signal from the leader, the first player of each team runs forward. The ball being nearer Team 1, the player from that team naturally reaches the ball first, but as he must turn to get back to his base, interesting situations develop. If the runner from Team No. 1 gets back before being tagged, his side scores one point. When all players have run, the sides exchange places, Team No. 2 being nearer to the ball. The side having the greatest number of runners untagged wins the game.

Another form of playing for younger players: The object is placed midway between the players. Upon signal from the leader the first player from each team runs forward. Either player may secure the object, and should he return to his side before being tagged by the opposing player, a point is scored by his side.   Should he be tagged, no point is scored by his side.   In either case the object is returned to the center and the next players start upon command.

An interesting variation of the game is had by placing an old hat (or a cap) on the box.   The player getting the hat must put it on his head before running for his base.   The pursuer has the right to snatch the hat off the runner's head and to put it on his own head while racing for his base.   Should he get there with the hat on his head, his side scores a point.   (The original possessor of the hat, naturally, tries to regain it.)

FOOT AND A HALF.

A boy, who is chosen by the usual method, is "down."   He is known as the "horse."   He chooses another boy, who is the leader.   (This position as leader is later occupied by the horse when relieved.)   A line is marked on the ground; the horse takes a stand in front of this line and bends over as in leapfrog, his head being in the direction of the jumping.   All players now, from a stand, execute a straddle vault over the horse.   Shouting "Foot and a half," the leader again vaults.   The horse then moves forward to the point where the leader landed.   The leader now decides how the next vault should be performed; for instance, "from a stand," "from a run of two steps," "from a stand, but jumping off with one foot"; "from a stand, but touching the back of the horse only with the right hand," etc.   The start in all attempts must be made from the scratch line.

We will say, in further explanation, that the leader decided that the second vault should be performed with a standing jump and touching the horse only with the left hand.   All players execute the vault as prescribed.   The leader, as last jumper, shouts "Foot and a half," whereupon the horse advances to the new mark.   The leader now decides how this distance is to be covered.   If, for instance, he calls for "three running steps and over, touching with both hands," and a player goes over with two steps or with using only one hand, the leader is "down," and the horse becomes leader.   This also happens if the leader jumps without shouting "Foot and a half."   The game now starts anew at the scratch line.   The leader must see that all vaults are straight over the center of the horse and from the scratch line.

HAT ON BACK.

This is a game of the "foot-and-a-half" order. A boy is chosen to be "down." He assumes the position of a horse, but stands crosswise (not lengthwise) to the direction of the vaulting. The approach may be as each player chooses; the jump-off, however, must be from the scratch line. After all players have had a "try," during the next vault each player deposits his hat or cap on the back of the horse. Who drops his hat or knocks off any other goes down as the next horse. If all hats are deposited on the back of the horse, the leader makes the succeeding vaults more difficult by adding some difficult feat—e. g., hopping off with the left foot, touching only with the right hand, etc., until some one knocks a hat off.

A variation of this game, making it more difficult, is to have all players who fail stay as horse and bucks. The horse takes the regular position, while the bucks go down on hands and knees between the horse and the take-off. The game in this form is admirable for developing courage, as well as skill.

HAT BALL. (Nigger Babies, Baby in the Hat, Pitch Cap.)

Eight or ten players put their hats (or caps) in a straight or curved row on the ground, each one standing near his hat. One of the players has a rubber ball or a soft indoor baseball. After making a number of deceptive passes he suddenly drops the ball into one of the hats. As soon as he drops the ball, all the players, except the one into whose hat the ball fell, run away in all directions. The player into whose hat the ball dropped grasps the ball and quickly throws it at one of the fleeing players. If he hits the player he also runs away. The player who was struck by the ball gets this as quickly as possible and, from where he picked up the ball, throws it at another player. If the thrower of the ball does not hit a player he gets a "nigger baby"—that is, a pebble (or a piece of coal, etc.) is placed in his hat. One of the players in the meantime recovers the ball and again starts the game. After a certain number of "nigger babies" have been distributed—usually as many as there are players—the second half of the game begins. A line is drawn, ten to fifteen steps from a wall. The first player who has a pebble in his hat steps up to the wall, facing it, and ducks his head. One after another, the other players then step up to the line and throw the (soft) ball at the player. If he had two or more pebbles in his hat he undergoes the ordeal so many times. Then the next victim steps to the wall to be thrown at, and so on, until all who have had pebbles in their hats have been targets.

DODGEBALL. (In a Circle.)

THE GAME.

Dodgeball is a game played by two teams of 12 players each. The object of the game is for the team on the outside of a large circle to score points by hitting the opponents within the circle with an inflated ball, the opponents dodging the ball whenever possible. During the first half of the game one team is in the center and one team is out. During the second half the positions are reversed.

RULE I.

SECTION 1. The circle shall be 40 feet in diameter, marked by a well-defined line at least 2 inches in width, and shall be at every point at least 10 feet from walls or other obstructions.

SEC. 2. The ball shall be round and shall consist of a rubber bladder covered with a leather case. It shall be not less than 26 nor more than 28 inches in diameter, and shall weigh not less than 14 nor more than 17 ounces.

SEC. 3. The home team shall provide the ball.

SEC. 4. In case the visiting team refuses to accept the ball furnished, the Referee shall decide which ball is to be used.

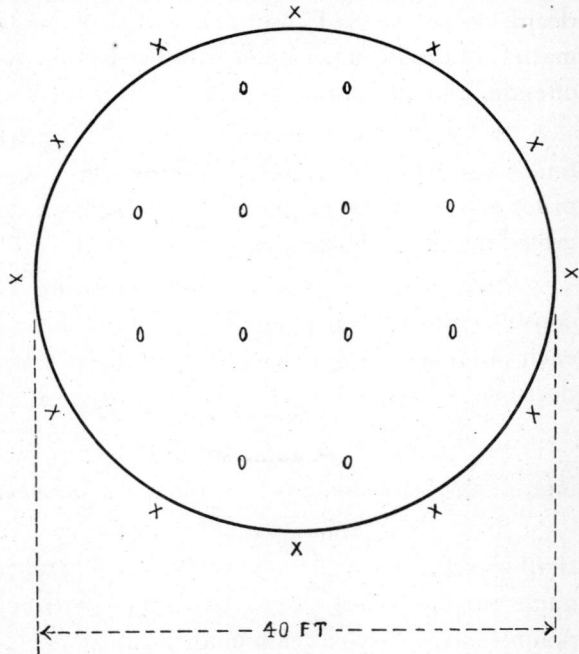

RULE II. PLAYERS AND SUBSTITUTES.

SECTION 1. A team shall consist of 12 players, one of whom shall be captain.

SEC. 2.   The captain shall be the representative of his team and may address any official on matters of interpretation or to obtain essential information. Before the game starts he shall furnish the Scorers with the names of the players.

SEC. 3.   A substitute may take the place of a player only when the ball has been declared dead. He shall first report to the Referee.

SEC. 4.   A player removed from the game may not re-enter the game during the same half, except as provided in Rule VIII, Section 2.

RULE III.   OFFICIALS AND THEIR DUTIES.

SECTION 1.   The officials shall be a Referee and two Timekeepers, who may also act as Scorers.

SEC. 2.   The Referee shall be the superior official of the game. He shall decide when the ball is in play, when it is dead, and when a point has been made. He shall impose penalties for all violations of the rules, designating the offender and offense.

SEC. 3.   The Timekeepers shall note when the game starts; shall note time consumed by "time out" during the game, and shall indicate by gong, pistol or whistle the expiration of the actual playing time in each half. It is suggested that the Timekeepers use one watch.

SEC. 4.   The Scorers shall record the points made. Their record shall constitute the official score of the game. They shall compare their scores after each point, and any discrepancy shall be referred at once to the Referee for decision.

RULE IV.   LENGTH OF GAME.

SECTION 1.   A game shall consist of two halves of 5 minutes each. An intermission of 3 minutes shall be given between halves.

SEC. 2.   A match shall consist of 3 games. A team winning 2 games shall win the match. If neither team wins two games (e. g., each team wins one game and ties one game), the winner shall be determined by the total of the points scored by each team in all 3 games.

SEC. 3.   In a match there shall be 5 minutes' intermission between games.

SEC. 4.   In championship matches, if after 3 games have been played and the winner not determined (i. e., neither team having won two games), the teams shall continue to play until one team wins a game.

Rule V.   Choice of Positions.

Section 1.   The captains shall toss for choice of positions (*i. e.*, for "ins" and "outs"). The teams shall exchange sides at the end of the first half.

Sec. 2.   The captains shall toss again for choice of court for each succeeding game.

Rule VI.   Playing Regulations.

Section 1.   PLAYING TERMS.

(a)   The team within the circle shall be "ins," and those outside the circle shall be "outs."

(b)   "Change Sides" is when the teams exchange positions at the end of the first half.

(c)   "Point" shall be called when a player standing on the outside of the circle hits an opponent within the circle on a fair throw.

(d)   "Foul throw" shall be called for stepping on or over the line when throwing the ball.

(e)   The ball is "dead" only when the Referee blows his whistle.

(f)   A "fair throw" is one thrown from without the circle.

Sec. 2.   The ball is put into play by the captain of the outside team when the Referee blows his whistle.

Sec. 3.   Players on the outside team must throw from outside the circle. If when throwing the ball a player touches the line, or the space within the line, with any part of his body, this shall be a foul throw, and no point may be scored.

Sec. 4.   As soon as an inner player is touched by the ball on a fly or a bounce on any part of his body or clothing the Referee shall signal and announce to the Scorer a point for the outside team. The player struck remains in the game, and the game continues without interruption.

Sec. 5.   If, in a throw, the ball strikes more than one member of the inner team, only one point shall be scored. The team securing the greater number of points during the game shall be the winner.

Sec. 6.   Should the ball, when thrown, remain in or rebound into the circle, a player from the outer team shall run in and get it. In order to make a fair throw he must, however, resume his place outside the circle; but he may (from within the circle) throw the ball to one of his teammates on the outside.

SEC. 7. If a player on the inside team steps out of the circle, one point shall be awarded to the outside team.

SEC. 8. If an inner player blocks the progress of an outer player, or handles the ball, the Referee shall award a point to the outside team.

SEC. 9. The whistle is blown only for starting and stopping the halves and when game is stopped for or resumed after "Time Out."

RULE VII. SCORING.

SECTION 1. One point is scored each time an outer player hits an opponent (provided the throw is fair).

SEC. 2. Only one point may be scored on any one throw, regardless of the number of players hit.

RULE VIII. CONDUCT OF PLAYERS.

SECTION 1. The Referee shall have the power to disqualify for the remainder of the game any player making derogatory remarks to or about the officials or opponents.

SEC. 2. A substitute shall take the place of the disqualified player.

RULE IX. DECISIONS.

SECTION 1. Decisions of the officials as to matters of fact are final.

SEC. 2. Decisions pertaining to the interpretation of the rules may be called into question at once, but only by the captains of the contesting teams.

SEC. 3. When a question pertaining to interpretation of the rules has not been settled conclusively, but is to be carried to higher authority for decision, the game shall proceed as before, the Referee making proper note of the protest.

RULE X. TIME OUT.

"Time Out" may be called by the Referee only, but the ball shall be in play until the whistle is blown by the Referee. He shall order "time out" at the request of a captain not more than 3 times for each team during the game.

RULE XI. COACHING.

There shall be no coaching from the side lines during the progress of the game by any one officially connected with either team, nor shall any such person go on the court during the game, except with permission of the Referee. Penalty—One point shall be awarded the opponents.

RULE XII.　FORFEITED GAME.

SECTION 1.　A team refusing to play after receiving instructions to do so from the Referee shall forfeit the game or match.

SEC. 2.　The score of a forfeited game shall be 1-0.

A SCIENCE OF DODGEBALL.

The game of Dodgeball may be made infinitely more interesting than the "hit-or-miss" affair to which it is so often relegated. The spectacle of a player receiving the ball and, not having an immediate target, throwing aimlessly into the circle or passing in an uncertain and indefinite manner to a member of his own team, is ofttimes disconcerting to coaches and spectators and players alike.

The following is a system designed to speed up the game. It has the advantage over the "hit-or-miss" system in that each child has something definite to do in the system of play. Dodgeball is made something more than a two or three player monopoly. There should be teamwork of a degree of co-ordination within the grasp of the thirteen-year-old boy or girl.

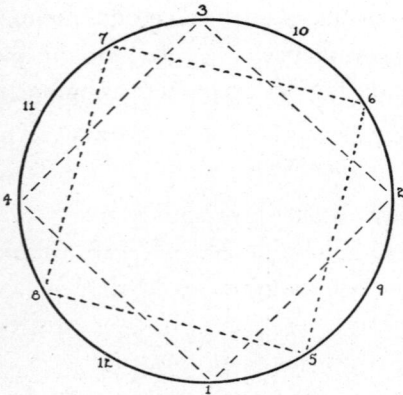

Nos. 1, 2, 3 and 4 constitute a cycle. Any member of this group not possessing a good target (defined as an opponent within his half of the circle) immediately passes either left or right to a player in his cycle.

Nos. 5, 6, 7 and 8 act in the same manner within their cycle.

Nos. 9, 10, 11 and 12 are the "go-getters." Their sole duty is to retrieve the ball as soon as it has failed of a target.

NOTE—Since a match usually consists of a series of three games, the "go-getters'" work may be assigned to a different group in each game.

DOUBLE DODGEBALL.

A very strenuous game for the higher grades, and a game in which the defending team seldom lasts long, is the regular game of dodgeball, played with two balls. Who is hit by a thrown ball leaves the circle. To pick the winning team, the game must be timed, the team staying in the circle longest winning the game.

BASE DODGEBALL. (Bull Pen.)

The present form of dodgeball in a circle seems to have descended from the game of "Bull Pen." The game of base dodgeball is played as follows: Place as many small circles (about two feet in diameter) around the periphery of a large circle having a diameter of from forty-five to fifty feet. The players of one team, the drivers, occupy the bases, and a like number of players are the bulls, who roam about inside of the pen (the large circle). An indoor baseball is used. This ball must always pass through the hands of three basemen (drivers) before it may be thrown at a bull. If the bull is hit he is out of the game. If, however, the bull catches the ball, he may, from where he caught the ball, throw this at a driver, who may not leave his base. If the driver is hit he is out of the game. Should he, however, catch the ball, he keeps his place and again starts the game by throwing the ball to one of his team mates. If one or more drivers are put out of the game the other basemen may run and occupy the empty bases.

After playing five minutes (or any other specified time), count the number of players left on each team, and then change places. At the end of the second half again count the players. The side having the greater number is the winner.

SOCCER FOOTBALL. (Form I.)

School-yard game, simplified, suitable for young boys and girls.

This game may be played in any large school yard. A soft rubber ball or an old tennis-ball will do for a ball. (See diagram for field.)

Players—Any number of players may play on a team, but care must be taken that too many do not try to play the ball at the same time.

Object of the Game—The object of the game is to kick the ball between the goals. At no time must the ball be touched with the hands or arms.

Goals—The goals shall be in the middle of the end lines, to be marked by stakes, posts (or by caps, coats, etc.)

A goal is scored when the ball has been kicked between the goals. A goal counts one point; the team having the greatest number of points wins the game.

Time of Game—The game is played in two halves of from ten to twenty minutes each, with an intermission of from five to ten minutes.

Choice of Goals and Kick-Off—The choice of goals is made by the toss of a coin, the winner choosing the goal and the loser getting the kick-off. Goals are changed between the halves.

Starting the Game—The game is started by a kick-off. The referee (who has full control of the game) places the ball on the center line in the middle of the yard. The side losing the toss kicks the ball toward their opponents' goal. No other player shall be within five yards of the ball when it is kicked, nor shall any player cross the center of the yard until the ball has been kicked off. (Should this happen the kick must be taken over.)

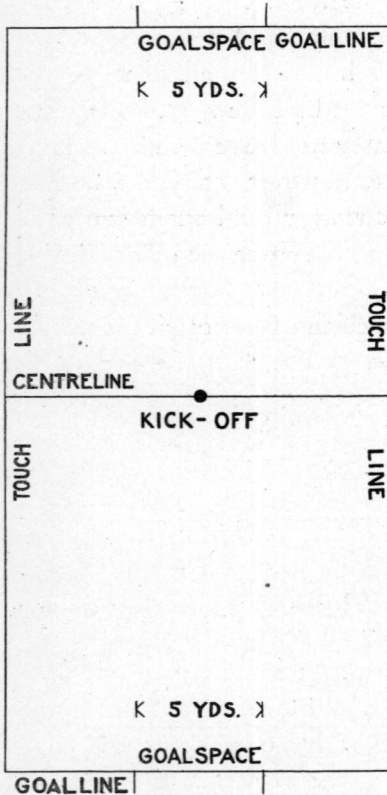

Out of Bounds—The ball is "out of bounds" when it has passed outside the field of play (the lines on the sides are called "touch lines," and the lines on the ends are called the "goal lines"). To put the ball into play again a player on the opposite side to that which caused the ball to go out of bounds stands on the line at the point where the ball went out, then throws the ball, with both hands completely over his head, into the field of play. He cannot again play the ball until it has been played by another player.

Fouls—Fouls are called for pushing, tripping, charging, unnecessary roughness and purposely touching the ball with the hands or arms.

Penalty for Fouling—In case of a foul the ball is given to the opposite side at the point where the ball was at the time the foul was made. The ball is placed on the ground and a free kick is given.

Officials—The officials shall be a referee, who has full charge of the game, two linesmen (one for each side of the field) and a timekeeper, who also acts as scorekeeper.

SAFETY TAG.

This is a rather intricate tag game that can be played in a limited space. It is suitable for pupils of the grammar grades and for adults. The players should not number more than sixteen. The game is played on a court as per diagram. The circles marked S are safety zones.

One player is chosen as chaser. The other players scatter within the lanes of the play court. No one is allowed to step outside of these lanes. He may, however, jump from one lane into another. Stepping on a line counts as out of bounds. When closely pursued any player, except the chaser, may enter one of the safety zones, where he may not be tagged. No two players may occupy one zone at the same time. If a zone is occupied, and later is entered by a second player, the first occupant must leave either by way of the lane leading to the zone, or by jumping into another lane. When the chaser tags another player this player becomes "it." Who steps out of the lanes or who in jumping steps on a line is "it." No back tagging is allowed.

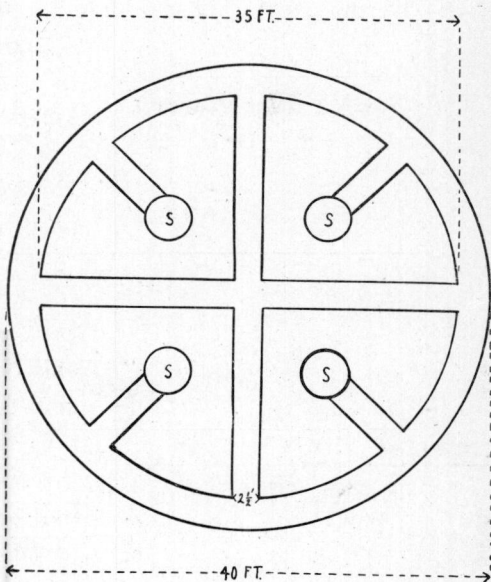

In laying out a diagram, if there is room enough it is advisable to have the outer circle 40 feet in diameter, and the inner circle 35 feet. This will make the rim 2½ feet wide. The other lanes also should be of this width.

BASKET ENDBALL.

The playing court is the same as in Girls' Basketball, except that each third of the court is again divided in half, making six sections in all. Each team has an equal number of centers, forwards and guards. The total number playing is determined by the size of the group to be accommodated.

At the start of the game the players are arranged as in the diagram.

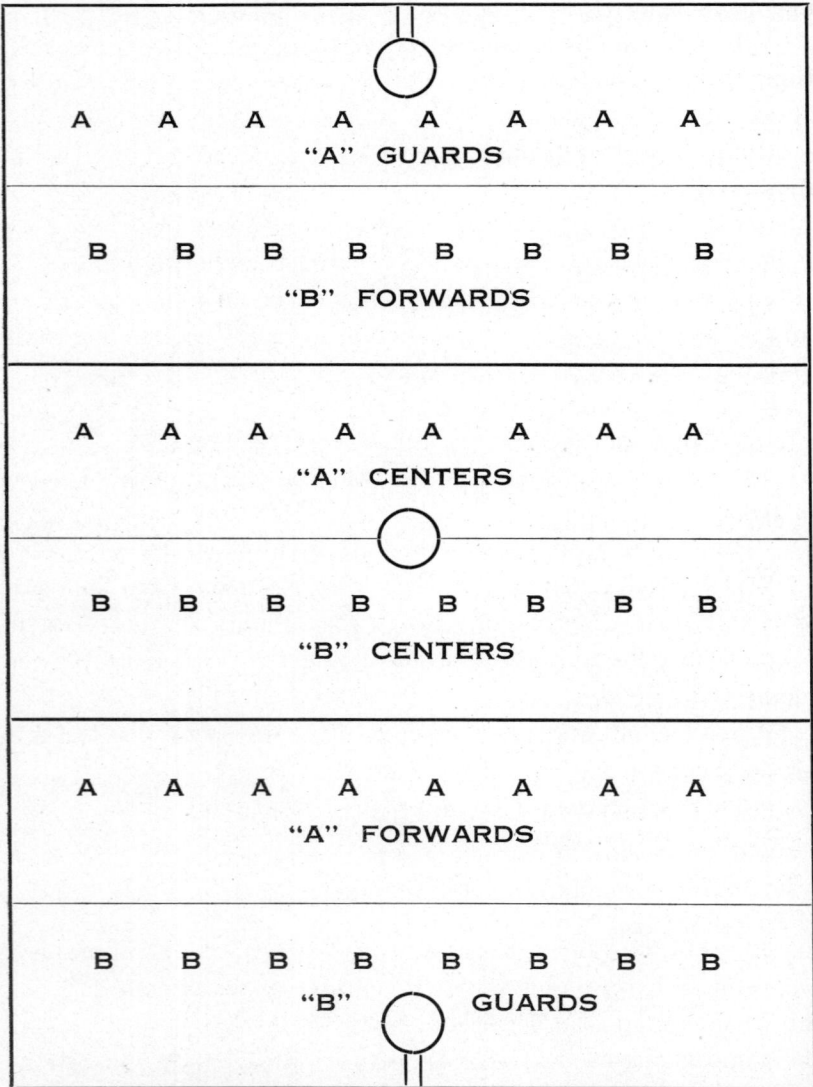

A   A   A   A   A   A   A   A
"A" GUARDS

B   B   B   B   B   B   B   B
"B" FORWARDS

A   A   A   A   A   A   A   A
"A" CENTERS

B   B   B   B   B   B   B   B
"B" CENTERS

A   A   A   A   A   A   A   A
"A" FORWARDS

B   B   B   B   B   B   B   B
"B"   GUARDS

The game is started by jumping at center between two players of opposing teams.

2. All players remain in their respective sections of the court, and the ball is passed from section to section, with the object of getting the ball into the possession of the forwards, who then shoot for the basket.

3. Whenever the ball is successfully passed into the hands of the forwards from the center or from the guards of the same team, one point is scored by that team.

4. If the shot then taken for the basket is successful, two additional points are scored.

5. In the event of a successful shot for the basket the ball is again put in play by jumping at center, otherwise play continues uninterruptedly.

6. The game is played in three innings of equal time intervals, with a change of position, so that at the termination of the game each player shall have had a chance to be a center, forward and guard.

7. Fouls are committed by:

(a) Stepping out of bounds of the players' position zone.

(b) Playing the ball when in the possession of another player of the opposing team.

(c) Running or walking with the ball or dribbling.

8. When a foul is committed, a free throw is taken from the basketball foul line by any forward of the offended team. If this trial is successful, one point is scored, and the ball is put in play at center. Otherwise play is continued uninterruptedly.

9. When the ball goes out of bounds at the end of the court, it is in possession of the guards at that end of the court.

The winner is determined by the highest total score made in the three innings.

HAND TENNIS.

The object of the game is to bat a tennis ball with the hand across a neutral space so that it will fall into the receiving area of the opponent.

The "court" is laid out as per diagram.

The game is played by two players, one on each side. In case of four players, i. e., two on each side, the court should be widened eight feet. In this case the measurements would be twenty by thirty-six feet. Each serving box, then, would be eight feet wide.

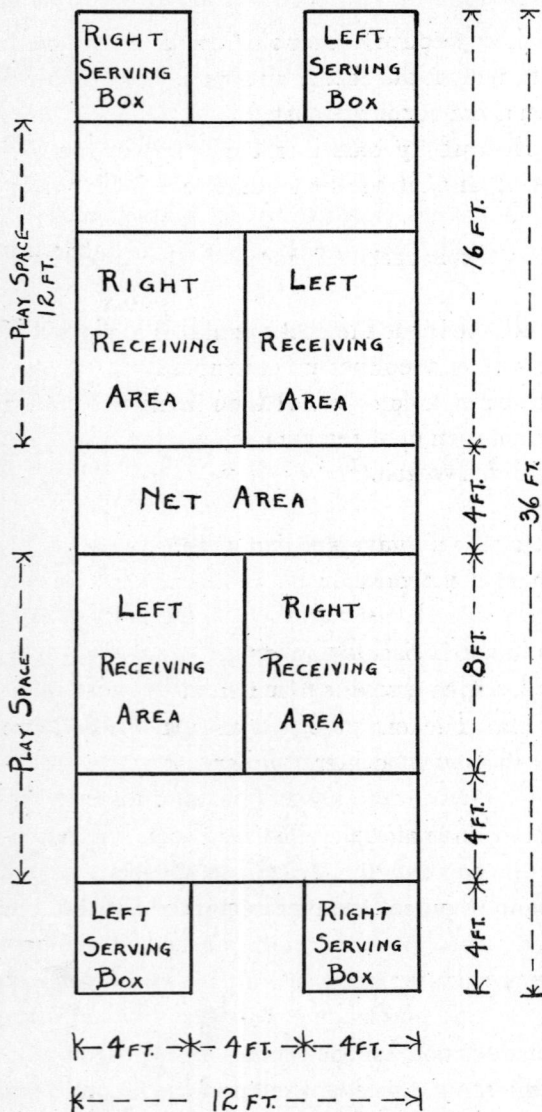

METHODS OF PLAY

Start—The players are a "server" and a "receiver," who face each other on opposite sides of the court. The "server" stands in the "Right Serving Box" and hits the ball (serves) across the court and "net" into the "Right Receiving Area."

Service—The "server" must bounce the ball (approximately knee high) before serving it into the "receiving area." He is allowed two trials. The receiver must allow the "service ball" to bounce before it may be hit.

After the ball has been put into play (by service) it may be hit before it bounces, or on the first bounce, and may be returned into any part of the opponents' "Playing Space." This continues until a point has been scored.

After a point has been made the "server" serves from the "Left Serving Box" into the "Left Receiving Area" and continues to alternate service until either player has scored 5 points. This constitutes a game. At the next game the "server" becomes "receiver," and *vice-versâ*, and play proceeds as in the beginning.

Diagram labels: Right Serving Box, Left Serving Box, Right Receiving Area, Left Receiving Area, Net Area, Left Receiving Area, Right Receiving Area, Left Serving Box, Right Serving Box, Play Space 12 ft, 16 ft, 36 ft, 8 ft, 4 ft, 4 ft, 4 ft, 12 ft.

Points—A point is scored:

1. When "server" fails to serve the ball successfully after two trials to the same "Receiving Area."

2. When "server" leaves serving box before the ball bounces in the "Receiving Area."

3. When the "receiver" hits the "Service Ball" before it bounces.

4. When a player fails to return any ball before the second bounce.

5. When a player hits the ball into net (except the first trial service).

6. When a player hits the ball out of the playing space (except the first trial service).

7. When a player hits the ball in any other manner than with either open hand.

8. When a player hits the ball more than once before it passes over the net.

The winner of a "game" is the player who succeeds in first making 5 points.

The winner of a "set" is the player who first wins five games.

BLOCK BASEBALL.

The object of the game is to toss a small disc into the playing field so as to make a run. The throwing discs are made of rubber, wood or metal and measure about two inches in diameter. Each player should have six or more discs.

Two teams of three members each play the game. The rules of the game are the same as in baseball. The method of play is as follows:

Player number one of Team A stands in the batter's box and tosses a disc into the playing space. If the disc lands in the territory marked "out," he retires, and the next batter is up. If, however, he lands in "strike," he throws a second disc. If the second and third also land in one of the places marked "strike," he is out, and the next batter is up. If a disc lands in the place marked "three-base hit," one additional base hit by the next batter scores a run for the player who made the three-base hit, and puts the next player on first base. The rules are as in baseball, except that a player does not run the bases.

When three players have been put out, the side is out and the second team comes to bat. A game consists of nine innings.

A player is out:

1. When disc fails to get into the playing space.

2. When disc falls in "out" block.

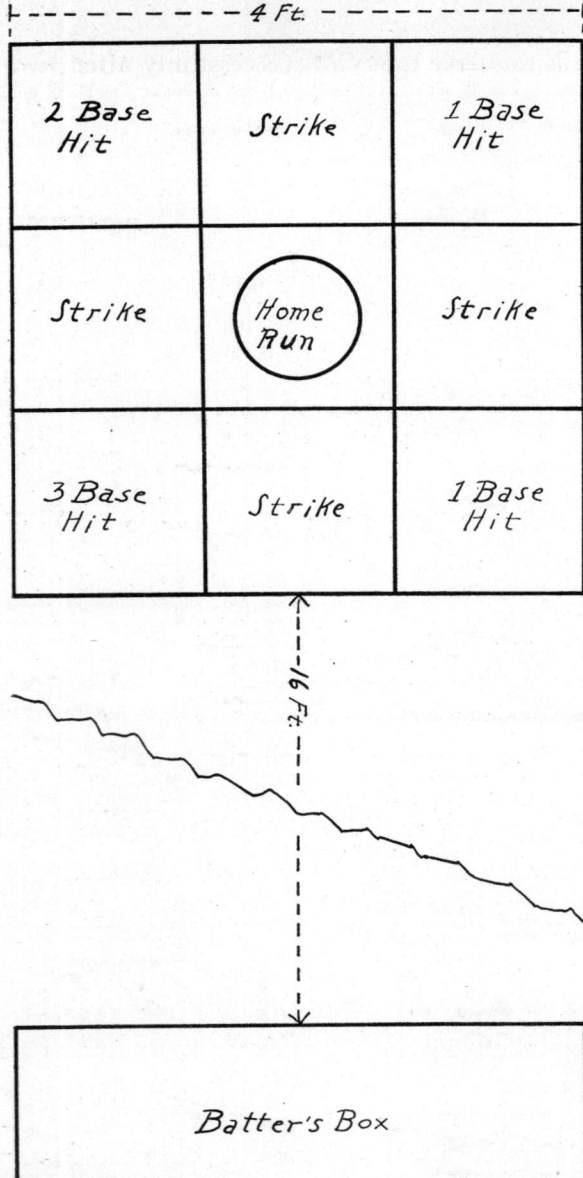

3. When disc rests on a line.
4. When disc lands in "strike" block three times in succession.
5. If batter touches any place outside of "Batter's Box."

GAMES AND DANCES
Eros.*
(SCHERZO VALSE.)

George Dudley Martin.

GAMES AND DANCES
Eros.

Eros.

GAMES AND DANCES
Eros.

BUTTERFLY DANCE.

Music: "Eros" by George Dudley Martin.

Any number of dancers can take part in this roundel. The class is arranged in open order at arm's-length distance. The music is written in three-quarter time. There are seven parts to both music and roundel, but parts 3, 5, 6 and 7 are repetitions.

INTRODUCTION.   (8 Measures.)

1 to 8.   Pose; raise the arms sideward and hold them there.

During the last measure of the introduction wave the left arm forward.

PART I.

Measures 1, 2, 3, 4, cross-balance step left, right, left and right sideward, waving the opposite arm forward—*i. e.*, when executing the cross-balance step left sideward the right arm is waved forward (and the left is again moved sideward). When executing the cross-balance step a slight trunk bending to the opposite side takes place—*i. e.*, when the cross-balance step left is performed the trunk is slightly bent to the right.

5.   Step left sideward (the arms are sideward).

6 and 7.   Curtsy (place the right leg crossed behind the left and bend both knees) and swing both arms down and onward in a circle to the side-position.

8.   Straighten the knees, slightly bend the trunk left, wave the right arm fore-upward and lower it sideward.

9 to 16.   Repeat 1 to 8 to the opposite side.

PART II.   (16 Measures.)

1, 2, 3.   Three glide-balance steps left sideward. The arms are held sideward in an easy position and sway slightly during the sideward movement.

4.   Place the right foot crossed in front, slightly bend the trunk right sideward, place the right knuckles on the hip and raise the left arm in a half circle overhead.

5, 6, 7 and 8.   Repeat measures 1 to 4 to the opposite side.

9 to 16.   Repeat measures 1 to 8.

PART III.　(16 Measures.　Repeat Part I.)

PART IV.　(32 Measures.)

1 to 2.　Pose, with the arms raised sideward.

3 to 4.　Cross-balance step obliquely left forward and right backward. When stepping left, the left arm is swung in a half circle overhead and the right knuckles are placed on the hip (*vice-versâ* when stepping right).

5, 6, 7 and 8.　Repeat measures 1 to 4.

9, 10, 11, 12.　Cross-swing hop forward (left, right, left and right), the knuckles placed on hips.　(Execution: On count 1 step left forward, on count 2 swing the bent right leg crossed in front of the left; on count 3 hop once on the left foot; on counts 4, 5 and 6 repeat right.)

13, 14, 15, 16.　Repeat measures 9 to 12, but step backward.　(The leg-crossing while hopping is, however, executed in front.)

17 to 32.　Repeat measures 1 to 16.

PART V.　(16 Measures.　Repeat Part I.)

PART VI.　(16 Measures.　Repeat Part II.)

PART VII.　(16 Measures.　Repeat Part I.)

NOTE—If at an exhibition a longer performance is wanted, this may be had (after executing the seven parts) by having the pupils face toward the center—*i. e.*, one-half of the class faces left and the other half right.　The side movements should then be performed to the front and the rear of the room or hall.　After the whole dance has been repeated in this formation, the pupils again face to the front and repeat Parts I to VII as written.

Santiago.

(VALSE ESPAGNOLE.)

A. Corbin.

A SPANISH COUPLE DANCE.

Music: "Santiago" by A. Corbin.

Formation: A column of front couples, inner hands grasped shoulder-high, outer hands at waist.

PART I.   (16 Measures.)

Beginning with the outer foot, step forward and hop, swinging the opposite leg forward; repeat with inner foot.   2 measures.

One-quarter turn inward, facing partner, and two draw-closing steps in the line of march; the grasped hands are held head-high, arms slightly bent. 2 measures.

Repeat three times, but finish with three stamps (on the first and third counts of the fifteenth and the first count of the sixteenth measure) instead of two draw-closing steps.   12 measures.

PART II   (16 Measures.)

Face forward and step forward with the outer foot in the line of march; place the inner foot forward, raising the grasped hands obliquely forward, upward; bend the trunk toward partner and look at partner over the inner shoulder.   This is executed on the first and second count of the first measure; pause during the last count and all of the second measure.   2 measures.

Rapid one-quarter turn inward, facing partner, and step sideward toward the last leader with the inner foot, and place the outer foot forward toward partner, raising the grasped hands obliquely upward and outward, and looking at partner; all executed as in the previous step—i. e., with pause.   2 measures.

Two draw-closing steps sideward in the line of march, as above.   2 measures.

Three stamps as above.   2 measures.

Grasp the opposite hands, and execute a rapid one-quarter turn toward the last leader and repeat the first eight measures in the opposite direction. 8 measures.

PART III.

Repeat Part I. 16 measures.

PART IV. (16 Measures.)

Repeat the first four measures of Part II. 4 measures.

Step sideward toward the first leader (in the line of march) with the outer foot, cross the inner foot in rear, bending knees. 2 measures.

Cross-turn step in the opposite direction (toward the last leader), releasing grasp of hands and immediately regrasping opposite hands. 2 measures.

Repeat the first eight measures in the opposite direction. 8 measures.

NOTE—Parts I and II may be used by themselves as a simple dance.

CRESTED HEN (Danish).

Victor Record 17,159 (Chord—Dance is played seven times).

Steps: Step hop (Hopsa step).
Formation: Groups of three. Boy and two girls, boy in center.
Music: Two parts of 8 measures each. Polka rhythm (2 counts to each measure).

PART I.

Measures:

Threes join hands in small circle.

8. Beginning with left foot, eight step hops in a circle, clockwise, a vigorous stamp on first count (counts 1 to 16).

8. Repeat in the opposite direction, beginning with a jump on both feet on the first count (counts 1 to 16).

PART II.

The two girls release hands and all face the front in a straight line.

2. Beginning left the girl on the right dances through the arch formed by the raised joined hands of the other two (counts 1 to 4).

2. The boy follows through the same arch (counts 5 to 8).

2. The girl on the left dances through the arch formed by the raised joined hands of the other two (counts 9 to 12).

2. The boy follows through the same arch (counts 13 to 16).

8. Repeat the above 8 measures (counts 1 to 16).

The step hop is used throughout and when not moving through an arch, the dancers do the steps in place.

Step hop left: Step on left foot, 1; raise the right foot back of left and hop on left foot, 2.

THE BLACK NAG (English).

Victor Record 18,004 (No introduction—Dance is played three times).

Steps: Glide, running, skipping.

Formation: Sets of three couples in column formation.

Music: Two parts of 8 measures each, A and B. B repeated. Polka rhythm (2 counts to a measure). All played three times.

PART I.

Measures:

A. 2. Right hands grasped. Beginning with outer foot, three small running steps forward and close (counts 1 to 4).

2. Same backward (counts 5 to 8).

4. Repeat above 4 measures (counts 9 to 16).

B. 2. Partners face. First couple join hands, take four glides sideward toward the front of room (counts 1 to 4).

2. Second couple the same (counts 5 to 8).

2. Third couple the same (counts 9 to 12).

2. All make a whole turn right in four running steps (counts 13 to 16).

8. Repeat above 8 measures back to places, the third couple leading (counts 1 to 16).

PART II.

A. 2. Beginning right, each takes four running steps forward, passing partner, left shoulder to left shoulder, turning toward partner on third and fourth counts (counts 1 to 4).

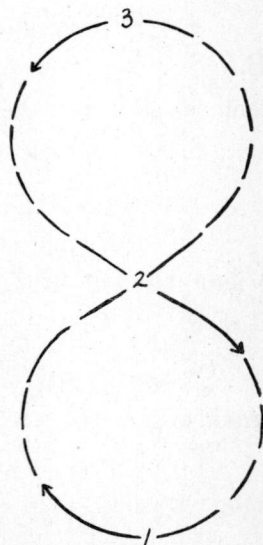

2. Repeat, passing right shoulder to right shoulder, returning to places (counts 5 to 8).

4. Repeat above 4 measures (counts 9 to 16).

B. 2. With four sideward glides, the first boy and the third girl change places (back to back) (counts 1 to 4).

2. In same way, the first girl and the third boy change places (counts 5 to 8).

2. In the same way, the second girl and the second boy change places (counts 9 to 12).

2. All make a whole turn right in four running steps (counts 13 to 16).

8. Repeat above 8 measures back to places (counts 1 to 16).

PART III.

A. 4. Beginning right, with running steps, partners linking right arms. Make a whole turn and with running steps backward return to places (counts 1 to 8).

4. Repeat, linking left arms. Finish facing front (counts 9 to 16).

B. 8. No. 1 faces about. The boys each execute a figure 8, with skipping, as shown in diagram (4 counts to each quarter) (counts 1 to 16).

8. Girls same (counts 1 to 16).

CZEBOGAR (Bohemian).

Victor Record 17,821 (Introduction, chord—Dance is played five times).

Steps: Glide, swing hop, lame step, stamp closing step.

Stamp closing step left: Step left sideward, stamping left and bending trunk to the left, 1; close right foot to the left and straighten trunk, 2.

Formation: Single circle of couples, facing center, boy on left of girl, all hands grasped.

Music: Two parts of 8 measures each, repeated. Polka rhythm (2 counts to a measure).

PART I.

Measures:

4. Seven glides left sideward, swing right leg forward, hopping on left foot (counts 1 to 8).

4. Same to right (counts 9 to 16).

PART II.

2. Beginning left, three steps forward and close with stamp (counts 1 to 4).

2. Repeat backward (counts 5 to 8).

4. Partners face, link right arms, raise left to half circle over head, and turn partner in place with four lame steps. (Hop right, step left, 1; step right, 2) (counts 9 to 16).

PART III.

4. Partners face, join both hands, arms sideward, and execute four stamp closing steps toward center (with leg swinging sideward to the step) (counts 1 to 8).

4. Repeat outward (counts 9 to 16).

4. Same, with two steps inward and outward (counts 1 to 8).

4. Link right arms and repeat turn in Part II (counts 9 to 16).

VIRGINIA REEL.

Victor Record 18,552 or 17,160 (Chord).

Steps: Running steps, glide.

Formation: Four couples, boys in one line, partners opposite, facing each other, 6 feet apart.

Music: Two step.

PART I.

Corners: Right corners execute figures first, then left corners.

With running steps:

Beginning left, forward diagonally, to center, nod, and return to places (counts 16).

Forward, diagonally to center, turn opposite corner, joining right hands, and return to places (counts 16).

Forward, diagonally to center, turn opposite corner, joining left hands, and return to places (counts 16).

Forward, diagonally to center, turn opposite corner, joining both hands, and return to places (counts 16).

Forward, diagonally to center, encircle opposite corner, back to back, right shoulder to right shoulder, and return to places (counts 16).

NOTE—In returning to places the movement is backward, looking toward opposite corner.

PART II.

With running steps forward beginning left, head couples link right arms and turn, then link left arms with next in line and turn (the girl turning the boys and the boy turning the girls); link right arms with partner and turn, and link left with next in line and turn, etc.

When end of line is reached, face partner, grasp hands, and glide through center to original position.

All face and follow leaders, who countermarch outward, the length of the lines. When partners meet they join inside hands and countermarch inward to original places. Partners face center, join both hands, raised to form arches. The head couple passes under arches to end of line.

The new corners then repeat the dance.

GAMES AND DANCES
FOR PLAYERS OF THIRTEEN YEARS AND OVER

Seventh to Twelfth School-Grades.

PRISONER'S BASE. (Darebase.)

The playfield is about thirty by seventy-five feet. A line across the field at each end marks the base of each team. At the right of each base a small space is marked off as a prison. The teams each consist of about ten players. The object of the game is to make prisoners of players of the opposite team. Any player may be made a prisoner by an opposing player who left his base later than the first player did. For instance, a player of Team No. 1 leaves his base and advances toward the base of Team No. 2. Having left his base, he may be tagged by any player on Team No. 2. When, therefore, an opposing player runs out to tag him, he quickly retreats to his own base before being tagged. If he is tagged before reaching his base he is a prisoner and is put into the prison of Team No. 2. If, however, a player from his own team runs out to support him and this new player (who left his base later than the pursuer) succeeds in tagging the player from Team No. 2, then this one is a prisoner and is placed in the prison of Team No. 1.

When a prisoner is made, the captain of the team designates a player whose duty it is to guard the prison. The capture of three prisoners by one team wins the game. Prisoners may be freed when one of the players succeeds in tagging a prisoner without himself being tagged. If there are two prisoners they may grasp hands and stretch out toward their team, thereby facilitating their release. If, then, the first one is tagged they are both free.

The referee must insist upon order. Do not allow too many players on the field at once. When a prisoner has been made all players must return to their own base before another play may be started. Only one prisoner may be made during a play. All players must stand behind the line which marks the front of their base. As soon as one foot is over the line they have left their base and may be made prisoners by an opposing player who still is on his base.

163

PUNCH BALL. (Fist Ball.)

This game is played with a basket-ball, which is struck with the closed fist, so that it will roll along the ground. The playfield is about twenty by forty feet. A lane, three feet wide, separates the two teams. The players are divided into forwards and backs. At the beginning of the game the ball is rolled (or bounced) forward into the center lane, the players from each side (who must not step into the lane) trying to get it. The object of the game is to cause the ball to roll over the end line of the opposite side by striking it as above described. The players are allowed to move about freely on their side, and may roll the ball up to the forwards. It may also be rolled from one player to another on the same side until a good opportunity is found to send it across the opposite goal line. Every goal made counts one point for the side making it.

PROGRESSIVE DODGEBALL.

For Three Teams.

Progressive dodgeball is a game suitable for pupils of 13 years and upward. Divide the players into three teams of equal size. With chalk (or paint) lay off the playfield in three squares, each 30 x 30 feet, joined in a straight line. (If so much space is not available shorten the outer fields.)

The teams may be designated "Red," "White" and "Blue," or any other name. The number of players on a team is governed by the space and players at command, and may be from five to twenty-five to each team.

At the beginning of the game the three teams line up as shown in the cut, and also at the beginning of the second and third innings, excepting that the teams will then have changed places:

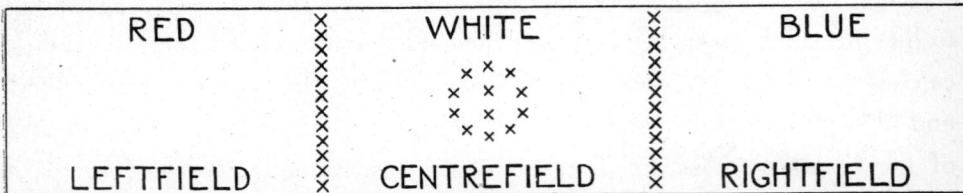

RED		WHITE		BLUE
LEFTFIELD		CENTREFIELD		RIGHTFIELD

Three innings are played, each of five minutes' duration (or any specified time). Each inning begins on the signal from the referee (blowing of a whistle) and ends with the call of time, when the teams change fields.

The outer teams always play against the team in the center.

A player on the center team may be hit by a player of the outer teams.

A player on either of the outer teams may be hit by a player on the center team, but it is not permissible for any player from either outer team to hit a player on the other, but a ball thrown by a player on either outer team, across the center territory, may be caught by a player on the other.

The referee begins the game by blowing the whistle and at the same time tossing the ball to the players of the center team (which in this case shall be "White," and standing in the center of their territory). The outer teams, "Red" and "Blue," are standing with one foot on the boundary lines of the center territory, and at the sound of the whistle run as far to the rear of their respective fields as they can to avoid being hit. The player of "White" who has caught the ball tossed by the referee runs up to either the left or the right boundary line of his field and throws at one of the end teams ("Red" or "Blue") ; or he may pass the ball quickly to a player of his side who has run near the boundary line, ready to throw, and he then must throw at his opponents.

The players of the teams may dodge in any manner to avoid being hit. The player from "White" having thrown and not hit an opponent, a player from the side thrown at—let us assume it to be the "Red"—tries to catch the ball before it rebounds or rolls into the center territory. If successful, he passes the ball or runs with it up to the boundary line and throws at the "White," who dodge and run to the opposite end of their field. If he fails to hit, one of the team at the other end—the "Blue"—standing in readiness, catches the ball and throws at the "White." Thus the two end teams, "Red" and "Blue," continue to play against "White" as long as they are in possession of the ball, and "White" keeps dodging and fleeing from one side of its territory to the other. Usually this does not last very long, for the ball frequently bounces or rolls into the center territory, when "White" again gets the ball and throws, as in the beginning, at either "Red" or "Blue."

Thus the game continues, "Red" and "Blue" playing against "White." Every time a player is hit "on a fly"—not on a bounce—the team throwing the ball is credited with a point, and the game continues without interruption until time is called.

INNING	1.	2.	3.	TOTAL, PLAYERS HIT.
RED	0			
WHITE	5			
BLUE	2			

At the conclusion of each inning the number of points of each team are counted and marked on the scoreboard or card, for instance, under first inning. (See diagram.)

The teams now change fields, from right to left, in the following manner. "Blue" moves to the center, "White" moves to the left, and "Red" moves to the right field. The teams form in exactly the same way as at the beginning of the game, and the referee again tosses the ball to the team in the center territory ("Blue"). The game continues as before, until time is called. The scores made are marked under the second inning, and the last change of fields takes place, so that in the three innings each team will have played in each field.

After the score of the third inning is marked, the scores of the three innings are added, and the team having the highest score wins the game.

A score is not made if a player is touched by a ball rebounding from the floor, a wall, an object, or from another player.

A score is not made if the thrower steps on or over the line.

A score is made only when a player is hit by a ball "on a fly" thrown from behind the line.

The ball belongs to the team of a territory (1) whenever it rolls or rebounds into its territory; (2) when stopped on a bounce subsequent to a throw from an opposing team.

In case of the ball going out of bounds it is brought back to the territory whose outer boundary line it crossed.

DODGEBALL IN THREE FIELDS.

FOR TWO TEAMS.

This form of dodgeball is designed to be used when but two teams shall play at a time. In all essentials it is played like the preceding game, with the following exceptions:

1. The teams shall have an even number of players; for a match-game sixteen players form a team.

2. The outer two fields, at the beginning of the first half, shall be occupied by eight players each of the attacking team. At the beginning of the second half a like number of the second team occupies these fields.

3. The time of each half shall be ten minutes, or a less number, as agreed upon before the game.

RUN DODGEBALL.

The object of the game is for the players on Team B to run across the field to the other end without being hit by the ball (a basket-ball) during their run.

Divide the players into two teams, A and B. The players on Team A are again divided, one-half standing on either side of the playfield. (See diagram.) All the players on Team B are at one end of the short end of the field. The field is approximately thirty by sixty feet.

To start the game the referee tosses the ball to one of the players on Team A, at the same time blowing his whistle as a signal for the players on Team B that they may run. Upon this the player of Team A who has the ball throws at the runners. Those who are hit are out. When all the untouched runners are over at B 1 the referee again gives the signal to run. The throwers must always stand behind their line when throwing at a runner. Should the ball roll into the field a player from Team A may run in and toss it to one of his teammates. Only the runners in the field of play may be thrown at. At the end

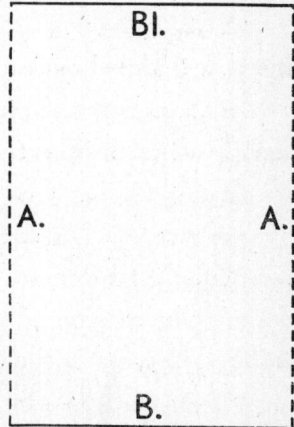

of three minutes (or any other specified time) count the number of players left on Team B and credit them with so many points. The teams then exchange places and activities. The team having the greatest number of points at the end of the game wins.

CIRCLE PINS.

Circle Pins is a game of skill that appeals to older boys and girls as well as to adults. It can be played either indoor or outdoor, and needs little space. The equipment consists of five bowling pins (blocks of wood will answer the same purpose), and a small bowling ball (a 17-inch indoor baseball or a square piece of wood will answer for this purpose.) The five pins are arranged as per diagram on a board 5 feet square (or on the ground). The ball is fastened to a strong cord and is suspended from the ceiling, a cross piece (a limb of a tree) 8 to 10 feet high directly above the center pin. The lower edge of the ball when hanging quietly is about one inch above the board.

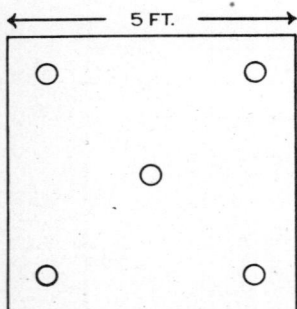

The object of the game is to swing the ball so as to knock down one or more pins. The player takes his stand at a mark from 6 to 10 feet from the pin board. The ball may be swung either forward and backward, or the player may swing it in an oval. The ball may pass over the board only during one swing—i. e., either forward and backward, or in a circular swing. If during this swing one pin is knocked down this counts one point for the player. One point is scored for each pin that is knocked down either by being struck by the ball or by another pin. If only the center pin is knocked down this counts 5 points. If only the four outer pins are knocked down this counts 10 points. Fifty points is a game. If played as a team game the total number of points to be scored is equal to the number of team members multiplied by 50—e. g., four members of a team must make 200 points.

WARBALL.

This game may be played by any number of players. It can be played in a large or a small gymnasium or playground.

The idea underlying the game is for the players of one side to hit with a ball one or more players on the other side. Soft indoor baseballs are used, or balls made of paper; i. e., newspapers wrapped with twine. According to the number of players, from twenty-four to forty-eight balls are needed. The game is in charge of a referee and two assistants, who are stationed as per diagram. The time of the game is from 15 to 20 minutes.

The field is an oblong about 40 by 60 feet, with a line through the center and two 3-foot lines. Each side

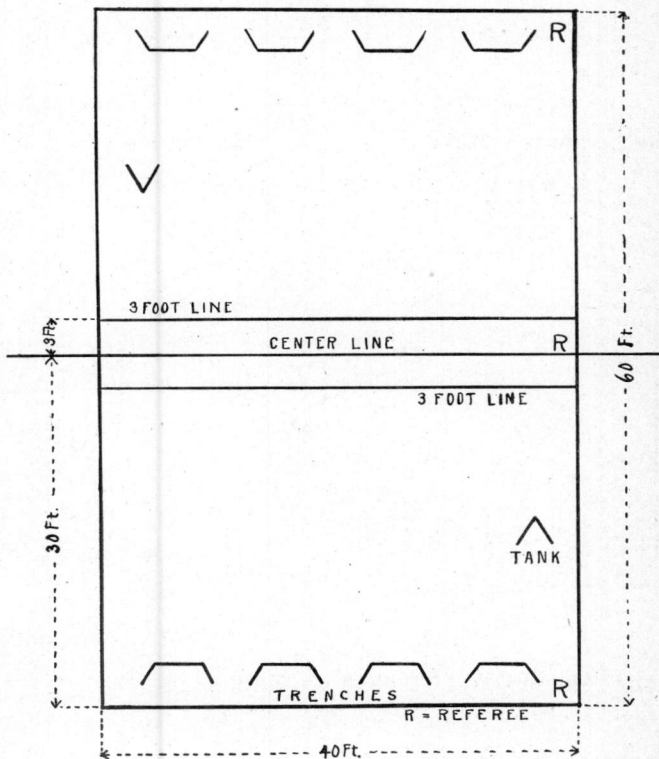

has from four to six movable trenches and one movable tank. The trenches are made of light wooden frames with canvas stretched over them. Gymnasium mats may also be used. The trenches should be from 24 to 30 inches high and about 5 feet long. The tanks should be made in the form of a triangle, open at the rear end, large enough to shield one person. Each trench should accommodate from four to six players. Each side has a captain. The trenches and tanks may fly the colors of their teams.

The players kneel, squat or lie behind the trench wall. Without exposing themselves too much they throw their balls at the enemy. A player hit by a thrown ball on any part of the body is disabled and must retire to the side line.   The players may move their trench in any direction up to the 3-foot line, but not over the side lines.   By order of the captain one player may go out in the tank to collect ammunition.   He may go in the tank to the center line, also over the side lines.   If he is hit he also must go to the side lines.   The captain then must call to some other player to run from his trench to man the tank.

At the end of the specified time the referee, by blowing a whistle, ends the game.   The side having most players left in the trenches wins the game.

VOLLEY BALL.   (Form II.)

(Bat the Ball.)

(For first form, see Fifth-grade games.)

Divide the players into two teams, of from eight to sixteen players each. The playfield is about twenty by forty feet, being divided into halves by a narrow net or a rope stretched across the short way, the top of the net being seven feet above the ground.   The object of the game is to keep a volley ball (a hollow ball, somewhat smaller and lighter than a basket-ball) passing from one side to the other over the top of the net or rope, by batting it either with one or two hands.

When playing with young or inexperienced players the ball may be returned over the line either on a "fly" or after one bounce.   If the ball is not returned over the line in this manner—that is, if it touches the ground twice before it is started on its return, or twice during its passage from one player to another of the same team—a point is scored against the side that has failed—i. e., the serving side scores one point.

If the serving side bats the ball outside of the bounds of the playfield it is a foul, and the opposite side then serves the ball.

Experienced players must return the ball on a "fly"—i. e., the ball must never touch the ground.   If it does, the side that last batted the ball over the net scores a point.   Teams may play either for a certain number of points or for a certain length of time.

CAPTAINBALL.

THE GAME.

Captainball is played by two teams with 10 players on each team. The object of the game is to score as many points as possible by throwing the ball from basemen to basemen of the same team, opposing guards trying to prevent this by securing the ball and throwing it to their basemen on the opposite side of the center line.

RULE I.   EQUIPMENT.

SECTION 1. THE COURT or playing space shall be a surface free from obstructions, 40 feet in width and 70 feet in length.

SEC. 2. It shall be divided into two equal parts (40 feet wide by 35 feet long) by a center line extended indefinitely.

Five bases, each 2 feet in diameter, shall be marked on each side of the court, according to the accompanying diagram:

SEC. 3. Center line and bases shall be marked by well-defined lines, which shall not be less than 2 inches in width.

SEC. 4. The ball shall be round. It shall consist of a rubber bladder, covered with a leather case not less than 26 nor more than 28 inches in circumference, and weighing not less than 14 nor more than 17 ounces.

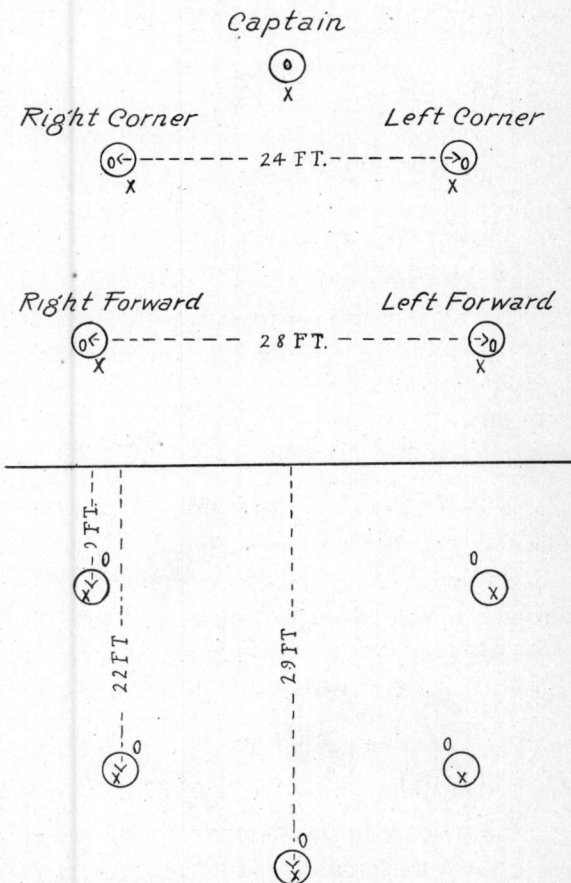

SEC. 5.   The home team shall provide the ball.

SEC. 6.   In case the visiting team refuses to accept the ball furnished, the Referee shall decide the ball to be used.

RULE II.   PLAYERS AND SUBSTITUTES.

SECTION 1.   Each team shall consist of ten players, five basemen (two forward basemen, two corner basemen and one captain baseman) and five guards (two forward guards, two corner guards and one captain guard). For positions see diagram, Rule I.

SEC. 2.   One member of each team shall be the captain. He shall be the representative of his team and may address any official on matters of interpretation or to obtain essential information.

SEC. 3.   A substitute may take the place of a player only when the ball has been declared dead. He shall first report to the Referee.

SEC. 4.   A player taken out of the game may not re-enter the game during the same half, except as provided for in Rule VIII, Section 2.

SEC. 5.   A player may be changed from one position to another position not more than once during the same half. The change shall be first reported to the Referee.

RULE III.   OFFICIALS AND THEIR DUTIES.

SECTION 1.   The Officials shall be a Referee and two Timekeepers, who may also act as Scorers.

SEC. 2.   The Referee shall be the superior official of the game. He shall put the ball in play, decide what points are scored, call fouls, decide who shall possess the ball in case of disagreement, and shall impose penalties for violations of rules. In the latter case he shall designate the offender and the offense. A foul shall not be called until the scoring play is completed.

SEC. 3.   The Timekeepers shall note when the game starts; shall note time consumed by "time out" during the game, and shall indicate by gong, pistol or whistle the expiration of the actual playing time in each half. It is suggested the Timekeepers use one watch.

SEC. 4.   The Scorers shall record the points made. Their record shall constitute the official score of the game. They shall compare their scores after each point, and any discrepancy shall be referred at once to the Referee for decision.

RULE IV. LENGTH OF GAME.

SECTION 1.   The game shall consist of two halves of 15 minutes each, with an intermission of 5 minutes between halves.

The teams shall change sides after the first half.

SEC. 2.   The game shall terminate by the sounding of the Timekeeper's signal. If a scoring play is in progress when the Timekeeper's signal sounds, the game shall continue until the ball comes into the possession of a player.

RULE V. CHOICE OF COURTS.

The captains shall toss for choice of courts.

RULE VI. PLAYING REGULATIONS.

SECTION 1.   The game shall be started by the Referee, who shall at center toss the ball up (at least 10 feet) between two opposing guards. As the ball is about to descend, the Referee shall blow his whistle. The ball is then in play.

SEC. 2.   The opposing guards shall jump at center in the following order:

(a)   Captain guards.

(b)   Right forward guards.

(c)   Left forward guards.

(d)   Right corner guards.

(e)   Left corner guards.

SEC. 3.   The ball shall be tossed up at center:

(a)   At the beginning of each half.

(b)   After the captain baseman has received the ball on a scoring play.

(c)   After each successful free throw.

(d)   After each double foul play.

(e)   After a scoring play started by the captain baseman, in which the ball has passed into the hands of all basemen.

SEC. 4.   When two opposing players (guard and baseman) get possession of the ball at the same time, the Referee shall give the ball to the guard. When two opposing guards get possession of the ball at the same time, the Referee shall toss the ball up at center between them.

SEC. 5.   If a captain baseman obtains possession of the ball from any player other than one of her basemen, she may start a scoring play. In this case no more than seven points may be made.

SEC. 6.   The penalty for a foul shall be a free throw for the opponents. The Referee shall award the ball to the captain baseman whose team did not foul, who shall try for a free throw to a baseman.

SEC. 7.   On a free throw the captain guard on the offending side is out of play until the throw is over, when he immediately re-enters the play.

SEC. 8.   A free throw shall be considered as successful when the ball has come into complete possession of any one of the four basemen on the offended side.

SEC. 9.   A free throw shall be considered unsuccessful when the ball comes into the possession of any player other than any of the four basemen. The free throw is therefore over, and play continues and a scoring play may begin.

SEC. 10.   In case of a double foul the ball is dead after each free throw and shall be put into play at center after the second throw. Time out shall be taken from the announcement of the double foul to the toss up at center.

SEC. 11.   If the ball strikes some obstruction at the sides of the court, the ball is given at that place to the guard who would otherwise have obtained it.

SEC. 12.   When a baseman other than a captain baseman gets a ball from a baseman, he has the privilege of continuing the scoring play by throwing the ball to any other baseman who has not had possession of it during the scoring play.

SEC. 13.   If a guard throws a ball to any baseman, no score is made. (See Section 5 of this rule.)

SEC. 14.   A scoring play is stopped as follows:

(a)   When the ball passes into possession of any guard or of an opposing baseman.

(b)   By a foul committed by a player on the team which is attempting to score. A baseman who fouls while receiving the ball scores no point. A baseman who fouls while throwing the ball scores no further point.

(c)   By the ball reaching the captain baseman from another baseman of the same team.

(d)   By the ball getting into the possession of any baseman for the second time during a scoring play. In this case the last pass of the ball does not score.

(e) By the ball striking any one or anything at the sides of the court other than the player, ground, floor or ceiling.

NOTE—A foul by a guard never stops the scoring play of the opponents. In such case a free throw is awarded *after* the scoring play is over.

SECTION 15. *It is a foul for any player:*

(a) Purposely to push, strike or trip an opponent.

(b) Purposely to touch a player. It is impossible to play the game without opposing players touching. When such touching becomes dangerous or interferes with plays or appears to be done purposely, the Referee shall call a foul on the player or players for each offense.

(c) Purposely to touch ball while in hands of opponent.

(d) To kick the ball. (Kicking is meeting the ball with the feet with the idea of propelling it.) Blocking with the feet is necessary and allowable.

(e) To delay the game unnecessarily. Delay for teamwork and signals must be brief.

SEC. 16. *It is a foul for a guard:*

(a) To touch a base with any part of his body.

(b) To touch the ground or floor on the opposite side of the middle line (except that a guard on the jump at center toss may drop with feet across the line).

(c) Who has crossed the line to touch the ball or interfere with play until he has returned to his side of the court.

(d) To touch the ball while it is going up at center.

(e) Jumping at center to catch the ball or to touch the ball a second time unless it has struck another player or the ground or floor.

(f) To carry ball more than one step or to roll or bounce it and take it again at an advanced point.

(g) To guard a captain baseman while he is making a free throw.

(h) When an opposing baseman has the ball to guard closer than one foot to the base. (The base is interpreted as being the surface enclosed by the circle and the column of air above it.)

(i) To straddle a base. All space above the base is property of the baseman, and may not be occupied by any part of the guard's body. While jumping to block high throws over the baseman's head the hands of the guard may be used above the base.

(j)   To guard a baseman already guarded.

SEC. 17.   *It is a foul for a baseman:*

(a)   Purposely to strike, trip or push an opponent.

(b)   To leave the base with both feet unless he jumps up in the air, in which case a foot must come down on base first.

(c)   When only one foot is on base to lift that foot from the base.

(Interpretations.)

Guards may:

(a)   Drop on other side of center line while jumping at center toss.

(b)   Reach across the center line at any time.

(c)   Guard any player at any time except captain baseman on free throw (see Rule VII, Section 2, j).

Basemen may:

(a)   Use a brief time for signals or teamwork.

(b)   Jump in air for ball.

(c)   Change base foot at any time.

SEC. 18.   The ball is "dead" after a scoring play has been completed or after any decision that temporarily suspends play.

RULE VII.   SCORING.

SECTION 1.   One point for throwing the ball from baseman to baseman, both basemen being on the same side of court, right or left.

SEC. 2.   Two points for throwing ball from baseman to captain.

SEC. 3.   Two points for throwing the ball across the court from a right baseman to a left baseman or vice versa. (See diagram.)

SEC. 4.   One point for throwing the ball from captain baseman to baseman when captain starts scoring play.

SEC. 5.   One point for throwing ball from captain baseman to baseman on a free throw.

NOTE—If the ball is touched or batted by an opposing guard, it does not prevent a score unless that guard has unmistakably had possession of the ball.

RULE VIII. CONDUCT OF PLAYERS.

SECTION 1. The Referee shall have the power to disqualify any player for the remainder of game for:

(a) Making derogatory remarks to or about officials or opponents.

(b) Rough play.

SEC. 2. A substitute shall take the place of a disqualified player.

RULE IX. FORFEITED GAME.

SECTION 1. Any team refusing to play, after receiving instructions to do so from the Referee, shall forfeit the game or match.

SEC. 2. The score of a forfeited game shall be 2-0.

RULE X. DECISIONS.

SECTION 1. Decisions of the officials as to matters of fact are final.

SEC. 2. Decisions pertaining to the interpretation of the rules may be called into question at once, but only by the captains of the contesting teams.

SEC. 3. When a question pertaining to interpretation of the rules has not been settled conclusively, but will be carried to higher authority for decision, the game shall proceed as before, the Referee making proper note of the protest.

RULE XI. TIME OUT.

SECTION 1. "Time out" shall be called by the Referee, but the ball shall be in play until the whistle is blown.

SEC. 2. The Captain or Faculty Representative may ask for "time out" only when the ball is in possession of her team.

RULE XII. COACHING.

There shall be no coaching from the side lines during the progress of the game by anyone officially connected with either team, nor shall any such person go on the court during the progress of the game, except with permission of the Referee. Penalty—Two free throws for the opponents.

HUMAN HURDLE RACE.

Each team forms a large circle. All players sit on the floor, facing outward, with legs straightened forward.

The first member of team No. 1 and the first member of team No. 2 are diametrically opposite each other on the circumference of the circles. Upon command, both competitors run in the same direction around the outside of the circle, hurdling over the legs of those sitting. The one returning first to his place scores a point for his team. The second members of the teams do the same, and so on until everyone has competed. The team having the highest score wins.

SOCCER FOOTBALL.   (Form II.)

The Field—The field should be between fifty and one hundred yards wide and between one hundred and one hundred and fifty yards long for a match-game (otherwise whatever space is available), divided into two equal parts by a line through the center, called the half-way line. The two long lines bounding the field are called the "touch lines," and the two short lines bounding the field are called the "goal lines." The center of the field shall be marked with a circle with a ten-yard radius.

Goals—Two posts with a crossbar are placed on the end lines in the middle. The posts are 8 yards apart. The crossbar is 8 feet above the ground.

Goal Area—Lines are marked 6 yards outside of each goal post at right angles with the goal line for a distance of 6 yards, and these lines are connected with a line parallel with the goal line. The space within these lines shall be known as the "goal area."

Players—Eleven players constitute a team. They are named as follows: Center, inside right, outside right, inside left, outside left, left halfback, center halfback, right halfback, right fullback, left fullback and goal-keeper. Their positions are shown in the diagram.

Time of Game—The game is played in two halves, of from twenty to forty minutes each, with an intermission of five or ten minutes.

Choice of Goals—The winner of the toss (toss of coin) has the option of the kick-off or the choice of goals. Goals are changed at half time (end of the first half).

Start of Game— The game is commenced by a place kick (kick-off) from the center of the field in the direction of the opponents' goal. No opponent may approach within 10 yards of the ball until it has been kicked off. Should this rule not be complied with, the kick must be taken over. After a goal has been made the losing side kicks off; after the change of goals at half time the ball is kicked off by the opposite side to that which kicked off at the start of the game.

Scoring a Goal —A goal is scored when the ball has passed between the goal posts and under

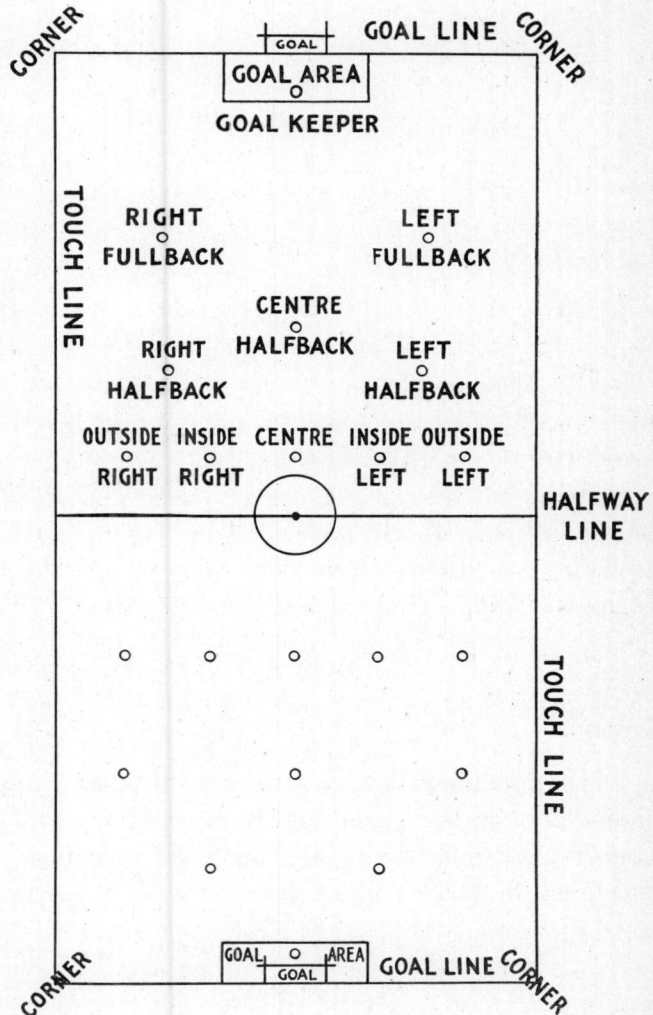

the crossbar, providing it has not been thrown, carried or touched by the hands or arms (knocked on) by any player of the attacking side. A scored goal counts one point.

Out of Play—The ball is out of play when it has crossed the goal line or touch line either on the ground or in the air.

Throw In—When the ball is "in touch"—that is, when the ball has crossed the touch or side line—a player on the opposite side to that which played it out shall, while standing outside the touch line facing the field of play, throw the ball with both hands, completely over his head, into the field of play. He must not, however, play the ball again until it has been played by another player. A goal cannot be scored from a "throw in."

Goal Kick—When the ball is played behind (over) the goal line by a player of the attacking side it shall be kicked off by any one of the players behind whose goal line it went, within that half of the goal area nearest the point where the ball left the field of play. If it be kicked across the goal line by one of the defending players a player on the opposite (attacking) team kicks the ball from within one yard of the nearest corner. No opponent is allowed within 10 yards of the ball until it has been kicked off (a kick of this kind is called a "corner kick").

Goal-Keeper Handling Ball—The goal-keeper may, within his own half of the field of play, use his hands, but must not at any time carry the ball. The goal-keeper cannot be changed without first notifying the referee.

Dangerous Play or Fouling—Tripping, kicking or jumping at a player is not allowed. Holding or pushing a player is not allowed. For the infringement of these rules a free kick is given to the opposing side at that place where the ball was at the time of such infringement of the rules.

Free Kick—A free kick is a kick at the ball without any interference, in which case the kicker's opponents must not be within 10 yards of the ball, unless they are standing on their own goal line. The kicker must not again play the ball until it has been played by another player.

Restarting the Game—In case of a temporary suspension of the game from any cause whatever, the ball shall again be put in play at the place it was at the time the play was suspended. The ball is thrown down where it was when the play ceased. The ball is in play as soon as it touches the ground, and the ball must not be played until it does touch the ground.

Officials—The officials shall be a referee (who has full charge of the game), two linesmen (one for each side of the field) and a timekeeper, who shall also act as scorer.

SHUTTLE BALL RELAY

The object of this team game is to throw a basketball rapidly "to and fro" from a leader to the first player of the team, then to the second, third, etc. The leader stands about 8 to 10 feet in front of the team, which is composed of six or more players (see diagram). As soon as the first player of the team receives the ball he immediately returns it to the leader. At the same time he takes one step to the left. This side stepping brings the next player in line to the head of the group. He now receives the ball, quickly returns it to the leader and steps to the left. This receiving the ball, returning it and stepping to the left continues until every team member except the last has received and returned the ball.

When the last team member receives the ball, he does not return it, but runs around the group and places himself where the leader originally stood. This leader in the meantime has gone over to the team and placed himself at its head.

The play then continues as described above (players stepping right sideward) until every player has been leader. The play ends when the player who began the game is again leader. The game is played with interest by players of all ages. When used in team competition the interest is great.

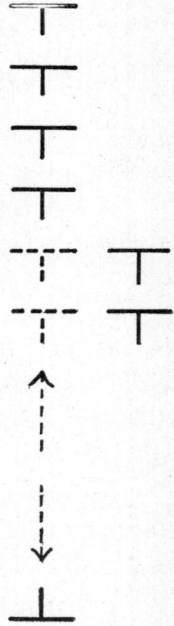

Variations.

1.   The player who receives the ball, instead of stepping to the left when returning it to the leader, bends his knees, thereby giving the team member standing behind him a chance to receive the ball.

2.   The last player, when running to place himself at the head as the leader, must first throw the ball into a basketball goal before play is resumed.

3.   The last player must dribble the ball forward and then shoot for the basket.

4.   The last player may be asked to perform any other kind of stunt before being allowed to shoot for the basket.

FOX AND CHICKENS DODGEBALL.

This is a game for two or more teams, of not more than seven players each. A circle, not less than 30 feet in diameter, and a basketball or soft baseball are required.

One team goes in the center, forming in line, one behind the other, with arms around the waist of the one in front. The other teams spread out around the outside of the circle. Each team is given the same length of time in the center, and the team with the smallest score wins.

The rules are the same as in Dodgeball in a Circle, with two exceptions: (a) A score is made only when the last one of the inner team is hit (unless the line breaks, when anyone in it may be hit); (b) The front player of the inner team may bat the ball, as he turns to keep his team protected.

May Day.

German.

MAY DAY.

The music is an old German folksong.

The dancers are arranged in couples. These stand either in a flank column or in a circle. In explaining the steps, the movements of those standing on the left (or inside) are described. The dancers on the right side begin with the opposite foot. The inner hands of the dancers are grasped shoulder-high, the outer knuckles are placed on the hips.

PART I.

1. Two mazurkas left forward and a half turn right in four quick steps (pause during the last beat).
2. Repeat 1 right and face left about.
3. Balance-step left and right obliquely forward, the opposite foot crossed in front, and a half turn right.
4. Repeat 3 right and left, facing left about.

PART II.

1. Six running steps forward and a half turn right (pause during the last beat).
2. Six running steps backward, beginning right, and a half turn left.
3. Repeat 1.
4. Repeat 2.

PART III.   (Partners Facing Each Other.)

1. Grasp partner's hands shoulder-high. Two mazurkas sideward, toward the leaders. Place knuckles on hips, and in four quick steps face right (left) about. (Pause during the last beat.)
2. Repeat 1 toward the foot of the column and face left about.
3. With hands grasped, balance-step left and right (right and left) obliquely forward, the opposite foot crossed in front. Knuckles on hips and a half turn right.
4. Repeat 3 right and left, facing left about.

PART IV.   (Partners Facing Each Other.)

1. Dancer No. 1 (on the left), in ten running steps, circles around No. 2, beginning to the left. Pause during the last beat. Knuckles placed on hips.
2. No. 2 encircles No. 1, beginning left.
3. Both grasp right hands, left on hips and, in ten running steps, circle around a common center.
4. Repeat 3, grasping left hands.

GAMES AND DANCES
Larkspur.
(MAZURKA.)

O. Heyer.

Larkspur.

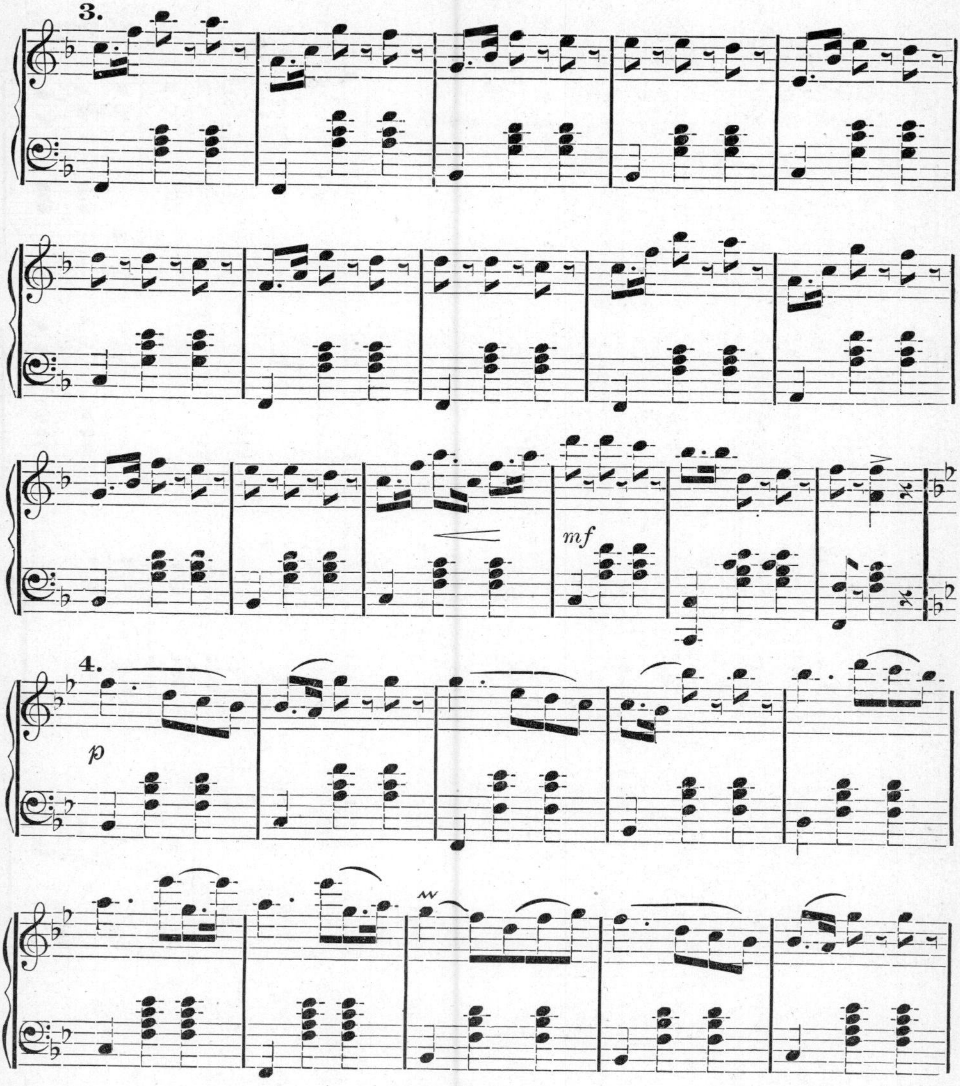

GAMES AND DANCES
Larkspur.

NORMAL SCHOOL MAZURKA.

Music : "Larkspur" by O. Heyer.

Formation: A column of front ranks in open order. Hands at waist (knuckles on hips).

PART I. (16 Measures.)

1. Three mazurkas to the left and a glide-balance hop left with a full turn left in two hops. 4 measures.

2. The same right. 4 measures.

3. Repeat 1 and 2, but finish with two stamps (left and right) in place of the glide-balance hop right, with a full turn. 8 measures.

PART II. (16 Measures.)

1. Three steps forward and point* right foot forward and pause. 2 measures.

2. Waltz-balance step obliquely forward right. 1 measure.

3. Glide-balance hop left, with a full turn left. 1 measure.

4. Repeat 1 to 3, beginning right. 4 measures.

5. Repeat 1 to 4, but taking three steps backward instead of forward (other parts precisely the same), and closing with two stamps. 8 measures.

PART III. (16 Measures.)

Repeat Part I, with arms folded in front, height of shoulder, during the step; replace hands at waist during the stamps.

PART IV. (16 Measures.)

1. Front crosscut left and two hops left, with the left arm raised to a half circle over head. 1 measure.

2. Rear crosscut right and hop twice on the right foot, replacing the left hand at waist. 1 measure.

3. Three steps left sideward, with a rear-cross step right, the arms raised sideward; point right foot forward and pause, with right arm moved in front of body. 2 measures.

*To "point" with a foot means to place the foot forward (or in the direction commanded), this movement being preceded by a slight and quick bending of the knee and a retraction of the foot.

4. Repeat 1 to 3, beginning right, and moving right sideward. 4 measures.

Repeat 1, 2, 3 and 4. 8 measures.

PART V. (16 Measures.)

1. Mazurka to the left and glide-balance hop left, with a full turn left, arms folded in front and kept shoulder-high. 2 measures.

2. As 1 to the right. 2 measures.

3. Repeat 1 and 2, but finish with two stamps. 4 measures.

Repeat 1, 2 and 3. 8 measures.

PART VI. (16 Measures.)

Repeat Part I.

GAMES AND DANCES
Cupid and Butterfly.
(INTERMEZZO GRAZIOSO.)

Revised and fingered by Carl Hofmann.

Claude d' Albret.

Cupid and Butterfly.

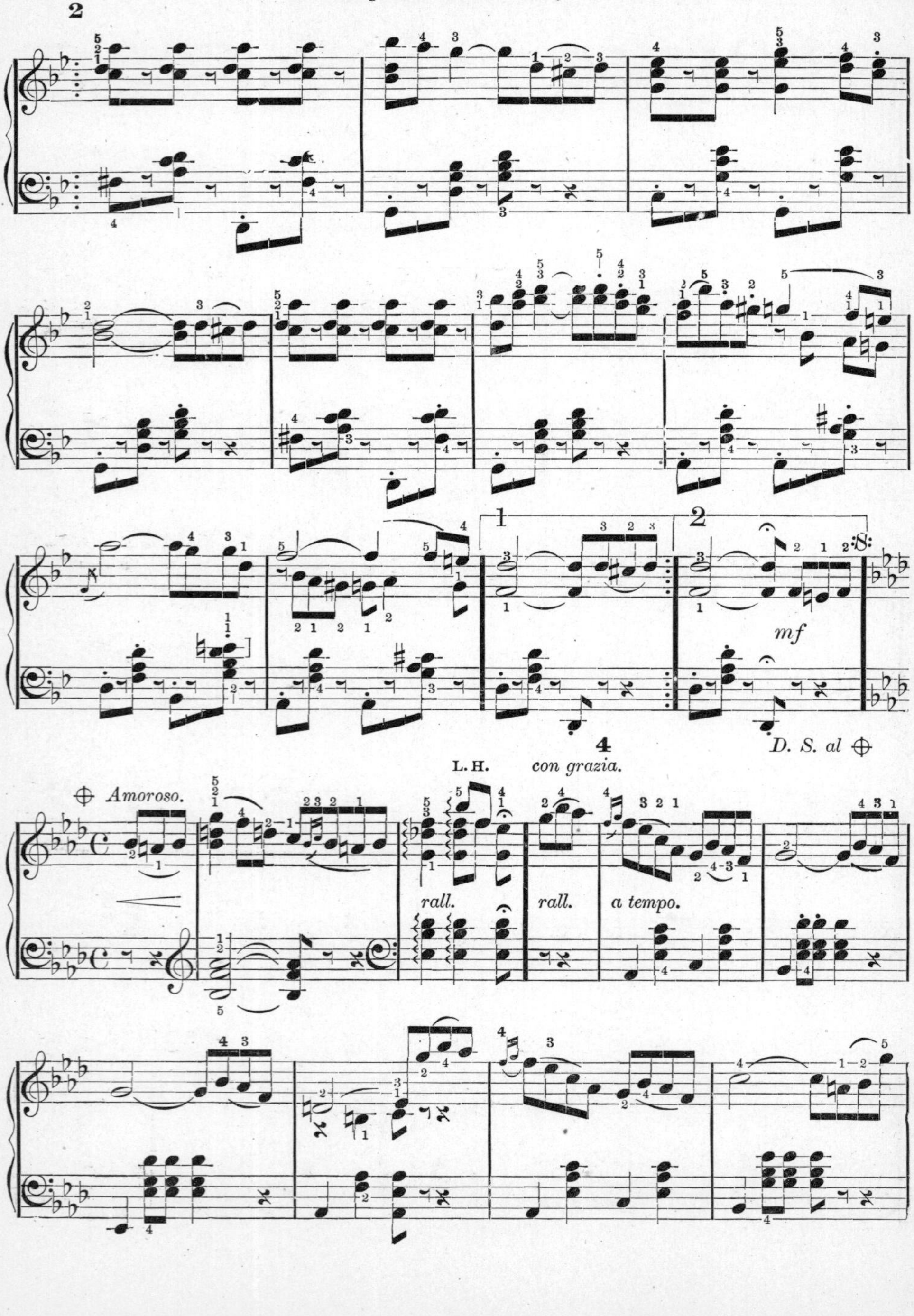

Cupid and Butterfly.

GAMES AND DANCES
Cupid and Butterfly.

Cupid and Butterfly.

CUPID AND BUTTERFLY—A SCHOTTISCHE.

Music: "Cupid and Butterfly," Intermezzo Grazioso, by Claude d'Albret.

INTRODUCTION.   (4 Measures.)

During the introduction the performers assume a pose chosen by the teacher.

PART I.   (16 Measures.)

Measures.   (Hands are placed at the waist.)

A. 1- 2   Schottische obliquely forward left and right.
    3- 4   Four swing-hops backward (left, right, left and right).
    5- 6   Schottische obliquely forward left and right.
    7   Two swing-hops backward (left and right).
    8   Two steps backward and close heels.
B.   Repeat A, 9-16, but beginning right (movements to the opposite side).

    Note:—Instead of the schottische-step beginners may perform a three-step swing-hop.

PART II.   (20 Measures.)

A. 1- 2   Three-step-turn left and point right.
    3- 4   Three-step-turn right and point left.
    5- 6   Step and curtsy left and right.
    7- 8   Place left foot forward, backward, then change-step forward.
    9-10   Repeat 7-8 right.
B.   Repeat A, 11-20.

PART III.   (Like Part I, 16 Measures.)

A. 1- 2   Schottische obliquely forward left and right.
    3- 4   Four swing-hops backward (left, right, left and right).
    5- 6   Schottische obliquely forward left and right.
    7   Two swing-hops backward (left and right).
    8   Two steps backward and close heels.
B.   Repeat A, 9-16, but beginning right (movements to the opposite side).

INTERLUDE. (2 Measures.)

PART IV. (16 Measures.)

A. 1   Cross-step to the left and then swing right leg forward.
   2   Balance-hop right forward, then swing-hop left.
   3   Repeat 2.
   4   Pirouette to the right.
   5- 8   Repeat 1-4 to the right side.
B. 9-16   Repeat 1-8.

PART V. (20 Measures.)

A. 1   With a quarter turn left two running steps and a balance-hop left forward.
   2   Repeat to the right.
   3- 4   Step left sideward, place right foot backward, bend trunk left and wave right arm upward; repeat to the opposite side.
   5- 6   Repeat 1-2.
   7- 8   Repeat 3-4.
   9-10   Repeat 3-4.
B.   Repeat A, 11-20.

PART VI. (Like Part IV, 16 Measures.)

A. 1   Cross-step to the left and then swing right leg forward.
   2   Balance-hop right forward, then swing-hop left.
   3   Repeat 2.
   4   Pirouette to the right.
   5- 8   Repeat 1-4 to the right side.
B. 9-16   Repeat 1-8.

INTERLUDE. (4 Measures.)

PART VII. (Like Part I, 16 Measures.)

A. 1- 2   Schottische obliquely forward left and right.
   3- 4   Four swing-hops obliquely backward (left, right, left and right).

5- 6   Schottische obliquely forward left and right.

7   Two swing-hops obliquely backward (left and right).

8   Two steps backward and close heels.

B.   Repeat A, 9-16, but beginning right (movements to the opposite side).

Note:—With advanced pupils the waving of one or both arms may be added to the different steps.

Arm "waving" corresponds to moving one or both arms to the commonly accepted "positions"—e. g., to the third position, or to the fifth position. etc.

GATHERING PEASCODS (English).

Victor Record 18,010 (No introduction—Dance is played once).

Steps: Glide, running.

Formation: Single circle of couples (five to eight), facing center, boy on left of girl.

Music: Three parts, A, B and C. A and B, 6 measures each, repeated. C, 8 measures, repeated. All played three times. Polka rhythm (2 counts to a measure).

PART I.

Measures:

A.   4.   Join hands, eight glides left sideward (counts 1 to 8).

     2.   Release hands and beginning right, make a whole turn right in four running steps (counts 9 to 12).

     6.   Repeat above 6 measures, gliding right (counts 1 to 12).

B.   6.   Boys: Twelve glides left sideward, joining hands in a circle to places (counts 1 to 12).

     6.   Girls: Same (counts 1 to 12).

C.   2.   Boys: Beginning right, three running steps forward and close, swinging arms obliquely fore-upward, clapping hands on count 3 (counts to 4).

2. Three running steps backward to places and close, as girls run forward and clap (counts 5 to 8).

2. Boys repeat measures 1 and 2 as girls return to places with three steps backward and close (counts 9 to 12).

2. Boys return to places making a whole turn right in four running steps (counts 13 to 16).

8. Repeat above 8 measures, girls beginning (counts 1 to 16).

PART II.

A. 2. Partners face. Beginning right take four running steps forward, passing partner left shoulder to left shoulder, turning inward toward partner on third and fourth counts (counts 1 to 4).

2. Repeat, passing right shoulder to right shoulder, returning to place (counts 5 to 8).

2. All make a whole turn right in four running steps (counts 9 to 12).

6. Repeat above 6 measures (counts 1 to 12).

B and C. Repeat B and C of Part I, girls beginning.

PART III.

A. 4. Partners face. Partners link right arms, and beginning right, with running steps, make a whole turn, and with running steps backward, return to places (counts 1 to 8).

2. All make a whole turn right in four running steps (counts 9 to 12).

6. Repeat above 6 measures, linking left arms (counts 1 to 12).

B and C. Repeat B and C of Part I, finishing with bow for boys and curtsy for girls.

NOTE—This dance is handed down from the religious ceremony of the Druids of Merrie England. In their nature worship to celebrate the coming of spring, they danced around a tree, and in order to secure a blessing, placed their hands on the tree. This is simulated in the clapping figure of the dance.

BLUFF KING HAL (English—May Pole Dance).

Victor Record 17,087 (Dance is played once).

Steps: Polka, heel-and-toe polka, skipping (light and joyous).

Polka left: Hop right, "and"; step left forward, 1; bring right foot to left and put the weight on it, "and"; step left forward, 2.

Heel and toe polka sideward left: Place the left foot forward, heel touching, 1; place the left foot backward, toe touching, 2; hop on the right foot, "and"; step left sideward, 3; bring the right foot to the left heel and put the weight on it, "and"; step left sideward, 4.

Formation: Double circle of couples, boy on left of girl, left sides toward center. Couples numbered 1, 2, 3, 4.

Music: Introduction of 4 measures. Three parts of 8 measures, A, B and C. All played six times. March rhythm (2 counts to a measure).

INTRODUCTION.

Measures:

4. With inside hands joined shoulder high, all stand with left foot pointed forward. Hold position through 4 measures of introduction (counts 1 to 8).

PART I.

A. 6. Beginning left, twelve skip steps around pole (two steps to a measure) (counts 1 to 12).

2. With four skip steps, couples swing in facing pole, forming single circle, joining hands (counts 13 to 16).

B. 2. Beginning left, advance toward pole in four skip steps, raising arms forward and upward (counts 17 to 20).

2. Same, moving backward (counts 21 to 24).

4. Repeat above 4 measures (counts 25 to 32).

C. 8. Partners face, join right hands and turn in sixteen skip steps. Finish with boy inside with back to pole (counts 33 to 48).

Part II.

A. 8. Beginning left, heel and toe polka sideward, repeat right, left, right (counts 1 to 16).

B. 8. Join right hands and turn partner in eight polkas. On the last polka swing into a single circle facing pole with hands joined (counts 17 to 32).

C. 8. Beginning left, sixteen skip steps around pole counter-clockwise (counts 33 to 48).

Part III.

A. 8. Same as B of Part I (counts 1 to 16).

B and C. 2. With four skip steps, all couples No. 1 advance toward pole and grasp ribbons with right hands (counts 17 to 20).

2. With four skip steps return to place and face partner, left toe pointed forward, the boy turned slightly toward pole, the girl away (counts 21 to 24).

4. Couples No. 2 repeat same (counts 25 to 32).

4. Couples No. 3 repeat same (counts 33 to 40).

4. Couples No. 4 repeat same (counts 41 to 48).

Part IV.

A and B. 16. Winding pole. Beginning left, with thirty-two skip steps, girls move clockwise, boys counter-clockwise, make "grand chain," partners passing right shoulders first (counts 1 to 32).

C. 2. Face center. With four skip steps all advance to pole, dropping ribbons (counts 33 to 36).

2. All join hands and with four skip steps move back from pole (counts 37 to 40).

4. Advance and retire again (counts 41 to 48).

FINALE.

At the finish of the dance, the circle breaks and the first one leads off the group in skip steps, during the repetition of the music.

NOTE—The May pole is about 12 feet high and should have a bright-colored streamer for each dancer.

The skips are vigorous, with high knee raising, accompanied by side-ward trunk swaying.

IRISH LILT (Irish).

Victor Record 17,331 (Introduction, Chord—Dance is played six times).

Steps: Cut, break, cut hop.

Cut: Displace right foot by hopping on left and raising right leg backward, 1 (cut backward); displace left foot by hopping on right and raising left leg forward, 2 (cut forward).

Break: Jump to a side stride, 1; jump with feet together, 2; hop left, raising right leg backward, 3; hop left, swinging right leg forward, 4.

Cut hop left: Cut backward with left, raising right leg backward, 1; hop left, swinging right leg forward, 2.

Formation: Dance for individual. Class in open order as for free exercises.

Music: Two parts of 8 measures each, repeated. Two-step rhythm (2 counts to each measure).

NOTE—The figures are arranged according to difficulty and any number of parts may be used.

PART I.

Measures:

6. Place left foot forward in preparation: Twelve cuts alternately backward and forward (counts 1 to 12).

2. Break right (counts 13 to 16).

8. Repeat above 8 measures, beginning with right foot, finishing with break left (counts 1 to 16).

Part II.

6. Beginning left, six cut hops backward (counts 1 to 12).
2. Break right (counts 13 to 16).
8. Repeat above 8 measures, beginning with right foot, finishing with break left (counts 1 to 16).

Part III.

2. Cut left backward, and place right foot backward (toe), 1; hop left and place right heel forward, 2; hop left and place right foot at left ankle, 3; hop left and swing right leg forward, 4 (counts 1 to 4).
2. Repeat, hopping right (counts 5 to 8).
2. Repeat, hopping left (counts 9 to 12).
2. Break right (counts 13 to 16).
8. Repeat above 8 measures, hopping right, left, right and break left (counts 1 to 16).

NOTE—Later add facing left on 1; facing right about on 2, and to the front on 3 and 4, and *vice versâ*.

Part IV.

2. Beginning left and crossing in front, seven short running steps right sideward, then swing right leg forward and hop left (counts 1 to 4).
2. Repeat left sideward, crossing right in front (counts 5 to 8).
2. Repeat right sideward, crossing left in front (counts 9 to 12).
2. Break right (counts 13 to 16).
8. Repeat above 8 measures, running left sideward first, finishing with break left (counts 1 to 16).

REAP THE FLAX (Swedish—An Industrial Dance).

Victor Record 17,002 (Introduction, Chord—Dance is played twice).

Steps: Running.

Formation: Front ranks of five, numbered from right to left. No. 1 of each rank is its leader.

Music: Two parts of 8 measures each, A and B, played four times. Fast waltz rhythm (three counts to a measure).

PART I (Gathering).

Measures:

A.　1.　Bend down to left as if gathering flax (counts 1 to 3).

　　1.　Straighten and bring hands to waist as if pulling flax (counts 4 to 6).

　　1.　Throw flax to right (counts 7 to 9).

　　1.　Hands on hips (counts 10 to 12).

　　4.　Repeat above 4 measures (counts 13 to 24).

B.　All make a quarter turn right, so as to be in single file.　No. 1 keeps hands on hips, others place hands on shoulders of ones in front.

　　7.　Beginning left, run in a circle, counter-clockwise, and return to place.　Three steps to a measure, stamping on first count of each measure and bending toward stamping foot (counts 1 to 21).

　　1.　All place hands on hips, and with two stamps (right, left) make a quarter turn left (counts 22 to 24).

PART II (Combing).

A.　1.　All reach down to the right (counts 1 to 3).

　　1.　Straighten as if picking the flax (counts 4 to 6).

　　1.　Throw forward as if over the hackle (counts 7 to 9).

　　1.　Jerk arms toward body as if pulling flax forcibly through hackle (counts 10 to 12).

　　4.　Repeat above 4 measures (counts 13 to 24).

B.　8.　Same as B of Part I (counts 1 to 24).

PART III (Spinning).

A.　4.　Nos. 2 and 5 step out of line, facing Nos. 3 and 4.　Nos. 2 and 4 and Nos. 3 and 5 join right hands.　With twelve running steps, beginning left, circle clockwise (three steps to a measure, stamping on the first count of each measure) (counts 1 to 12).

　　4.　All face right about, grasp left hands and circle opposite (counts 13 to 24).

　　During these 8 measures No. 1 turns, facing other four.　On first count of each measure clap hands and stamp with left foot, as if treading wheel. All finish in a straight line.

B.　8.　Same as B of Part I (counts 1 to 24).

PART IV (Weaving).

A. 8. All take same position as for A of Part III. In twenty-four running steps No. 1 (the shuttle) runs under arches, passing between 2 and 3, 5 and 4, turns right, and passes between 2 and 5, 3 and 4; turns right, and passes between 4 and 5, 3 and 2, back to original position. All finish in a straight line (counts 1 to 24).

B. 8. Same as B of Part I (counts 1 to 24).

VARIATIONS OF STANDARD GAMES AND EVENTS

Many of the games and events described on the preceding pages, by variations, may be made more difficult or more interesting for older pupils. Some of the more valuable of these variations are as follows:

Three-Deep Variation—The players are grouped by twos, the rear player grasping around the waist of the one in front. The pairs are scattered about the gymnasium or play space. Two players are then designated as the runner and the catcher (or chaser). Upon command the runner tries to get into a safe place by grasping around the waist of the last player of one of the pairs. The pairs try to make this difficult by turning around or by moving from place to place. The catcher in the meantime is chasing the runner, trying to tag him. If he tags him, the roles of these two players are reversed. If, however, the winner grasps someone, as designated above, he is safe, whereupon the one standing in "front" becomes the runner. Using two couples as runners and catchers adds greatly to the enjoyment.

This variation appeals to players of all ages. It also is a usable parlor game.

Snake Race—For this race the players are arranged in teams of six to eight. The players stand one behind the other, grasping around the waist of the one in front. During the race this formation must not be broken. About ten to twenty steps away, place in front of each team a club or some other object. At the signal each team runs forward and circles around the club twice (or three times) and returns to its starting position, *i. e.*, standing as it originally did. If the club is upset, or if a team breaks its formation, the team is out.

Centipede Race—Divide the players into teams of a like number. Get as many poles as there are teams, the poles being about ten to twelve feet long. The teams that are to race line up at the starting place. Each team member is astride of a pole, grasping the same with one hand. Upon command, each "centipede" races around a designated spot or obstacle and back to the starting line.

Running twice or oftener around the obstacle before returning adds greatly to the fun.

Combination Races—Combining two or more different types of locomotion in a race often adds a splendid element of interest for the player as well as for the spectator. Several such combinations are as follows:

(a) Run to a given mark, but when returning to the starting place run on hands and feet; that is, "on all fours."

(b) Run to a given mark, but when returning jump or leap forward on hands and feet; that is, by means of a "rabbit jump."

(c) Run to a given mark, but when returning run sideways; that is, like a crab.

(d) Run to a given mark, but when returning run backward.

The above-named forms of racing can also be used during relay races. In such races one-half of a team performs ordinary running, while the other half returns in one of the forms spoken of above, or all the runners perform definitely prescribed stunts.

Tag Games—Tag games as a rule need a large play space. Often only a restricted space is available. Under such conditions the following variations are useful:

Ankle.Tag—In this game a person may not be tagged when he has hold of the ankle of another player. As players generally are moving about, this is a rather strenuous game.

Turkish Tag—In this game a person may not be tagged who is kneeling and bending forward until his forehead touches the ground.

Turtle Tag—In this game a person may not be tagged who is lying on his back, both arms and legs being off the floor.

Ostrich Tag—In this game a person may not be tagged who, while stooping forward, has put the left arm under the left knee and grasped his nose with the left hand. Naturally, the right arm and leg also may be used.

Who Am I?—This game belongs to the I Spy type. The players are divided into two teams standing opposite to each other. While shielded behind the others, one player from each team gets behind a curtain (blanket, sheet, etc.), which he holds before him with upstretched arms. These two players advance toward each other, and by all kinds of turns and maneuvers try to find out who is behind the other screen, and calling that person's name as soon as a good guess is possible. The winning side scores a point. Play continues until each player has had a chance to guess. The game is a good parlor game.

Tug-of-War Variations:

1. The players, instead of standing with faces to the rope, turn around and, during the pull, have their backs to the rope.

2. The players stand at the side of the rope, which is lying on the ground. At a signal from the teacher the rope is grasped, and the tug begins.

3. The players are lined up ten to twenty feet from the rope, which is lying on the ground. At a signal from the teacher the players run forward, grasp the rope and begin to pull.

4. The players are lined up some distance from the rope, which is lying on the ground. At a signal from the teacher the players execute a roll forward (or some other stunt), run forward and begin to pull.

5. A progressive tug. The pupils are lined up some distance from the rope. At a signal from the teacher the first four of each team rush forward and begin to pull. After a half minute (or less), at a signal the next four run forward to help. Then, at a third signal, the rest of the team members run forward to help their side.

NOTE—As the tug-of-war is a very strenuous exercise, great care should be taken to see that children do not have long pulls. It is better to have two short pulls than to have only one pull, even if this one pull lasts no longer than the aggregate time devoted to two.

Novelty Races—At exhibitions or play days it often is wise to change some of the standard forms of racing by introducing novelties. In the following some of the more amusing forms are described.

Obstacle Race—Place various obstacles in the path of the runners. Obstacles like barrels or bags to be crawled through, hoops to be pulled over the body, a barricade to be climbed over, a carpet to be crawled under, a pair of overalls to be donned at one place and discarded at another place, are forms that can be used anywhere.   In a gymnasium the various pieces of apparatus can be used as obstacles.

Stunt Races—The runners in races of this kind must perform some stunt like Dribble a Ball, Juggle a Ball, Roll a Hoop, Turn Cartwheels, Skip a Rope, Balance a Stick, Carry an Egg in a Spoon.

Races by Pairs—1.   The Wheelbarrow. This race is run by pairs. One of the players gets down on his hands. The other player grasps the feet of the first one, and the race is run in this formation.

2.   With crossed arms. The pair cross arms in the front chain lock and run in this formation.

3.   Chain gang. The players stand one behind another, the rear player with his hands on the shoulders of the one in front. The foremost player has his arms crossed on his chest.

4.   The travelers. The pair carry a traveling bag or grip between them. In the bag are various articles of clothing. When arriving at a designated place, the bag is opened and the apparel is put on. The race then proceeds to the starting place.

Racing by Threes—The camel. Three players form a group. Player number one is in front, facing in the direction of the race. Player number two, standing behind number one, bends forward and grasps the hands of number one. Player number three jumps to a straddle seat on the back on number two and places his hands on the shoulders of number one.

The chain gang described above can also be run by threes or more.

GAMES AND DANCES
FOR PLAYERS OF FOURTEEN YEARS AND OVER

Eighth to Twelfth School-Grades.

RIDER BALL.   (Mount Ball, Horse and Rider.)

The players pair off according to height, strength and agility, and form a double circle, faces to the center, with from two to six paces interval between the pairs. Those forming the inner circle are the "horses" and those in the outer the "riders." The horses take a stride position sideways, bracing themselves by placing both hands on the knees (which should be kept extended). The body is bent forward, in order that upon the command of the leader of the game to mount, the riders may readily mount by straddling their backs. The riders having mounted, a basket-ball is thrown from one to the other. The riders must hold themselves in place by the pressure of their knees, so that both hands are free for catching and throwing. When a rider misses catching the ball, all riders immediately dismount and flee. A horse quickly picks the ball up and commands all to halt. All riders then stand still while the horse endeavors to hit any one of them, who may dodge, but not leave his place.

If the player who aims at a rider succeeds in hitting him, places are exchanged, horses becoming riders and riders horses. If not successful, the game continues as before. The ball must at no time be held by a rider, but tossed as quickly as caught. The horses must not leave the circle, but may prance or turn around. The leader gives the commands to mount and determines the hits and misses.

BATTLE BALL.   (Bombardment—if played without clubs.)

The playfield is about thirty by sixty feet, a center line dividing the field. The members of each team are divided into forwards and guards. Six or more clubs, or other suitable objects, are placed equally apart on the rear line of each field. Each club is guarded by a player. The object of the game is to knock down an opponent's club with a ball, or to throw a

207

basket-ball through the opposing lines. When a club is knocked down the attacking side scores two points; when the ball passes through the opposing line (not higher than the heads of the players) the attacking side scores one point. The ball may be thrown by any player who may run up to the center line. As a rule, it is wiser to let the forwards do the throwing. If played with a medicine ball or with two basket-balls the game becomes very strenuous.

HANDBALL.   (Fives.)

Handball is a strenuous game for a small number of players. Either one, two or three players constitute a team. The object of the game is to bat a small rubber ball with the hand against the wall. The ball must not make more than one bounce before being batted. It must be batted first by a member of one team and then by a member of the other team. The playfield, which should be perfectly flat, is about twenty feet square, lying in front of a wall of the same length and approximately ten to fifteen feet high.

The game is played by four players, as follows: A player from Team No. 1 steps close to the wall, and with his hand bats the ball so vigorously against the wall that it rebounds beyond the "short line" drawn on the ground, usually about eight feet from the wall. If it falls short—i. e., within the short line territory—he tries again. If he again fails, or if the ball strikes him, he is out, and his team-mate plays the ball. We will suppose that the team-mate is successful and that he bats the ball across the line. The ball then must be returned (batted) by one of the players of Team 2 before it has bounced twice. If this is not done the side on the "ins" (Team 1) counts one point. The second player of Team 1 then begins a new play. This continues until the players on Team 1 do not return the ball correctly. Both players are then out. Team 2 thereupon is "in" and begins its scoring play. The players on the "ins" always are the ones who may score. The team first scoring 21 points wins the game. The ball played with is generally from two to three inches in diameter. A lively tennis-ball will answer.

TETHER BALL.   (Tether Tennis.)

The object of the game is to bat a ball, which is hung (tethered) from the top of a pole by a stout cord until the cord is all wound around the pole. The ball may be batted either with a tennis racket, or a flat, wooden bat, about twelve inches long and four inches wide at the end.

Two players may play the game, or the two sides may be composed each of two or three players.

Tether ball is an organized team game, for the conducting of which definite rules have been formulated.

1. The pole shall be 12 feet above the ground, and shall be set in the center of a 5-foot circle. (See diagram.) The pole shall have a line marked around it 5 feet from the ground.

2. A 12-foot line passing through the center of the circle shall divide the play space into two courts. (See diagram).

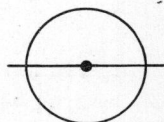

3. The 9-inch ball shall be attached to a strong cord, so that it hangs 3 feet from the ground.

4. A team shall consist of three players; each player to take part in a game.

5. The game shall be started by a player of the side winning the toss taking hold of the ball and batting it either to the right or left. The opposing player bats in the opposite direction.

6. A point is made by winding the whole cord around the post, above the 5-foot line.

7. After a point has been made, a player from the team opposite to the one that began the game starts the play. The third start is made by the last player of the first team (making three innings).

8. The side scoring most points in the three innings wins the game. In a match three games shall constitute a set.

9. Fouls are called as follows: (a) Stepping into the circle; (b) stepping into the opponents' court.

10. A foul gives the ball into the hands of the opponent. He may, for the first strike, step into the circle on his side of play, in case the cord is wound up so far that he cannot bat the ball when standing outside the circle.

FIELD BALL.

Field ball has some of the features of basket ball and of captain ball. Its advantages are that the field of play may be adjusted to accommodate any number of players. Every four players have a field of approximately eight by sixteen feet for themselves, excepting the captains' fields, which have only three players. See the diagrams which show the playfields and the positions for either eight, eighteen or thirty-eight players.

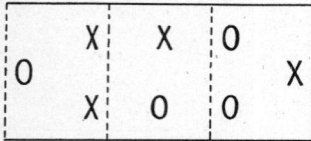

8 PLAYERS

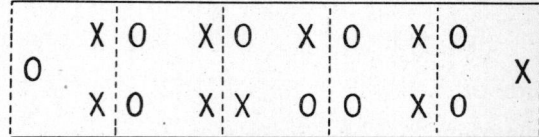

18 PLAYERS

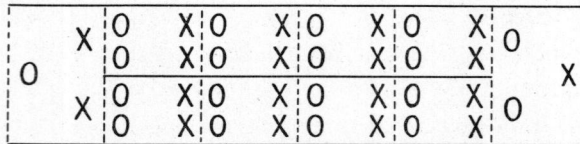

38 PLAYERS

The object of the game is to get a large, hollow ball (a basket ball) into the hands of the captain. At the beginning of the game (also of the second half) the referee tosses the ball up between two opposing players in the center of the field of play. Whenever a point has been made the ball is again tossed up in the center. Every time the captain of a side catches the ball his side scores one point. Every player has one guard, except the captain, who has two guards.

Players are not allowed to step on or over the lines of their field. Within the field they may move about freely. If a ball is thrown out of bounds a player from the opposite side gets it and throws it in from the point where it crossed the side or end line. A foul shall be called on every player guilty of tackling, tripping, or any other form of rough and unfair play. If a foul is called the referee shall give the ball to a player of the opposite side standing nearest the center of the field of play for a free throw toward his captain. The guards in the thrower's field shall not interfere with this free throw.

After five minutes of play the sides change places.

CAPTAIN DODGEBALL.

The object of the game is for the players on Team A to hit the members of the opposing Team B with a large, hollow ball (basket-ball), except as noted below.

Divide the players into two teams. Team A is placed on the outer side of the circle, which should be from forty to fifty feet in diameter. (See diagram.) The members of Team B are scattered around the inside of the circle, their captain being in the small circle in the center. This circle is 5 feet in diameter.

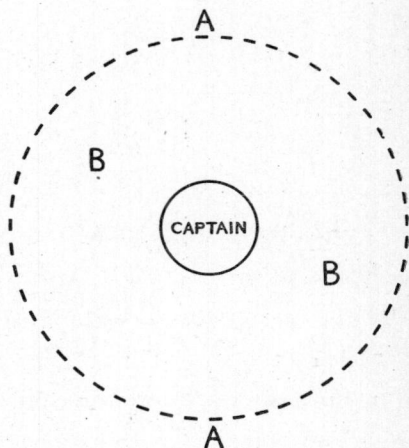

To start the game the referee blows the whistle, at the same time tossing the ball to one of the players on Team A. The players on Team B defend their captain by trying to intercept the thrown ball. This may be done only by raising one's foot so that the ball rebounds from the sole. (Warding off the ball with the forearm may also be used.) If the ball touches any other part of the body of a player on Team B he is out and leaves the circle. If the captain is struck (who may not leave his circle) he remains in the game, but the captain of Team A has the right to pick two players of Team B and put them out. Members of the attacking team must always stand behind the line when throwing. Should a ball roll into the field of play a player of Team A may run in and toss the ball to one of his team-mates. At the end of three minutes (or any other specified time) count the number of players remaining on Team B and credit them with so many points.

The sides are then changed and the second half of the game played.

"KICK BALL IN A CIRCLE."

The object of the game is to kick a basket-ball or a round football through the line of the opposing players.

The game is played in a divided dodgeball circle, 45 feet in diameter, having two foul fields as shown in the diagram.

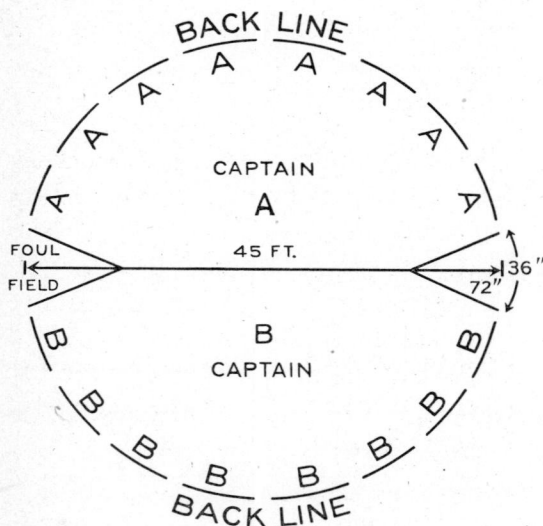

In a match game sixteen players form a team.

The players are arranged to guard the back line (the circle).

Two chasers or rovers stationed near the center line are captains.

A goal is made when a player on one side kicks the ball across the line of the opposing side below the shoulders of the opponents. The ball must be kicked. It may be stopped by the feet and body only, not with hands or arms.

The player who kicks the goal becomes captain. It is the duty of the captain to move around in the field of play, while his men guard the back or goal line. The men on the line as well as the captain may attempt to score whenever possible.

The captains make all tries for free goals. A free goal is an attempt to score without any interference from the opposing captain, who must retire to the back line with his players during the try.

A free try for goal is earned when the opposing side kicks the ball above the heads of the opponent players.

Each player is expected to guard the space to his right. Should a ball pass between the legs of a player or anywhere between two players (below the shoulders), a point is made by the opposite side. The ball is then put in play by the captain of the side scoring the point.

Fouls are made: (1) When the ball is kicked through the foul fields. (2) When the ball is "handled"—*i. e.*, touched by the hands or arms. (3) When an offside (crossing the center line) occurs.

N. B.—The ball may be handled when thrown in from the outer field, or by the captain in placing the ball for a free try for goal. A free try for goal may be kicked from any point behind the center line.

The game is 21 points.

WALL BASEBALL.

This game, requiring much skill, is played by two teams of nine players each. The players on the outs are placed as per diagram. If more or less players take part, these are placed to the best advantage. The diamond may be regulation size. An indoor bat is used, and a lively ball the size of a regular baseball, but covered with yarn. The home base is 12 feet from a blank wall. Five feet back of this is the pitcher's place. There is no catcher, but there are two shortstops. (See diagram.) The batter faces the wall, away from the diamond. On the wall are four upright lines, 8 feet high. The inner two lines mark the pitching space, which is 3 feet wide; the outer two the batting space, which is 9 feet wide.

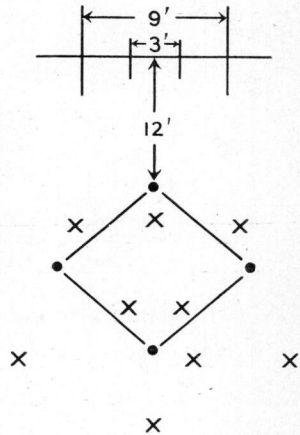

In starting the game the pitcher throws the ball toward the wall, so that it strikes the ground somewhere in front of the wall, then strikes the wall within the pitching space, and finally rebounds toward the batter. As soon as he has thrown the ball he quickly steps to one side.

When the ball reaches the batter he bats it against the wall, so that it strikes this inside of the batting lines. If the batted ball strikes outside of the batting space, or on the ground, it is a foul. The batter in trying to bat the ball is allowed to move forward and sideward, but not backward. From here on the regular baseball rules apply.

This game can also be played by batting a tennis ball with the hand. The wall, in this case, should be closer to the diamond.

THREE PINS.

The object of the game is to throw an indoor baseball from the scratch line, so that when rebounding from a wall the ball knocks down the pins (clubs, sticks, etc.), placed as per diagram. A team is composed of from six to ten players. Each player has three balls that he throws as explained above. If the three pins are knocked down by the first, or by the first and the second ball, they are replaced. It therefore is possible for a player to make nine points with his three throws. After the first player of one side has had his three throws, the first player of the opposite team throws. This alternation continues until all team members have thrown. The team having the highest number of points wins.

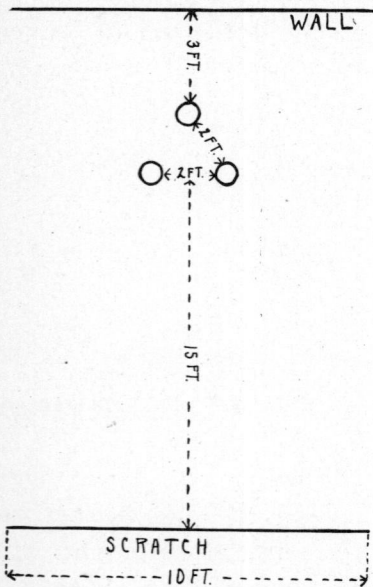

With inexperienced players the distance between the pins and the scratch line may be shortened to 10 feet.

The game also can be played with a basket-ball. In this case the pins should be placed farther apart.

JUMPING CIRCLE RACE.

Formation—Two teams, each with about ten to fifteen players, form two circles, facing outward.

The opposing runners always begin on opposite sides of the circle, both running in the same direction around the outside of the circle. Each runner holds a wand in his hand, the tip of which he drags on the floor, compelling the members in the circle to jump over it as it approaches them. The one returning first to his place scores a point for his team. The second members of the teams do the same, and so on until every one has competed. The team having the highest score wins.

CIRCLE RELAY RACE.

Formation—A line of front ranks of twos in a circle formation, the members of the ranks being numbered one and two from left to right, all facing inward.   All members numbered one belong to team No. 1 and likewise members numbered two compose team No. 2.   Anywhere from eight to fifteen players on a side may be used.   (See diagram.)

The first members of each team should be as nearly as possible diametrically opposite each other on the circumference of the circle.   The first two start the game by running once around the outside of the circle and tagging the next member of their team. When the runners are going left around the circle then the second member of their team is to their right.   (See diagram.)   The second member after being tagged takes up the race, runs once around the circle and tags the third member, and · so on until every member of the team has taken part.   Each member after finishing steps into the circle and returns to his original place.   The team finishing first wins.

To avoid confusion all members in the circle may sit on the floor, allowing only the two who are to run next to stand.

The runners may also be made to carry an object such as a basket-ball, a small medicine-ball or a dumbbell, around the circle and pass it to the next one.

HUMAN HURDLE CIRCLE RELAY RACE.

This game is similar to the Circle Relay Race, all members of the circle, however, sitting on the floor and facing outward with legs straightened forward.   Each runner while going around the outside of the circle must hurdle over the legs of those sitting in the circle.   Otherwise this game is identical with the Circle Relay Race.

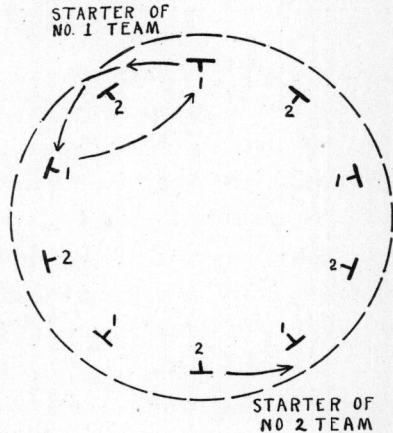

JUMPING CIRCLE RELAY RACE.

This game is a combination of the Circle Relay Race and the Jumping Circle Race. The formation is a line of front ranks of twos, the members of the ranks being numbered one and two, all facing outward.

The first members of the two teams begin on opposite sides of the circle and run in the same direction around the outside. Each one carries a wand, the tip of which is dragged on the floor, compelling the members of the circle to jump over it. After completing the circuit the wand is given to the next team member, who does likewise. After passing the wand the runner steps into the circle and returns to his original place. The team finishing first wins.

The members of the circle should be at least a double arm's length distance apart, and there should be at least eight players on a side, so that the circle will be sufficiently large.

It may happen that one runner will try to overtake the other. In this case the runner who is doing the overlapping must pass on the outside of his competitor and must constantly keep the tip of the wand on the floor.

COMBINATION VOLLEY BALL.

If a teacher has players of great difference of skill in one class a game may be played that is a combination of batting and catching.

From ten to twenty players on a side may be used. The unskilled play against the skilled on opposite sides of the net. The unskilled are allowed to catch the ball and return it by means of a throw. The skilled must bat the ball with the open hand and are not allowed to handle it. The rules concerning the service, out of bounds, etc., are the same as those of the regular volley ball game.

In some cases it may be proper to play a girls' team against a boys' team by modifying the rules similar to the above.

TAG FOOTBALL.

Tag football is a team game which may be as highly organized as regular football. It will develop the same skill and great physical activity as football does, without subjecting the players to serious injury.

It is particularly adapted to players of fourteen years or more, and is played either as a yard and gymnasium game, or as a match game on a regular football field.

The object of the game is to advance the ball across the opponents' goal line, either by running with the ball, by passing or by throwing it.

A basket-ball or football may be used for the yard or gymnasium game. The regulation football must be used for a match game, and such game should be played on a regular football field.

Organization for a Yard or Gymnasium Game—The players are organized into two teams, each containing eleven players, or more if the occasion requires this. There should be an equal number on each side, and there should be but seven players on the forward line. The rest would be regarded as backs.

The teams toss up a coin for possession of the ball or for the defense of a selected goal line.

The teams line up the same as in a regular American football game, and the game is started by the blowing of the referee's whistle.

After the calling of signals the ball is snapped back by the center to any one of the backs, who may pass it to any one of the members of the team. The players then endeavor to advance the ball toward their opponents' goal line.

As soon as any member of the defending team succeeds in tagging the player who has the ball, the progress of the ball stops and a "down" is called. The game is then resumed from this spot.

The attacking team is allowed four trials to advance five yards. (In an ordinary gymnasium the number of trials and the distance may have to be reduced.) If they do not succeed the ball is given to the opposing team. If the team in possession of the ball is successful in advancing five yards, "first down" is called, and they try to advance another five yards. If at any time during the play one player who is carrying the ball succeeds in getting past the opposing team and across their goal line, this play counts as a touchdown.

A touchdown scores six points.

The game should be in charge of a referee who calls all fouls, and decides all questions as to rules.

The ball should never be kicked in this form of the game. Penalty, a loss of five yards.

Suggestions for Playing the Game—End runs and forward passes are especially adapted to this game. When held for "downs" the team may throw the ball into the opposing team's territory (instead of kicking it). However, the caller of signals must call out "kick formation," in order to distinguish it from a forward pass, and no other play must be attempted.

Rules Regarding a Match Game—The players are organized as in regular football; *i. e.*, two teams of eleven members each.

The regular football field is used, and the rules of regular football are applied with a few modifications.

The team winning the toss either makes or receives the kick-off. After this the ball is snapped back by the center of the team in possession of the ball, at the beginning of every play.

The team in possession of the ball is given three trials to advance ten yards. Failing to do so in the three trials the ball is given to the opposing team.

The teams may form interference for end runs and other trick plays, but they may not use line bucking plays. Forward passes and end runs are best adapted to tag football because no tackling is allowed. When the runner carrying the ball is touched on any part of his clothing or person, he must stop and the number of the down is called.

The penalty for fouls such as "off side," "tackling," etc., is a loss of five yards by the team making the offense.

There shall be a referee, an umpire, a timekeeper and two linesmen.

The game should be played in four quarters of fifteen minutes each. The time between quarters should be not less than two minutes.

Tackling is not allowed. As mentioned above, the runner with the ball must be tagged. The decision of the referee is absolute and final on this part of the play.

Penalty for tackling, loss of five yards by the team making the foul.

The ball is kicked off at the beginning of each quarter and after a touch-down is made. The goal is kicked and a goal from field may be made from either a drop or a place-kick. The ball may be punted at any time by the team in possession of the ball.

A touchdown shall count six points for the team which makes it. When a goal from touchdown is kicked it shall count one point. A goal from field shall count three points.

Goal Shooting—The object of the game is to shoot a basketball into the basket as often as possible during a given length of time by a team composed of three players who play successively. There are but few rules. Player number one of team one begins by shooting from the free-throw line. Player number two immediately runs to where he expects the ball to fall and, as soon as he gets the ball, shoots from this spot. Player number three thereupon runs to where he expects the ball to fall and shoots from there. He is followed by player number ber one, and so the play goes on until time is called. Every ball that falls in the basket counts one point. Players are not allowed to walk or run with the ball. If under such circumstances a goal is made, it does not count.

As this is a strenuous game, it is advisable to have short innings, say, about three minutes. As soon as the first team has finished its inning the second team begins play and proceeds in the same manner. Three innings constitute a game. The team having most goals wins the game.

While it is possible to have more than three players on a team, it is not advisable to increase the number, as this slows down the game to such an extent that much of the interest is lost. If large numbers are to play the game, it is better to use four or more baskets and have two teams play at each basket.

Variation—A variation of the game described above is to have both teams play at the same time. Each team uses only its own ball. This, naturally, makes a very strenuous game that should be played only for a very short length of time. The team that at the end of the time limit has most goals wins.

If played in this manner, a second group of teams may begin to play when the first group has finished.

GOAL BALL.

Goal ball is a combination of basket-ball and soccer. It is especially adaptable to schoolyards and to cold weather, with the additional advantage that it may be played with large or small numbers with the same degree of interest.

Little is required in the way of lines. The absolutely necessary ones are the goals and goal-keeper's space—described hereafter—while the others only facilitate the duties of the referee. Two posts (or perpendicular lines on a fence will answer) are placed 6 feet apart and 6 feet high at each end of the playing space (diagram, *a*). A rope or bar is placed across the top of these posts (diagram, *b*). This constitutes the goal (G). With the line connecting the base of these posts as a base line, a square is marked out toward the middle of the field, which necessarily must be 6 feet square. This constitutes the goal-keeper's space (K). A circle, 18 inches in diameter, is placed in the middle of the field (O), and another concentric to this with a diameter of 20 feet (C). A line, 6 feet long, is placed parallel to the near edge of goal-keeper's space and 15 feet away, as a free-throw line (F). From the center of

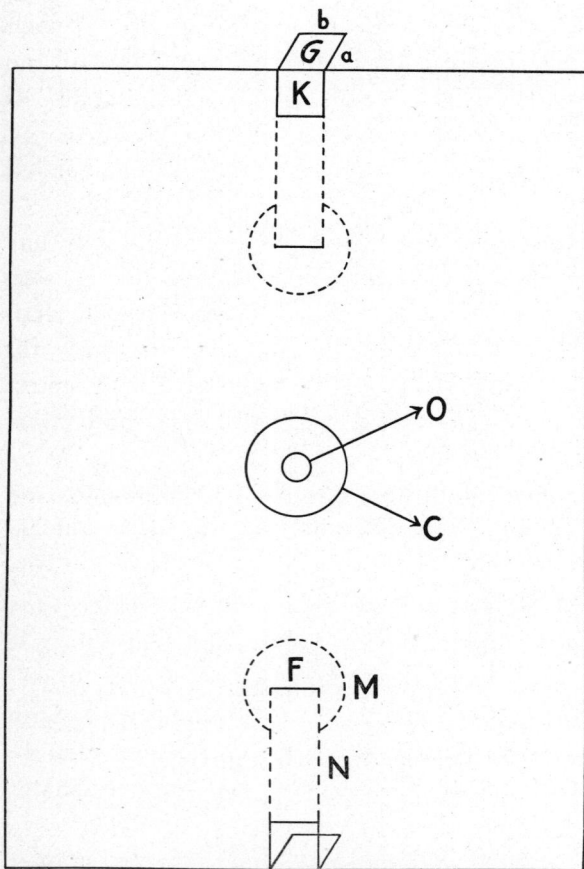

FIELD OF PLAY, 6000 TO 30,000 SQUARE FEET.

this line a circle 20 feet in diameter is marked (M) and an alleyway laid out from the free-throw line to the near edge of goal-keeper's space (N).

(All of these 20-foot circles and alleyways are not necessary except in regulation games.)

The playing space may be any size or shape. It is immaterial whether it is 6000 square feet or 10,000 square yards, only the smaller the space the less should be the number of players.

The players are divided into equal sides. A dodgeball or basket-ball is placed in the small, central circle. Two players, one from each side, with no other players nearer than ten feet, stand with one foot, toeing the 18-inch circle, and at a given signal seize the ball. The ball is advanced toward the goal by passing, a score being made when it is thrown between the goalposts and under the crosspiece. There should be two halves with a change of goals.

The following rules are suggested, though they may have to be changed with the evolution of the game:

1. There shall be one goal-keeper for each side, who is the only one who may enter the goal-keeper's space, though he is not compelled to stay there. If any one of those defending the goal, except the goal-keeper, shall enter this space, the ball shall be given to the other side, 5 yards away, for a free throw. If any part of the body of one of the aggressive team enters this space, the goal, if made, shall not count, and the goal-keeper shall throw the ball out with no one nearer than 10 feet.

2. Running with or advancing the ball by one's self is prohibited, and in such case the ball shall be given to a player of the opposite side with no one nearer than 10 feet.

3. Kicking the ball, holding, tripping, pushing and any unnecessary roughness shall be penalized in the same way as advancing with the ball. (See 2.)

4. A free throw consists of a trial for a goal, at a distance of 5 yards from the near edge of the goal-keeper's space, with no one nearer than 10 feet and no one in the alleyway between the goalkeeper and the one making the throw.

5. There are no out of bounds, and the play shall only be stopped as in above-mentioned cases and after scoring, in which case it shall be put in play at the center.

6. One official is all that is necessary in a small field, though two may be an advantage when a large field is to be covered.

PINBALL.

Pinball is one of the many variations of Baseball. The game can be played in a limited space, both in the playground or in the gymnasium. The diamond is 27 feet square. Eighteen inches back of the home plate, three Indian clubs (or any similar or appropriate device) are placed on a triangle, the sides of which measure 15 inches. An indoor baseball and bat are used. Nine players placed like in baseball form a team. The pitcher may either roll or bowl the ball. In some places there is a rule that, in order to be fair, the ball must bounce once in front of the pins.

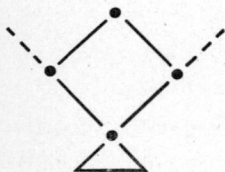

If one club is knocked down by a pitched or rolled ball the batter is out. If two pins are knocked down the batter, as well as the next player, are out. If three pins are knocked down, three players are out. This retires the side just as if three players had been put out under the ordinary rules of baseball. Should a batter accidentally or intentionally knock down one or more pins the rules described above apply. The balance of the rules are like in baseball.

FOOT BASEBALL.

This is a game for older players, presenting a combination of several features of football and baseball. Like in baseball, the object of this game is to circle around the four bases and thereby score a run for the team.

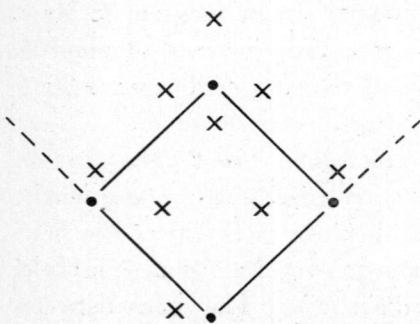

1. Teams are composed of nine players standing as indicated in the diagram (in large classes more players may be placed in the field.)

2. No pitcher is needed. An oval football is used. The diamond is regulation size.

3. The player opening the game takes the ball and, standing on the home

plate, kicks it into the field either by means of a punt, a dropkick or a place-kick. In doing this he is not allowed to step beyond the home plate. If he wishes to take one or more steps before kicking the ball he must begin behind the home plate.

4. Except as follows, the regular baseball rules then apply:

(a) If the ball is kicked outside the foul line on a fly the player is out.

(b) If the ball lands inside the foul lines and then bounces or rolls out, this is a fair play.

(c) A player on a base cannot leave this base to run for the next one until the ball is kicked.

(d) After a kick a player on a base may run until he is put out, according to the rules governing baseball, or thrown out (see (e)) or until the ball has been placed on the home plate by an opposing player. If a runner already has passed first base and is approaching second (or third) base after the ball has been placed on the home plate, he may continue until he reaches this base. This rule, however, shall not apply to a runner approaching the home plate; in order to score a run he must reach the home plate without being touched with the ball.

(e) A player is out who when off the base is tagged with the ball in the hands of an opponent, or who when off a base is hit with the thrown ball.

(f) A fielder may throw or kick the ball to his team-mates.

(g) Three outs shall end an inning, and nine innings shall constitute a game.

WICKET BALL.

Wicket Ball is a modified form of Soccer Football. It may be played on any good sized gymnasium floor (or playground). The diagram shows a field 40 x 80 feet. It is wise to have some space outside the field of play, in order to keep the ball in play when it rebounds into the field when kicked across the side line.

Divide the playfield into two parts of equal size (40 x 40). In the center of this line place a pair of jumping standards 5 feet apart. At a height of 5 feet place a jumping stick on the standards. At each end of the field place six wickets, equally spaced. At the center of each half of the playfield draw a cross line (call one Line X and the other Y). The space between Line X and the wickets is for the wicket guards, and can be invaded only by the goal tender and forwards of the opposite team. The same holds good of the space between Line Y and the wickets at the other end. The space between Lines X and Y is the scrimmage field for the forwards and the goal

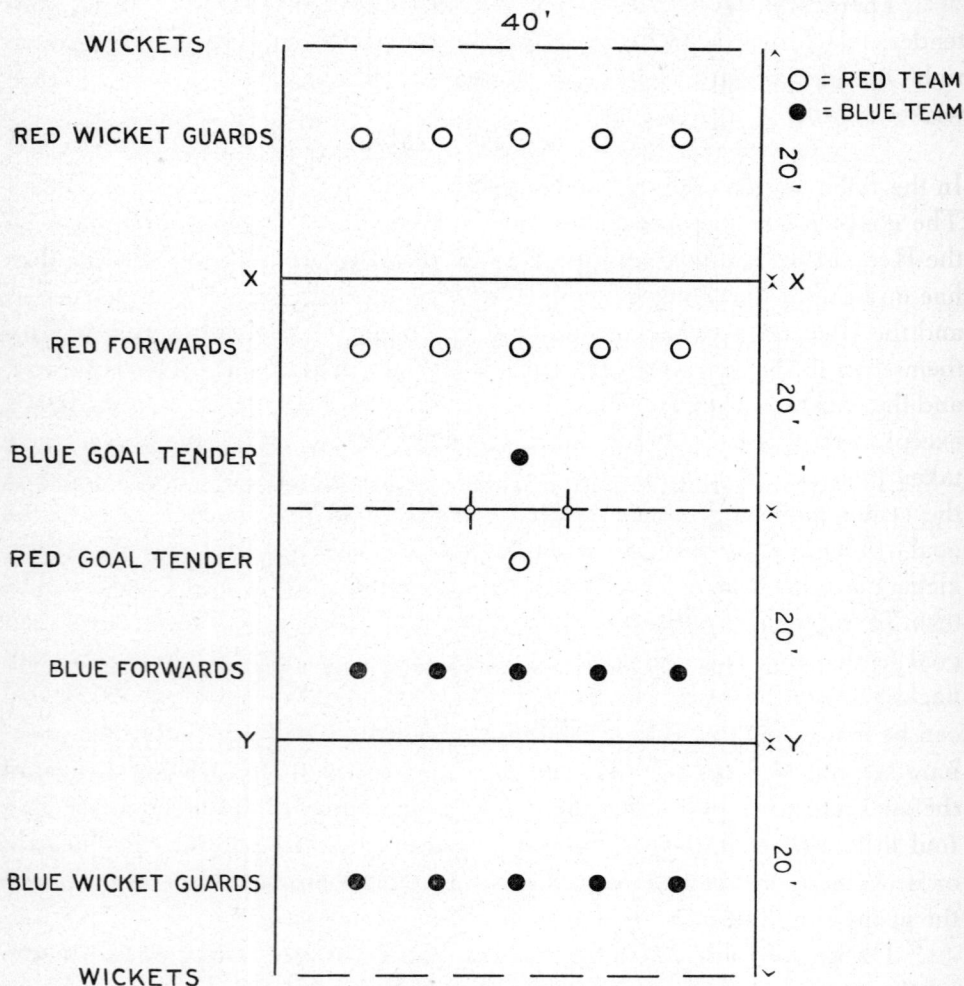

WICKETS

40'

RED WICKET GUARDS

O = RED TEAM
● = BLUE TEAM

20'

X   X X

RED FORWARDS

20'

BLUE GOAL TENDER

RED GOAL TENDER

20'

BLUE FORWARDS

Y   Y

20'

BLUE WICKET GUARDS

WICKETS

DIAGRAM OF FIELD.

tender of both teams. The goal is the space between the jumping standards, both above and below the crossbar.

The wickets made of wood are three feet high and two and a half feet wide. (They are of light frame construction and may be made by the players.)

The ball is a soccer football.

There are eleven players on a team, divided as follows: One goal tender, five forwards (who are named center forward, right inside forward, right outside forward, left inside forward, left outside forward) and five wicket guards.

The game is commenced by the players taking their places upon the field. In the following description one team is called "Red," and the other "Blue." The goal tenders line up near the goal, the Blue tender taking his position on the Red side of the goal and the Red on the Blue side. The forwards then line up back of the center line, the Reds 10 feet back of the Blue goal tender, and the Blues 10 feet back of the Red goal tender. The wicket guards place themselves in the space between Line X and the wicket and between Line Y and the wicket. They are not allowed to leave this space throughout the game, except to recover balls kicked out of the field of play. After the players have taken their places, the referee stations himself on either side directly opposite the center goal, and calling "Play," rolls the ball into the field toward the goal. The goal tenders rush upon the ball and skirmish until one succeeds in kicking it to his team. The forwards shall not take part in this skirmish. The team having gained possession of the ball, by its being kicked to them by their goal tender, tries to retain it, and, by kicking and passing (see fouls) the ball backward and forward between their own men, they attempt to score. A goal can be made, first, by kicking the ball through the center goal under the cross-bar; second, by carrying (see fouls) it down the field and kicking it against the wickets; third, by kicking the ball over the crossbar; fourth, by score on a foul kick. If the forwards succeed in knocking over a wicket with the ball, or if a score is made from a foul kick, play is stopped and the referee begins the game again by rolling the ball toward the center goal.

Points are made as follows: First, by one team kicking the ball underneath the crossbar of the jumping standards, this counts two points; second, by kicking the ball over the crossbar and between the jumping standards, this counts four points (called a top goal kick); third, by kicking the ball against and knocking down any one of the wickets of their opponents, this counts four points; fourth, by scoring from a foul kick, this counts two points.

The game is played in halves of ten minutes each. At the expiration of this time the team having the highest score wins. If the game ends with a tie, it is continued by starting with the ball rolled towards the center goal by the referee, and continues until one side scores, and so wins the game.

Fouls—Fouls are made by any player touching the ball with his hands while the ball is in play; by pushing, tripping, striking and unnecessary roughness, or encroaching upon that part of the field set apart for certain designated players.

Penalties—When a foul is made, a free kick is given to the opposing team from a line fifteen feet in front of the center of their line of wickets. The ball must be kicked from this line over the crossbar and between the jumping standard apparatus. By doing this, the side kicking the ball scores two points. In the event of not scoring, the ball continues in play without any stop in the game. If the ball is kicked out of bounds on any side of the field, it goes to the opposite team, and any player on that team has a free throw into the field of play from a point opposite the place where the ball went out of bounds. In the event of scoring from a foul kick, or kicking the ball against a wicket and knocking the wicket over, the referee stops the game and throws the ball into the center of the field again for a skirmish between the goal tenders, and the game goes on as before. In the event of a score being made by either team while kicking the ball up and down the field (by kicking the ball above or beneath the crossbar and between the jumping standards) the game continues.

Officials—A referee has charge of the game. Two scorers mark down scores as they are made, being especially watchful of the points made by kicking the ball underneath and over the crossbar and between the jumping standards. The referee's duty is to call out "ball under" or "ball over," whenever the ball is scored in the above manner, in order to aid the scorers in their duty.

The referee has sole charge of the ball and the players. He calls all fouls.

The scorers put down the points made by each team, giving credit to the players making the points. They also mark down the fouls made against the player making the foul.

Timekeeper—A timekeeper shall be appointed by the referee before the game commences.

VOLLEY BALL.   (Form III.)

THE GAME.

Volleyball is a team game of skill and moderate physical activity. It is played by two teams of nine players each, the ball being batted back and forth over a net. The object is to bat the ball into the opponents' court so that it will be impossible for them to return it.

RULE I.   EQUIPMENT.

SECTION 1. The court shall be 25 feet by 60 feet and free of obstructions for at least 15 feet above its surface.

SEC. 2. The court shall be marked by well-defined lines not less than two inches in width. The lines on the short side of the court shall be termed the "End Lines"; those on the long sides the "Side Lines."

SEC. 3. The court shall be divided into two equal parts, 25 by 30 feet, by a line parallel to and midway between the End Lines. This line shall be known as the "Center Line." A line parallel to and 25 feet from the Center Line at each end of the court shall be known as the "Serving Line."

SEC. 4. The ball shall be round and shall consist of a rubber bladder, covered with a leather case, not less than 25 inches nor more than 27 inches in circumference, and weighing not less than 10 ounces nor more than 13 ounces.

SEC. 5. The home team shall provide the ball.

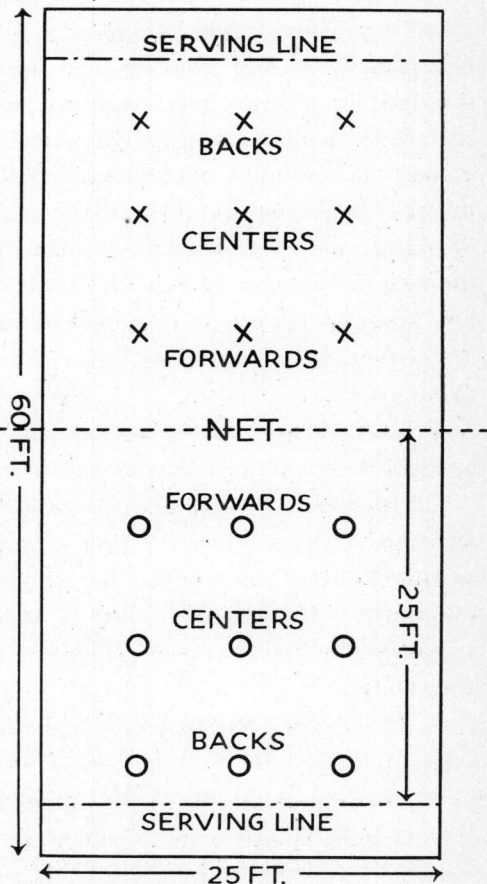

Sec. 6.   In case the visiting team refuses to accept the ball furnished, the Referee shall decide the ball to be used.

Sec. 7.   The net shall be at least one foot wide and of sufficient length to reach from boundary to boundary. The meshes shall be small enough to prevent the passage of the ball through the net. It shall be tightly stretched by the four corners across the court, above the center line. The top of the net at the middle shall be eight feet from the ground.

Rule II.   Players and Substitutes.

Section 1.   The teams in all official games shall be composed of 9 players each.

Sec. 2.   Each team shall have a captain. The captain shall be the representative of his team and may address any official on matters of interpretation or to obtain essential information. Before the game starts he shall furnish the scorers with the names of the players.

Sec. 3.   A substitute may take the place of a player only when the ball has been declared dead. He shall first report to the Referee.

Sec. 4.   A player taken out of the game may re-enter the game once.

Rule III.   Officials and Duties of Officials.

Section 1.   The officials shall be a Referee and two Linesmen, who may also act as timekeepers and scorers.

Sec. 2.   THE REFEREE shall be the superior official of the game. He shall decide when the ball is in play, when dead, when a point has been made, when side is out, and shall impose penalties for violation of rules. In the latter case he shall designate the offense and the offender.

Sec. 3.   THE LINESMEN shall be stationed so that the entire court is in plain view and shall assist the Referee, should he so request, in deciding whether the ball is out of bounds.

Sec. 4.   The Timekeepers shall note when the game starts; shall note time consumed by "time out" during the game, and shall indicate by gong, pistol or whistle the expiration of the actual playing time in each half. It is suggested the timekeepers use one watch.

Sec. 5.   The Scorers shall record the points made. Their record shall constitute the official score of the game. They shall compare their scores after each point, and any discrepancy shall be referred at once to the Referee for decision.

RULE IV. LENGTH OF GAME.

SECTION 1. The game shall consist of two halves of 15 minutes each, with an intermission of 5 minutes between the halves. The teams shall change sides after the first half.

SEC. 2. The sounding of the Timekeeper's signal shall indicate the ending of the game. If the ball is in play when the Timekeeper's signal is sounded, the play in progress shall continue until "side out" is declared or "point" is scored.

RULE V. CHOICE OF COURTS AND SERVICE.

SECTION 1. The captains shall toss for courts or service. The winner of the toss may choose either to take the first service or his choice of courts.

SEC. 2. At the opening of the game the ball shall be put in play by the "server" on the serving team which is to begin service.

SEC. 3. The serving team at the end of the first half shall be the serving team at the beginning of the second half.

SEC. 4. The server shall continue to serve until the Referee calls "side out." The opponents shall then serve.

SEC. 5. When a served ball touches the net, passes under the net or touches any player, surface or object before entering the opponents' court, "side out" shall be called.

RULE VI. PLAYING REGULATIONS.

SECTION 1. PLAYING TEAMS.

(a) The court occupied by a team shall be called its "own court"; that occupied by the opponents, the "opponents' court."

A "service" is the putting of the ball in play by the server batting it over the net into the opponents' court in any direction with one or both hands while standing with *both feet wholly behind* the serving line of the court.

(b) The player putting the ball in play is called the "server"; his team, the "serving" team; and the continuation of his putting the ball in play, "service."

The opposite team is called the "receiving" team.

(c)   "Point shall be called when the team receiving fails to return the ball legally to the opponents' court.

(d)   "Side out" shall be called when the team serving fails to win its point or plays the ball illegally.

(e)   The ball is "dead" after "point," "side out," or any other decision temporarily suspending play.

(f)   A player who touches the ball, or is touched by the ball when it is in play, shall be considered as "playing the ball."

(g)   The ball is "out of bounds" when it touches any surface or object or the ground outside of the court. A ball touching a boundary line is good.

(h)   When the ball momentarily comes to rest in the hands or arms of a player, he shall be considered as "catching" or "holding the ball." The ball must be clearly batted. Scooping, lifting, shoving or following the ball shall be considered as holding.

(i)   A player touching the ball more than once with any part of his body when the ball meanwhile has not been touched by another player shall be considered as "dribbling."

(j)   Any player committing any act which, in the opinion of the Referee, tends to slow down the game unnecessarily shall be considered as "delaying" the game.

(k)   "Time out" may be declared only when the ball is dead.

SEC. 2.   ROTATION.

(a)   The shifting of the players in position shall be called "Rotation."

(b)   The order in which the teams are to serve shall be called the serving order.

(c)   Players on forward line and back line shall move from left to right (facing net), and centers shall move from right to left. The player who has just served shall cross diagonally to left forward position. (See diagrams.)

(d)   At the beginning of the game the ball shall be put into play by the first player on the serving order of the team serving. (Diagram 1.)

(e)   The server shall continue to serve until the Referee calls "side out."

(f)   Service shall change as "side out" is called.

(g)   Team receiving the ball for service shall immediately rotate one position.

(h)   If a player serves out of turn, "side out" shall be called, and any points made on his service before the error was discovered shall not be scored.

(i)   A center or back may not play a forward position until rotation brings him to the forward line.

Penalty—"Side out" or "Point."

NOTE—The purpose of Section 2 is to prevent a one-man monopoly and to encourage all-round team play.

SEC. 3.   A ball other than a service touching the top of the net and going over into the opponents' court is still in play.

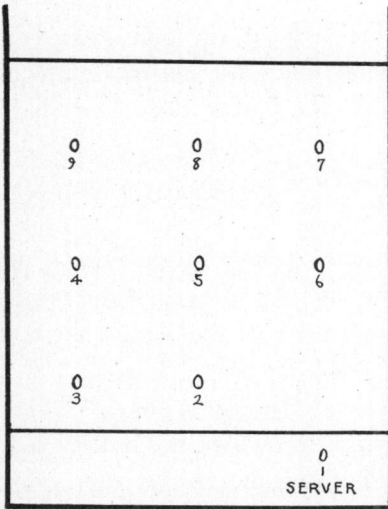

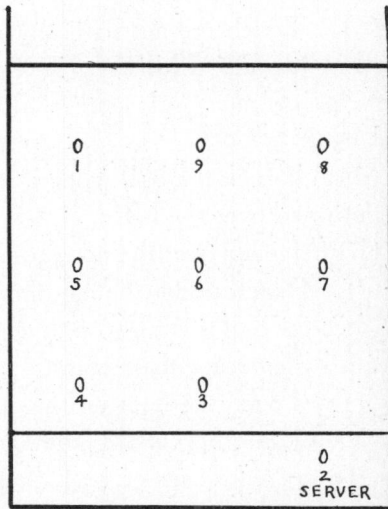

0 9	0 8	0 7		0 1	0 9	0 8
0 4	0 5	0 6		0 5	0 6	0 7
0 3	0 2			0 4	0 3	
		0 1 SERVER			0 2 SERVER	

SEC. 4.   A ball other than a service may be recovered from the net, provided the player avoids touching the net.

SEC. 5.   The ball may be touched only three times by one team before being returned over the net.

NOTE—(a)   This does not prevent a man from playing the ball twice, provided the rule against dribbling is not violated; that is, a man may be the first and third to play the ball. This means, of course, that he is also eligible on his second play to return the ball over the net.

(b)   Two players of the same team touching the ball simultaneously shall count as two players having played the ball.

SEC. 6.   POINTS AND "SIDE OUT." If a player of the serving team commits any of the following acts, it shall be "side out"; if a player of the receiving team commits any of the following acts, one point shall be scored for the serving team:

(a)   Cause the ball to go out of bounds or under the net.

(b)   Catch or hold the ball.

(c)   Dribble.

(d)   Allow the ball to touch his person or clothing below the hips.

(e)   Play the ball while he is raised off the ground by any player or object.

(f)   Touch the net with any part of the body at any time except when the ball is "dead." However, if two opponents touch the net simultaneously, neither "point" nor "side out" shall be called; the ball is dead and shall be served over.

(g)   Touch the ball when it already has been played three times before being returned over the net.

(h)   Reach over the net under any circumstances whatsoever.

(i)   Reach under the net and touch the ball or a player of the opposing team when the ball is in play on that side, or interfere with the play of the opposing team by entering their court.

(j)   Touch the floor on the opposite side of the center line.

(k)   Enter opponents' court in an attempt to recover the ball (reaching under the net with one or both hands, but keeping the feet in own court is allowed).

(l)   Persistently delay the game.

(m)   Play substitute who has not reported to Referee.

SEC. 7.   When a player steps on or over the serving line while serving, "side out" shall be declared.

SEC. 8.   When two opposing players commit infractions of the rules simultaneously, it shall be called a "double foul," and the ball shall be served over.

RULE VII.   SCORING.

SECTION 1.   Failure of the receiving team to return the ball legally over the net into the opponents' court shall score one point for the team serving.

RULE VIII. CONDUCT OF PLAYERS.

SECTION 1. The Referee shall have the power to disqualify for the remainder of the game any player making derogatory remarks to or about the officials or opponents.

SEC. 2. A substitute shall take the place of the disqualified player.

RULE IX. FORFEITED GAME.

SECTION 1. Any team refusing to play after receiving instructions to do so from the Referee shall forfeit the game.

SEC. 2. The score of a forfeited game shall be 1-0.

RULE X. DECISIONS.

SECTION 1. Decisions of the officials as to matters of fact are final.

SEC. 2. Decisions pertaining to the interpretation of the rules may be called into question at once, but only by the captains of the contesting teams.

SEC. 3. When a question pertaining to interpretation of the rules has not been settled conclusively, but is to be carried to higher authority for decision, the game shall proceed as before, the Referee making proper note of the protest.

RULE XI. TIME OUT.

"Time out" may be called by the Referee only when the ball is dead. He shall order "time out" at the request of a captain not more than three times for each team during the game.

RULE XII. COACHING.

There shall be no coaching from the side lines during the progress of the game by anyone officially connected with either team, nor shall any such person go on the court during the progress of the game except with permission of the Referee. Penalty—One point or "side out."

SOCCER FOOTBALL.　(Form III.)

Officials of the Game—A referee and two linesmen. The referee to decide all points of the game and warn players against rough playing. He may put a player out for rough playing.

The linesmen mark the place where the ball went out of bounds and decide, when necessary, who put it out.

The team shall consist of eleven (11) players, as follows: Goal-keeper. Fullbacks—Right fullback, left fullback. Halfbacks—Right halfback, center halfback, left halfback. Forwards—Outside right, inside right, center forward, inside left, outside left.

These players, in general, work as follows: The goal-keeper tries to prevent the ball from going between the goal posts. He may use any part of his body to do so while within his own penalty area (hands included).

The fullbacks act as extra guards to the goal, and at least one of them keeps in the vicinity of the goal during the progress of the game, while the other one advances and retreats whenever it is necessary. They should as a rule make long passes. They form the second line of defense.

The halfbacks keep some distance behind the forwards who are to advance the ball and score goals whenever possible. They form the first line of defense.

The forwards should play up against the halfbacks of their opponents.

THE GAME.

The duration of the game shall be 40 minutes, divided into two 20-minute halves, with an intermission of 5 minutes.

Teams must change ends at the end of the first half.

The winner of the toss shall have the option of the kick-off or the choice of goals.

The game shall begin by a place kick from the center of the field (see plan of field) in the direction of the opponents' goal line. The opponents shall not approach within the circle until the ball has been kicked off; nor shall a player pass beyond the center of the field until the ball has been kicked off,

GOAL LINE 75 YDS.

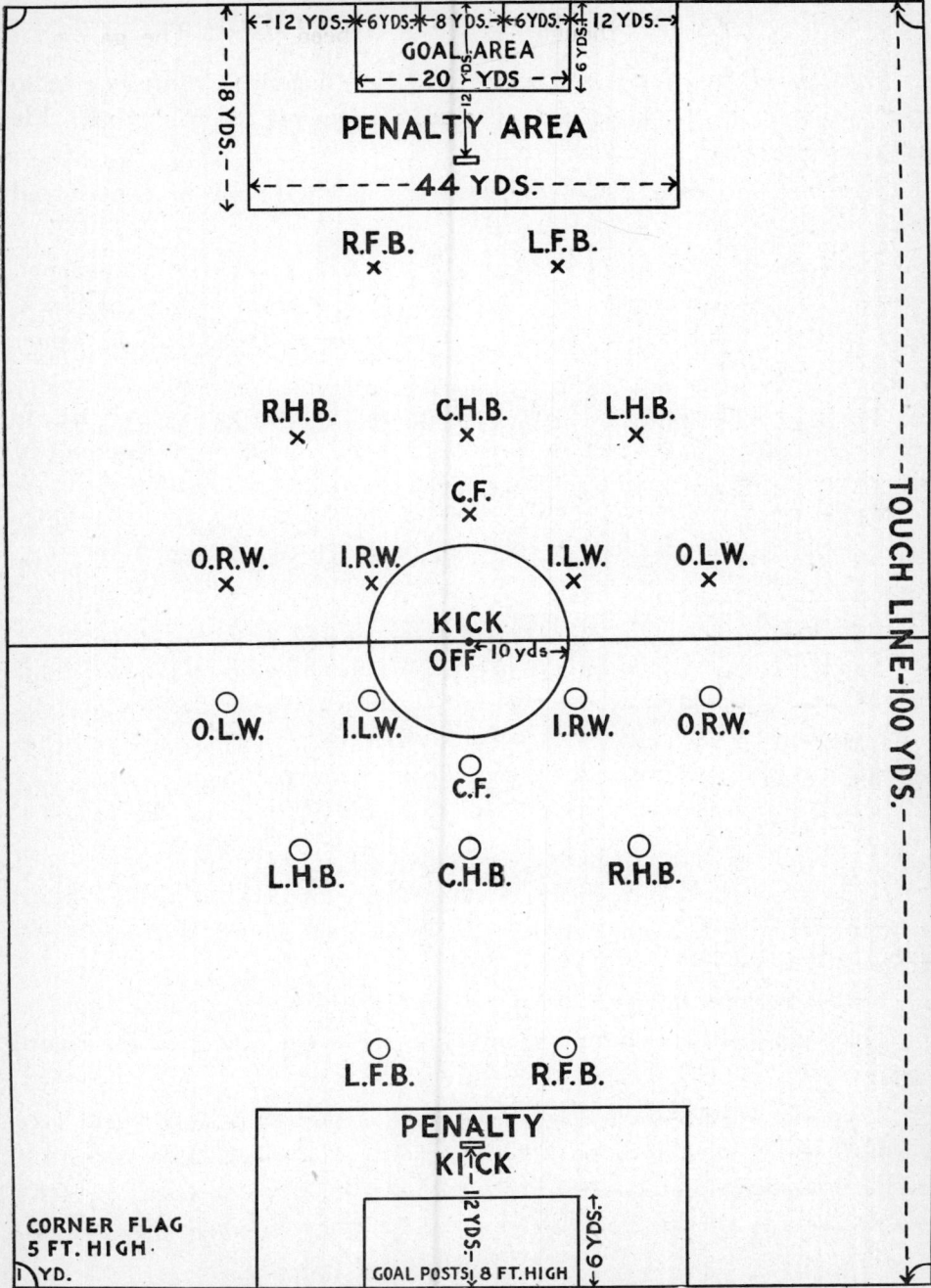

12 YDS. — 6YDS. — 8 YDS. — 6YDS. — 12 YDS.

GOAL AREA
— 20 YDS —

6 YDS.

18 YDS.

PENALTY AREA

44 YDS.

R.F.B. ×   L.F.B. ×

R.H.B. ×   C.H.B. ×   L.H.B. ×

C.F. ×

O.R.W. ×   I.R.W. ×   I.L.W. ×   O.L.W. ×

KICK
OFF ← 10 yds →

TOUCH LINE-100 YDS.

O.L.W. ○   I.L.W. ○   I.R.W. ○   O.R.W. ○

C.F. ○

L.H.B. ○   C.H.B. ○   R.H.B. ○

L.F.B. ○   R.F.B. ○

PENALTY
KICK

12 YDS.   6 YDS.

CORNER FLAG
5 FT. HIGH.

1 YD.   GOAL POSTS 8 FT. HIGH

even though the whistle has been blown.   The game officially starts when
the ball has been kicked off—not at the blowing of the whistle.

After the change of ends at half time, the ball shall be kicked off by the
side opposite to the one that originally kicked it off.   The ball shall be kicked
about the field until a goal is scored, or until the referee blows his whistle.

The Throw-In—When the whole of the ball has crossed the goal line,
other than between the goal posts, or passed beyond the side or touch lines,
either on the ground or in the air, it is out of play.   If it has crossed the side
line it is thrown in by a player on the side opposite to the one that put it out.
The player (usually a halfback) must throw the ball in by standing with both
feet outside the touch line and by raising the ball with both hands completely
over his head.   The thrower cannot play the ball until it has been played by
another player.

Goal Kick—When the ball is passed beyond the goal line by a player
of the opposite side, it shall be returned to play by the goal-keeper or a
fullback kicking it into the field from a point 6 yards in front of the goal post
nearest which it was when it passed over the line.

Corner Kick—If the ball is played, accidentally or otherwise, behind
the goal line by a player whose goal line it is, then a corner kick is awarded
to the opponents.   A corner kick is taken from the corner flag nearest which
the ball was put out.   A goal cannot directly be scored from a corner kick.
In all kick-offs no opposing player shall be within 10 yards of the ball.

Fouls—Fouls are committed as follows:
1.   When the ball is touched intentionally by any part of the hands
or arms of a player.   The referee is the sole judge of this.   (Goal-keeper
excepted as above.)
2.   When the referee catches a player dangerously charging, pushing,
holding, tripping an opponent, playing unfairly, kicking at, or jumping at an
opponent.

Penalty for a Foul—A free kick in the direction of the goal of the player
who made the foul shall be awarded at the place where the foul took place.
Opponents must keep 10 yards away from the ball in a free kick.   See
Law 9, Referees' Chart.

Penalty Kick—When a foul is committed intentionally within the penalty area (or within 18 yards of the goal) a penalty kick is awarded the unoffending side. The ball is to be kicked from a point 12 yards in front of the goal. The penalty area must be cleared of all players except the kicker and the goal-keeper. The ball is in play as soon as kicked.

Goals—The side scoring the greatest number of goals is the winner. (Each goal counts one point.) A goal is scored when the ball has passed between the goal posts and under the bar; not being thrown in, knocked on, or carried by any player of the attacking side. (If there is no bar the referee has the power to decide the scoring of a goal, if within his judgment the entire ball has passed through within bounds.) A goal may be scored from a penalty kick or as the result of a free kick awarded for a foul mentioned under No. 2 above. After a goal is scored the losing side shall kick off the ball from the center of the field as in the start of the game.

Restarting the Game—In case of a temporary suspension of the game from any cause whatever by the referee, the ball shall again be put in play at the place it was at the time the play was suspended. The ball is dropped by the referee where it was when the play ceased. The ball is in play as soon as it touches the ground, and the ball must not be played until it does touch the ground.

Change of Players—A player may be changed during the game by notifying the referee at the time of change. (An adaptation.) A player removed by the referee for any offense cannot be replaced.

SUGGESTIONS FOR THE GAME.

1. The game is best played by passing the ball from player to player along the wings, and then centered for a shot at the goal.

2. Each player should play an opponent and stick to him unless he gets too far out of position.

3. Pass the ball by short passes (except fullbacks).

4. It is better to let the ball hit the body to stop it before kicking it than to attempt to kick it on the bounce or while it is in the air. A ball may at times be "headed" in preference to kicking in order to clear it.

5. The center halfback should ever be on the alert and be one of the best players. This is the pivotal position on the team.

6. The referee should decide when a player is "off side" and award a foul accordingly. (For "off side" see Referees' Chart.)

Some Don'ts for the Game.

1. Don't use your hands (except the goal-keeper).
2. Don't let the ball intentionally hit the hands or arms.
3. Don't charge violently, push, hold, trip, or kick an opponent.
4. Don't get into a bunch; much running will thus be avoided.
5. Don't get too far out of position (get back quickly).
6. Don't charge the goal-keeper unless he is holding the ball or obstructing an opponent.
7. Goal-keeper, don't carry the ball; throw or kick it away from the goal quickly . Do not carry the ball more than two steps.
8. Don't stop playing until the whistle blows.
9. Objections to referee's decisions or profane language should not be tolerated at any time.

Lastly, do not be dressed too warmly. Take extra clothing to put on after the game or leave the field immediately. If possible, have a "rub-down" and change of clothing after playing.

Literature on the Subject.

"The Football Association Game and Laws." (Price, 3 pence.) 104 High Holborn, London, W. C., England.

"Referees' Chart." (Price, by post, 2 pence.) F. J. Wall, 104 High Holborn, London, W. C., England. (Recommended for Managers.)

"How to Play Soccer." (Price, 10 cents.) Spalding's Athletic Library.

"Association Football Rules and Diagrams." (Price, 5 cents.) Wood & Guest, 1227 Arch Street, Philadelphia, Pa.

FROLIC OF THE BROWNIES. (Form I.)

Music: "Frolic of the Brownies," by Harry S. Romaine. Published by Henry P. Vogel, Albany, N. Y.

Moderate schottische tempo. The measure equals 4 counts. Omit the introduction.

Formation: A column of front ranks of threes (fours or more), standing in open order. Hands at waist.

PART I. (8 Measures.)

Raise the left foot sideward in preparation for the first step. (After the dance is learned this may be omitted and a quick side-cut executed with the left foot.)

1. Side-cut left (raising the right leg sideward) (a) and hop on the left foot (b); the same right (c and d). 1 measure.

2. Rear cross-step left (a), side-step right (b); front cross-step left (c), hop on the left and raise the right leg sideward (d). 1 measure.

3. Repeat 1, beginning right. 1 measure.

4. Four side-cuts, beginning right (right, left, right and left). The displaced leg is always raised sideward. 1 measure.

5. As 1, beginning right. 1 measure.

6. As 2, beginning right (moving back to the starting point). 1 measure.

7. As 1. 1 measure.

8. Jump to the side-stride stand (a); jump to cross-stride stand, left in front (b); jump to position (c); pause (d). This "finish" is frequently used and will be referred to as the finish of step a. 1 measure.

PART II. (8 Measures.)

The same as Part 1, except that all movements are executed forward and backward instead of sideward. It begins with a front-cut and hop, etc.; then the movements from place consist of three forward-running steps and hops with leg swings. To return to the starting place, these steps are later executed backward. The finish is the same as in step a, but beginning from the front- and rear-cut and hop instead of the side-cut and hop, as in step a. 8 measures.

PART III. (8 Measures.)

Part I is repeated.

PART IV. (8 Measures.)

This part should be played *pp.*, although marked *f*, as the steps are arranged accordingly.

1. Step left forward on the toes, knee slightly bent (a), raise the right foot rear of left ankle and rise high on the toes of the left foot. A rocking movement should be apparent (b). The same movements backward, the left foot being raised in front of the right ankle (c and d). 1 measure.

2. Three steps forward on toes, with leg swing forward, right, rising high on the toes of the left foot (not hopping). 1 measure.

During these two measures the left index finger is raised to the chin, indicating silence, while the right arm is raised obliquely side-downward, with the index finger pointing. On the last count of these two measures perform one-quarter turn right. The step may at first be practiced left and right forward without the one-quarter turn.

3. As 1, beginning right. 1 measure.

4. As 2, beginning right (one-quarter turn right on 4). 1 measure.

During the execution right, the positions of the hand and arm are, of course, changed.

5. Repeat 1 to 4, always adding the one-quarter turn right on the last count of each step, so that the whole step will be performed on a right square. Finish with a small jump instead of leg swing on the last count of the last step. 4 measures.

PART V. (8 Measures.)

1. Jump to side-stride stand with stamping (knees slightly bent) and straighten arms sideward, palms up (a); jump to stand, crossing left foot in front of right (knees slightly bent) and crossing arms (b); repeat (c) and (d).

2. Step on left foot, raising right leg backward and hop three times with whole turn left, raising left arm to half circle overhead and right arm sideward.

3. Same as 1, with crossing right foot in front of left on (b) and (d).
4. Same as 2, only right.
5. Repeat 1 to 4.

PART VI. (8 Measures.)

As IV, but performed on a left square.

PART VII. (8 Measures.)

As I, with alternate arm swings left and right sideward, accompanying the leg movements—*e. g.*, when the left leg is raised sideward the left arm is raised sideward, etc. During the finish both arms move with the legs.

PART VIII. (8 Measures.)

As II. Hands at waist during the step.

PART IX. (8 Measures.)

As VII.

FROLIC OF THE BROWNIES. (Form II.)

I. (16 Measures.)

1. Side cut hop left and right (cut right foot away with left—1, hop on left foot—2, cut left foot away with right—3, hop on right foot—4), both arms swing right sideward on cut-hop left and left sideward on cut-hop right. 1 measure.
2. Rear cross-step left—1, step right sideward—2, front cross-step—3, hop on left foot and swing right leg sideward—4. Arms swinging 4 times as before. 1 measure.
3. Repeat 1, beginning right. 1 measure.
4. Four side cuts, beginning right (right, left, right, left), arm swings repeated. 1 measure.
5. Repeat 1, beginning right. 1 measure.
6. Repeat 2, beginning right. 1 measure.
7. Repeat 1. 1 measure.
8. Finish with: Jump to a cross-stride stand, left foot in front, arms cross

in front of body—1, jump to side-stride stand—2, jump to position—3 (moving arms sideward on 2 and 3), pause—4. I measure.

This will be referred to as "Finish."

9. Repeat all, beginning with right foot. 8 measures.

II. (16 Measures.)

1. Step left forward on the toes, knees slightly bent—1, raise the right foot in rear of left ankle and rise high on the toes of the left foot—2 (a rocking movement should be apparent). The same movement backward on the right foot, the left foot raised in front of right ankle—3 and 4. During this measure the left index finger is raised to the chin (indicating silence), while the right arm is raised obliquely side-downward with the index finger pointed. I measure.

2. Three steps forward on toes with leg swing right forward, rising high on the toes of the left foot (not hopping), making a quarter turn left. During these steps forward the arm positions change, the right index finger being raised to the chin. I measure.

3. Repeat 1, beginning right. 1 measure.

4. Repeat 2, beginning right, leg swing left, making a quarter turn left. I measure.

5. Repeat 1 to 4, always making a quarter turn left each time with the leg swing, the whole being executed on the lines of a square. 4 measures.

6. Repeat all on lines of a square to the right, turning right instead of left with leg swing, finishing with jumping to a close stand and lowering arms on last movement. 8 measures.

III. (16 Measures.)

1. Cut-hop left backward and right forward (swing the left foot from in front, displacing the right—1, hop on left foot—2; then displace the left foot with the right—3, and hop on right foot—4). The left arm is forward and right arm obliquely backward on these cut-hops. I measure.

2. Three-step swing hop (run forward 3 steps, beginning left—1 to 3, hop on left foot and swing right leg forward—4). The arms change positions during these forward movements. I measure.

3. Cut-hop right backward and left forward (right foot swings from the front and displaces the left, and the left swings from the rear and displaces the

right, as explained before). The arms remain in the previous position during these two cut-hops. 1 measure.

4. A cut right backward and left forward and repeat (right foot displaces the left foot backward, and the left immediately displaces the right foot forward and repeat). Arm positions are same as before. 1 measure.

5. A cut-hop right backward and left forward with the same arm positions as before. 1 measure.

6. Three-step swing hop backward, beginning with the right foot, changing arm positions as before. 1 measure.

7. Cut-hop left backward and right forward, same arm positions as before and close with "Finish," as in (1). 2 measures.

8. Repeat all, beginning with right foot. 8 measures.

IV. (8 Measures.)

1. Repeat Part II to the left (turning left at corners), adding the jump "Finish"; some pupils whistling and some humming the melody. 8 measures.

V. (8 Measures.)

1. Jump to a side-stride stand with stamping—1 (knees slightly bent), and straighten arms sideward, palms up; the arms move quickly from a crossed position in front of body. Jump to a cross stand, left foot in front of right, crossing arms forward in front of chest at about the wrists—2. Repeat 3 and 4. 1 measure.

2. Step left sideward, raising right leg backward, and hop three times with a whole turn left. Left arm to a half circle overhead and right arm sideward. 1 measure.

3. Repeat 1, crossing right foot in front of left. 1 measure.

4. Repeat 2, making the turn to the right. 1 measure.

5. Repeat 1 to 4. 4 measures.

VI. (8 Measures.)

1. Repeat Part II to the right, some pupils whistling and some humming the melody. 8 measures.

VII. (8 Measures.)

1. Repeat Part I, beginning left.

GAMES AND DANCES
Venus–Reigen.
(WALZER.)

Josef Gung'l.

GAMES AND DANCES
Venus–Reigen.

GAMES AND DANCES
Venus–Reigen.

VENUS REIGEN WALTZ. (Form I.)

Music: "Venus Reigen" by Josef Gung'l.

The music should be played very fast.

Formation: Front column of any number, standing in open order. Hands at the waist.

PART I. (32 Measures.)

1. Step left sideward, cross right in rear, bending the knees; the same in the opposite direction. 4 measures.

2. Two glides left sideward (2 measures), step left sideward, and cross right in rear, bending the knees. 4 measures.

3. Repeat to the right. 8 measures.

4. Repeat left and right. 16 measures.

PART II. (32 Measures.)

1. Step left sideward (1 measure), hop and swing the right leg forward (1 measure); the same right. 4 measures.

2. Three steps forward, one step to each measure, beginning left, and place the right foot forward. 4 measures.

3. Repeat the first four measures. 4 measures.

4. Three steps backward, beginning with the right foot, and place the left foot forward. 4 measures.

5. Repeat forward and backward. 16 measures.

PART III. (32 Measures.)

1. Glide left forward (1 measure), and hop, raising the right leg backward (1 measure); step right backward and hop, swinging the left leg forward (2 measures). 4 measures.

2. Two glides left sideward (2 measures), step left sideward, and cross right in rear, bending the knees (2 measures). 4 measures.

3. Repeat to the right. 8 measures.

4. Repeat left and right. 16 measures.

PART IV.　(32 Measures.)

1.　Step left sideward, cross right in rear, bending the knees (2 measures); repeat to the right and left (4 measures); cross-step turn to the right (2 measures).　8 measures.

2.　Repeat to right.　8 measures.

3.　Repeat left and right.　16 measures.

PART V.　(32 Measures.)

Repeat Part I, with neighbors' hands grasped shoulder-high, arms slightly bent, and with ranks moving in opposite direction—*i. e.*, the first rank begins left, the second right, etc.

NOTE—The first four parts may also be executed with hands grasped as in the fifth part.

VENUS REIGEN.　(Form II.)

The dance may be executed in the following manner, which adds interest and variety:

Formation: Single circle, facing center, hands grasped about waist high, arms obliquely side-downward.

Step 1:　Same as description, moving left and right in the circle.

Step 2:　The first three steps are taken forward toward the center of the circle with raising arms upward. The next three steps are taken backward away from center, with lowering arms sideward. Otherwise same as written.

Step 3:　On the glide hop forward, arms are raised upward, and on the swing hop backward arms are lowered sideward. Remainder of the dance is repeated as written.

Step 4:　On the cross step turn the grasped hands are released and re-grasped immediately after the turn. Otherwise the step is danced as written.

The Dorothy.

(THREE STEP.)

Mazurka or Redowa.

by J. Bodewalt Lampe.

1

GAMES AND DANCES
The Dorothy.

The Dorothy.

The Dorothy.

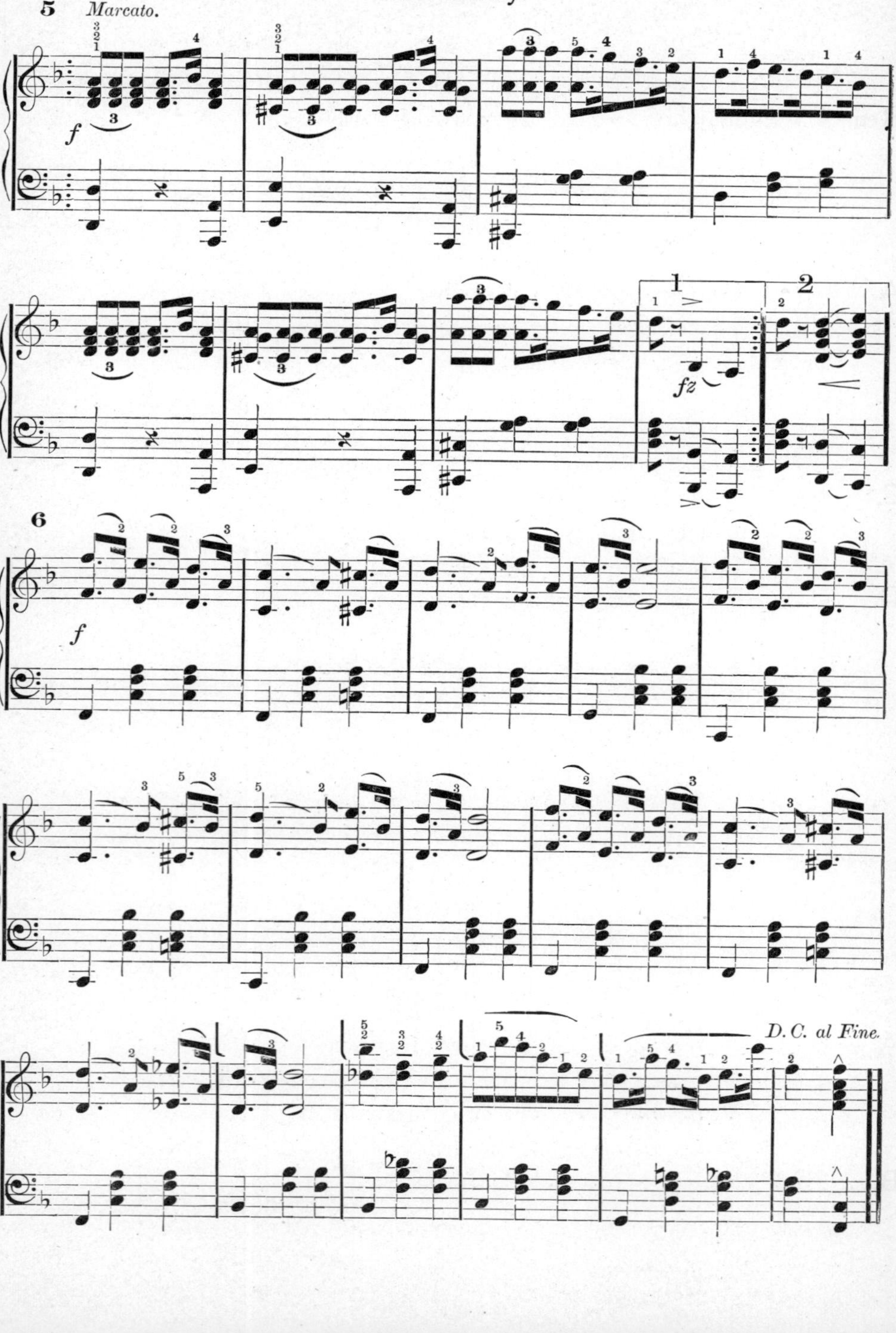

ALUMNI THREE-STEP.

Music: "The Dorothy," by J. B. Lampe. Published by Jerome H. Remick Company, New York and Detroit.

PART I. (16 Measures.)

Hands at Waist.

			Measures
A.	1	Glide-cut-leap left sideward......................	1
	2	Place right foot crossed in rear and bend knees (curtsy)	2
	3- 4	Repeat 1 and 2 right sideward....................	3- 4
B.	5	Two mazurka-hops left sideward..................	5- 6
	6	Glide-cut-leap left sideward......................	7
	7	Place right foot crossed in rear and curtsy..........	8
C.	8	Glide-cut-leap right sideward....................	9
	9	Place left foot crossed in rear and curtsy...........	10
	10-11	Repeat 8 and 9 left sideward....................	11-12
D.	12	Two mazurka-hops right sideward................	13-14
	13	Glide-cut-leap right sideward....................	15
	14	Place left foot crossed in rear and curtsy...........	16

Note—The change-step may be substituted for the glide-cut-leap, to make this part of the dance easier. To increase the difficulty of the dance, appropriate arm-waving may be added to the mazurkas or to any other part.

PART II. (16 Measures.)

Arms Are Raised Sideward.

			Measures
A.	1	Three glides obliquely left forward...............	1
	2	Waltz-balance (or mazurka-balance) left sideward....	2
	3	Waltz-balance right sideward....................	3
	4	Waltz-balance left sideward.....................	4
B.	5- 8	Repeat 1-4 to the opposite side..................	5- 8

C.   9-12   With a slight turn left repeat 1-4 obliquely left backward 9-12

D. 13-16 With a slight turn right repeat 1-4 obliquely right backward 13-16

Note—During the balance-steps the arm on the side opposite to the step is waved forward—*e. g.*, balance-step obliquely left forward and wave right arm forward. The waving can also be obliquely upward.

PART III. (16 Measures, like Part I.)

Hands at Waist.

Measures

A.   1   Glide-cut-leap left sideward..................... 1

     2   Place right foot crossed in rear and bend knees (curtsy) 2

   3- 4   Repeat 1 and 2 right sideward.................... 3- 4

B.   5   Two mazurka-hops left sideward................. 5- 6

     6   Glide-cut-leap left sideward..................... 7

     7   Place right foot crossed in rear and curtsy........... 8

C.   8   Glide-cut-leap right sideward.................... 9

     9   Place left foot crossed in rear and curtsy 10

  10-11   Repeat 8 and 9 left sideward.................... 11-12

D.   12   Two mazurka-hops right sideward................. 13-14

    13   Glide-cut-leap right sideward.................... 15

    14   Place left foot crossed in rear and curtsy............ 16

PART IV TRIO. (16 Measures.)

Arms Are Raised Sideward.

Measures

A.   1   Three steps forward........................... 1

    2   Point right forward, bend trunk forward and lower right hand over right foot........................ 2

<table>
<tr><td></td><td></td><td></td><td align="right">Measures</td></tr>
<tr><td></td><td>3</td><td>Straighten trunk and again raise right arm sideward....</td><td align="center">3</td></tr>
<tr><td></td><td>4</td><td>Bend trunk right sideward and wave left arm obliquely upward ....</td><td align="center">4</td></tr>
<tr><td>B.</td><td>5- 8</td><td>Repeat 1-4 to the opposite side...................</td><td align="center">5- 8</td></tr>
<tr><td>C.</td><td>9</td><td>Three steps backward.........................</td><td align="center">9</td></tr>
<tr><td></td><td>10</td><td>Point right forward, bend trunk forward and lower right hand over right foot......................</td><td align="center">10</td></tr>
<tr><td></td><td>11</td><td>Straighten trunk and again raise right arm sideward....</td><td align="center">11</td></tr>
<tr><td></td><td>12</td><td>Bend trunk right sideward and wave left arm obliquely upward ....</td><td align="center">12</td></tr>
<tr><td>D.</td><td>13-16</td><td>Repeat 9-12 to the opposite side.................</td><td align="center">13-16</td></tr>
</table>

PART V. (16 Measures.)

Hands at Waist.

<table>
<tr><td></td><td></td><td></td><td align="right">Measures</td></tr>
<tr><td>A.</td><td>1- 2</td><td>Two mazurka-hops obliquely left forward...........</td><td align="center">1- 2</td></tr>
<tr><td></td><td>3</td><td>Double balance-hop-turn left (arabesque) ....</td><td align="center">3</td></tr>
<tr><td></td><td>4</td><td>Two stamp-steps (right, left)...................</td><td align="center">4</td></tr>
<tr><td>B.</td><td>5- 8</td><td>Repeat 1-4 to the right.........................</td><td align="center">5- 8</td></tr>
<tr><td>C.</td><td>9-10</td><td>With a slight turn left two mazurka-hops obliquely left backward ....</td><td align="center">9-10</td></tr>
<tr><td></td><td>11</td><td>Double balance-hop-turn left.....................</td><td align="center">11</td></tr>
<tr><td></td><td>12</td><td>Two stamp-steps (right, left)...................</td><td align="center">12</td></tr>
<tr><td>D.</td><td>13-16</td><td>Repeat 9-12 to the right.......................</td><td align="center">13-16</td></tr>
</table>

Note—During the mazurkas the opposite arm may be raised upward. During the balance-hop-turns the arms may be raised diagonally.

PART VI.   (Like Part IV Trio, 16 Measures.)

Arms Are Raised Sideward.

<table>
<tr><td></td><td></td><td></td><td align="right">Measures</td></tr>
<tr><td>A.</td><td>1</td><td>Three steps forward...........................</td><td align="center">1</td></tr>
</table>

Measures

	2	Point right forward, bend trunk forward and lower right hand over right foot.......................	2
	3	Straighten trunk and again raise right arm sideward....	3
	4	Bend trunk right sideward and wave left arm obliquely upward	4
B.	5- 8	Repeat 1-4 to the opposite side...................	5- 8
C.	9	Three steps backward..........................	9
	10	Point right forward, bend trunk forward and lower right hand over right foot.......................	10
	11	Straighten trunk and again raise right arm sideward....	11
	12	Bend trunk right sideward and wave left arm obliquely upward	12
D.	13-16	Repeat 9-12 to the opposite side.................	13-16

Parts VII, VIII and IX are like parts I, II and III.   Repeat these as written.

HIGHLAND SCHOTTISCHE (Scotch).

Victor Record 17,331 (Introduction, Chord—Dance is played six times).

Steps: Schottische, or three step swing hop.

Schottische step (right sideward): Step right sideward, 1; cut the right foot sideward, 2; step right sideward, 3; hop on the right foot, swinging the left leg forward (knee slightly bent), 4.

Three step swing hop left: Three running steps forward (left, right, left), 1, 2, 3; hop on left foot and swing the right leg forward, 4.

Formation: Single circle of couples, facing center, boy on the left of the girl.

Music: Two parts of four measures each.   Schottische rhythm (four counts to each measure).

PART I.

Measures:

1.   Partners face.   With left arm raised to a half circle overhead, right hand on hip.   Hop left and place right foot sideward, 1; hop left and raise

right foot in rear of left knee, 2; hop left and place right foot sideward, 3; hop left and raise right foot in front of left knee, 4 (counts 1 to 4).

1. Schottische step right sideward (counts 5 to 8).

2. Repeat above 2 measures opposite (counts 9 to 16).

PART II.

2. Partners link right arms, and beginning right execute two schottische steps forward (same as sideward, but stepping forward) (counts 1 to 8).

2. Repeat above 2 measures, linking left arms (counts 1 to 8).

NOTE—The dance may be made progressive by partners moving forward and in opposite directions on the last schottische step.

The three step swing hop may be substituted in Part II.

OXDANSEN (Swedish).

Victor Record 17,003 (Chord—Dance played six times).

Formation: Couples; partners in two different lines three feet apart. Those in the line on the left are No. 1, others No. 2.

Music: Three parts of 8 measures each, A, B and C, all played six times. Polka rhythm (2 counts to a measure).

PART I (Salutation).

Measures:

Partners face. Hands on hips.

A. 2. No. 1 makes a deep bow (lower trunk forward), 1, 2; and straightens, 3, 4; while No. 2 bends knees, 1, 2, and straightens, 3, 4 (counts 1 to 4).

2. No. 1 bends knees while No. 2 bows (counts 5 to 8).

4. Repeat above 4 measures (counts 9 to 16).

B. 8. Same as A, with quicker rhythm, 2 counts to a movement (counts 1 to 16).

C. 2. No. 1 with hands clenched in front of chest, elbows high, two gallops left sideward, flinging the arms sideward, 1, 2; step left sideward, 3;

close right foot to the left with a stamp, bringing the fists in front of the chest, 4 (counts 1 to 4).

2.   Repeat right (counts 5 to 8).

4.   Repeat above 4 measures (counts 9 to 16).

No. 2 does the same, beginning to the right, moving in the same direction as partner.

PART II (Treading on Toes).

A.   2.   With hands on hips, hop on right foot and place left foot forward and hold position (counts 1 to 4).

2.   With a hop change position of feet and hold (counts 5 to 8).

4.   Repeat the above 4 measures (counts 9 to 16).

B.   8.   Same as A, with quicker rhythm, 2 counts to a movement (counts 1 to 16).

C.   8.   Same as C of Part I (counts 1 to 16).

PART III (Jostling of Elbows).

A.   2.   With hands on hips, all make a quarter turn left, with a jump (so that right elbows touch) and hold, each looking directly at the other (counts 1 to 4).

2.   Both make a half turn right (jumping), with left elbows touching, and hold (counts 5 to 8).

4.   Repeat the above 4 measures (counts 9 to 16).

B.   8.   Same as A, with quicker rhythm, 2 counts to a movement.   Finish facing partner (counts 1 to 16).

C.   8.   Same as C of Part I (counts 1 to 16).

PART IV (Hair Pulling).

A.   2.   Each places right hand on partner's head.   No. 1 pulls No. 2's head forward and holds (counts 1 to 4).

2.   No. 2 raises head and pulls No. 1's head forward (counts 5 to 8).

4.   Repeat above 4 measures (counts 9 to 16).

B.   8.   Same as A, with quicker rhythm, 2 counts to a movement (counts 1 to 16).

C.   8.   Same as C of Part I (counts 1 to 16).

PART V (Punching).

A. 2. Hands on hips. Thrust right diagonally forward, turning and bending trunk to left (fist under partner's right arm), and hold (counts 1 to 4).

2. Same, thrusting left, replacing right hand on hip (counts 5 to 8).

4. Repeat the above 4 measures (counts 9 to 16).

B. Same as A, with quicker rhythm, 2 counts to a measure (without replacing hands on hips) (counts 1 to 16).

C. 8. Same as C of Part I (counts 1 to 16).

PART VI (Boxing).

A. 2. Hands on hips. No. 1 makes a vigorous movement with right arm, as if boxing No. 2's left ear, and holds position. At the same time No. 2 bends trunk right and claps hands at the right side, flinching as if struck (counts 1 to 4).

No. 2 boxes ears while No. 1 claps (counts 5 to 8).

4. Repeat the above four measures (counts 9 to 16).

B. 8. Same as A with quicker rhythm, 2 counts to a movement (counts 1 to 16).

C. 8. Same as C of Part I (counts 1 to 16).

At the end they hold the position, with clenched hands, looking sternly at each other, then shake hands.

This dance had its origin in the beginning of the eighteenth century at a college in Karlstad, Sweden, when freshmen, nicknamed "oxen," were made to perform it before the sophomores. The movements represent a mock fight.

RUFTY TUFTY (English).

Victor Record 18,009 (No introduction—Dance is played once).

Steps: Running, balance step.

Balance step: Step right sideward, 1; place the left foot front of right, and rise on toes, "and"; lower heels, 2; repeat left, 3 and 4.

Formation: Sets of four, consisting of two couples facing each other, boy on the left of girl.

Music: Three parts, A, B and C. A and B, 4 measures each, repeated. C, 6 measures, repeated. All played three times. Polka rhythm (2 counts to a measure).

PART I.

Measures:

A. 2. Beginning right, all take three short running steps forward and close (counts 1 to 4).

2. Same backward (counts 5 to 8).

4. Repeat above 4 measures (counts 1 to 8).

B. 4. Partners face, balance step (with leap on first count) right and left sideward and a whole turn right in four running steps (counts 1 to 8).

4. Repeat above 4 measures (counts 1 to 8).

C. 2. Couples face away from each other, partners join left hands, and beginning right, three short running steps forward and close (counts 1 to 4).

2. Face about, turning inward, join right hands and repeat measures 1 and 2 to places (counts 5 to 8).

2. Whole turn right in four running steps (counts 9 to 12).

2. Boys face left, girls right, join right hands with opposite. Beginning right three short running steps forward and close (counts 1 to 4).

2. Face about, turning inward, join left hands and repeat measures 1 and 2 to places (counts 5 to 8).

2. Whole turn right in four running steps (counts 9 to 12).

PART II.

A. 2. Partners face. Beginning right, take four running steps forward, passing partners left shoulder to left shoulder. Turn inward toward partner on third and fourth counts (counts 1 to 4).

2. Repeat, passing right shoulder to right shoulder, returning to places (counts 5 to 8).

4. Repeat above 4 measures (counts 1 to 8).

B and C. Same as B and C of Part I.

PART III.

A. 4. Beginning right, with running steps, partners link right arms, make a whole turn, and with running steps backward, return to places (counts 1 to 8).

4. Repeat, linking left arms (counts 9 to 16).

B and C. Same as B and C of Part I.

RITKA (Hungarian).

Victor Record 17,003 (Csardas) (Introduction, Chord—Dance is played three times. The remainder of the record is not used).

Steps: Schottische, balance step, lame step.

Schottische step left forward: Step left forward, 1; cut the left foot forward, 2; step left forward, 3; hop on the left foot, swinging the right leg forward (knee slightly bent), 4.

Step obliquely forward with outer foot, 1; bring the instep of the inner foot to the heel of the outer foot and rise on toes, "and"; lower heels, 2 "and"; step obliquely backward inward with inner foot, 3; bring the outer foot to the instep of the inner foot and rise on toes, "and"; lower heels, 4 "and."

Formation: Double circle of couples, boy on left of girl, left sides toward center, inner hands grasped, outside arms raised obliquely side-upward.

Music: Two parts of 8 measures each. Schottische rhythm (4 counts to a measure).

PART I.

Measures:

2. Beginning with the outer foot, two schottische steps forward (counts 1 to 8).

1. Balance step obliquely forward outward, 1, 2; balance step obliquely backward inward, 3, 4 (counts 9 to 12).

1. Jump to a cross stride (outer foot in rear), 1; to a side stride, 2; feet together, 3; pause, 4 (counts 13 to 16).

4. Repeat the above 4 measures, beginning with the inner foot (counts 17 to 32).

PART II.

1.   Partners face.   Right arm raised to a half circle overhead, left hand at waist.   Each moves to the left.   Beginning left, step left sideward, 1; cut left foot, bending right knee slightly, 2; repeat, 3, 4 (counts 1 to 4).

1.   Jump to a cross stride, 1; side stride, 2; feet together, 3; and pause, 4 (with arms moving from a crossed position in front, 1; to a sideward position, 2; hold, 3, 4) (counts 5 to 8).

1.   Link right arms with new partner, outer arms obliquely side-upward. Whole turn in two lame steps.   (Hop right and step left forward, 1; step right forward, 2; repeat, 3, 4) (counts 9 to 12).

1.   Jump to a cross stride, 1; side stride, 2; feet together, 3; and pause, 4 (arms moving as above) (counts 13 to 16).

4.   Repeat the first 4 measures of Part I (counts 17 to 32).

APPENDIX I.

*A Selection of Drills and Dances Suitable for Exhibitions, Play Days,
Field Days, Pageants, Etc.*

GROUP I.   (Free Exercise Drills.)

Several of these drills can be used with wands or dumbbells. In these
cases the teacher can easily make the few changes that the use of such hand
apparatus demands.

COMPOSITION No. 1.

The following exercises were written to "Old Faithful," a march by
A. Holzman. The music is in 6-8 time; count two for each measure of music.

The order of the exercises should be as follows: After the ranks have
been opened the music plays the introduction, 4 bars equals 8 counts. The
exercises of Part I, 64 counts, should then be performed. After an intermission of 16 counts filled in by drum beats come the exercises of Part II,
64 counts. Then after a similar intermission comes Part III, 64 counts,
then Part IV, 96 counts, and, as the last, after a similar intermission, comes
Part V, 96 counts. The music is played exactly as written, with the exception
of the 16 drum beats between each two parts.

PART I.   (64 Counts.)

I.

1 to 4. Raise arms sideward.
5 to 8. Raise arms upward.
9 to 12. Lower arms sideward.
13 to 16. Arms down.

Repeat twice, 2 counts for each movement, 1 to 16.

II.

1 to 4. Raise arms forward.
5 to 8. Raise arms upward.
9 to 12. Lower arms forward.
13 to 16. Arms down.
Repeat twice, 2 counts for each movement, 1 to 16.
Sixteen counts for intermission.

PART II. (64 Counts.)

I.

1 to 4. Stride left sideward and place hands on shoulders.
5 to 8. Bend left knee and straighten arms sideward.
9 to 12. Reverse the foregoing movement.
13 to 16. Return to the starting position.
Repeat twice, 2 counts for each movement, 1 to 16.

II.

1 to 4. Stride left forward and place hands on shoulders.
5 to 8. Bend left knee and straighten arms upward.
9 to 12. Reverse.
13 to 16. Return.
Repeat twice, 2 counts for each movement, 1 to 16.
Sixteen counts for intermission; on the ninth count let pupils bend arms for thrust.

PART III. (64 Counts.)

I.

1 to 4. Lunge left sideward and thrust sideward.
5 to 8. Bend trunk left and bend left arm over back, right arm over head.
9 to 12. Reverse.
13 to 16. Return.
Repeat twice, 2 counts for each movement, 1 to 16.

II.

    1 to 4. Lunge left forward and thrust upward.

    5 to 8. Bend trunk forward and swing arms fore-downward.

    9 to 12. Reverse.

    13 to 16. Return.

Repeat twice, 2 counts for each movement, 1 to 16.

Sixteen counts for an intermission; on the ninth count let the pupils lower the arms.

PART IV. (96 Counts.)

I.

    1 to 4. Two steps left sideward.

    5 to 8. Mark time, four steps.

    9 to 10. Raise arms sideward.

    11 to 12. Raise arms upward.

    13 to 14. Lower arms sideward.

    15 to 16. Arms down.

Repeat, but march to the right, 1 to 16.

II.

    1 to 4. Four steps forward.

    5 to 8. Mark time, four steps.

    9 to 10. Raise arms forward.

    11 to 12. Raise arms upward.

    13 to 14. Lower arms forward.

    15 to 16. Arms down.

Repeat, but march 4 steps backward, 1 to 16.

III.

    1 to 4. Two steps left sideward.

    5 to 8. Mark time, four steps.

    9 to 10. Stride left sideward and hands on shoulders.

    11 to 12. Bend left knee and straighten arms sideward.

    13 to 14. Reverse to former position.

    15 to 16. Return to fundamental position.

Repeat marching to the right and then stride right sideward, etc., 1 to 16.

Sixteen counts intermission; let the pupils bend arms for thrust on the ninth count.

I.   PART V. (96 Counts.)

1 to 4.   Two steps left sideward.

5 to 8.   Mark time, four steps.

9 to 10.   Lunge left sideward and thrust sideward.

11 to 12.   Bend trunk left and swing left arm down and across the back, right arm up and bend it over the head.

13 to 14.   Reverse to preceding position.

15 to 16.   Return to starting position.

Repeat to the opposite side, 1 to 16.

II.

1 to 4.   Four steps forward.

5 to 8.   Mark time, four steps.

9 to 10.   Lunge left forward and thrust upward.

11 to 12.   Bend trunk forward and swing arms fore-downward.

13 to 14.   Reverse to preceding position.

15 to 16.   Return to starting position.

Repeat, but marching backward, and lunge right forward, 1 to 16.

III.

1 to 4.   Two steps left sideward.

5 to 8.   Mark time, four steps.

9 to 10.   Lunge obliquely left forward and thrust diagonally, the left arm obliquely fore-side-upward, the right arm in opposite direction.

11 to 12.   Turn trunk left (one-eighth of a turn), reverse the arm positions and draw the head well backward.

13 to 14.   Reverse to preceding position.

15 to 16.   Return to starting position.

Repeat in the opposite direction, lunging right, 1 to 16.

COMPOSITION No. 2.

Music: "In the Arena" march, by H. Engelman; published by Theo. Presser Company, Philadelphia, Pa. The march is written in 4-4 time. Two counts are taken for each measure. When taking the exercises count up to 16, and then repeat. The "Introduction" to the march has 4 measures. There are five parts in the march, of 32 measures each; the fourth part (in the form of an interlude) is skipped.

There are two groups of exercises. For each group the complete march (excepting the interlude) should be played. After the first group of exercises has been performed there should be an intermission of 16 drum-beats. Then the whole march should again be played for the second group.

The exercises in Parts III and IV of each group are tactics (marching exercises), Part IV being exactly like Part III, except that the following words should be sung while marching:

FIELD DAY SCHOOL SONG.

With heads erect and flashing eyes
    We march upon the field;
With hearts so true, with courage bold,
    We fear not, nor shall yield.
Our sports and games, our races, too,
    Are more to us than play;
They give us health, and strength and grace,
    Lead us the honest way.

INTRODUCTION. (4 Measures, 8 Counts. All Stand in Position.)

Group I.

PART I. (32 Measures Equal 64 Counts.)

I. Measures.
    1 to 2. Raise the arms sideward. Counts 1 to 4.
    3 to 4. Raise the arms upward. Counts 5 to 8.
    5 to 6. Lower the arms forward. Counts 9 to 12.
    7 to 8. Lower the arms. Counts 13 to 16.

II.
    9 to 16. Repeat the exercises of I twice, giving two counts to each movement. Counts 1 to 16.

III.
    17 to 18. Raise the arms forward. Counts 1 to 4.
    19 to 20. Raise the arms upward. Counts 5 to 8.

21 to 22.   Lower the arms sideward.   Counts 9 to 12.

23 to 24.   Lower the arms.   Counts 13 to 16.

IV.

Repeat the exercises of III twice, giving two counts to each movement, 1 to 16.

PART II.   (32 Measures Equal 64 counts.)

The arm movements of Part I are repeated with striding.

I.

1 to 2.   Raise the arms sideward and stride left sideward.   Counts 1 to 4.

3 to 4.   Raise the arms upward and replace the left foot.   Counts 5 to 8.

5 to 6.   Lower the arms forward and stride left forward.   Counts 9 to 12.

7 to 8.   Lower the arms and replace the left foot.   Counts 13 to 16.

II.

Repeat the exercises of I, giving two counts to each movement, 1 to 16.

III.

1 to 2.   Raise the arms forward and stride right forward.   Counts 1 to 4.

3 to 4.   Raise the arms upward and replace the right foot.   Counts 5 to 8.

5 to 6.   Lower the arms sideward and stride right sideward.   Counts 9 to 12.

7 to 8.   Lower the arms and replace the right foot.   Counts 13 to 16.

IV.

Repeat the exercises of III twice, giving two counts to each movement, 1 to 16.

PART III.   (32 Measures Equal 64 Counts.)

Marching in a cross.

I.

1 to 2.   In four steps face to the left.   Counts 1 to 4.

3 to 4.   Four steps forward.   Counts 5 to 8.

5 to 6. In four steps face left about. Counts 9 to 12.

7 to 8. Four steps forward. Counts 13 to 16.

II, III and IV are exactly like I. Each part takes 16 counts and consists of marching on one part of the cross.

NOTE—The interlude as written in the march is not played.

PART IV. (32 Measures Equal 64 Counts.)

The air is exactly like Part III. The same marching movements are performed as in Part III, with the addition of singing the words of the Field Day Song.

Interlude of 16 drum-beats. Get into line in case the alignment has been lost. On count 9 bend arms for thrust. The music should now be repeated without the introduction.

Group II.

PART I. (32 Measures Equal 64 Counts.)

I.

1 to 2. Lunge left sideward. Counts 1 to 4.

3 to 4. Thrust upward. Counts 5 to 8.

5 to 6. Bend the arms. Counts 9 to 12.

7 to 8. Replace the left foot. Counts 13 to 16.

II.

Repeat the exercises of I twice, giving two counts to each movement, 1 to 16.

III.

1 to 2. Lunge right forward. Counts 1 to 4.

3 to 4. Thrust upward. Counts 5 to 8.

5 to 6. Bend the arms. Counts 9 to 12.

7 to 8. Replace the right foot. Counts 13 to 16.

IV.

Repeat the exercises of III twice, giving two counts to each movement, 1 to 16.

I.　　　　　　　　PART II.　(32 Measures Equal 64 Counts.)

1 to 2.　Lunge left sideward.　Counts 1 to 4.
3 to 4.　Bend the trunk left and thrust right upward.　Counts 5 to 8.
5 to 6.　Straighten the trunk and bend the right arm.　Counts 9 to 12.
7 to 8.　Replace the left foot.　Counts 13 to 16.

II.

Repeat the exercises of I twice, giving two counts to each movement,
1 to 16.

III.

1 to 2.　Lunge right forward.　Counts 1 to 4.
3 to 4.　Bend the trunk forward and thrust downward.　5 to 8.
5 to 6.　Straighten the trunk and bend the arms.　Counts 9 to 12.
7 to 8.　Replace the right foot.　Counts 13 to 16.

IV.

Repeat the exercises of III twice, giving two counts to each movement,
1 to 16.

PART III.　(32 Measures Equal 64 Counts.)

Marching in a square.

I.

1 to 2.　In four steps, face to the left.　Counts 1 to 4.
3 to 4.　Four steps forward.　Counts 5 to 8.
5 to 6.　In four steps face to the left.　Counts 9 to 12.
7 to 8.　Four steps forward.　Counts 13 to 16.

II.

9 to 16.　Repeat I.　Counts 1 to 16.

III.

1 to 2.　In four steps face to the right.　Counts 1 to 4.
3 to 4.　Four steps forward.　Counts 5 to 8.
5 to 6.　In four steps face to the right.　Counts 9 to 12.
7 to 8.　Four steps forward.　Counts 13 to 16.

IV.

9 to 16.　Repeat III.　Counts 1 to 16.

PART IV.　(32 Measures Equal 64 Counts.)

This is exactly like Part III, with the addition of the song.

COMPOSITION No. 3

The exercises were written to the music, "National Emblem March," by E. E. Bagley. Victor record.

The pupils are arranged in ranks of four. Upon command, the ranks are opened left sideward.

INTRODUCTION. (20 Counts. Clinch Hands on 17th Count.)

PART I. (64 Counts.)

1. (a) Raise arms side-upward over head to strike (knuckles back), 1-2.
   (b) Strike sideward, 3-4.
   (c) Reverse, 5-6.
   (d) Return, 7-8.
2. (a) Jump to side stride position and raise arms side-upward over head to strike, 1-2.
   (b) Strike sideward, 3-4.
   (c) Reverse, 5-6.
   (d) Return, 7-8.
3. (a) Turn head left and raise arms left sideward (knuckles out), 1-2.
   (b) Circle right arm down and outward to strike over head (knuckles back), 3-4.
   (c) Reverse, 5-6.
   (d) Return, 7-8.
4. (a) Lunge right sideward, turn head left and raise arms left sideward, 1-2.
   (b) Circle right arm down and outward to strike over head, 3-4.
   (c) Reverse, 5-6.
   (d) Return, 7-8.
5. (a) Raise arms side-upward over head to strike, 1-2.
   (b) Strike sideward, 3-4.
   (c) Reverse, 5-6.
   (d) Return, 7-8.
6. (a) Jump to side stride position and raise arms side-upward over head to strike, 1-2.
   (b) Strike sideward, 3-4.
   (c) Reverse, 5-6.
   (d) Return, 7-8.

7. (a) Turn head right and raise arms right sideward (knuckles out), 1-2.
   (b) Circle right arm down and outward to strike over head (knuckles back), 3-4.
   (c) Reverse, 5-6.
   (d) Return, 7-8.

8. (a) Lunge left sideward, turn head right and raise arms right sideward, 1-2.
   (b) Circle left arm down and outward to strike over head, 3-4.
   (c) Reverse, 5-6.
   (d) Return, 7-8.

PART II.   (64 Counts.)

1. (a) Face left and raise arms obliquely fore-upward (knuckles up), 1-2.
   (b) Swing right arm down and back, 3-4.
   (c) Reverse, 5-6.
   (d) Return, 7-8.

2. (a) Raise arms sideward (knuckles up), 1-2.
   (b) Swing arms in half circle down and inward and bend knees (finish with left forearm above and parallel with right), 3-4.
   (c) Reverse, 5-6.
   (d) Return, 7-8.

3. (a) Face right and raise arms obliquely fore-upward, 1-2.
   (b) Swing left arm down and back, 3-4.
   (c) Reverse, 5-6.
   (d) Return, 7-8.

4. (a) Raise arms sideward, 1-2.
   (b) Swing arms in half circle down and inward and bend knees (finish with left forearm above and parallel with right), 3-4.
   (c) Reverse, 5-6.
   (d) Return, 7-8.

5. (a) Face left, lunge left forward, raise arms obliquely fore-upward, 1-2.
   (b) Swing right arm down and back and turn trunk right, 3-4.
   (c) Reverse, 5-6.
   (d) Return, 7-8.

6. (a) Raise arms sideward, 1-2.
   (b) Swing arms in half circle down and inward, 3-4.
   (c) Reverse, 5-6.
   (d) Return, 7-8.

7. (a) Face right, lunge right forward and raise arms obliquely fore-upward, 1-2.
   (b) Swing left arm down and back and turn trunk left, 3-4.
   (c) Reverse, 5-6.
   (d) Return, 7-8.

8. (a) Raise arms sideward, 1-2.
   (b) Swing arms in half circle down and inward, 3-4.
   (c) Reverse, 5-6.
   (d) Return, 7-8.

EXTRA MEASURE.   (Mark Time, 4 Counts.)

PART III. (96 Counts.)

1. (a) Face left and mark time, 4 counts (begin with left foot), 1-4.
   (b) Raise arms forward, 5.
   (c) Raise arms upward, 6.
   (d) Reverse, 7.
   (e) Return, 8.

2. (a) Face right and mark time, 4 counts (begin with right foot), 1-4.
   (b) Raise arms sideward, 5.
   (c) Raise arms upward, 6.
   (d) Reverse, 7.
   (e) Return, 8.

3. (a) Face right and mark time, 4 counts (begin with right foot), 1-4.
   (b) Raise arms forward, 5.
   (c) Raise arms upward, 6.
   (d) Reverse, 7.
   (e) Return, 8.

4. (a) Face left and mark time, 4 counts (begin with left foot), 1-4.
   (b) Raise arms sideward, 5.
   (c) Raise arms upward, 6.
   (d) Reverse, 7.
   (e) Return, 8.

5. (a) Raise left leg sideward, 1-2.
   (b) Swing left leg across in front (straight knee), 3-4.
   (c) Step left sideward, 5.
   (d) Jump left sideward (landing with bent knees), 6.
   (e) Straighten knees, 7-8.

6. (a) Face left and jump to cross stride position (left foot forward and right foot back), 1.
   (b) With a jump, change position of feet, 2.
   (c) With a jump, change position of feet, 3.
   (d) With a jump, change position of feet, 4.
   (e) With a jump, face right and stand in position, 5-8.

7. (a) Raise right leg sideward, 1-2.
   (b) Swing right leg across in front, 3-4.
   (c) Step right sideward, 5.
   (d) Jump right sideward (landing with bent knees), 6.
   (e) Straighten knees, 7-8.

8. (a) Face right and jump to cross stride position (right foot forward and left foot back), 1.
   (b) With a jump, change position of feet, 2.
   (c) With a jump, change position of feet, 3.
   (d) With a jump, change position of feet, 4.
   (e) With a jump, face left and stand in position, 5-8.

9. (a) Raise left leg sideward, 1-2.
   (b) Swing left leg across in front, 3-4.
   (c) Step left sideward, 5.
   (d) Jump left sideward, 6.
   (e) Straighten knees, 7-8.

10. (a) Face left and jump to cross stride position (left foot forward and right foot back), raising left arm forward and right arm back, 1.
    (b) With a jump, change position of feet and arms, 2.
    (c) With a jump, change position of feet and arms, 3.
    (d) With a jump, change position of feet and arms, 4.
    (e) With a jump, face right and stand in position, arms down, 5-8.
11. (a) Raise right leg sideward, 1-2.
    (b) Swing right leg across in front, 3-4.
    (c) Step right sideward, 5.
    (d) Jump right sideward, 6.
    (e) Straighten knees, 7-8.
12. (a) Face right and jump to cross stride position (right foot forward and left foot back), raising right arm forward and left arm back, 1.
    (b) With a jump, change position of feet and arms, 2.
    (c) With a jump, change position of feet and arms, 3.
    (d) With a jump, change position of feet and arms, 4.
    (e) With a jump, face left and stand in position, arms down, 5-8.

After 32 counts for an intermission, repeat the whole drill.

COMPOSITION No. 4.

The exercises were written to the music "Marche des Petits Pierrots" ("Here, There and Everywhere"), by August Bosc, published by the Theodore Presser Company, Philadelphia. There is also a Victor record.

The pupils are arranged in ranks of four. Upon command, the ranks are opened left sideward.

The entire march is played through three times as it is written. Each time the march is played one group of exercises is performed, each group consisting of four parts. There should be either 16 or 32 drum-beats intermission between the groups of exercises.

Group I.

INTRODUCTION. (8 Counts.)

PART I. (64 Measures, 128 Counts.)

1. (a) Raise arms sideward, 1-4.

(b) Raise arms upward and place hands on shoulders, 5-8.
(c) Reverse, 9-12.
(d) Return, 13-16.

2. (a) Raise arms forward, 1-4.
(b) Raise arms upward and place hands on shoulders, 5-8.
(c) Reverse, 9-12.
(d) Return, 13-16.

3. (a) Face left and raise arms forward, 1-4.
(b) Turn trunk right, swing right arm upward and sideward (arms sideward, palms down), 5-8.
(c) Reverse, 9-12.
(d) Return, 13-16.

4. Repeat 3; opposite, 1-16.

5. Repeat 1, 2, 3 and 4, two counts for each movement instead of four (32 counts).

6. Repeat 5 (32 counts).

PART II.   (48 Measures, 96 Counts.)

1. (a) Stride left sideward and raise arms sideward, 1-4.
(b) Bend left knee and arms, hands in front of chest (palms downward), 5-8.
(c) Reverse, 9-12.
(d) Return, 13-16.

2. Repeat, opposite, 1-16.

3. (a) Stride left forward and swing arms foreupward, 1-4.
(b) Face right (on heels) and lower arms forward, 5-8.
(c) Reverse, 9-12.
(d) Return, 13-16.

4. Repeat 3; opposite, 1-16.

5. Repeat 1, 2, 3 and 4, two counts for each movement instead of four (32 counts).

PART III.   (32 Measures, 64 Counts.)

1. (a) Raise arms sideward, 1-4.

    (b) Deep knee bend and move arms forward, 5-8.

    (c) Reverse, 9-12.

    (d) Return, 13-16.

2. Repeat, 1-16.

3. (a) Jump to sidestride and raise arms sideward, 1-2.

    (b) Raise arms upward, 3-4.

    (c) Reverse, 5-6.

    (d) Return, 7-8.

4. Repeat 3; 1-8.

5. (a) Face left, jump to sidestride and raise arms forward, 1-2.

    (b) Raise arms upward, 3-4.

    (c) Reverse, 5-6.

    (d) Return, 7-8.

6. Repeat 5; opposite, 1-8.

Group II.

INTRODUCTION.   (8 Counts; on Fifth Count Clinch Hands.)

PART I.   (64 Measures, 128 Counts.)

1. (a) Jump to sidestride and raise arms sideward, 1-4.

    (b) Raise arms upward and bend arms to strike (over shoulders; knuckles back), 5-8.

    (c) Reverse, 9-12.

    (d) Return, 13-16.

2. (a) Jump to sidestride and raise arms forward, 1-4.

    (b) Raise arms upward and bend arms to strike (over shoulders), 5-8.

    (c) Reverse, 9-12.

    (d) Return, 13-16.

3. (a) Face left, stride left forward and raise arms forward, 1-4.

    (b) Face right (on heels), swing right arm upward and sideward (arms sideward), 5-8.

    (c) Reverse, 9-12.

    (d) Return, 13-16.

4. Repeat 3; opposite, 1-16.

5. Repeat 1, 2, 3 and 4, two counts for each movement instead of four (32 counts).
6. Repeat 5 (32 counts).

PART II.　(48 Measures, 96 Counts.)

1. (a) Lunge left sideward and raise arms sideward, 1-4.
   (b) Bend arms to strike over head (knuckles back), 5-8.
   (c) Reverse, 9-12.
   (d) Return, 13-16.
2. Repeat, opposite, 1-16.
3. (a) Lunge left forward and swing arms foreupward, 1-4.
   (b) Straighten left knee, face right and lower arms forward, 5-8.
   (c) Reverse, 9-12.
   (d) Return, 13-16.
4. Repeat 3; opposite, 1-16.
5. Repeat 1, 2, 3 and 4, two counts for each movement instead of four (32 counts).

PART III.　(32 Measures, 64 Counts.)

1. (a) Raise arms sideward, 1-4.
   (b) Deep knee bend and move arms forward, 5-8.
   (c) Reverse, 9-12.
   (d) Return, 13-16.
2. Repeat, 1-16.
3. (a) Jump to sidestride and raise arms sideward, 1-2.
   (b) Raise arms upward, 3-4.
   (c) Reverse, 5-6.
   (d) Return, 7-8.
4. Repeat 3; 1-8.
5. (a) Face left, jump to sidestride and raise arms forward, 1-2.
   (b) Raise arms upward, 3-4.
   (c) Reverse, 5-6.
   (d) Return, 7-8.
6. Repeat 5; opposite, 1-8.

COMPOSITION No. 5.

A Free Exercise Drill

Music: "Officer of the Day March"—Hall. Victor Record No. 35,284.

INTRODUCTION. (4 Measures, 8 Counts.)

Stand at attention.

PART I. (32 Measures, 64 Counts.)

A.

1. Raise arms sideward, 1-2; move arms upward, 3-4; reverse, 5-6; return 7-8.
2. Stride left sideward and raise arms sideward, 1-2; move arms upward, 3-4; reverse, 5-6; return, 7-8.
3. Stride left forward and raise arms forward, 1-2; move arms upward, 3-4; reverse, 5-6; return, 7-8.
4. Two steps left sideward, 1-4; three steps in place, 5-7; hold, 8.

B.

Repeat A, opposite (32 counts).

PART II. (32 Measures, 64 Counts.)

A.

1. Bend arms to strike, 1-2; strike obliquely side upward, 3-4; reverse, 5-6; return, 7-8.
2. Face left and march three steps forward (beginning with the left foot), raising arms forward and upward (2 counts to each movement), 1-4; march three steps backward (beginning with the right foot), lowering arms forward and down (2 counts to each movement), facing front on last two counts, 5-8.
3. Repeat 1 (8 counts).
4. Repeat 2, opposite (8 counts).

B.

1. Jump to side stride and bend arms to strike, 1-2; strike obliquely side upward, 3-4; reverse, 5-6; return, 7-8.
2. As 2 of PART II A (8 counts).
3. As 1 of this part (8 counts).
4. As 4 of PART II A, but bend arms to thrust on count 7 (8 counts).

PART III. (32 Measures, 64 Counts.)

A.

1. Face left, stride left forward and thrust upward, 1-2; lower arms forward, 3-4; reverse, 5-6; return, 7-8.
2. Thrust sideward and bend knees, 1-2; move arms upward, 3-4; reverse, 5-6; return, 7-8.
3. Three double-arm circles left, 1-8.
4. Lunge obliquely left forward and thrust left arm obliquely fore-side-upward and right arm obliquely back-side-downward, 1-2; change arm positions by swinging left arm down and right arm up, 3-4; reverse, 5-6; return, 7-8.

B.

Repeat A, opposite, but return to fundamental position on next to last count (32 counts).

INTERLUDE. (4 Measures, 8 Counts.)

Stand at attention.

PART IV. (32 Measures, 64 Counts.)

A.

1. Raise arms sideward, 1-2; move arms upward, 3-4; reverse, 5-6; return, 7-8.
2. Lunge left sideward and raise arms sideward, 1-2; move arms upward and bend trunk left, 3-4; reverse, 5-6; return, 7-8.
3. Lunge left forward and raise arms forward, 1-2; move arms upward and bend upper trunk backward, 3-4; reverse, 5-6; return, 7-8.
4. Two steps left sideward, 1-4; three steps in place, 5-7; hold, 8.

B.

Repeat A, opposite (32 counts).

PART V. (32 Measures, 64 Counts.)

Same as Part II.

PART VI.   (32 Measures, 64 Counts.)

A.

1. Face left, lunge left forward, and thrust upward, 1-2; lower trunk and
    arms forward (knuckles touching the floor), 3-4; reverse, 5-6; return
    7-8.
2. As in Part III A (8 counts).
3. As in Part III A (8 counts).
4. As in Part III A (8 counts).

B.

Repeat A, opposite (32 counts).

COMPOSITION No. 6.

A Free Exercise Drill That Can Be Used With Indian Clubs.

Music—"Sari" (Waltz)—E. Kalman. Columbia Record 5542.

NOTE—Starting position is with knuckles on hips, hands clinched, assum-
ing this position upon command. The entire drill will be executed with hands
clinched. Introduction, 1 count.

PART I.   (64 Measures.)

A.

(a) Straighten arms obliquely sideupward, 1-2; perform an outward circle
     to arms crossed overhead (left arm in front), 3-4; inward circle to
     arms sideward, 5; outward circle to arms bent in front of chest (left
     arm above), 6; full arm circle inward and return to starting posi-
     tion, 7-8.
(b) Repeat (a).
(c) and (d)   Repeat (a) and (b), but full arm circles inward on counts
     5 to 7, returning to starting position on count 8.

B.

(a) Stride left forward and straighten arms obliquely sideupward, 1-2, out-
     ward circle to arms crossed overhead and bend upper trunk back-
     ward, 3-4; inward circle to arms sideward and straighten the trunk,

5; outward circle to arms bent in front of chest, 6; full arm circle inward, return left foot and replace knuckles on hips, 7-8.

(b)   Repeat (a), but stride right forward.

(c) and (d)   Repeat (a) and (b), but full arm circles inward on counts 5 to 7, returning to starting position on count 8.

Part II.   (32 Measures.)

(a)   Two closing steps left sideward, 1-4; bend knees, 5; straighten, 6; bend knees, 7; straighten, 8.

(b)   Repeat (a) to the right, 1-8.

(c)   Step curtsy left sideward, 1-2; step curtsy right sideward, 3-4; three step turn left sideward, 5-8.

(d)   Repeat (c), beginning right, 1-8.

Part III.   (40 Measures.)

(a)   Straighten arms upward to position crossed overhead (left in front), 1-2; inward circle to arms obliquely sideupward, 3-4; outward circle to position crossed in front of chest, 5; inward circle to arms sideward, 6; three-quarter arm circle outward and return to starting position, 7-8.

(b)   Repeat (a).

(c) and (d)   Repeat (a) and (b), but full arm circles outward on counts 5 to 7, returning to starting position on count 8.

(e)   Straighten arms upward to position crossed overhead, 1; hold position in pose to count 7; return to starting position, 8.

Part IV.   (32 Measures.)

(a)   Lunge left sideward and straighten arms obliquely left sideupward, 1-2; bend trunk left, swing arms down and up to obliquely right sideupward, turning head right, 3-4; straighten trunk and swing arms down to left sideward, turning head front, 5; swing arms down and right sideward, 6; three-quarter (double) arm circle right, and return to starting position, 7-8.

(b)   Repeat (a), beginning to the right, 1-8.

(c) and (d)   Repeat (a) and (b), but full arm circles on counts 5 to 7, returning to starting position on count 8.

PART V. (32 Measures.)

(a) Stride left backward and straighten arms upward to crossed position, 1-2; inward circle to arms sideward and lower trunk forward, 3-4; straighten trunk and outward circle to position crossed in front of chest, 5; inward circle to arms sideward, 6; three-quarter arm circle outward and return to starting position, 7-8.

(b) Repeat (a), but stride right backward, 1-8.

(c) and (d). Repeat (a) and (b), but full-arm circles on counts 5 to 7, returning to starting position on count 8.

PART VI. (40 Measures.)

(a), (b), (c), (d) Repeat Part I, B (a, b, c and d).

(e) Step left forward, kneel on right knee and straighten arms obliquely side-upward, 1; hold position in pose to count 6; return to starting position, 7; hold, 8.

On command, lower hands.

GROUP II. (Free Exercises With Dance Steps or Hopping.)

COMPOSITION No. 7.

The exercises were written to the music of "Teddy Bears' Pic Nic," a two-step by John W. Bratton, published by Witmark & Sons.

The music is written in 6-8 time. When exercising, count two for each measure of music.

The pupils should be arranged in open ranks of four: ⊤ ⊤ ⊤ ⊤.

The exercises of Parts I, II and III are alike for both girls and boys. Parts IV, V and VI are, however, composed of different exercises for each sex. If desired, both sexes may perform the same exercises throughout.

A—MASS EXERCISES FOR GIRLS.

INTRODUCTION. (8 Measures, 16 Counts. All Stand in Position.)

PART I. (32 Measures, 64 Counts. Four Divisions of 16 Counts Each.)

1. Four steps forward 1 to 4; face left about 5 to 8.
   Four steps forward 9 to 12; face left about 13 to 16 (on count 15 place hands on hips).

2. Straighten arms sideward 1 to 2; replace hands 3 to 4, repeat 5 to 8.

Straighten arms upward 9 to 10, replace hands 11 to 12, repeat 13 to 16 (on count 15 lower arms to side).

3. Repeat the exercises under 1, 1 to 16.
4. Repeat the exercises under 2, 1 to 16.

NOTE—When marching four steps, take three steps forward and a closing step. The facing in all parts is done while marching.

PART II. (32 Measures, 64 Counts.)

1. Two steps left (sideward) 1 to 4; face left about 5 to 8.
Two steps left 9 to 12; face left about 13 to 16 (on count 15 place hands on hips).
2. Bend trunk left and straighten arms sideward 1 to 2; return 3 to 4, repeat 5 to 8.
Bend trunk backward and straighten arms upward 9 to 10; return 11 to 12, repeat 13 to 16 (on count 15 lower arms to side).
3. Repeat the exercises under 1, 1 to 16.
4. Repeat the exercises under 2, 1 to 16.

PART III. (16 Measures, 32 Counts.)

1. Four steps forward 1 to 4; face left about 5 to 8.
Four steps forward 9 to 12; face left about 13 to 16 (on count 15 place hands on hips).
2. Straighten the arms sideward 1 to 2; return 3 to 4, repeat 5 to 8.
Straighten the arms upward 9 to 10; return 11 to 12, repeat 13 to 16 (on count 15 place knuckles on hips).

PART IV. (Trio. 32 Measures, 64 Counts.)

The movements in parts 4, 5 and 6 are performed alternately left and right.

1. Two steps left 1 to 4, two steps right 5 to 8.
Four gallops left (sideward) 9 to 12, four gallops right 13 to 16.
2. Two steps left and (on count four) place the right foot crossed in front 1 to 4.

Two steps right and place the left foot crossed in front 5 to 8.

Three gallops left, and (on count 4) place the right foot crossed in front 9 to 12.

The same exercise right sideward 13 to 16 (on count 15 straighten the arms sideward).

3. Repeat the exercises under 1, 1 to 16.

4. Repeat the exercises under 2, 1 to 16 (on count 15 lower the arms; on count 16 close feet).

PART V. (16 Measures, 32 Counts.)

1. Each rank of four forms a small circle, hands grasped shoulder-high 1 to 4, mark time 5 to 8.

Face left and march forward (in the circle) 9 to 16 (hands remain grasped).

2. Face right about and march forward (in the circle) 1 to 8.

Re-form the front ranks 9 to 12, mark time 13 to 16.

PART VI. (32 Measures, 64 Counts.)

1. Form circles of four, hands grasped shoulder-high 1 to 4, mark time 5 to 8.

Eight gallops left (sideward) 9 to 16.

2. Eight gallops right (sideward) 1 to 8.

Re-form the front ranks 9 to 12, mark time 13 to 16.

3. Repeat the exercises under 1, but when galloping raise the grasped hands upward 1 to 16.

4. Repeat 2 with grasped hands up 1 to 16.

All parts I to VI are now repeated. While the introduction of 16 counts is being played see that the ranks and files are again straightened.

B—MASS EXERCISES FOR BOYS.

The same piece of music is used.

Parts IV, V and VI for boys are different from those for girls. While this is of no consequence in classes composed exclusively of boys, it must be taken into consideration in mixed classes.

The pupils in mixed classes must be arranged in two columns, each composed of ranks of four ⊤ ⊤ ⊤ ⊤ | ⊤ ⊤ ⊤ ⊤. If
Boys   Girls
the space for exercising is not large enough it is advisable to place the girls in the front half of the column and the boys in the rear half.

INTRODUCTION.   (All Stand in Position.)

PART I.   (Like the Exercise for Girls.)

PART II.   (Like the Exercise for Girls.)

PART III.   (Like the Exercise for Girls. On Count 15 Bend Arms for Thrust.)

PART IV.   (Trio. 32 Measures, 64 Counts.)

The exercises in the last parts are performed alternately, left and right (not twice to the same side as in the first parts).

1. Turn trunk left and thrust forward 1 to 2, return 3 to 4; turn trunk right and thrust forward 5 to 6, return 7 to 8.
   Turn trunk left and thrust upward 9 to 10, return 11 to 12; turn trunk right and thrust upward 13 to 14, return 15 to 16.
2. Lunge left sideward, turn trunk left and thrust forward 1 to 2, return 3 to 4; the same right, 5 to 8.
   Lunge left sideward, turn trunk left and thrust upward 9 to 10, return 11 to 12; the same right 13 to 16.
3. Repeat the exercises under 1.
4. Repeat the exercises under 2 (on count 15 lower the arms).

PART V.   (16 Measures, 32 Counts.)

1. Four steps forward, four steps in place, 1 to 8.
   Four steps backward, four steps in place 9 to 16.
2. Repeat 1 (on count 15 bend arms for thrust).

PART VI.   (32 Measures, 64 Counts.)

1. Lunge left sideward and thrust sideward 1 to 2, return 3 to 4.
   The same exercise right 5 to 8.
   Lunge left sideward and thrust upward 9 to 10, return 11 to 12.
   The same exercise right 13 to 16.

2. Lunge left sideward, bend trunk left and thrust sideward 1 to 2, return 3 to 4.   The same exercise right 5 to 8.
Lunge left sideward, bend trunk left and thrust upward 9 to 10, return 11 to 12.   The same exercise right 13 to 16.
3. Repeat the exercise under 1.
4. Repeat the exercise under 2 (on count 15 lower the arms).

The whole performance, Parts I to VI, is now repeated.   While the introduction is being played, see that the ranks and files are again straightened.

COMPOSITION No. 8.

The exercises are written to the music "In Lilac Time," march, by Engleman; published by Theodore Presser Company, Philadelphia.

The pupils are arranged in ranks of four.   Upon command, the ranks are opened left sideward.

The entire march is played through three times as it is written, except the third part, which is not repeated as is indicated in the music.

Each time the march is played one group of exercises is performed, each group consisting of three parts.   There should be either 16 or 32 drum-beats intermission between the groups of exercises.

Group I.

PART I.   (32 Measures, 64 Counts.)

1. (a) Face left and raise arms forward, 1-4.
    (b) Raise arms upward, 5-8.
    (c) Reverse, 9-12.
    (d) Return, 13-16.
2. (a) Raise arms sideward, 1-4.
    (b) Raise arms upward, 5-8.
    (c) Reverse, 9-12.
    (d) Return, 13-16.
3. (a) Face right and raise arms forward, 1-4.
    (b) Raise arms upward, 5-8.
    (c) Reverse, 9-12.
    (d) Return, 13-16.

4. Like 2 of this part, 1-16. On the last count place hands at waist in preparation for next part.

PART II. (32 Measures, 64 Counts.)

1. (a) Step-hop left and right sideward, 1-4.
   (b) Four gallops left sideward, 5-8.
   (c) Step-hop right and left sideward, 9-12.
   (d) Four gallops right sideward, 13-16.
2. (a) Step-hop left and right sideward, 1-4.
   (b) Four steps forward (closing heels on 8), 5-8.
   (c) Step-hop right and left sideward, 9-12.
   (d) Four steps backward (closing heels on 16), 13-16.
3. Repeat 1 of this part.
4. Repeat 2 of this part, lowering hands on last count.

Intermission of 4 measures, in which lines are straightened.

PART III. (32 Measures, 64 Counts.)

1. (a) Face left and bend knees, 1-4.
   (b) Lunge left forward, 5-8.
   (c) Reverse, 9-12.
   (d) Return, 13-16.
2. (a) Jump to side stride, 1-2; and return, 3-4.
   (b) Jump to side stride and return, 5-6.
   (c) Jump to side stride and return, 7-8.
   (d) Repeat (a), (b) and (c), 9-16.
3. Like 1 of this part, facing right and lunging right forward, 1-16.
4. Like 2 of this part, 1-16.

Group II.

PART I. (32 Measures, 64 Counts.)

1. (a) Face left, lunge left forward, and raise arms forward, 1-4.
   (b) Raise arms upward, 5-8.
   (c) Reverse, 9-12.
   (d) Return, 13-16.
2. (a) Lunge left sideward and raise arms sideward, 1-4.

(b) Raise arms upward, 5-8.

(c) Reverse, 9-12.

(d) Return, 13-16.

3. As 1 of this part, facing right and lunging right forward, 1-16.

4. As 2 of this part, lunging right sideward, 1-16. On the last count place hands at waist.

Part II.   (32 Measures, 64 Counts.)

1. (a) Step-hop left and right sideward, 1-4; on 2 raise the left arm in half circle over head and on 4 the right arm in half circle over head.

(b) Four gallops left sideward, with arms raised sideward, 5-8.

(c) Step-hop right and left sideward, 9-12, raising the right arm in half circle over head on 10, and the left on 12.

(d) Four gallops right sideward, with arms raised sideward, 13-16.

2. (a) Step-hop left and right sideward, 1-4, with left and right arms in half circle over head on 2 and 4.

(b) Four steps forward, with arms raised sideward, closing heels on 8, 5-8.

(c) Step-hop right and left sideward, 9-12, raising right and left arms in half circle over head on 10 and 12.

(d) Four steps backward, with arms raised sideward, 13-16.

3. Repeat 1 of this part, 1-16.

4. Repeat 2 of this part, 1-16, lowering hands on last count.

Intermission of 4 measures.

Part III.   (32 Measures, 64 Counts.)

1. (a) Face left, bend knees and raise arms forward, 1-4.

(b) Lunge left forward and raise arms upward, 5-8.

(c) Reverse, 9-12.

(d) Return, 13-16.

2. (a) Jump to side stride and raise arms sideward, 1-2, return and lower arms, 3-4.

(b) Jump to side stride and return, raising and lowering arms, 5-6.

(c) Jump to side stride and return, raising and lowering arms, 7-8.

(d) Repeat (a), (b) and (c), 9-16.

3.   Like 1 of this part, facing right and lunging right forward, 1-16.
4.   Like 2 of this part, 1-16.

Group III.

PART I.   (32 Measures, 64 Counts.)

1.   (a) Face left, lunge forward and raise arms forward, 1-4.
     (b) Lower trunk and arms forward, 5-8.
     (c) Reverse, 9-12.
     (d) Return, 13-16.
2.   (a) Lunge left sideward and raise arms sideward, 1-4.
     (b) Bend trunk left and raise right arm upward and place left hand on
          hip, 5-8.
     (c) Reverse, 9-12.
     (d) Return, 13-16.
3.   Like 1 of this part, facing right and lunging right forward, 1-16.
4.   Like 2 of this part, lunging right and bending right with opposite arm
     work, 1-16.   On last count place hands at waist.

PART II.   (32 Measures, 64 Counts.)

Like Part II of Group II.

Intermission of 4 measures.

PART III.   (32 Measures, 64 Counts.)

1.   (a) Face left, bend knees and raise arms forward, 1-4.
     (b) Lunge left forward, raise arms upward and lower trunk half for-
          ward, 5-8.
     (c) Reverse, 9-12.
     (d) Return, 13-16.
2.   Like 2 in Part III of Group II.
3.   (a) Face right, bend knees and raise arms forward, 1-4.
     (b) Lunge right forward, raise arms upward and lower trunk half for-
          ward, 5-8.
     (c) Reverse, 9-12.
     (d) Return, 13-16.
4.   Like 2.

COMPOSITION No. 9.

A Combination Drill.

Music: "Our Director March"—Bigelow. Victor Record No. 35204.
NOTE—In all arm circles the movements must be continuous.

INTRODUCTION. (8 Counts.)

Stand at attention.

PART I. (64 Counts.)

A.

1. Raise arms sideward, 1-2; upward, 3-4; reverse, 5-6; return, 7-8.
2. Two steps left sideward, 1-4; jump to side stride, 5; return, 6; jump to side stride, 7; return, 8.
3. Repeat 1, 1-8.
4. Face right and, beginning right, march three steps forward, facing front on count 4, 1-4; 4 steps in place, 5-8.

B.

Repeat A, opposite (32 counts).

PART II. (64 Counts.)

A.

1. Swing arms foreupward, 1-2; bend trunk foredownward, and swing arms downward, 3-4; reverse, 5-6; return, 7-8.
2. Hop twice on left foot, 1-2; hop twice on right foot, 3-4; three cuts sideward, 5-7; close right to left, 8. (NOTE—The opposite leg should be raised sideward during the hops).
3. Repeat 1, 1-8.
4. Repeat 2, opposite, 1-8.

B.

Repeat A, 1-32.

INTERLUDE. (20 Counts.)

1. Stand at attention, 1-4.
2. Face left, bend knees deeply and place hands on floor (squat stand), 1-2; straighten legs backward, 3-4; reverse, 5-6; return, 7-8.
3. Repeat 2, but face right, and on the last count bend arms to thrust, 1-8.

PART III.   (128 Counts.)

A.

1. Stride left sideward, 1-2; turn trunk left and thrust forward, 3-4; reverse, 5-6; return, 7-8.
2. Three arm circles outward, 1-6; bend arms to thrust, 7-8.
3. Repeat 1, opposite, 1-8.
4. Three arm circles inward, 1-6; bend arms to thrust, 7-8.

B.

Repeat A, 1-32.

C.

1. Lunge left sideward, 1-2; turn trunk left and thrust forward, 3-4; reverse, 5-6; return, 7-8.
2. Three arm circles outward, 1-6; bend arms to thrust, 7-8.
3. Repeat 1, opposite, 1-8.
4. Three arm circles inward, 1-6; bend arms to thrust, 7-8.

D.

1-2-3. Repeat 1, 2, 3, of Part C (24 counts).
4. Three and one-half arm circles inward, finishing with hands at sides, 1-8.

INTRODUCTION.   (8 Counts.)

Stand at attention.

PART IV.   (32 Counts.)

1. Jump to side stride and raise arms sideward, 1-2; raise arms upward, 3-4; reverse, 5-6; return, 7-8.
2. Two steps left sideward, 1-4; jump to side stride, 5; return, 6; jump to side stride, 7; return, 8.
3. Repeat 1, 1-8.
4. Face right and, beginning right, march three steps forward, facing front on count 4, 1-4; four steps in place, 5-8.

PART V.   (32 Counts.)

1. Lunge left forward and swing arms foreupward, 1-2; bend trunk fore-downward, and swing arms downward, 3-4; reverse, 5-6; return, 7-8.

2. Hop twice on left foot, 1-2; hop twice on right foot, 3-4; three cuts sideward, 5-7; close right to left, 8. (The opposite leg should be raised sideward during the hops).

3. Repeat 1, opposite, 1-8.

4. Repeat 2, opposite, 1-8.

INTERLUDE. (20 Counts.)

1. Stand at attention, 1-4.

2. Face left, bend knees deeply, and place hands on floor (squat stand), 1-2; straighten legs backward, 3-4; reverse, 5-6; return, 7-8.

3. Repeat 2, but face right, and on last count bend arms to thrust, 1-8.

PART VI. (64 Counts.)

A.

1. Lunge left sideward, 1-2; turn trunk left, bend foredownward and thrust downward, 3-4; reverse, 5-6; return, 7-8.

2. Three arm circles outward, 1-6; bend arms to thrust, 7-8.

3. Repeat 1, opposite, 1-8.

4. Three arm circles inward, 1-6; bend arms to thrust, 7-8.

B.

1-2-3. Repeat 1, 2, 3 of preceding part (Part VI-A) (24 counts).

4. Three and one-half arm circles inward, finishing with hands at sides, 1-8.

GROUP III. (Free Exercises and Marching. A Marching Drill.)

COMPOSITION No. 10.

A Marching and Free Exercise Drill.

Music: "Keeping Step With the Union"—Sousa. Victor Record No. 18929.

Formation: The pupils are arranged in fours, the tallest on the right. They march forward in closed ranks and, upon command, open ranks left sideward in twelve counts.

INTRODUCTION. (8 Counts.)

Hold position, 1-8.

PART I. (64 Counts.)

A.

1. Raise arms sideupward, 1-2; lower sideward, 3-4; reverse, 5-6; return, 7-8.
2. Raise arms foreupward, 1-2; lower forward, 3-4; reverse, 5-6; return, 7-8.
3. As 1, 1-8.
4. As 2, 1-8.

B.

1. Stride left sideward and raise arms sideupward, 1-2; lower sideward, 3-4; reverse, 5-6; return, 7-8.
2. Stride left forward and raise arms foreupward, 1-2; lower forward, 3-4; reverse, 5-6; return, 7-8.
3. As 1 of B, but stride right sideward, 1-8.
4. As 2 of B, but stride right forward, 1-8.

PART II. (64 Counts.)

A.

1. Stride left sideward and raise arms sideward, 1-2; swing left arm down, across and up (three-quarter arm circle outward), 3-4; reverse, 5-6; return, 7-8.
2. Raise arms foreupward, 1-2; bend trunk foredownward and swing arms foredownward, 3-4; reverse, 5-6; return, 7-8.
3. As 1, but opposite, 1-8.
4. As 2, 1-8.

B.

1. Lunge left sideward and raise arms sideward, 1-2; swing left arm down, across and up (three-quarter circle outward), 3-4; reverse, 5-6; return, 7-8.
2. Jump to side stride and raise arms foreupward, 1-2; bend trunk foredownward and swing arms foredownward, 3-4; reverse, 5-6; return, 7-8.
3. As 1, but opposite, 1-8.
4. As 2, 1-8 (bend arms to thrust on count 7).

PART III. (64 Counts.)

A.

1. Stride left sideward and thrust upward, 1-2; turn trunk left and lower arms forward, 3-4; reverse, 5-6; return, 7-8.
2. Three arm circles outward, 1-6; bend arms to thrust, 7-8.
3. As 1, but to the right, 1-8.
4. As 2, 1-8.

B.

1, 2, 3. As 1, 2, 3 of A, 1-24.
4. Three and one-half arm circles outward, finishing with hands at sides, 1-8.

PART IV. (48 Counts.)

1. Four steps in place, 1-4; close ranks through marching forward, 5-8; four steps forward, 9-12; four steps in place, 13-16.
2. Full wheel left, 1-16.
3. Four steps in place, 1-4; four steps backward, 5-8; open ranks through marching forward, 9-12; four steps in place, 13-16 (bending arms to thrust on count 15).

PART V. (32 Counts.)

1. Lunge left sideward and thrust upward, 1-2; turn trunk left and lower arms forward, 3-4; reverse, 5-6; return, 7-8.
2. Three arm circles outward, 1-6; bend arms to thrust, 7-8.
3. As 1, but to the right, 1-8.
4. Three and one-half arm circles outward, finish with hands at sides, 1-8.

PART VI. (48 Counts.)

As Part IV.

PART VII. (32 Counts.)

1. Lunge left sideward and thrust upward, 1-2; turn trunk left, bend trunk forward and swing arms foredownward, 3-4; reverse, 5-6; return, 7-8.
2. Three arm circles outward, 1-6; bend arms to thrust, 7-8.
3. As 1, but to the right, 1-8.
4. Three and one-half arm circles outward, finish with hands at sides, 1-8.

COMPOSITION No. 11.

A Free Exercise Drill, Including Marching Steps.

Music: "Marcia Militaire"—Vessella. Victor Record No. 35258.

(Record should be played at 72 revolutions per minute.)

INTRODUCTION. (8 Measures, 16 Counts.)

Stand at attention, 1-4; four marching steps in place, beginning left, 5-8; two closing steps left sideward, raising arms sideward, 9-12; two closing steps right sideward, lowering arms on last count, 13-16.

PART I. (32 Measures, 64 Counts.)

A.

1. Place hands on shoulders, 1-2; straighten arms forward, 3-4; reverse, 5-6; return, 7-8.
2. Place hands on shoulders, 1-2; straighten arms sideward, 3-4; reverse, 5-6; return, 7-8.
3. Repeat 1, 1-8.
4. Repeat 2, 1-8.

B.

1. Stride left forward and place hands on shoulders, 1-2; straighten arms forward, 3-4; reverse, 5-6; return, 7-8.
2. Stride left sideward and place hands on shoulders, 1-2; straighten arms sideward, 3-4; reverse, 5-6; return, 7-8.
3. Repeat 1, but stride right forward, 1-8.
4. Repeat 2, but stride right sideward, 1-8.

PART II. (32 Measures, 64 Counts.)

A.

1. Raise arms foreupward, 1-2; lower sideward, 3-4; reverse, 5-6; return, 7-8.
2. Beginning with the left foot, seven marching steps forward, 1-8.
3. Repeat 1, 1-8.
4. Beginning with the left foot, seven marching steps backward, 1-8.

B.

1. Raise arms sideupward, 1-2; lower forward, 3-4; reverse, 5-6; return, 7-8.
2. Four closing steps left sideward, 1-8.
3. Repeat 1, 1-8.
4. Four closing steps right sideward, 1-8.

INTERMISSION. (4 Measures, 8 Counts.)

Stand at attention, 1-6; bend arms upward, 7; hold position, 8.

PART III. (32 Measures, 64 Counts.)

A.

1. Stride left sideward and straighten arms upward, 1-2; turn trunk left and lower arms forward, 3-4; reverse, 5-6; return, 7-8.
2. Repeat 1, but to the right, 1-8.
3. Repeat 1, 1-8.
4. Repeat 2, 1-8.

B.

1. Lunge left sideward and straighten arms upward, 1-2; turn trunk left and lower arms forward, 3-4; reverse, 5-6; return, 7-8.
2. Repeat 1, but to the right, 1-8.
3. Repeat 1, 1-8.
4. Repeat 2, returning to the fundamental standing position, lowering arms foredownward on count 7, 1-8.

INTERLUDE. (16 Measures, 32 Counts.)

Four marching steps in place, 1-4; close ranks through forward marching, 5-8; full wheel left, 9-24; open ranks through forward marching, 25-28; four marching steps in place (bending arms upward on count 31), 29-32.

PART IV. (16 Measures, 32 Counts.)

1. Lunge left sideward and straighten arms upward, 1-2; turn trunk left, bend trunk forward and lower arms forward, 3-4; reverse, 5-6; return, 7-8.
2. Repeat 1, but to the right, 1-8.
3. Repeat 1, 1-8.

4. Repeat 2, returning to the fundamental standing position, lowering fore-downward on count 7, 1-8.

INTRODUCTION.   (8 Measures, 16 Counts.)
Repeat the Introduction at the beginning of the Drill.

PART V.   (32 Measures, 64 Counts.)
A.
1. Lunge left forward and place hands on shoulders, 1-2; straighten arms forward, 3-4; reverse, 5-6; return, 7-8.
2. Lunge left sideward and place hands on shoulders, 1-2; straighten arms sideward, 3-4; reverse, 5-6; return, 7-8.
3. Repeat 1, but lunge right forward, 1-8.
4. Repeat 2, but lunge right sideward, 1-8.

B.
1. Lunge left forward and place hands on shoulders, 1-2; bend trunk forward and straighten arms forward, 3-4; reverse, 5-6; return, 7-8.
2. Lunge left sideward and place hands on shoulders, 1-2; bend trunk left sideward and straighten arms sideward, 3-4; reverse, 5-6; return, 7-8.
3. Repeat 1, but to the right, 1-8.
4. Repeat 2, but to the right, 1-8.

PART VI.   (32 Measures, 64 Counts.)
Same as Part II.

COMPOSITION No. 12.

A Combination Drill; Marching and Free Exercises.

Music: "The Jolly General"—Neil Moret. Victor Record No. 35608.

INTRODUCTION.   (8 Counts.)
A.
PART I.   (64 Counts, 2 Counts to Each Movement.)
(a) 1. Raise arms sideupward, 1-2.
2. Three-quarter arm circle outward (to position front of chest, left arm over right), 3-4.

3. One-half arm circle inward (to position of arms sideward), 5-6.

4. Lower arms, 7-8.

(b) 1. Jump to side-stride position and raise arms sideward, 1-2.

2. Lower trunk forward, swing arms downward and clap hands, 3-4.

3. Reverse, 5-6.

4. Return, 7-8.

(c)   Repeat (a), 1-8.

(d) 1. Face left and jump to side-stride position, raising arms sideward, 1-2.

2. Swing arms forward, clapping hands, 3-4.

3. Reverse, 5-6.

4. Return, 7-8.

B.

Repeat (a), (b), (c) and (d), but face right in (d).

PART II. (64 Counts.)

(a) 1. Four steps in place, 1-4.

2. Four steps forward (last step a closing step), 5-8.

3. Close ranks (through forward), 9-12.

4. Four steps in place, 13-16.

(b) 1. Four steps forward, 1-4.

2. One-quarter wheel left, 5-8.

3. Four steps forward, 9-12.

4. One-quarter wheel left, 13-16.

(c)   Repeat (b), 1-16.

(d) 1. Four steps in place, 1-4.

2. Four steps backward (last step a closing step), 5-8.

3. Open ranks (through forward), 9-12.

4. Four steps in place; on last count bend arms to thrust, 13-16.

PART III. (64 Counts, 2 Counts to Each Movement.)

(a) 1. Thrust sideward, 1-2.

2. Bend arms to strike overhead, 3-4.

3. Reverse, 5-6.

4. Return, 7-8.

(b) 1. Thrust sideward, 1-2.
     2. Swing arms, left bent overhead, right behind back, 3-4.
     3. Reverse, 5-6.
     4. Return, 7-8.
(c)   Repeat (a), 1-8.
(d)   Repeat (b), but right arm bent overhead, left arm behind back, 1-8.
(e)   Repeat (a), 1-8.
(f) 1. Jump to side-stride position and thrust sideward, 1-2.
     2. Swing arms sideupward, 3-4.
     3. Reverse, 5-6.
     4. Return, 7-8.
(g) 1. Jump to cross-stride position left forward and thrust left arm obliquely foreupward and right arm obliquely back downward, 1-2.
     2. Jump to cross-stride position right forward and swing arms to opposite position, 3-4.
     3. Reverse, 5-6.
     4. Return, 7-8.
(h)   Repeat (f), 1-8.

PART IV.   (24 Counts.)

(a) 1. Balance hop left forward, left arm sideward, right arm curved overhead, 1-2.
     2. Balance hop right forward, opposite arm position, 3-4.
     3. Two gallops left sideward, arms sideward, 5-6.
     4. Step and curtsy left sideward, waving right arm forward, 7-8.
(b)   Repeat (a), opposite, 1-8.
(c) 1. Swing hop left backward, arms sideward on count 1, wave right arm forward on count 2.
     2. Swing hop right backward, opposite-arm position, 3-4.
     3. As 1, 5-6.
     4. Step right backward on count 1 (arms sideward), close left to right on count 2, bending arms to thrust, 7-8.

PART V. (64 Counts, 2 Counts to Each Movement.)

(a) 1. Lunge left forward and thrust sideward, 1-2.
    2. Bend arms to strike overhead, 3-4.
    3. Reverse, 5-6.
    4. Return, 7-8.
(b) 1. Lunge left sideward and thrust sideward, 1-2.
    2. Swing arms, left bent over head, right behind back, 3-4.
    3. Reverse, 5-6.
    4. Return, 7-8.
(c)   Repeat (a), but lunge right forward, 1-8.
(d)   Repeat (b), opposite, 1-8.
(e)   Repeat (a), 1-8.
(f), (g), (h) Same as (f), (g), (h) of Part III.

PART VI. (24 Counts.)

Same as Part IV.

PART VII. (64 Counts, 2 Counts to Each Movement.)

(a) 1. Lunge left forward and thrust sideward, 1-2.
    2. Bend arms to strike overhead and bend upper trunk backward, 3-4.
    3. Reverse, 5-6.
    4. Return, 7-8.
(b) 1. Lunge left sideward and thrust sideward, 1-2.
    2. Swing arms, left bent over head, right behind back, and bend trunk right, 3-4.
    3. Reverse, 5-6.
    4. Return, 7-8.
(c)   Repeat (a), but lunge right forward, 1-8.
(d)   Repeat (b), opposite, 1-8.
(e)   Repeat (a), 1-8.
(f), (g), (h) Same as (f), (g), (h) of Part III, but come to fundamental position on last 2 counts.

PART VIII.　(32 Counts, 2 Counts to Each Movement.)

(a) 1. Swing arms sideupward and rise on toes, 1-2.
   2. Three-quarter arm circle outward (to position front of chest, left arm over right) and bend knees, 3-4.
   3. One-half arm circle inward (to position of arms sideward) and straighten knees, rising on toes, 5-6.
   4. Lower arms and heels, 7-8.

(b) 1. Jump to side-stride position and raise arms sideward, 1-2.
   2. Lower trunk forward, swing arms downward and clap hands, 3-4.
   3. Reverse, 5-6.
   4. Return, 7-8.

(c)　　Repeat (a), 1-8.

(d)　　Repeat (b), 1-8.

PART IX.　(32 Counts.)

(a) 1. Four steps in place, 1-4.
   2. Four steps forward (last step a closing step), 5-8.
   3. Close ranks through forward, 9-12.
   4. Four steps backward, 13-16.

(b) 1. Four steps in place, 1-4.
   2. Four steps forward (last step a closing step), 5-8.
   3. Open ranks through forward and halt, 9-12.
   4. Hand salute, 13-14; lower hand, 15-16.

COMPOSITION No. 13.

A Marching Drill.

Music: "The Thunderer"—Sousa. Victor Record 35531.

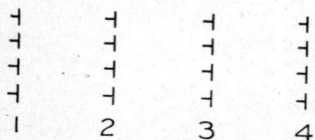

The marching squad consists of 16 pupils, arranged in a column composed of four front ranks of four pupils each (see Figure 1), the taller ones on the right.

The drill has four parts of four divisions (A, B, C, D) each. Each part has 128 counts.

FIG. 1.

PART I.

DIVISION A. (32 Counts.)

(a) The ranks quarter wheel left and four steps forward; 8 counts (see Figure 2).

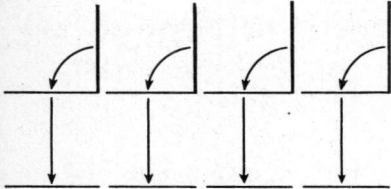

(b) (c) and (d) repeat three times; 24 counts; 32 counts in all.

DIVISION B. (32 Counts.)

Repeat Division A, but wheel right instead of left; 32 counts.

FIG. 2.

DIVISION C. (32 Counts.)

Ranks 1 and 3 repeat Division A (wheel left and march forward).

Ranks 2 and 4 repeat Division B (wheel right and march forward); 32 counts.

DIVISION D. (32 Counts.)

Ranks 1 and 3 repeat Division B (wheel right and march forward).

Ranks 2 and 4 repeat Division A (wheel left and march forward); 32 counts.

PART II.

DIVISION A. (32 Counts.)

(a) The ranks quarter wheel left and 4 steps forward; 8 counts.

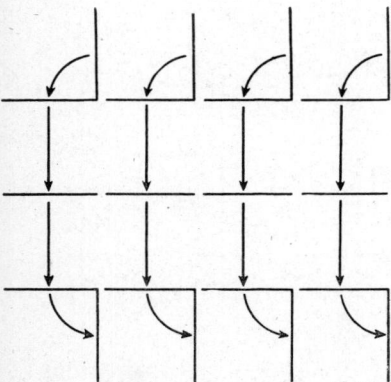

(b) Four steps forward and the ranks quarter wheel left; counts 9 to 16 (see Figure 3).

(c) and (d) repeat (a) and (b); 16 counts; 32 counts in all.

DIVISION B.

Repeat Division A, but wheel right instead of left; 32 counts.

DIVISION C.

Ranks 1 and 3 repeat Division A (wheel left and march forward).

FIG. 3.

Ranks 2 and 4 repeat Division B (wheel right and march forward);
32 counts in all.

Division D.

Ranks 1 and 3 repeat Division B (wheel right and march forward).
Ranks 2 and 4 repeat Division A (wheel left and march forward);
32 counts in all.

Part III. (Cross.)

Division A.

(a) (b) Rank 1, a complete wheel left.
          Rank 2, 4 steps forward and three-quarters wheel left.
          Rank 3, 8 steps forward and half wheel left.
          Rank 4, 12 steps forward and quarter wheel left; 16 counts.
(c) and (d) The cross a complete wheel left; counts 17 to 32.

Division B.

(a) and (b) The ranks a complete wheel right; counts 1 to 16.

(c) and (d) The cross a complete wheel left; counts 17 to 32.

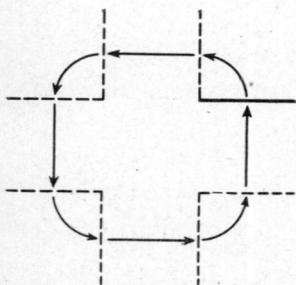

FIG. 4.

Division C.

(a) The ranks quarter wheel left and 4 steps forward; 8 counts (see Figure 4).

(b) (c) and (d) repeat 3 times; counts 9 to 32.

Division D.

(a) The ranks 8 steps forward; 8 counts.

(b) The ranks half wheel left; counts 9 to 16 (see Figure 5).

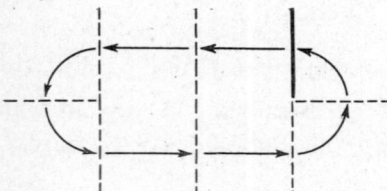

FIG. 5.

(c) Repeat (a); counts 17 to 24.

(d) The cross half wheel left; counts 25 to 32.

PART IV. (First Formation.)

DIVISION A.

(a) (b) Rank 1, 8 steps forward and 8 steps in place; 16 counts.
Rank 2, quarter wheel left, 4 steps forward and 8 steps in place.
Rank 3, half wheel left, and 8 steps in place.
Rank 4, quarter wheel left, 4 steps forward and half wheel left; 16 counts.

(c) and (d) The ranks quarter wheel left and 12 steps in place; counts 17 to 32.

DIVISION B.

(a) The ranks half wheel left; 8 counts.
(b) 8 steps forward; counts 9 to 16.
(c) The ranks half wheel left; counts 17 to 24.
(d) 8 steps forward; counts 25 to 32.

DIVISION C.

(a) Ranks 1 and 3, quarter wheel left and 4 steps in place.
Ranks 2 and 4, quarter wheel right and 4 steps in place; 8 counts (see Figure 6).

(b) Ranks 1 and 3, quarter wheel left backward and 4 steps in place.
Ranks 2 and 4, quarter wheel right backward and 4 steps in place; counts 9 to 16.

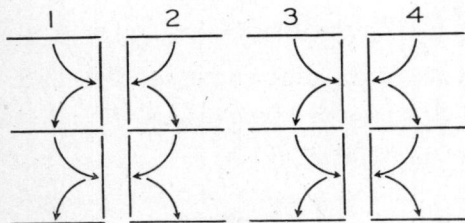

FIG. 6.

(c) Ranks 1 and 3, quarter wheel left backward and 4 steps in place.
Ranks 2 and 4, quarter wheel right backward and 4 steps in place; counts 17 to 24.

(d) Ranks 1 and 3, quarter wheel left forward and 4 steps in place.
Ranks 2 and 4, quarter wheel right forward and 4 steps in place; counts 25 to 32.

DIVISION D.

(a) and (b) 8 steps backward and 8 steps in place; 16 counts.

(c) Quarter wheel right, four steps in place and halt; count 17 to 24.

(d) Salute: raise right arm obliquely forward (2 counts); raise right hand to head (2 counts); straighten forward (2 counts); lower to side (2 counts); counts 25 to 32.

GROUP IV.   (Free Exercises and Athletic Events. A Stunt Drill.)

COMPOSITION No. 14.

A Combination Drill, Marching, Free Exercises and Athletic Events.

Music: "Moon Winks," Three-step—Stevens-Frey. Victor Record 16069. Record is played through once for each group of exercises.

Formation: The pupils are arranged in a column of fours, the tallest on the right. They march forward in closed ranks and, upon command, open ranks left sideward in 12 counts.

NOTE—The music is written in three-four time. Where one measure is allowed for an action, the movement is taken on the first count and held for counts two and three.

First Group.   (Free Exercises and Marching.)
PART I.   (32 Measures.)

A. 1. Raise arms sideward, 1 measure; move arms upward, sideward and side-downward, 1 measure; repeat all, 2 measures; face left and three steps forward, 1 measure; two steps in place and hold, 1 measure; face front and two steps right sideward, 2 measures.

2. Repeat 1, but marching steps in opposite direction, 8 measures.

B.   Repeat A, 16 measures.

PART II.   (16 Measures.)

A. 1. Jump to side-stride and raise arms sideward, 1 measure; turn trunk left and immediately bend trunk right, 1 measure; straighten trunk and face front, 1 measure; return to position, 1 measure.

2. Face left and jump to squat stand, 1 measure; extend legs backward, 1 measure; return to squat stand, 1 measure; return to position, facing front, 1 measure.

B. 1. Repeat 1 of A, but opposite, 4 measures.
   2. Repeat 2 of A, but to the right, 4 measures.

PART III. (16 Measures.)

A. 1. Jump to side stride and raise arms sideward, 1 measure; move arms upward, sideward and side-downward, feet together on last count, 1 measure; repeat the preceding two measures, 2 measures; face left and three steps forward, 1 measure; two steps in place and hold, 1 measure; face front and two steps right sideward, 2 measures.
   2. Repeat 1, but marching steps in opposite direction, 8 measures.

PART IV. (32 Measures.)

A. 1. Lunge left sideward and bend arms to thrust, 1 measure; turn trunk left and thrust forward, 1 measure; reverse, 1 measure; return, 1 measure.
   2. Raise arms sideward and hop three times on the left foot, 1 measure; hop three times on right foot, 1 measure; four cuts sideward and close, lowering arms when closing, 2 measures.
   3. As 1, but to the right, 4 measures.
   4. As 2, but opposite, 4 measures.

B. 1. Lunge left sideward and bend arms to thrust, 1 measure; turn trunk left, bend trunk forward and thrust downward, 1 measure; reverse, 1 measure; return, 1 measure.
   2. Hop three times on the left foot, raising the left arm obliquely side-upward, 1 measure; repeat opposite, 1 measure; four cuts sideward with corresponding arm raising and lowering, finish with feet together and arms at sides, 2 measures.
   3. As 1, but to the right, 4 measures.
   4. As 2, but opposite, 4 measures.

Second Group.   (Athletic Activities.)

PART I.   (32 Measures.)

A. 1. *Pitching* (right hand as though holding a baseball). Raise right arm sideward and immediately one and three-quarter right arm circles outward, hands meeting overhead ("Wind up"), 1 measure; raise left knee high, bring hands down toward right hip, 1 measure; with a quarter turn left, lunge left forward and throw ball forward, swinging left arm backward, 1 measure; return to position, facing front, 1 measure.

2. *Batting* (hands as though grasping a baseball bat). Stride left sideward, bend slightly forward, touching bat on home plate 3 times, 1 measure; bend right knee, swing bat over right shoulder, 1 measure; change knee-bend and strike forward, the body making a quarter turn left (the bat shoulder high in front), 1 measure; return to position, facing front, 1 measure.

3. Repeat 1, but pitch left handed, 4 measures.

4. Repeat 2, but bat left handed, 4 measures.

B.   Repeat A, 16 measures.

PART II.   (16 Measures.)

A. 1. *Ballthrow Overhead.*
Stride left sideward, lower trunk and arms forward (as though grasping ball), 1 measure; raise trunk and swing arms foreupward, ball overhead, 1 measure; throw ball forward, arms obliquely foreupward, palms front, 1 measure; return to position, 1 measure.

2. *Standing Broad Jump.*
Face left, raise arms obliquely foreupward and rise on toes, 1 measure; bend knees, swing arms down and back, 1 measure; jump forward, landing on toes, with knees bent and arms forward, 1 measure; return to position, facing front, 1 measure.

3. As 1, but stride right sideward, 4 measures.

4. As 2, but to the right, 4 measures.

PART III. (16 Measures.)

1. *Catching Ground Ball and Throwing.*

   Stride left sideward and place hands on knees, 1 measure; bend left knee, clap hands to catch ball outside left knee, 1 measure; lunge obliquely right forward with the left foot, throwing ball in the same direction with right hand, 1 measure; return to position, 1 measure.

2. *Running, Catching High Ball and Tagging.*

   Run three steps forward, beginning left, 1 measure; jump upward, clap hands to catch ball overhead, landing with slight knee bend, 1 measure; lunge right sideward, bend trunk right sideward and tag with ball in right hand, 1 measure; return to position, 1 measure.

3. As 1, 4 measures.

4. As 2, but running steps backward instead of forward, 4 measures.

PART IV. (32 Measures.)

A.   1. *Sprinting* (on a square left).

   "On your mark," right knee on the ground, 1 measure; "Get set," 1 measure; run three steps forward, 1 measure; face left and three running steps in place, 1 measure.

   2, 3, 4. Repeat 1 three times, 12 measures.

B.   1. *Boxing* (Files 1 and 2, 3 and 4 immediately face each other).

   Lunge right backward, extend the slightly bent left arm forward, right arm bent at right angles against the waist, 1 measure; attack right, 1 measure; quickly attack left, right, left, 1 measure; attack right and return to position, 1 measure.

   2. Lunge left backward, extend the slightly bent right arm forward, left arm bent against the waist, 1 measure; attack left, 1 measure; quickly attack right, left, right, 1 measure; attack left and return to position, 1 measure.

   3. As 1, 4 measures.

   4. As 2, but immediately after attacking left (last measure) step left forward toward partner and grasp right hands, 4 measures. Hold until signal to face front is given.

NOTE—Attack right means to vigorously extend the right arm forward, slightly bending the trunk forward and turning the right shoulder forward (punching) and bringing the bent left arm against the waist (guarding). Attack left means the opposite movements.

COMPOSITION No. 15.

An Athletic Drill.

Music: "Hindustan." Victor Record 18507. Fox-trot rhythm.

NOTE—*In all positions or movements requiring two or four counts for completion the movement must be executed on the first count and the position held during the remaining one or three counts.*

PART I.   (42 Measures, 168 Counts.)

Introduction.   (8 Counts.)

1.   (a)   Raise arms sideward, 1-2; upward, 3-4; lower forward, 5-6; downward, 7-8 (8 counts).

  (b)   As (a) (8 counts).

  (c)   Raise arms forward, 1-2; upward, 3-4; lower sideward, 5-6; downward, 7-8 (8 counts).

  (d)   As (c) (8 counts).

2.   Basketball Far Throw.

  (a)   Stride left sideward, slightly bend knees, bend trunk foredownward, arms forward, 1-2; straighten trunk and bend slightly backward, raising arms foreupward and then bending arms, 3-4; straighten trunk and move arms quickly to obliquely foreupward position, 5-6; return to fundamental position, 7-8 (8 counts).

  (b)   Four marching steps forward, beginning left, 1-4; four marching steps in place, facing left on the first step, 5-8 (8 counts).

  (c)   As (a) and (b), repeated 3 times on the lines of a square left (48 counts).

3.   Crouch Start and Dash.

  (a)   Kneel on right knee, hands placed about four inches in rear of left toe ("on your mark"), 1-4; raise right knee off ground, raise back until parallel to ground, weight shifted slightly forward ("get set"), 5-8 (8 counts).

  (b)   Straighten up and run forward 4 steps (arms bent), beginning right, 1-4; face left about in 4 running steps in place, 5-8 (8 counts).

(c) As (a) and (b) in the new direction (to the rear) (16 counts).

(d) As (a) and (b) (16 counts).

(e) As (c) (16 counts).

PART II.   (40 Measures, 160 Counts.)

1.   As 1 of Part I (32 counts).

·2.   Standing Broad Jump.

(a) Raise arms foreupward and rise on toes, 1-2; half knee bend, swing arms down and back, slightly bending trunk forward, 3-4; jump forward (about 3 feet), swinging arms forward, and alight with knees full bend, arms forward and body erect, 5-6; rise to fundamental position, 7-8 (8 counts).

(b) In 8 steps countermarch left to starting position and face front (8 counts).

(c) As (a) and (b), repeated 3 times (48 counts).

3.   Boxing.

(a) Face left, stride right backward, bending both knees slightly, raise and hold the bent left arm forward, right arm bent over pit of stomach ("on guard"), 1-4; thrust right arm forward and bend left arm over pit of stomach, turning right shoulder forward and straightening right leg, 5-8 (8 counts).

(b) Thrust left arm forward and bend right over pit of stomach, 1; reverse, 2; left forward and right bent, 3; reverse, 4; fundamental position, 5-8 (8 counts).

COMPOSITION No. 16.

A Stunt Drill for Boys.

By Otto A. Wurl.

NOTE—The pupils are arranged in a column of closed ranks of three, smaller pupils in front. The ranks are numbered in twos from the front to the rear. The lightest boy in each rank should be in the center. The column marches forward to its place with a distance of ten feet between ranks.

Music: "Spirit of Independence March"—Holzmann. Victor Record 18559.

NOTE—The eight counts of preparation are to be divided into two parts of 4 counts each; return to position on count 1; hold counts 2, 3 and 4. Prepare for and assume the next grouping on counts 5 to 8.

INTRODUCTION. (4 Measures, 8 Counts.)

Prepare for first grouping on last 4 counts.

PART I. (64 Counts.)

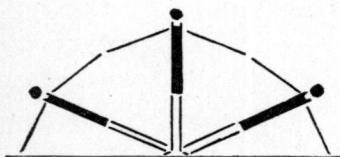

1st

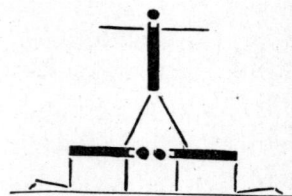

2nd

A.

Hold first grouping (8 counts).
Return and prepare for second (8 counts).
Hold second grouping (8 counts).
Return and prepare for first (8 counts).

B.

Repeat A, but during last 4 counts prepare for third grouping (32 counts).

PART II. (64 Counts.)

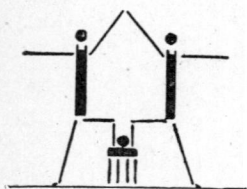

3rd

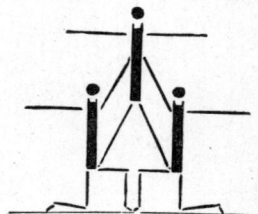

4th

A.

Hold third grouping (8 counts).
Return and prepare for fourth (8 counts).
Hold fourth grouping (8 counts).
Return and prepare for third (8 counts).

B.

Repeat A, but during last 4 counts prepare for fifth grouping (32 counts).

PART III. (64 Counts.)

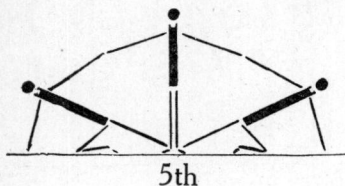

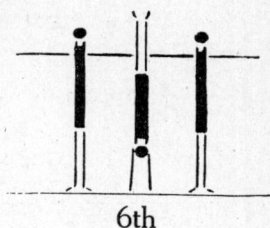

5th   6th

A.

Hold fifth grouping (8 counts).
Return and prepare for sixth (8 counts).
Hold sixth grouping (8 counts).
Return and prepare for fifth (8 counts).

B.

Repeat A, but during last 4 counts stand at attention (32 counts).

PART IV. (24 Counts.)

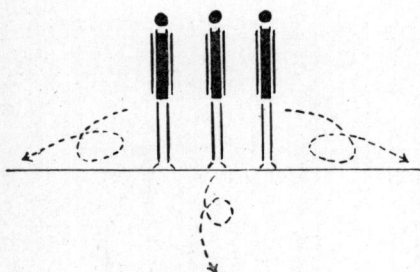

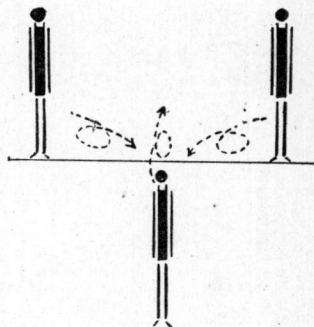

Outer ones take a cartwheel outward; center one face left and take cartwheel right, and face front (4 counts).

Stand at attention (4 counts).

Center one face right, and all take a cartwheel back to position (4 counts).

Stand at attention (4 counts).

Prepare for seventh grouping (8 counts).

PART V.   (64 Counts.)

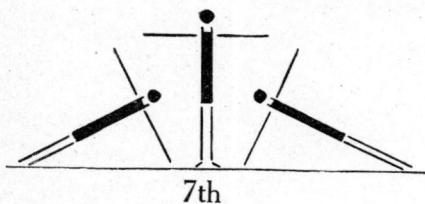

7th   8th

A.

Hold seventh grouping (8 counts).
Return and prepare for eighth (8 counts).
Hold eighth grouping (8 counts).
Return and prepare for seventh (8 counts).

B.

Repeat A, but during last 4 counts stand at attention (32 counts).

PART VI.   (24 Counts.)

Repeat cartwheels of Part IV (16 counts).

Rank No. 2 run forward to Rank No. 1 (outer ones of Rank 1 open outward, outer ones of Rank 2 step between center and outer ones of Rank 1; center of Rank 2 takes place behind center of Rank 1) and prepare for ninth grouping (8 counts).

PART VII.   (64 Counts.)

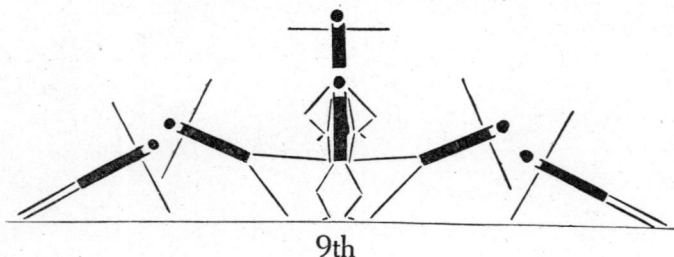

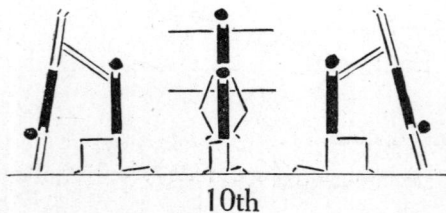

9th

10th

A.

Hold ninth grouping (8 counts).
Return and prepare for tenth (8 counts).
Hold tenth grouping (8 counts).
Return and prepare for ninth (8 counts).

B.

Repeat A, but during last 8 counts return to original column formation (32 counts).

GROUP V. (Dances.)

COMPOSITION No. 17.

A Dance for Boys and Girls.

"THE PLAYFUL SPRITES"

Music: "Parade of the Wooden Soldiers"—Jessel. Victor Record 73400.

Formation: Groups of eight—four boys and four girls—numbered from one to eight, beginning at the right (girls, odd numbers; boys, even), standing in a front line, hands joined shoulder high.

INTRODUCTION. (8 Counts.)

Hold position.

PART I. (32 Counts.)

1. Double glide balance hop obliquely right forward, 1-2; obliquely left forward, 3-4; glide polka right sideward, 5-8 (8 counts).
2. Double glide balance hop obliquely left forward, 1-2; obliquely right forward, 3-4; three steps backward and close, 5-8 (8 counts).
3. Repeat 1, opposite (8 counts).
4. Repeat 2, opposite (8 counts).

PART II. (28 Counts.)

1. Jump to side stride, 1; return, 2; jump to side stride, 3; return, 4; beginning left, three steps forward and close, 5-8 (8 counts).

2. Repeat 1, but steps backward and close, 5-8 (8 counts).

3. Double glide balance hop obliquely left forward, 1-2; cut forward, 3; cut backward, "and"; cut forward, 4 (4 counts).

4. Jump to side stride and hold, 1-2; return and hold, 3-4; beginning left, three steps backward and close, 5-8 (8 counts).

PART III. (32 Counts.)

Repeat Part I.

PART IV. (8 Counts.)

The boy on the extreme left leads the members of his group into a circle, joining hands with the girl on the extreme right to complete the circle (8 counts).

PART V. (64 Counts.)

1. Swing hop left sideward, 1-2; swing hop right sideward, 3-4; glide polka left sideward, 5-8 (8 counts).

2. Repeat 1, opposite (8 counts).

3. Repeat 1 (8 counts).

4. Swing hop right sideward, 1-2; swing hop left sideward, 3-4; release hands, and in four steps turn right-about, immediately rejoining hands, 5-8. (Backs are now toward center of the circle.) (8 counts.)

5 to 8. Repeat 1 to 4, opposite. (At finish all will be facing the center of the circle.) (32 counts.)

PART VI. (20 Counts.)

1. Beginning left, four steps toward center, swinging arms upward, 1-4; four steps backward, lowering arms, 5-8 (8 counts).

2. Repeat 1 (8 counts).

3. Release hands and in four steps turn left-about, 1-4. (Backs are now toward center of circle). (4 counts.)

PART VII. (32 Counts.)

Repeat 1, 2, 3 and 4 of Part V. (Finish facing center of the circle.)

PART VIII.   (8 Counts.)

Numbers 1 and 8 release hands, and Number 1 leads the members of the group back to a straight line (8 counts).

PART IX.   (44 Counts.)

1.   Repeat 1 of Part I (8 counts).
2.   Repeat 2 of Part I (8 counts).
3.   Repeat 3 of Part I (8 counts).
4.   Double glide balance hop obliquely right forward, 1-2; double glide balance hop obliquely left forward, 3-4; step right backward and close left to right, 5 (5 counts).
5.   Twenty-one quick running steps backward, 1-7 (7 counts).
6.   Release hands, three step turn right and close, joining hands, 1-4; lower trunk forward, swinging the arms down and backward, 5-6; straighten trunk, swing arms upward and hold, 7-8 (8 counts).

COMPOSITION No. 18.

A Dance for Girls.

Music: "Entr' Acte Gavotte"—E. Gillet. Victor Record 19143.

Formation: Eight couples in flank circle formation, facing to move anti-clockwise, No. 1 on the right, No. 2 on the left. The group will march forward in a column of twos, and on reaching the designated place on the field will circle anti-clockwise.

INTRODUCTION.   (8 Measures.)

Partners facing, inside hands joined and arms raised sideward, outside foot placed sideward; hold. On the last two notes step sideward on the outside foot, place inside foot in rear and curtsy.

PART I.   (16 Measures.)

A.   1. Place inside foot forward and backward, 1 measure, and change step forward, 1 measure; facing partner, two glides sideward, 1 measure; a full turn outward in two steps, 1 measure.

2. Place outside foot forward and backward, 1 measure; and change step forward, 1 measure; facing away from partner, two glides sideward, 1 measure; a full turn outward in two steps, 1 measure.

B.   Repeat A, finishing with feet together, 8 measures.

PART II.   (21 Measures.)

A. 1. Partner No. 1, four short running steps forward in line of progression (arms obliquely sidedownward), as though running from partner, 1 measure. Partner 2, four short running steps forward, pursuing No. 1, who stands in place with knuckles on hips, 1 measure.

2. Repeat 1, 2 measures.

3. No. 1 circles outward with 6 small running steps in place (raising right arm overhead) and finishes with stamp left, while No. 2 stands in place (with knuckles on hips), 2 measures.

4. No. 2 circles outward with 6 small running steps in place (raising left arm overhead), and finishes with two stamps, while No. 1 stands in place, 2 measures.

B. 1, 2, 3. Repeat 1, 2 and 3 of A, 6 measures.

4. No. 2 (right arm around No. 1's waist) turns No. 1 in a circle left with 8 running steps, 2 measures; 8 running steps forward, 2 measures; 4 running steps backward, 1 measure; step on the inside foot and hold, finishing in same position as at start of dance, then on the last two notes step sideward on the outside foot, place the other foot in rear and curtsy, 2 measures.

PART III.   (16 Measures.)

Repeat Part I.

PART IV.   (56 Measures.)

A. 1. Partners join left hands (right arms sideward) and turn in a circle left, with eight walking steps, 4 measures; all face center of circle, join hands and walk four steps forward (raising joined hands upward), 2 measures, and four steps backward (lowering arms), 2 measures.

2. Repeat 1, 8 measures.

B. 1. Step on right foot, crossing front of left, step on left, step on right, crossing front of left, and swing left leg sideward, 2 measures; repeat opposite, 2 measures.

2. Repeat 1, 4 measures.

3. Release hands, step on right foot, crossing front of left, step on left, balance hop right (left arm overhead), 2 measures; opposite, 2 measures; three steps backward and hold, 2 measures; pirouette left (waving arms forward and sideward), step forward on left foot, transfer weight to right foot, 2 measures.

C. Repeat A, 16 measures.

D. No. 2 steps front of and faces No. 1. Step on left foot, step on right rear of left, balance hop left (arms sideward), 2 measures; repeat opposite, 2 measures; partners circle back to back in eight running steps (arms sideward), finishing in position taken at start of dance and hold, then on last two notes step on outer foot, placing inside foot in rear and curtsy, 4 measures.

PART V.   (16 Measures.)
Repeat Part I.

PART VI.   (21 Measures.)
Repeat Part II.

PART VII.   (17 Measures.)

A. Repeat A of Part I, 8 measures.

B. 1. Place inside foot forward and backward, 1 measure, and change step forward, 1 measure; facing partner, two glides sideward, 1 measure; a full turn outward in two steps, 1 measure.

2. Place outside foot forward and backward, 1 measure; change step forward, 1 measure; eight small running steps backward, face partner, step on inside foot and hold, curtsy right, step on left and hold the position as at start of dance, 3 measures.

COMPOSITION No. 19.

An Aesthetic Dance for Girls.

Music: "Marsovia Waltz"—Belcher-Lampe. Victor Record 16069.

Formation: The pupils are arranged in fours, the tallest ones on the right. They march forward in closed ranks and, upon command, open ranks left sideward in 12 counts.

PART I. (32 Measures.)

A. 1. Step on right foot, crossing front of left, step on left (arms sideward), balance hop right forward (left arm overhead), 2 measures; repeat opposite, 2 measures.

    2. Swing hop right backward (arms sideward on step, left arm forward on hop), swing hop left backward (opposite arm positions), 2 measures; pirouette right (arms forward and sideward), 2 measures.

    3. Polka obliquely right forward (right arm forward, left arm sideward), 2 measures; same left (opposite arm positions), 2 measures.

    4. Two glides right sideward (arms sideward), 2 measures; step and curtsy right sideward (left arm forward on the curtsy), 2 measures.

B. 1, 2, 3. Repeat 1, 2 and 3 of A, opposite, 12 measures.

    4. Two glides left sideward (arms sideward), 2 measures; pirouette left (arms forward and sideward), 1 measure; balance hop left forward (right arm overhead), 1 measure.

PART II. (32 Measures.)

A. 1. Double balance hop turn right (right arm overhead, left arm sideward), 2 measures; balance step left and right sideward with opposite foot placed in front (opposite arm forward), 2 measures.

    2. Balance hop left forward, right arm overhead (left arm sideward), then swing hop right backward (left arm forward, right arm sideward), 2 measures; repeat, 2 measures.

    3. Repeat 1 opposite, 4 measures.

    4. Two two-step-turns right sideward (arms forward and sideward), 2 measures; step right sideward (arms sideward), place the left foot in front (left arm forward), 2 measures.

B.   Repeat A opposite, 16 measures.

PART III. (32 Measures.)

Same as Part I.

PART IV. (32 Measures.)

All face right.

A.
1. Balance hop right forward (left arm overhead, right arm sideward) and swing hop left backward (right arm forward, left arm sideward), 2 measures; repeat, 2 measures.
2. Four skips forward (arms sideward), facing left about on last two skips, 4 measures.
3. Repeat 1, 4 measures.
4. Repeat 2, 4 measures, facing front instead of left about.

B.
Files 1 and 2, 3 and 4 face each other. Those facing are partners.
1. With right hands joined (left arms sideward), balance hop right forward and swing hop left backward, 2 measures; repeat, 2 measures.
2. Four skip steps in a circle clockwise, partners changing places, 4 measures.
3. Repeat 1, 4 measures.
4. Eight running steps in a circle clockwise, back to place facing front, 4 measures.

PART V. (32 Measures.)

A.
1. Place right foot forward, sideward, backward and feet together (right arm forward, sideward, overhead and sideward, left arm sideward), 4 measures.
2. Repeat 1, opposite, 4 measures.
3. Three step turn right and raise left leg sideward (arm forward and sideward), 2 measures; same in opposite direction, 2 measures.
4. Balance hop right forward (right arm sideward, left arm overhead), 1 measure; balance hop left forward (opposite arm positions), 1 measure; repeat right and left, 2 measures.

B.
1, 2, 3. Repeat 1, 2 and 3 of A, 12 measures.
4. Swing hop right backward (right arm sideward, left arm forward), 1 measure; swing hop left backward (left arm sideward, right arm forward), 1 measure; repeat right and left, 2 measures.

PART VI. (37 Measures.)

A.   As A of Part I, 16 measures.

B.   1, 2, 3 as B 1, 2, 3 of Part I, 12 measures.

    4. Two glides left sideward (arms sideward), 2 measures; two steps forward, left, right (arms sideward), and balance hop left forward (right arm overhead), 2 measures; two steps forward, right, left (arms sideward), and balance hop right forward (left arm overhead), 2 measures; swing hop left backward (right arm forward), 1 measure; swing hop right backward (left arm forward), 1 measure; step left backward (arms sideward), and place the right foot backward (right arm overhead), 1 measure.

COMPOSITION No. 20.

An Aesthetic Dance.

Music: "April Smiles"—Depret. Victor Record 19054.

Formation: Pupils are arranged in fours, the tallest ones on the right. They march forward in closed ranks and, upon command, open ranks left sideward in 12 counts.

PART I. (48 Measures.)

A. 1. Balance hop right forward, left arm overhead, right arm sideward, 1 measure; swing hop left backward, right arm forward, left arm sideward, 1 measure. Repeat, 2 measures (4 measures).

    2. Rear cross step right sideward (right, left, right), arms sideward, and curtsy, left arm forward, 4 measures.

    3. Repeat 1 opposite, 4 measures.

    4. Step left sideward, step on right foot in rear of left, arms sideward, pirouette left, wave arms forward and sideward, balance hop left forward, both arms overhead, 4 measures.

    5. Polka obliquely right forward (swinging straight leg forward on first count), right arm forward, left arm sideward, 2 measures; repeat opposite, 2 measures (4 measures).

6. Three step turn right sideward, arms sideward, forward, sideward, and place left foot in rear, left arm overhead, 4 measures.

B. Repeat A opposite, 24 measures.

PART II. (32 Measures.)

A. 1. Stamp right (facing right and raising left leg as in balance hop) and hold, 1 measure; hop twice right, completing turn right, 1 measure. The right arm is high overhead and the left arm sideward. Balance step left sideward, right arm forward; right sideward, left arm forward, 2 measures. The balance step is to be done with a leaping movement on the first count and with opposite foot placed in front (4 measures).

2. Repeat 1 opposite, 4 measures.

3. Two glides right sideward, arms sideward, 2 measures; three step turn right, arms forward and sideward, and swing left leg forward, left arm forward, 2 measures (4 measures).

4. Repeat 3 opposite, 4 measures.

B. Repeat A, 16 measures.

PART III. (32 Measures.)

A. 1. Balance hop right forward, left arm overhead, right arm sideward, 1 measure; swing hop left backward, left arm sideward, right arm forward, 1 measure; step right foot rear of left, step left sideward, step right foot front of left, arms sideward, 2 measures (4 measures).

2. Repeat 1 opposite, 4 measures.

3. Swing hop right forward, left arm forward, right arm sideward, 1 measure; swing hop left forward, right arm forward, left arm sideward, 1 measure; swing hop right forward, 1 measure; swing hop left forward, 1 measure (4 measures).

4. Three steps backward, arms sideward, and point left foot forward, left arm forward, 4 measures.

B. Repeat A opposite, 16 measures.

PART IV. (32 Measures.)

A. 1. Step and curtsy right sideward, arms sideward on step, left arm forward on curtsy, 2 measures; repeat opposite, 2 measures (4 measures).

2. Three step turn right, arms sideward, forward, sideward, 2 measures; place left foot in rear of right and hold left arm overhead, 2 measures (4 measures).

3. Repeat 1 opposite, 4 measures.

4. Repeat 2 opposite, 4 measures.

B.   Repeat A, 16 measures.

PART V. (48 Measures.)

Repeat Part I, 48 measures.

COMPOSITION No. 21.

An Aesthetic Dance.

"THE NYMPHS"

Music: "The Watz Is Made for Love"—Kalman. Victor Record 18972.

Formation: The pupils are arranged in fours, the tallest ones on the right. They march forward in closed ranks and, upon command, open ranks left sideward in 12 counts.

Beginning at the right, number the girls 1, 2, 3, 4; Numbers 1 and 2, and Numbers 3 and 4 are partners.

PART I. (32 Measures.)

1. Moving obliquely right forward, swing hop right forward, wave left arm forward, 1 measure; swing hop left forward, wave right arm forward, 1 measure; two steps forward, arms sideward, 1 measure; balance hop right forward, left arm overhead, right arm sideward, 1 measure (4 measures).

2. Moving obliquely left backward, swing hop left backward, wave right arm forward, 1 measure; swing hop right backward, wave left arm forward, 1 measure; pirouette left, wave arms forward and sideward, 2 measures (4 measures).

3. Repeat 1 opposite, 4 measures.

4. Repeat 2 opposite, 4 measures.

5. Repeat 1, 4 measures.

Repeat 2, 4 measures.

7. Hop on the right foot, raising the left straight leg obliquely forward, 1 measure; change step left forward (short steps), left arm raised forward, 1 measure; repeat opposite, 2 measures (4 measures).

8. Three steps backward, place the right foot in rear of left and bend knees very slightly, arms sideward, 4 measures (4 measures).

PART II. (32 Measures).

Partners grasp hands across.

1. Numbers 2 and 4, beginning with the right foot, make a bounding turn right, landing to the right of partners, 2 measures; Numbers 1 and 3 repeat this, 2 measures. Partners release hands and take a three-step-turn right, waving arms forward and sideward, 3 measures; place the left foot in rear and slightly bend the knees, arms sideward, 1 measure (8 measures).

NOTE—At the end of the bounding turn there is a transfer of weight in order to be ready for the three-step-turn.

2. Repeat 1 opposite, 8 measures.

3. Repeat 1, 8 measures.

4. Repeat 2, 8 measures.

PART III. (10 Measures.)

1. Face right, step right forward, 1 measure; swing the left leg forward, waving the left arm forward, 1 measure; swing the left leg backward, waving the left arm sideward, 1 measure; turn left about and change step left forward, arms sideward, 1 measure (4 measures).

2. Swing the right leg forward, waving the right arm forward, 1 measure; swing the right leg backward, waving the right arm sideward, 1 measure; turn right about and change step right forward, arms sideward, 1 measure (4 measures).

3. Face front and balance step left sideward, waving right arm forward, 1 measure; balance step right sideward, waving left arm forward, 1 measure (2 measures).

PART IV. (32 Measures.)

Repeat Part I, beginning left, but take the three steps backward toward partner, facing partner on the last count, right shoulder to right shoulder. The arms are sideward, the right arm extending back of partner.

PART V.   (15 Measures.)

1.   Balance hop left forward, 1 measure; swing hop right backward, 1 measure; balance hop left forward, 1 measure; swing hop right backward, 1 measure (4 measures).

2.   Beginning left, in eight running steps circle clockwise around partner (back to back), finishing left shoulder to left shoulder, 4 measures.

3.   Repeat 1, 4 measures.

4.   Beginning left, in four steps circle anti-clockwise (back to back), 2 measures. Return to places, facing front, 1 measure (3 measures).

(A left-about turn is necessary for Numbers 2 and 4 to return to places.)

PART VI.   (17 Measures.)

1.   Moving obliquely left forward, three short running steps, arms sideward, 1 measure; balance hop right forward, left arm overhead, 1 measure; three steps obliquely right backward, arms sideward, 2 measures (4 measures).

2.   Repeat 1 opposite, 4 measures.

3.   Repeat 1, 4 measures.

4.   Three-step-turn right, waving arms forward and sideward, 3 measures; face partner and take two steps toward partner, finishing right shoulder to right shoulder, arms sideward, right arm extending back of partner (as at finish of Part IV), 2 measures (5 measures).

PART VII.   (15 Measures.)

Repeat Part V.

PART VIII.   (17 Measures.)

1.   Three steps forward, arms sideward, 1 measure; balance hop right forward, left arm overhead, 1 measure (2 measures).

2.   Repeat 1, 2 measures.

3.   Repeat 1, 2 measures.

4.   Three steps forward, arms sideward, 1 measure; pirouette right, both arms overhead, 1 measure (2 measures).

5.   Step right sideward, step on left foot crossed in rear of right (bending knees), 2 measures.

6. Repeat 5, 2 measures.

7. Pirouette right, waving arms forward and sideward, 1 measure; repeat, 1 measure (2 measures).

8. Step right sideward, arms sideward, 1 measure; place left foot in rear, left arm overhead, and hold, 2 measures (3 measures).

APPENDIX II.

The Revival of the Play Spirit in America—A Pageant.

In a beautiful country, many years ago, so a real story tells us, every one led a free and happy life, until one day an evil appeared. The evil, small at first, by and by grew so big that misery and discontent prevailed throughout the land. Then, one day, a fairy came and, wafting her wand, dispelled the evil, and so brought happiness once more to all.

So it was in our country before the time of cities, when every man's playground lay before his own door. The happy life in the open was free to all. This passed with the establishment of villages and towns, which, through the advantages of closer living, grew into cities.

The lure of the city, with its promise of wealth and success, attracted great numbers of men and women. Their gain proved their loss when the city robbed their children of the chance to play and the active life of their forefathers.

In recognition of this loss the gospel of purposeful physical education is now being preached, so as to give to every one the great knowledge of how best to use his leisure so that health and happiness may once more be the privilege of all, and in a small measure compensate for the adventure, romance and beauty that have passed.

THE PROGRAM.

OVERTURE—"Zampa" . . . .*Herold*

PROLOGUE.

The Suppression of the Play Spirit.

The Play Spirit of the human race, symbolized by little children, expresses itself in dance and play.

"The Secret". . . . . *Gautier*

The play is interrupted by the appearance of Civilization, who majestically advances.

The Play Spirit is suppressed as Civilization, with its modern economic conditions, dominates the scene.

"Pomp and Circumstance". . . . . *Elgar*

329

Scene I.

The Land of the Red Man.

(America an Ideal Playground.)

"The Red Man"..*Sousa*

The Indian chief and braves come seeking new hunting grounds. The squaws and children follow, bringing to the new village the trappings of the tribe, which they put in order while the youths and men engage in games and dances.

"Natoma"..*Victor Herbert*

An Indian youth brings news of strange white men coming toward the village. In great excitement all gather together and await their approach.

Scene II.

Arrival of the White Man.

A group of early settlers, in their explorations, come upon the Indian village. They wish to trade for the land. The Indians agree, after much bargaining, to give up land for the finery and trinkets offered them.

The new settlers establish the claim and go to bring their fellow-colonists.

Scene III.

The Playground Occupied by the White Man.

During the early years of our history, the settlers had to hunt, fish, clear and plant the land and build homes. Yet in their leisure there was time and spirit for the rollicking dances of the farmers and milkmaids and for the celebration of the hunters' and fishermen's day's success.

"The Shepherds' Dance".....................................*German*

"Gathering Peascods"—Folk Dance Music................*Cecil Sharpe*

Scene IV.

Establishment of the City.

"Polonaise Militaire".......................................*Chopin*

The spirit of progress prompts men and women to seek new careers through the various avenues of manufacturing, education, commerce, science and the arts.

The country of yesterday becomes the city of today.

SCENE V.
The Mad Rush of Modern Times.
(A Typical Street Scene.)

In the tenseness and crowdedness of city life, of modern competition and eagerness for careers, money becomes the great driving power, and in the blind rush of the motley throng, there is no time for play.

SCENE VI.
Revival of the Play Spirit.
"Marcia Militaire"..*Vessella*

Modern physical education recalls the lost Play Spirit.

The dance of the little children typifies the revival of the Play Spirit—the hope of modern physical education is realized.

SCENE VII.
Evidences of the Reawakened Play Spirit.

Camp-fire girls, boy scouts and similar organizations afford opportunities to boys and girls for playful activities.

SCENE VIII.
Effect of the Revived Play Spirit in Our Modern System of Education.

Baseball Drill—"Chin-Chin".....................*Caldwell and Caryll*
Aesthetic Dance—"Isoline"............................*Messenger*
Folk Dance—"Crested Hen".............................*Burchenal*
Folk Dance—"Come, Let Us be Joyful".....................*Mozart*

EPILOGUE.
The Play Spirit Re-established.

The modern conception of play brings joy to the little children, symbolizing the Play Spirit, and in gay mood they dance.

"Amaryllis"........................*Louis XIII, arranged by Ghys*

CONCERNING THE PAGEANT.

The pageant requires from two to two and a half hours for its performance, and may be given outdoors or indoors. The outdoor setting should have a semi-circular background of trees, if possible. Indoors, choose a woodland scene for all scenes except Scene V, in which an American street background should be used.

The pageant is so written that it is possible for a number of schools to take part, as the dances are done in groups, each school training one or more groups. Some whole scenes can be given by one school, as the Indian scene, the Street scene, and the Establishment of the City. In the Philadelphia production forty schools took part.

School orchestras can be utilized for playing part of the music.

ACTION OF THE PAGEANT.

PROLOGUE.

Musical selection, overture, "Zampa," Victor Record 35,584, Parts I and II.

During Part II of the overture, the Play Spirits enter in a natural manner, walking, skipping, running, or picking flowers, from entrance right rear, and gradually move to their places for their dance.

At the end of the overture groups of six join hands, facing front, in position for their dance.

Dance by Play Spirits, "The Secret," Victor Record 17,689.

At the end of the dance, the children scatter, some to play, others to gather flowers, talk in groups, etc.

One Play Spirit near entrance is startled by the approach of Civilization. She turns and runs to the other children, pointing to what she sees. All gather closer together at the far end of the field and look on in awed surprise while some run off as Civilization advances in pantomime march.

Dance by Civilization, "Pomp and Circumstance," Victor Record 35,247.

The remaining Play Spirits, in spite of their fear, try to dance, but as Civilization draws nearer, the children scatter, rushing off in all directions. Civilization turning slowly, follows Play Spirits off the field with arms raised.

SCENE I.

Musical Selection, "The Red Man," Sousa.

This music is incidental to the action.

An Indian chief and a few Indian men enter, gesticulating to show the idea of looking over the ground for a new village, and decide upon this place. An Indian boy comes on with a pack horse, followed by squaws carrying tents, etc. Horses, men, children follow. Men of the first group order the women to pitch tents, pointing to location.

The chief and other men, after having carefully looked over the entire space chosen for the village, lie on the ground in groups, smoking, mending bows, etc. The boys form a circle and play near the men, while the latter watch.

Game by Indian Boys, "Ten Little Indian Boys."

They move off to try their bows and arrows, while the men rise slowly and form a circle for their dance.

Dance by Indian Men, "Natoma," Victor Record 70,049.

An Indian runner enters at the end of the dance, goes to the chief and tells of the approach of white men, pointing in their direction. All gather and watch their approach.

SCENE II.

A group of white men enter and halt in the background. The leader advances as the Indian chief steps forward. By gestures the white man shows his friendliness and desire to buy the land. The Indians come closer and the chief turns to his braves for conference. The Indians show their willingness to exchange land for the offerings of the white men. They gather about them curiously and look over the trinkets. The chief accepts the finery, while the braves turn and hurry the squaws to gather their belongings and take up tents, etc. As the Indians depart the white men explore the ground, expressing satisfaction by gestures on the exchange made with the Indians. They establish their claim by planting a flag, as they sing.

Song by White Men, "Oh God, Our Help in Ages Past," "St. Anne's."

They go out to bring their fellow-colonists.

SCENE III.

Farmers and Milkmaids enter in couples, dancing, as they move around in a large circle, and separate into smaller circles.

Entrance Dance by Farmers and Milkmaids, "Shepherds' Dance," Victor Record 35,530.

At its conclusion, by facing inward, they are in position for the next dance.

Dance by Farmers and Milkmaids, "Gathering Peascods," Victor Record 18,010.

After this the couples move to a semi-circular formation at the back of stage, singing and dancing.

Dance and Song by Farmers and Milkmaids, "Coming Thro' the Rye."

They act as audience to Fishermen and Hunters, and help them to sing their songs.

The Fishermen enter (Farmers and Milkmaids cheer, waving handkerchiefs), and take center stage, singing.

Song by Fishermen, "Fisher's Song."

They retire up stage right as the Hunters enter, singing, and advance down stage left (action suited to song as they put down game).

Song by Hunters, "The Mountain Bear."

Farmers, Milkmaids and Fishermen go off during the last verse, as the Hunters take up game and march around the field and exit.

SCENE IV.

Musical Selection, "Polonaise Militaire," Victor Record 35,241.

This music is incidental to the scene.

A platform should be placed down stage at the left.

Enter at center back, twelve heralds in twos, with trumpets raised in playing position. They march forward and group themselves on each side of the platform. All mark time in this position until Progress and followers are on the platform—lower trumpets and halt.

Progress follows the heralds at a distance of twenty feet. She marches to the front and takes position on center of the platform. At distances of eight feet, Manufacturing, etc., follow in this order: (1) Manufacturing, (2)

Commerce, (3) Education, (4) Science, (5) The Arts, and group around Progress as central figure.

The Seekers of Progress enter from rear in groups in scattered fashion, approach the front of the platform, and kneel with extended arms, appealing to Progress.

Progress takes Manufacturing by the hand and steps out to the center front of the platform, and bids (by gesture) the Seekers of Manufacturing to follow. Manufacturing steps down from the platform and leads down center to exit. The seekers of Manufacturing rise at the bidding of Progress and follow.

Progress repeats this pantomime with each in turn—Commerce, Education, Science and The Arts.

As The Arts lead off, Progress steps down from the platform and with arms raised obliquely upward, marches down center from the platform and off.

The heralds march forward to center and meet partners, where they turn to rear and follow Progress, trumpets raised.

SCENE V.

Enter a hurdy-gurdy man, who takes his place in middle of stage and begins to play. Children enter, running after the hurdy-gurdy and group themselves about it. Girls gallop around. Boys watch, hands in pockets, for a while, and then begin to play marbles. Girls begin skipping rope.

People enter from opposite directions, showing the movement, to and fro, of a busy street. Some enter in twos, others alone, carrying market baskets, traveling bags, etc. A newsboy follows men, trying to sell papers. Two others come on and take positions, one near the hurdy-gurdy man, the other near the far end of the street.

Fakers and newsboys call out wares.

Enter, on stilts, the "Money Man," who passes down the street, followed by a mob. All turn and rush after him, as he exits. As the hurdy-gurdy man stops, the orchestra plays.

Musical Selection, any popular air.

SCENE VI (If Shown Outdoors).

Musical Selection, "Marcia Militaire," Victor Record 35,258.

The Spirit of Physical Education enters on a horse, gallops around the field, waving a scarf overhead to recall the Play Spirits. The Play Spirits appear, peeping from behind trees. They beckon to each other as they step forward timidly, pointing to the rider. To express their joy at coming back, they jump up and down, clapping their hands, and then run forward to their places for the dance, while the rider wheels her horse to the left, down stage, and watches the dance.

Dance by the Play Spirits, "The Secret," Victor Record 17,689.

At the end of the dance, Physical Education makes exit.

The Play Spirits retire up stage right, where they watch with animation and great interest, the numbers following, showing their joy by applause.

SCENE VI (If Shown Indoors).

Musical Selection, "Marcia Militaire," Victor Record 35,258.

The Spirit of Physical Education dances in to music, and by her dancing and gestures, shows that she wants to recall the Play Spirits.

The Play Spirits appear, peeping from behind trees. They beckon to each other, and step forward timidly and follow the dancer, trying to imitate her. She goes down stage left, where she watches the dance of the Play Spirits.

Dance by the Play Spirits, "The Secret," Victor Record 17,689.

At the end of their dance, the Play Spirits join the Spirit of Physical Education down stage, where they watch with animation and interest the numbers following, showing their appreciation by applause.

SCENE VII.

Camp Fire Girls in their ceremonies (and exit).
Boy Scouts in their maneuvers (and exit).

SCENE VIII.

Baseball Boys run on, and take their places for Baseball Drill, after which they run off in a natural manner.

Drill by Baseball Boys, "Chin Chin," Victor Record 35,432.

Dance by Girls, "Isoline," Victor Record 37,201.

Musical Selection, "The Thunderer," Victor Record 16,151.

Folk Dancers enter in threes (a boy and two girls) and march to places for the first dance.

Dance by Boys and Girls, "The Crested Hen," Victor Record 17,159.

After this the sets face for the next dance.

Dance by Boys and Girls, "Come Let Us Be Joyful," Victor Record 17,161.

Musical Selection, "The Thunderer," Victor Record 16,151.

At the end they face in line of march and exit.

When "Come Let Us Be Joyful" is being done the last time, the Play Spirits exit quietly, get balloons and advance to positions for their last dance as the Folk Dancers are marching off.

Epilogue.

Dance by Play Spirits, "Amaryllis," Victor Record 16,174.

On the last four measures of "Amaryllis," the Play Spirits gradually, by twos and threes, let go of their balloons and slowly back off the stage, gazing after them.

CHARACTERS AND PROPERTIES.

(The numbers mentioned were used in the Philadelphia production.)

The characters may all be chosen from school children, using the taller ones for the men and women.

The numbers may be increased or diminished according to the size of the stage.

Prologue.

Eighty-four Play Spirits (very little girls), twenty-four Civilization (tall girls).

Costumes.

SCENE I.

Thirty Indian Men, fifteen squaws, twenty-five Indian Boys, twelve Indian Girls.

Costumes, five tents, six horses, three papooses, one tripod and kettle, fire.

SCENE II.

Twenty White Men.

Costumes, one flag, guns, beads, trinkets.

SCENE III.

Thirty-six Farmers, thirty-six Milkmaids, forty Fishermen, forty Hunters.

Costumes, fishing rods, guns or bows and arrows, game.

SCENE IV.

Twelve Heralds, one Progress, one Education, one Manufacturing, one Commerce, one Science, one Dancing, one Painting, one Sculpture, one Music, forty Seekers of Progress.

Costumes, twelve trumpets, one palette, one lyre, one vase, one wheel, one retort, one globe.

SCENE V.

Sixty-five Men (including policeman, candy man, white wings, balloon man), fifty-four Women, twenty-five Boys (including newsboys, telegraph boy), one Money Man.

Modern costumes, hurdy-gurdy, push cart, balloons, jumping ropes, newspapers.

SCENE VI.

One Girl, same eighty-four Play Spirits.

Costume, horse (for outdoor).

SCENE VII.

Fifty Camp Fire Girls, fifty Boy Scouts.

Costumes.

SCENE VIII.

Seventy-two Baseball Boys, eighty Girls in Aesthetic Dance, one hundred and eight Folk Dancers.

Suits, costumes.

EPILOGUE.

Eighty-four Play Spirits (same as in Prologue).

Eighty-four balloons.

Total, nine hundred and thirty-four participants.

COSTUMES.

PROLOGUE.

The Play Spirits—The colors used for these costumes were orange, yellow-orange and yellow, with an underslip of yellow. In each group of six there were two of each color, the colors in a different order in each group.

The style was Grecian, of knee length, with low neck and no sleeves and a slightly raised waist line, the width at the shoulder seam, one and a half inches. No stockings were worn and the hair hanging.

For a girl four and a half feet tall the costume required two yards of cheesecloth for the dress, and one yard and twenty-five inches for the slip, the skirt of which was slit at the sides.

Civilization—The colors used were dark and light violet and cerise, with an underslip of dark blue. There were twice as many dark violet as light.

The style was Grecian, of ankle length, full and draped to the slip below the waist line. The sleeves were long and tight, with a flowing piece lined with cerise. This was attached to the shoulder and sleeve to the wrist, falling to the bottom of the skirt. A piece of the violet bunting was drawn tight across the forehead and allowed to fall just below the shoulders in the back, so as to cover the hair. Black shoes were worn.

The costume required eleven yards of violet cheesecloth, three and three-quarter yards of cerise, and two and one-half yards of dark blue.

SCENE I.

The Indians—The colors used were dark and light brown with red and yellow trimmings. Beads and feathers were used for decoration. The chief wore a long trailing headdress of feathers.

The papooses were made from flat grape basket lids with a stuffed rag baby.

The squaws wore no feathers. A little variation was made in the dress of the squaws by having them wear the costume of the Indians of the southwest, with brilliant red coloring and leg wrappings of white, and a red head cloth, falling in veil fashion from behind the ears.

SCENE II.

The White Men—The colors used were dark and light orange, brown, green, red and black.

The styles used were taken from the historic early settlers' costumes.

SCENE III.

The Farmers—The colors used were dark orange, bright blue and orange.

The trousers were long and of the dark orange. A tight-fitting double-breasted jacket of waist length, with an upstanding collar worn over a long-sleeved white shirt. The cap was orange, and full, being drawn into a band, as a chef's cap. Black slippers and white stockings were worn.

The costume required two yards of dark orange cambric, one yard of bright blue cambric and three-eighths of a yard of orange cambric.

The Milkmaids—The colors used were bright blue, yellow, orange, black, dark orange and white.

The skirt was a plain full skirt of bright blue. It came below the knee.

A long-sleeved blouse of white, with a round neck, was worn under a sleeveless black bodice, laced up the front.

An apron of yellow with a border on the bottom of black, two and one-half inches wide, between two orange bands one and one-quarter inches wide, was worn over the skirt and bodice.

The cap was of dark orange with a white flaring turnback in the front. They wore yellow hair, made of raveled rope, and white stockings and black slippers.

The costume required three and two-thirds yards of bright blue cambric, one yard of unbleached cheesecloth, three-quarters of a yard of yellow cambric, one-quarter of a yard of orange cambric, one yard of black, one-quarter of a yard of dark orange.

The Hunters—The colors used were dark and bright green, brown, and orange. The hunters wore dark green bloomers of knee length; an orange blouse, with a round collar, which turned over a brown Eton jacket.

A bright green Robin Hood's cap with an orange feather, and brown shoes and stockings complete this costume.

The costume required one and one-half yards of dark green cambric, one and one-quarter yards of orange cheesecloth, one and three-quarters yards of brown cambric, one-quarter of a yard of bright green cambric.

The Fishermen—The colors were brown, blue and orange.

The fishermen wore light brown trousers, blue blouses, with orange handkerchiefs knotted at the throat, and large round straw hats.

SCENE IV.

The Heralds—The heralds wore black bloomers and white blouses, under a jumper open at the sides, fastened only at the shoulders. The cape was made of black and white squares alternately arranged, the back the reverse of the front.

The heralds held brass trumpets, to which were attached banners on one side, black with a design of white, and on the other side the scheme reversed. A small black, turned-up hat with a white feather, and black shoes and stockings were worn.

Progress—Progress wore a long, full, rose Grecian gown, with flowing angel sleeves, weighted with a green tassel. A golden girdle with two green tassels passed in a high waist line in front, crossed in rear at the waist and passed to the front, where it was tied, the ends falling to the hem. A royal purple cloak, lined with green and bordered with canton flannel to represent ermine, was worn over the dress.   A golden bandeau studded with simulated jewels, held her flowing hair in place.

Manufacturing—Manufacturing wore short knee pants of light brown, a long narrow over-blouse of orange, a flowing light brown cloak with wide kimona sleeves lined with orange.   The brown belt of the cloak was worn across the orange blouse at the waist line.   He wore a small, round light brown cap and carried a wheel.

Commerce—Commerce wore a long, plain, blue-green coat with narrow sleeves.   A bright blue cape fell from the shoulders, with a belt of the same color fastened with a large golden buckle.   He wore a small hat of the blue-green, with a narrow turned-up brim of the bright blue and carried a large globe.

Education—Education wore a cap and gown.

Science—Science wore a sapphire blue gown, not unlike a man's dressing gown, with a black corded girdle.   The sleeves and neck were faced on the outside with a two-inch border of light brown.   He wore a blue skull cap and dark-rimmed spectacles.   He carried a retort.

Painting—Painting wore a yellow-green dress in Empire style.   The material had a large figure in it, like batik work.   A flowing cape of bright blue hung from the shoulders to the hem of the dress.

Dancing—Dancing wore a short green Grecian dancing costume.

Sculpture—Sculpture wore a long full white sleeveless robe after the Grecian style, with an over-slip below the waist line in front, and longer toward the sides and back.   She carried a white vase on her shoulder.

Music—Music wore a long, full yellow Grecian gown, caught in at a high waist line.   She wore a laurel wreath and carried a lyre.

Seekers of Progress—The colors were dark green, light green, red, dark blue, bright blue, orange, yellow and white.

Seekers wore a costume made by taking double width of the material the full length of back and front and cutting a hole in the middle for the neck.   The material then fell over the arms, simulating sleeves.   A band of the same color was worn around the head.

SCENE V.

Money Man—The money man wore a long yellow coat to which were sewn representations of gold coins and paper money.

SCENE VI.

Spirit of Physical Education—Outdoors—The spirit of physical education wore over a riding habit a light green-blue cape lined with yellow and waved a blue scarf.

Indoors—She wore a white Grecian dancing costume.

SCENE VIII.

Baseball Boys—The baseball boys wore modern baseball suits and caps.

Aesthetic Dancers—The colors were pink, light lavender, dark lavender and light blue. There were the same number of costumes of each color, but arranged irregularly.

The style was Grecian, draped to a high waist line and in line with the hips, no sleeves and low neck, the width at the shoulder seam two inches. There was an under-slip of white and the dress reached below the knees. The hair was worn hanging. The costume required three yards of colored cheesecloth and two and one-half yards of white cheesecloth for the slip.

Folk Dancers—Girls—The colors were red, black, white and green.

The girls wore a straight full skirt of red cambric, with a square-necked sleeveless waist of the same. A black band five inches wide bordered the skirt, four inches from the bottom, and bands two inches wide over the shoulders and around the bodice above the waist. There was a guimpe of unbleached muslin with long sleeves and black cuffs, and an apron of the same with two-inch wide strings of green cambric. There was a full cap of green with a white band across the front that had tabs at the side that extended to the shoulders. White stockings and black slippers were worn. The costume required four and three-quarters yards of red cambric, one and one-quarter yards of black cambric, two and one-eighth yards of white unbleached muslin, one-half yard of green cambric.

Boys—The colors were black, green, orange and white.

The boys wore short black trousers tied in below the knee, a long-sleeved unbleached muslin blouse with a Buster Brown collar, over which was a green Eton jacket, a sash of orange two yards long (one-half width of the material), which encircled the waist twice and tied at the side. They wore long pointed orange caps joined to a black band. The costume requires one and one-half yards of black cambric, three-quarters of a yard of green cambric, one and one-half yards of orange cambric, one and one-quarter yards of unbleached muslin.

NOTE—The material for the costumes was bought wholesale and distributed to the schools taking part. The costumes were made at the schools, through the co-operation of the schools and the homes, after colored designs made by the Art Department.

CHORUSES.

Scene II—Song by the White Men—St. Anne's, "Oh God, Our Help in Ages Past." (Franklin Assembly Song Book, page 93.)

Scene III—Song by the Fishermen—"Fishers' Song." (Educational Music Course, Fourth Reader, page 92.)

Song by the Hunters—"The Mountain Bear." (Educational Music Course, Fourth Reader, page 86.)

DESCRIPTION OF THE DANCES.

THE SECRET (Gautier).
Victor Record 17,689.

PART I. (16 Measures.)

Groups of six, facing front, hands joined.

Introduction, 2 measures.

All face to right and place left foot forward.

A. 1. Four skip-change steps forward, beginning left. 4 measures.

2. With half face left, one glide balance hop left, obliquely right forward, swinging joined hands obliquely fore-side-upward. 1 measure.

3. Three small running steps backward, arms sideward, dropping hands. 1 measure.

4. Pirouette left sideward, arms waving downward and inward and outward to position obliquely side-downward. 1 measure.

5. One step left sideward with arms sideward and place right foot obliquely left forward, turning trunk slightly to left, waving right arm obliquely right forward. 1 measure.

B. Repeat A to opposite side. 8 measures.

PART II. (16 Measures.)

A. 1. Glide balance hop left forward, waving both arms fore-upward. 1 measure.

2. Swing hop right backward, waving arms down and backward. 1 measure.

3. Four-fourths turn left with small running steps; wave left arm across body and from position obliquely side-downward right, wave arms to open position obliquely side-downward. 2 measures.

B. Repeat A, beginning right forward. 4 measures.

C. Nos. 1 and 2, 3 and 4, 5 and 6 face and join right hands and repeat A, running in circle, with free arm sideward. 4 measures.

D. Partners join left hands and beginning with right foot repeat C. 4 measures.

NOTE—This brings each back to place.

PART III. (16 Measures.)

A. Same as Part I, forming circle with four skip change steps. 8 measures.

B. Same as A, in opposite direction and return to place with running steps backward, pirouette and step and point. 8 measures.

PART IV. (16 Measures.)

Nos. 1, 3, 5 one-eighth turn left.

Nos. 2, 4, 6 three-eighths turn right and partners will be facing in an oblique position.

A. 1. Glide balance hop obliquely left forward, waving right arm overhead, left arm sideward. 1 measure.

2.   Step back right and point left obliquely forward, waving left arm obliquely forward and right arm sideward. 1 measure.

3.   Two glides left sideward, arms sideward. 1 measure.

4.   Step and deep curtsy left, waving right arm forward. 1 measure.

B.   Same to opposite side.   4 measures.

C.   Facing front, repeat A.   4 measures.

D.   Facing front, repeat B.   4 measures.

PART V.   (16 Measures.)

A.   1.   Nos. 2, 4, 6 clap three times, turning to left slightly.   1 measure.

2.   Nos. 1, 3, 5 run in three steps to other side of partners.   1 measure.

3.   With both hands joined partners in eight running steps swing around in a four-fourths turn left.   2 measures.

B.   Repeat A, Nos. 2, 4, 6 clapping to right three times.   Nos. 1, 3, 5 returning to place with the three running steps and four-fourths turn is taken to the right.   4 measures.

C.   Repeat A.   4 measures.

D.   Repeat B.   4 measures.

PART VI.   (16 Measures.)

Repeat Part IV.

PART VII.   (16 Measures.)

Repeat Part I.

At the end of Part VII children run away to the last measures of music.

CIVILIZATION.

Music, "Pomp and Circumstance," Elgar.   Victor Record 35,247-A.

NOTE—In single flank line with arms' length distance count off by threes.   No. 3 stands still, No. 2's march sideward right one step, No. 1's march sideward right two steps.   Enter in this formation.

PART I. (16 Measures.)

A. On an oblique line toward the middle of the left side of the stage, sixteen walking steps, beginning with the right foot, two counts to each step. The left arm is raised obliquely fore-upward and the right arm backward during the first four steps. Reverse arm positions every fourth step. 8 measures.

NOTE—At end of the 8 measures all are on the stage.

B. 1. With three steps a full turn to the right on place (right, left, right, hold), swinging right clenched hand overhead. 1 measure.

2. Hold threatening attitude. 1 measure.

3. Two steps forward (left counts 1 and 2), (right counts 3 and 4). 1 measure.

4. Three steps forward, counts 1, 2, 3, and hold count 4. 1 measure. Repeat B. 4 measures.

INTERLUDE. (3 Measures.)

1. Eight crouching steps in circle left. 2 measures.

2. With three steps on place a full turn to the right and hold. 1 measure.

PART II. (14 Measures.)

A. 1. Starting left four walking steps forward (2 counts to each step). 2 measures.

2. Step left forward, swing arms obliquely fore-upward and hold. 1 measure.

3. Swing arms down and backward, hands clenched. 1 measure.

4. Repeat 2, stepping right forward. 1 measure.

5. Repeat 3. 1 measure.

6. Stamp left forward and swing right arm to bent position over head. 1 measure.

7. Stamp right forward and swing left arm to bent position over head. 1 measure.

8. Three steps forward and hold, left, right, left. 1 measure.

9. Twirl to right five times and hold attitude toward rear with arms raised obliquely fore-upward. 4 measures.

Turn to front, keeping weight on left foot, which is back. 1 measure.

PART III. (20 Measures.)

A. 1. Seven steps forward and close heels, raising arms fore-upward to position obliquely side-upward. 4 measures.

2. Stand still, waving arms forward to a crossed position, shoulder high, and then sideward. 4 measures.

B. Repeat A. 8 measures.

C. 1. Step obliquely forward right, waving left arm obliquely side-upward, right arm obliquely side-downward and turn trunk to right. 2 measures.

2. Repeat 1 to opposite side. 2 measures.

PART IV. (14 Measures.)

Like Part II, but facing front.

PART V. (24 Measures.)

A. Like A of Part III, but stepping backward. 8 measures.

B. Like B of Part III. 8 measures.

C. Like C of Part III. 4 measures.

D. Twirl right seven times to rear and pose facing rear, arms obliquely side-upward. 4 measures.

NOTE—During Part I, Interlude and Part II the line of direction is a circle right, finishing with the three lines facing front, parallel to the front of stage. During the whole dance individuals keep the same relative positions. During the last seven twirls of dance all should get into a single line, so as to be able to step back of nearest trees for exit.

THE INDIANS—Song for Indian Boys.

PART I.

Music, "Playing Indian," The Song Series, Book I, Alys E. Bentley.

	Line
Come, let's play we're Indian chiefs •	1
Way out in the West;	2
I will be the Big Chief, because	3
I'm braver than the rest.	4
Let's take a bow and arrow	5
And go hunting every day,	6
With the *Indians* who live	7
Across the way. (Indian war whoop.)	8

NOTE—During lines 1, 2, 3 and 4 of Part I all with crouching steps walk in circle left.   During line 3 one boy goes to center of circle to be chief. During lines 5, 6, 7 and 8 all kneel and assume position of shooting with bow and arrow.

PART II.

Music, "Children's Singing Games," Mari Hofer.

	Line
John Brown *had* a little Indian,	1
John Brown *had* a little Indian,	2
John Brown *had* a little Indian,	3
One little Indian boy,	4
One little, two little, three little Indians,	5
Four little, five little, six little Indians,	6
Seven little, eight little, nine little Indians,	7
Ten little Indian boys.	8

NOTE—On "had," of lines 1, 2 and 3, of Part II, children stamp once (same foot each time).   During lines 5, 6, 7 and 8, of Part II, the chief chooses children to go into the ring until there are ten children chosen.

PART III.

	Line
Round the ring with a boom-za-la,	1
A boom-za-la, a boom-za-la.	2
Round the ring with a boom-za-la,	3
Ten little Indian boys.	4

During lines 1, 2, 3 and 4, of Part III, all children in both circles gallop sideward left.

PART IV.

Yell

A boosh! A bash! A rick chick chick,
A boosh! A bash! A rick chick chick,
Ten little Indian boys!

Pull right ear on word *a boosh*, count 1 and.
Pull left ear on word *a bash*, count 2 and.
Pull right ear on word *a rick*, count 1.
Pull left ear on word *chick*, count and.
Pull right ear on word *chick*, count 2 and.

PART V.

Ten little, nine little, eight little Indians,
Seven little, six little, five little Indians,
Four little, three little, two little Indians,
One little Indian boy.

During Part V Indians go to places one by one until all are back into first circle.

Play the game twice.

INDIAN DANCE FOR MEN.

Music, "Natoma," Victor Herbert. Victor Record 70,049.

INTRODUCTION. (2 Measures.)

NOTE 1—During introduction all form into circle for dance.

NOTE 2—Execute all walking steps with knee raising, stepping on toes on first count and coming down with heel on second count. Unless otherwise stated, forearms are raised forward to little more than a right angle, the left arm slightly higher than right, fingers are spread and thumbs pointed up. During walking steps reverse arm positions on each step, the movement done from the elbows. During side jumps arms are held in bent position. During forward jumps arms move to a position obliquely side-upward and during backward jumps arms are brought back to bent arm position.

PART I. (16 Measures.)

A. 1. In circle left, beginning with right foot, four walking steps forward. 2 measures.

2. Facing center, two jumps sideward right and hold two counts. 1 measure.

3. Two jumps sideward right and hold two counts. 1 measure.

NOTE—Jumps executed with heels, toes and knees together.

B. Repeat A. 4 measures.

C. 1. As 1 of A. 2 measures.

2. As 2 of A, jumping forward toward center. 1 measure.

3. As 3 of A, jumping forward toward center. 1 measure.

4. Two jumps backward, counts 1 and 2, hold third count and step back with right foot on fourth count. 1 measure.

5. One jump backward on first count and hold three counts. 1 measure.

6. One step right backward and jump backward, counts 1 and 2, hold counts 3 and 4. 1 measure.

7. Hold. 1 measure.

INTERLUDE. (2 Measures.)

During interlude stand still with arms folded.

PART II. (16 Measures.)

Like Part I.

PART III. (10 Measures.)

A. 1. In circle left, march in place three steps, beginning with right foot (right, left, right), and hold left knee up on fourth count. 1 measure.

2.   Replace left foot and bend knees on first count, straighten knees on second, bend on third, and straighten on fourth.   In bending keep knees and feet closed, and moving from elbows swing arms down and return on knee straightening.   1 measure.

3.   As 1.   1 measure.

4.   As 2.   1 measure.

B.   1.   Step sideward right with right foot on first count, crossing in rear, step on left foot on second count, step right sideward on third count, and crossing in front step on left foot on fourth count.   1 measure.

2.   Step back on right foot on first count, step sideward left with left foot on second count, crossing in front step on right foot on third count and step sideward left on fourth count.   1 measure.

C.   As A of this part.   4 measures.

PART IV.   (16 Measures.)

Like Part I.

PART V.   (7 Measures.)

A.   Like A, of Part III.   4 measures.

B.   1.   Facing center, bend trunk fore-downward, lowering arms.   1 measure.

2.   Straighten trunk and fling arms upward.   1 measure.

3.   Hold and give Indian yell.   1 measure.

ENTRANCE FOR FARMERS AND MILKMAIDS.

SCENE III.

Music, "Shepherd's Dance," Ed. German (Henry VIII).   Victor Record 35,530.

NOTE—In the following steps only the first 16 measures of the music are used, repeating these as often as is necessary.

Enter in couples, man on lady's left, inside hands joined, outside hands placed below hip.

A.   1.   Beginning with outside foot, three steps forward and point inside foot forward.   1 measure.

2. Repeat 1, beginning with the inside foot. 1 measure.
3. Repeat 1. 1 measure.
4. Repeat 2. 1 measure.

In line of March:

B. 1. Partners facing, four glides sideward. 1 measure.
2. Partners back to back, four glides sideward. 1 measure.
3. Repeat 1. 1 measure.
4. Repeat 2. 1 measure.

C. 1. Beginning with outside foot, four steps forward. 1 measure.
2. Partners facing, lady steps right sideward on counts 1 and 2, and steps backward on left foot, bending left knee deeply, counts 3 and 4. Man steps sideward left, counts 1 and 2, closes right foot to left and bows, counts 3 and 4. 1 measure.
3. Like 1. 1 measure.
4. Like 2. 1 measure.

D. 1. Facing front, begin with outside foot and take two swing-hops forward. 1 measure.
2. Four walking steps forward. 1 measure.
3. Repeat 1. 1 measure.
4. Repeat 2. 1 measure.

GATHERING PEASCODS.

Victor Record 18,010. For description of dance see page 196.

COMING THROUGH THE RYE.

If a body meet a body comin' thro' the rye,
If a body kiss a body, need a body cry?
Ev'ry lassie has her laddie,
    Nane, they say, ha'e I;
Yet a' the lads they smile on me,
    (When) comin' thro' the rye.

Couples, inside hands joined, outside hands with knuckles on hips. Begin with outside foot.

A. 1. Place the foot forward, heel touching, 1 "and"; place the foot backward, toe touching, 2 "and." 1 measure.

2. Change step, 3 "and" 4 "and."

3. Like 1, inside foot, 5 "and," 6 "and."

4. Like 2, inside foot, 7 "and," 8 "and" (facing inward and about), (8 counts). 1 measure.

B. Same as A, finishing by facing partner (8 counts). 2 measures.

NOTE—As heel is placed forward lower trunk forward, as toe is placed backward, raise trunk and turn head over opposite shoulder.

C. Four swing hops sideward, bending trunk to opposite side (8 counts). 2 measures.

(First swing hop is taken toward leaders.)

D. Four glides sideward in the line of direction and facing front, four slow walking steps forward, closing on heels on last count (8 counts). 2 measures.

BASEBALL DRILL FOR BOYS.

Use as many groups of nine as wanted.

Music, "Chin Chin Fox Trot," Victor Record 35,432-A.

INTRODUCTION.

Boys at attention, facing front, arranged as in diagram (8 counts).

PART I.

A. Pitching. (Hands clinch) (8 counts).

1-2. Raise right arm sideward, two and one-quarter right arm circles outward.

3. Raise arms fore-upward, hands meet overhead.

4. Hold position.

5-6. Raise left knee, lunge sideward left, throw ball to left with right hand. (During this movement the body makes a quarter turn left, left arm swings backward and right heel is raised.) (See Fig. 1.)

FIG. 1.

7-8. Position.

B. Batting (8 counts).
   1-2. Stride sideward left, hit bat on home-plate in front.
   3-4. Bend right knee, swing bat over right
        shoulder.
   5-6. Change knee bend, raising right heel. Strike
        forward. (During this movement the
        body makes a quarter turn left, and bat
        is shoulder high in front.) (See Fig. 2.)
   7-8. Position.

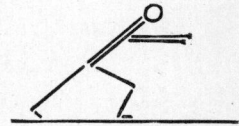

FIG. 2.

C. Pitching. Repeat A. (8 counts.)
D. Batting. Repeat B. (8 counts.)
E. Interlude. (8 counts.)
   1-2. Two gallops sideward left.
   3. Jump sideward left to deep knee bend,
      catch ball low in front. (See Fig. 3.)
   4. Throw right forward, left arm swings backward.
   5-8. Repeat 1-4 to the opposite side (40 counts).

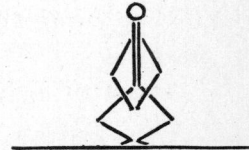

FIG. 3.

Part II.

A. Catching and Throwing. (8 counts.)
   1-2. Stride sideward left, hands on knees.
   3-4. Bend left knee, clap hands to catch ball
        outside left knee. (See Fig. 4.)
   5-6. Lunge obliquely forward right with left leg. Throw ball in
        same direction with right hand. (Right arm remains shoulder
        high, left arm swings backward.)
   7-8. Position.

FIG. 4.

B. Running, Catching and Tagging. (8 counts.)
   1-2. Run forward three steps, start left.
   3. Jump forward, clap hands to catch ball
      overhead. (See Fig. 6.)
   4. Land with slight knee bend, heels closed.
   5-6. Lunge sideward right, bend trunk right. Tag
        with ball obliquely downward with right hand. (See Fig. 5.)

FIG. 5.

7-8. Position.

C. Catching and Throwing. Repeat A. (8 counts.)

D. Running, Catching and Tagging. (8 counts.)

1-2. Run backward three steps, start left.

3. Jump backward, clap hands to catch ball overhead. (See Fig. 6.)

4-8. Repeat, same counts as B.

E. Interlude. (4 counts.)

1. Lunge left forward. Throw ball straight forward right, left arm swings backward.

2-3. Hold position.

4. Position. (36 counts.)

FIG. 6.

PART III.

Like Part II. (36 counts.)

PART IV—Base Running.

Bases are at least 8 feet apart.

Nos. 1, 3, 7, 9, fielders, face No. 5.

Nos. 2, 4, 6, 8, runners, face No. 5.

Batters (on home-plate) left shoulder to No. 5.

No. 5, pitcher, left shoulder to home-plate.

A. Following exercises (a, b, c, d, e) are executed at same time in unison (counts 1 to 8).

(a) Pitcher, No. 5 (hands clinch, raise right arm sideward).

1. Two and one-quarter right arm circles outward.

2. Raise arms fore-upward, hands meet overhead, raise left knee.

3. Lunge sideward left, throw ball to left with right hand. (The body makes a quarter turn left, right arm is forward, left arm swings backward.)

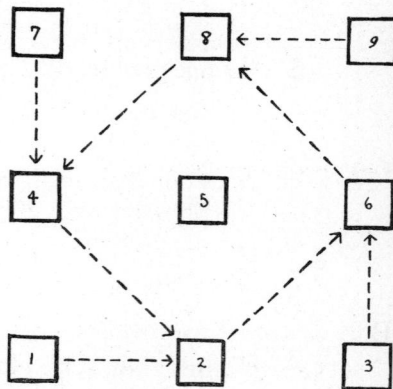

4.   Hold position.

5-6.   Position.

7.   Turns to receive ball from fielder No. 3.

8.   Position.

(b)   Batter No. 2.

1.   Stride sideward left, hit bat on home-plate in front.

2.   Bend right knee, swing bat over right shoulder.

3.   Change knee bend, raise right heel, strike forward.   (The body makes a quarter turn left, and the bat is shoulder high in front.)

4.   Hold position.

5-6.   Run three steps (right, left, right) to base. Slide right foot for base.

7-8.   Position.

(c)   Runners Nos. 4, 6, 8.

1-2-3-4.   Two steps right sideward toward diagonal base.

5-6.   Run three steps (right, left, right) to base.

7-8.   Position on base.

(d)   Fielder Catching and Tagging, No. 3.

1-2.   Stride sideward right, hands on knees.

3.   Hold position.

4.   Jump up to catch ball overhead.

5-6.   Run to base on right and tag runner.

7.   Throw ball to pitcher with right hand.

8.   Position (left side of base).   During next counts 1, 2, 3, 4, return to own base, 5, 6 hands on knees, 7, 8 position.

(e)   Fielders, Nos. 1, 7, 9.

1-2.   Stride sideward right, hands on knees.

3-4-5-6.   Hold position.

7-8.   Position.

B.   Counts 9 to 16.

(a)   Pitcher, No. 5.   Repeats exercise A (a), but catches ball from No. 9.

(b)   Batter, No. 4.   Like A (b).

(c) Runners, Nos. 2, 6, 8. Like A (c).
(d) Fielder catching and tagging, No. 9. Like A (d).
(e) Fielders, Nos. 1, 3, 7. Like A (e).
C. Counts 17 to 24.
  (a) Pitcher, No. 5. Repeats exercise A (a), but catches ball from No. 7.
  (b) Batter, No. 8. Like A (b).
  (c) Runners, Nos. 2, 4, 6. Like A (c).
  (d) Fielder catching and tagging, No. 7. Like A (d).
  (e) Fielders, Nos. 1, 3, 9. Like A (e).
D. Counts 25 to 32.
  (a) Pitcher, No. 5. Repeats exercise A (a), but catches ball from No. 1.
  (b) Batter, No. 6. Like A (b).
  (c) Runners, Nos. 2, 4, 8. Like A (c).
  (d) Fielder catching and tagging, No. 1. Like A (d).
  (e) Fielders Nos. 3, 7, 9. Like A (e).

PART V.
Like Part IV. (32 counts.)

PART VI.
Like Part II. (36 counts.)

PART VII.
Like Part I. (40 counts.)

PART VIII.
Like Part II. (36 counts.)

AESTHETIC DANCE—"ISOLINE."

Formation, Class in open order.
Music, "Isoline," Messager. Victor Record 67,201.

INTRODUCTION.
1. Small running steps to places. 10 measures.

2. Step right sideward, cross left foot in rear and salute. 1 measure.

3. Repeat 2 in opposite direction. 1 measure.

4. Repeat 2 and 3. 2 measures.

PART I. (16 Measures.)

A. 1. Glide hop right forward, left arm overhead, right arm sideward, swing hop left backward, right arm forward, left arm sideward. 1 measure.

2. Step on the right foot, crossing in rear, waving right arm sideward, 1, 2; step left sideward, waving left arm forward, 3; glide obliquely left forward on right foot, holding arm position, 5, 6. 1 measure.

3. Waltz turn left (two waltz steps, beginning left), on line obliquely left forward, left arm in a circle overhead and right arm down and inward; reverse arm position on second waltz step. 1 measure.

4. Step obliquely left forward, arms sideward, swing right leg forward and wave right arm forward. Step right forward in the same direction, swing left leg forward, arms in opposite position. 1 measure.

B. 1. Like A 1, beginning left. 1 measure.

2. Like A 2. 1 measure.

3. Like A 3, turning right and moving obliquely right backward. 1 measure.

4. Pirouette right, waving arms down, inward and sideward. (Pirouette: Step right sideward with a quarter turn right, cross left leg in front placing left foot in rear of right, rise on toes and complete turn, transferring weight to left foot and pointing right forward.) 1 measure.

C. Like A. 4 measures.

D. Like B. 4 measures.

PART II. (8 Measures.)

A. 1. Pas de Basque right forward, waving left arm forward. Pas de Basque left forward, waving right arm foreward. (Pas de Basque: Leap right sideward, 1; glide on the left foot obliquely right forward, 2; cut right forward, 3.) 1 measure.

2. Like 1 of this part. 1 measure.

3. Three step turn right, arms sideward, place left foot obliquely right

backward with both arms raised to a circle overhead and trunk turned slightly to the left. Hold position. (Three step turn: While executing a whole turn right, take three steps right sideward.) 2 measures.

B. 1. Like A 1, beginning left and moving backward. 1 measure.
2. Like B 1. 1 measure.
3. Like A 3, opposite. 2 measures.

INTERMISSION.

With weight on left foot and right foot placed in rear, bend knees and bend trunk forward, waving arms downward and inward. 1 measure.

Straighten knees and raise trunk and wave arms to an open position sideward. 1 measure.

PART III. (16 Measures.)

Like Part I. 16 measures.

PART IV. (8 Measures.)

A. 1. Pas de Zephyr turn right. (Cut hop right backward, swinging left leg forward, waving left arm forward, 1, 2, 3; cross left foot over right and with a cut hop left make a whole turn right, swinging the right leg forward, waving the right arm forward, 4, 5, 6.) 1 measure.
2. Pas de Basque right, waving right arm sideward and left arm forward, same left with opposite arm movements. 1 measure.
3. Step right sideward with arms sideward, 1, 2, 3; step left, crossing in rear, bending knees slightly and waving arms forward, 4, 5, 6. 1 measure.
4. Step curtsy right sideward, waving arms forward. 1 measure.
B. Like A, to opposite side. 4 measures.

PART V. (20 Measures.)

A. Like A of Part I. 4 measures.
B. 1. Like B 1 of Part I. 1 measure.
C. 2. Like B 2 of Part I. 1 measure.
3. Like B 3 of Part I. 1 measure.
4. Pas de Zephyr turn right. 1 measure.
5. Pas de Basque right and left. 1 measure.

6. Like A 3 of Part IV. 1 measure.

7. Twelve running steps backward with arms sideward. 2 measures.

8. Three pirouettes right. (See B 4 of Part II.) Three measures.

9. Three running steps backward with arms sideward. 2 measures.

10. Glide right sideward, cut left sideward, 1, 2, 3; step right sideward, 4, 5, 6. 1 measure.

11. Place left foot obliquely right backward, bend knees deeply, bend trunk, circling arms forward, 1, 2, 3; straighten knees and trunk, 4, 5, 6. 1 measure.

12. Wave arms sideward and hold position, head back and chest up. 1 measure.

CRESTED HEN.

Victor Record 17,159. For description see page 157.

COME, LET US BE JOYFUL.

Victor Record 17,761. For description see page 121.

BALLOON DANCE.

Music, "Amaryllis," Victor Record 16,474.

NOTE—Hold string of balloon with both hands so as to allow free movement of balloon; right hand near balloon, left hand near end of string.

PART I. (16 Measures.)

(Begin dance on down beat; first note of second measure.)

A. 1. Starting with right foot obliquely right forward, two running steps and a balance hop right. Start with right arm down and backward and swing it to a position obliquely fore-upward. 1 measure.

2. Three running steps obliquely left backward, swinging the balloon down and back, and hold last beat of measure. 1 measure.

3. Two whole turns right in seven running steps, holding last beat of second measure. Right arm raised sideward during turns. 2 measures.

B. Repeat A to opposite side. 4 measures.

C. Repeat A. 4 measures.

D. Repeat B. 4 measures.

PART II.   (8 Measures.)

A.   1.   Step left with right foot crossing in front, 1; step left sideward, "and"; step left with right foot crossing in front, 2; swing the left leg sideward, "and."   1 measure.

2.   Repeat to the opposite side.   1 measure.

3.   Repeat A 1, making four cross steps.   2 measures.

B.   1.   Repeat A 1, 2, 3 to the opposite side, executing a pirouette instead of the last cross step.   4 measures.

Hold balloon in an easy bent arm position, hand about shoulder high, during cross steps, and during pirouette circle right arm down and inward to a position obliquely side-upward.

PART III.   (16 Measures.)

Like Part I, alternate files facing.   Individuals keep to right of opposite and move straight forward instead of obliquely forward.

PART IV.   (16 Measures.)

NOTE—The first 12 measures are done on the sides of a triangle.   Start from the apex obliquely right forward, completing the first side with measures 1 to 4; the base with measures 5 to 8; the third side with measures 9 to 12, finishing at the apex.

A.   1.   Pas de Basque sideward right.   1 measure.

2.   Pas de Basque sideward left.   1 measure.

3.   Six quick running steps forward.   1 measure.

4.   Place right foot forward.   1 measure.

B.   Repeat A on base of triangle.   4 measures.

C.   Repeat A on third side of triangle.   4 measures.

D.   Repeat A to the front.   4 measures.

During Pas de Basque right, wave right arm sideward, during Pas de Basque left, wave right arm forward and left arm sideward.   During running steps the right arm is raised backward, and with a big circling of the arm backward, upward, fore-downward, touch the balloon to the right foot as it is placed forward.

PART V. (8 Measures.)

Like Part II.

PART VI. (8 Measures.)

A. 1. Pas de Basque right sideward. 1 measure.
   2. Pas de Basque left sideward. 1 measure.
   3. With a quarter turn right six quick running steps forward. 1 measure.
   4. Place the right foot forward. 1 measure.
B. 1. As 1 of A. 1 measure.
   2. As 2 of A. 1 measure.
   3. With quarter turn left repeat 3 of A. 1 measure.
   4. As 4 of A. 1 measure.
   NOTE—Arm work like Part IV.

PART VII. (16 Measures.)

Like Part I.

PART VIII. (4 Measures.)

During the last 4 measures the balloons are gradually released and the children move backward and exit.

APPENDIX III.

Suggestions for Coaching.

The following events and suggestions were put in their present form to assist the classroom teacher in conducting track and field events. They are not intended for the use of trained or experienced coaches. When the teacher has reached this stage of experience the more advanced and technical books on these events are suggested.

It will be of great value and assistance in all athletic and physical training work to have the girls wear bloomers.

SPRINTING.
50-, 75-, 100-YARD DASH.

A sprint is a run at top speed for a distance of 20 to 220 yards. It is also the final effort at the end of a long run. In a sprint the athlete taxes himself to the utmost to secure the greatest possible speed.

The start is of great importance. In starting there are two forms, the standing start and the crouch start. The more successful form of starting on a dirt or cinder track is the crouch start. In this the stronger leg is placed forward and its distance from the scratch varies with the size of the athlete, but the distance generally ranges from 4 inches to 7 inches from the scratch. A hole, usually, is dug for the rear foot. This hole should be at right angles to the surface. Its proper distance behind the forward foot is found by placing the rear knee beside the instep of the forward foot. The arms are straight, and no part of the hands may overlap the starting line.

The athlete should take a deep breath on the signal to "get set," and rise, balancing on hands and feet, at the same time leaning a little forward. The hands and fingers assist in maintaining a firm balance. When the signal to go is given the athlete should spring forward with both feet. The arms at once move in correct opposition to the legs. After leaping forward from the impetus given by the push-off, the runner should not straighten up immediately, as this retards his progress, but should straighten up gradually. The athlete should run straight forward with natural strides, the first stride not being lengthened or shortened.

For class work the standing start is suggested as the best and most practical. The stronger leg should be placed forward, and a slight crouching position should be assumed; the forward knee should be bent and the arms should be held so they will give immediate correct opposition to the legs. The stride should be easy, natural and not forced. The knees should be brought well up; the legs should not be crossed in the rear; the toes should grip the ground; running should be on the ball of the foot. The arms should swing forward and backward, and should not cross the chest in front.

The runner should not slow up as he approaches the finish line, but should put forth his greatest effort at this point. He should keep his movements well under control, and not throw his hands up as he crosses the line, as this retards his speed. The tape at the finish must not be touched by the hands. After crossing the line the runner should slow up gradually, running from 5 to 10 yards past the finish.

Suggestions to Teachers—Class running, in couple or in squad formation, is very useful in developing form. Allow the pupils to run slowly, raising the knees high in front, weight on the ball of the foot. The arms should swing naturally, not crossing in front. In timing dashes of children a false finish may be used; that is, have the children run 5 to 10 yards past the real finish line; this avoids slowing up before the finish line is reached. Warn the children to keep their speed whether they are first or second, as they are running against time.

Occasional practice in starting will prove very beneficial—a quick getaway is very helpful. A short race is usually decided by a good start.

SHUTTLE RELAY RACE.

The equipment consists of two posts or standards placed upright in the ground 100 yards apart (for girls 75 yards apart) for each team, a baton, also a cord or rope connecting the two posts to divide the lanes.

A team consists of ten members. Five of these form in the rear of one post in a flank rank, and the other five form in rear of the other post at the opposite end of the course. At the starting signal the first runner runs along one side of the rope, holding the baton in the right hand, to the other end of the course. Here he passes the baton to the first runner at this end, who runs down the opposite side of the rope and passes the baton to the next runner. This continues until all the members of the team have run. The time is taken as the last runner crosses the starting line.

If the baton is dropped it must be recovered by the runner who dropped it.

The baton must be passed around the post. The receiver stands in rear of the post with one hand outstretched to receive the baton.

Fouls—Dropping the baton and failing to recover it. Passing the baton in front of the post.

Penalty—Disqualification of the team.

Suggestions to Teachers—As a classroom game where the teacher does not have the necessary equipment, the following is suggested: Divide the class into four teams; two of boys, two of girls. Then divide each team into two parts. Teams take their position at the end of the required distance. The race is then run as a regular shuttle relay.

Board erasers or rulers may be used as batons. If it is impossible to place posts, the last child to run on each end may be placed to act as the post around which the baton must be passed.

PURSUIT RELAY RACE.

The equipment consists of an oval or circular track and a baton. The touch-off may be made within 10 yards of either side of the scratch line, and a running start is permissible by all except the first runner. A team usually consists of four runners.

Coaching Suggestions—Special attention should be paid to the placing of the runners. The speediest man should run last, the next speediest should run first in order to get a good lead for No. 2 and No. 3 men who are slower. If both No. 2 and No. 3 men are fairly speedy, have the fastest man run third. This placing is very important if a greater number of runners than four are participating in the event on each team.

The pursuit relay may be run over any distance, the recognized relays being the 440-, 880-yard, 1-mile and 2-mile races. The training for the event depends entirely upon the distance to be run. Practice the starting and the passing of the baton. Special attention should be paid to this feature. It is advisable to have the runner who is receiving the baton stand with his back toward the inside of the track, his left foot extended forward, and have him receive the baton with the right hand.

Occasional jogs for a greater distance than the required run are beneficial in developing the wind.

Suggestions to Teachers—For class work, where a suitable track is available, the entire number participating may be divided into two teams, and if the track is narrow, one team may be placed on each side of the oval or circle. The runners from both teams encircle the track in the same direction; *i. e.*, counter-clockwise; the team having its last runner cross its own finish line first being the winner.

STANDING BROAD JUMP.

The standing broad jump must be started by toeing the mark. Where spiked shoes are used the toes should be placed up to, but not over the line. The feet should be placed fairly close together. The arms should be swung forward and upward, and at the same time the pupil should rise upon the toes. Then, bending the knees, swing the arms downward and backward. Jump on the forward swing of the arms, bringing the knees well up toward the chin, and holding a crouch position while in the air.

The landing should be made on both feet in a crouched position. The arms should be forward about shoulder high, the jumper trying to reach as far forward as possible. Where children are jumping on a dirt surface or in a pit, distance will be added to the jump by a slight straightening of the leg just before the landing is made.

Where ordinary shoes or rubber-soled shoes are used a slight toe hold over the take-off board is permissible.

A jump is measured from the edge of the take-off board to the impress nearest to the board or to the impression of the nearest heel.

Note—If the jumper falls backward measure to the nearest impress, whether it be that of hands, feet or head.

Fouls are made by the following: One-step jump; double jump; touching the pit in front of the take-off with the feet, or falling into the pit.

Suggestions to Teachers—Jumping used as a class exercise is beneficial for developing form. Teachers should watch and eliminate step jumps, double jumps, bent-arm position when jumping, etc.

Encourage children to get as much height as possible when jumping.

RUNNING BROAD JUMP

No particular physical build is necessary, as a rule, but good broad jumpers are usually persons who are tall, and who have good sprinting ability.

The equipment consists of a smooth, level runway to a pit. The take-off should consist of a joist 8 inches wide sunk into the ground. In front there is a 6- to 8-inch dug-out, beyond which extends an area of loosened soil about 25 to 30 feet in length and 8 to 10 feet in width.

The run must be at full speed, allowing about 26 feet for a start. Don't hit the take-off at too great a speed or else the spring will be broken. Two methods of measuring exist, either measuring from the edge of the take-off board or measuring from where the take-off is actually taken. The latter method is advisable in novice meets.

From the spring soar into the air, draw the knees well up. The arms should be raised fore-upward. As you are about to land, vigorously straighten the legs forward, this adds greatly to the distance. Some jumpers use the scissors kick, which consists of trailing the take-off leg with the knee bent, and then with a scissors motion snap this leg forward.

Coaching Suggestions—Have the athlete constantly practice the take-off, taking it squarely and without altering his stride, in order to hit it just right. A mark is often made about ten or twelve paces back from the board, at which the proper foot (athlete must find out which is the correct one) must strike in order to strike the board with the take-off foot without changing the stride or speed. About fifteen paces behind the first mark another is made for the start. This extra space is for gradually increasing the speed, so that by the time the first mark is reached full speed is nearly attained.

HOP, STEP AND JUMP.

Strong legs, good spring, fair speed and good body control are necessary. Broad jumpers usually excel in this event.

The equipment consists of a take-off and a level stretch beyond it about 30 feet long, at the end of which is a jumping pit 12 to 15 feet long.

With a good running start, take off with either foot and hop (landing on the same foot) then step forward with the other foot, following with a broad jump, landing on both feet. The hop must not be too long nor too high. Increase the size of the step by getting a good spring. The step is generally the weakest point in a jumper. The final effort is the same as in the broad jump, the arm movement being very important.

This event is also taken from a stand, starting either from one or from both feet.

Coaching Suggestions. They are the same as for the broad jump. Arouse the athlete's interest by measuring each part of his jump. Look for faulty interfering movements.

RUNNING HIGH JUMP.

No definite rule as to size can be made in this event, as both small and large persons have made good jumpers. Girls between 8 and 12 years may take up jumping. After menstruation is firmly established they may again participate in jumping.

The tall, strong-limbed person has the advantage. All jumpers need a good, natural spring and strength in the legs, hips and abdomen.

The equipment consists of two movable uprights, placed 6 to 8 feet apart with holes at 1-inch intervals from 1 foot 8 inches to 7 feet. Pegs fitting the holes are needed to support the crossbar. The crossbar is made of bamboo, or of light metal tubing. A line is drawn 3 feet in front of the standards, called the balk line. On the other side of the stands is the jumping pit, filled with loose soil or sawdust. Extremely peculiar styles of take-off should not be imitated by beginners. The object to be worked for is to throw the body head-high or higher, and to get the hips out of the way with a quick turn or twist. This requires practice, and should be mastered before trying for height.

There are three distinct styles of high jumping, each modified a little by individual jumpers:

1. THE STRAIGHT-OVER JUMP.

The athlete should not take too long a running start, but begin with a slow run, making the last six steps longer and with increased speed.   It is not necessary to run hard at the bar, but bound easily along.   The free leg is swung powerfully forward and upward, followed by the other leg and a sudden arching of the body, then snap the legs down quickly, landing on one or both feet.   A slight turn, left or right, may be taken to assist in getting the hips out of the way.

2. THE SCISSORS JUMP.

This is the jump most frequently used by beginners.   The landing should be made on the same foot that is used to take off with.   A turn is necessary if a good height is expected. Taking off with the left foot, start straight in front, or a little to the left, of the crossbar.   Nearing the bar, a small arc is described.   Spring from the left foot, and at the same time the right leg is powerfully kicked up.   Nearing the bar, the body is sharply turned left, thereby jerking the hips and left leg over.   If taking off with the right foot reverse this.

3. FRONT VAULT JUMP.

In this jump a half turn in either direction is made when the body is clearing the bar, the front of the body passing over the surface of the bar. When clearing the bar the free leg is swung backward and upward, the body clearing the bar facing it.   This is a spectacular jump, and the one with which the best results are attained, but is not used very often, as it requires skillful control of the body, as the result of long practice.

Coaching Suggestions—Don't do too much.   Take up practice for form first, and stay at it until it is perfect.   Call attention to the free leg. Observe the natural style of the jumper, and don't try to change it unless it prevents a good jump.   The take-off varies according to the physical build, and may be 3 feet 6 inches from the bar.   Marks to gauge the stride may also be made, similar to those in the broad jump.

BASKETBALL OVERHEAD FARTHROW.

The start should be made by toeing the line, with the feet in a side stride position. The ball should be held with the hands slightly in the rear of the ball, the fingers in a spread position. Now bend the trunk forward, bending the knees slightly, meanwhile watching the ball. Straighten the trunk, straightening the knees, and bring the ball in rear of the head, arms bent slightly, trunk bent backward. Repeat this movement several times, then, on the forward movement, deliver the ball at an angle of 45 degrees. The ball should be thrown from overhead with both hands. The delivery of the ball should always be accompanied by a "follow through" of the hands. The feet should not be moved from place (heels may be raised) until the ball touches the ground. A lane in front of the take-off should be marked with lines 1 foot apart—lines running parallel to the scratch line.

Fouls are made by hopping, jumping, touching the ground in front of the scratch line with the hands or feet, or by moving the feet in any direction, or lifting the feet before the ball touches the ground.

Coaching Suggestions—Teachers should look for fouls and warn children of the same. Use class exercise to develop form.

Have pupil use an eye mark about 50 feet away from the scratch line.

KNEE-RAISING.

Jump to a straight arm, still hang on the horizontal bar. Draw up both knees until the thighs are parallel to the floor, knees level with the hips, the upper leg forming a right angle with the trunk. Toes are pointed toward the floor.

The raising and lowering should be done in a slow, steady rhythm. Avoid all swinging of the body. Do not attempt a fast, jerky rhythm, as this causes a swinging motion of the body. Repeat the exercise as often as possible.

CHINNING.

Jump to a straight arm, still hang on the horizontal bar. Either over or under grip may be used. From this position pull up slowly until the chin is slightly above the bar. Lower slowly to the straight arm hang, and repeat as many times as possible. The legs should hang straight, and the feet should be together, and the toes pointed toward the ground.

POTATO RACE.

Equipment: Six wooden cubes about 2 by 2 by 3 inches. One basket (box or bucket) for each team.

The receptacle is placed on the scratch line (starting line). The first block is placed 6 feet beyond the start, and the other blocks every 6 feet thereafter. The finish is 10 feet in the rear of the starting line. (See diagram.)

The blocks may be gathered in any order, one at a time. They should be picked up with the right hand and transferred to the left as the runner is returning. The reverse may be used if the runner is left-handed.

The following order is suggested as being the quickest and giving the best results in competition: 6, 5, 2, 1, 4, 3.

Care should be taken not to overrun the block that the runner intends to pick up, and runners should place (not throw) the blocks in the receptacle.

Suggestions to Teachers—In place of blocks, board erasers, potatoes, stones or any small objects of uniform size may be used. If receptacles are not handy a small circle (1 foot in diameter) may be marked on the ground, into which blocks may be placed. The event may be used as a relay by having the runners alternately plant and pick the potatoes, and having a circle on the ground instead of a receptacle.

TUG OF WAR.

The team usually consists of ten members. The rope should be from 30 to 35 feet long, and at least 1 inch in diameter, and should be free from knots or holdings for the hands.

A center tape shall be affixed to the center of the rope and 3 feet on each side of center tape a side tape shall be affixed to the rope.

A center line shall be marked on the floor (or ground) and 3 feet on each side of center line a side line parallel thereto.

At the start the rope shall be taut and the center tape shall be over the center line, and the competitors shall be outside of the side line.

The pull shall be started by any prearranged signal.

The end of the pull is announced by the blowing of a whistle or by pistol.

A pull shall be won where one team has pulled the opposing team over, so that the center tape shall be over the side line. If neither team succeeds in pulling the opponents over the side line, the event shall be won when one team has secured the advantage of 6 inches at the expiration of one minute.

Suggestions to Teachers—Select contestants who have weight and strength. The best results are secured by placing the team in alternate positions along the rope. The heavier contestants should be placed toward the rear. The arms, legs and the body should be straight and inclined backward. This position should be maintained throughout the entire time of the pull. Breathing should be normal. Street clothes may be worn, also rubber-soled shoes or rubbers to prevent the feet from sliding. Individual pulling should not be tolerated. A starting signal should be used so that all will pull together.

As a class event divide the number participating into two equal teams, and pit them against each other.

HURDLING.

A good hurdler must be tall and have long and strong legs, and must be well proportioned. He must be an excellent sprinter, and have a good natural spring, also courage and determination. Timid persons rarely make good at the hurdles.

The equipment consists of ten low hurdles, each 2 feet 6 inches high, placed over a distance of 220 yards (20 yards apart). From the start to the first hurdle the distance is 20 yards; from the last hurdle to the finish the distance is also 20 yards.

High hurdles are ten in number, each 3 feet 6 inches high, placed over a distance of 120 yards. The hurdles are 10 yards apart, there being 15 yards between the start and the first hurdle, and 15 yards between the last hurdle and the finish.

Each hurdler has a separate row of hurdles.

Low Hurdles—The high and the low hurdles each demand a different style. In the high hurdles three strides are taken between the hurdles; in the low, seven strides. The take-off is about two yards from the hurdles. In the jump over each hurdle 12 to 13 feet is covered. The shorter that distance can be made the faster the time. It is important to reach the first hurdle with the correct foot. The clearing should be as low as possible without hitting. Don't soar over, but take the hurdle in the stride. The forward leg is swung directly forward and pointed somewhat upward. The rear leg immediately follows in a way that the entire exertion resembles an elongated stride. This is where long legs assist. Seven strides between jumps is used by all champions. Clearing the hurdles in 13-foot strides leaves the remaining 47 feet to be covered in seven strides. In all other respects this race is the same as the 220-yard dash.

High Hurdles—This event is essentially different from the low, in that there are but three strides between the jumps. Take the hurdles at a moderate speed. The forward leg is swung forward and pointed well up. The rear leg follows with a lateral motion, turning the leg outward. This will bring the knee over without soaring too high. The same rule to skim over the hurdles applies here. The rear foot must be well pointed, so the toes don't hook. The jump covers 12 feet or less. In landing, the forward leg snaps down in a forward direction. Be careful not to lose balance, for in regaining it time is lost.

Coaching Suggestions—Teach first, form in clearing the hurdles. Then the start and taking the first hurdle. Practice springs to acquire speed and quarter-mile runs for endurance. Pay especial attention to skimming the hurdle, the correct take-off and the landing, with the forward leg pointing directly forward. Then practice on three hurdles, increasing the number of hurdles as greater efficiency is developed.

If the athlete tries out for both hurdles, start him on the high ones first. Care should be taken that form for each style is taught correctly, as faults once acquired are hard to break.

Suggestions to Teachers—The above rules are for standard hurdle races.

In the elementary schools or for girls it is suggested that the number of hurdles be decreased, and that the height of the hurdles be lowered to suit the individuals. The distance between hurdles should be decreased, but the fundamental distance should be kept; that is, keep seven strides between the low hurdles, and three strides between the high hurdles. In this manner correct form can be taught.

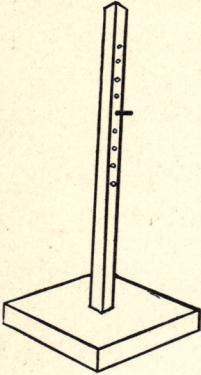

If it is impossible to obtain regulation hurdles an imitation of the regulation jumping standard may be made in the shop.

A wooden base 1½ feet square and an upright made of 2-inch square wood, the height to be determined by the size of the athletes. Starting at 1 foot above the base and continuing every 2 inches dowel pins are placed, extending outward about 1 inch. Then use as a crossbar a light wooden bar or a rope with weighted ends.

APPENDIX IV.

Competitive Mass Athletics.

The success of mass competition in athletic sports as a means for rapidly improving the physical fitness of young men drafted for army service has created a great interest in these forms of bodily exercise.

Most communities, naturally, do not have the space nor the time or equipment necessary to undertake all the forms of competition that were used in the army training camps. In the following we have, therefore, gathered a number of standard events and indicated methods of conducting them that will be useful in competition among individuals as well as among teams.

These events have been grouped as follows:

A. Track Events.
B. Field Events.
C. Combative Events.
D. Team Games of Low Organization.
E. Handicap and Combination Races.
F. Stunts.

A. TRACK EVENTS.

1. *Running*—It is wise to use standard distances, so as to be able to compare your results with those obtained elsewhere.

The standard distances are 40, 50, 75, 100, 220, 440 yards, ½ mile and 1 mile.

The team events are the straight relay, the shuttle relay race, and the return relay race. (See notes, p. 365.)

2. *Hopping*—Because of the strenuous nature of the exercise the distances should be short.

The standard distances are 10, 15, 20 and 25 yards.

The team events are the straight relay, the shuttle relay and the return relay race.

3. *Hurdling*—Hurdling is a combination of running and step-jumps. The standard distances are 120 and 220 yards, with ten hurdles.

The hurdles are either low, with 2 feet 6 inches or high, with 3 feet 6 inches. For children and for women these heights and distances, also the number of hurdles should be reduced.

B. FIELD EVENTS.

1. *Jumping*—Broad, high, or broad-high.

The jump may be performed from a stand or after a preliminary run or hop.

The exercise itself may be either a jump, or a hop, or a step.

The distance may be covered by a succession of jumps, or hops, or steps; or by a combination of two or three. The most frequently used jumps of the combination type are the hop, step and jump, and the triple standing broad jump.

2. *Throwing*—An object may be thrown for distance, for height or for accuracy. The throw may be from a stand, from a run, from a spring-start and from a turn. The possibilities are mentioned (in parentheses) at the end of each event.

The standard events are:

1. Basketball farthrow, (a) overhead forward, (b) overhead backward (stand).
2. Round arm basketball farthrow (stand, spring-start, run).
3. Baseball farthrow, also for accuracy (stand, run).
4. Hurlball farthrow (stand, spring-start, run, turn).

Additional events are:

5. Javelin farthrow, also for accuracy (stand, run).
6. Discus farthrow (stand, turn).

3. *Putting*—Putting always is for distance. As a rule a solid shot is used, although a medium weight medicine ball also can be used. The standard weights are 8, 12, 16 pounds (stand, turn).

4. *Football Kicking*—As a rule the oval ball is used for these events, although the round football also may be used. The standard events are:

1. A kick-off.
2. A drop kick.
3. A punt.

NOTES RELATING TO A AND B.

Running may be done forward, sideward with crossing legs, and backward.

There are also the following additional forms: Bent-knee running; bent-body running; running with a complete turn at some specified place, or with a roll forward or backward. Run forward on all fours, also backward and sideward, rabbit jump forward (frog jump). Use a jumping rope or hoop and perform various stunts during the race. Roll over a player placed in the center of the track, then continue the run. Egg-race; balance a basketball overhead on one hand while running; man lifting at some specified place; wheelbarrow race.

The following are the commonly accepted terms for relay races, and the forms of their execution:

1. Straight relay (straight away).
2. Shuttle relay (to and fro).
3. Return relay (run to a certain place and back again; useful in gymnasium for stunts on apparatus, obstacles).
4. Double return relay (perform some stunt in the middle and return).
5. Double shuttle relay (perform some stunt in the middle and then run and touch off the player on the opposite side).

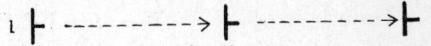

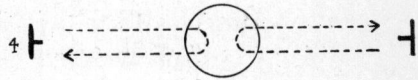

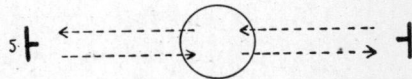

"Double" means that the first player on both parts of the team starts off at the same time, and performs some stunt in the middle before running to the opposite side and touching off the next player (shuttle) or before returning to the same side.

Jumping in team competition may be in the form of "progression," during which the next team member begins where the preceding one finished. It also may be in the form of "jump and return," "to and fro." In this form the first team member jumps, whereupon the first member of the opposite team "returns" by jumping in the opposite direction from the landing spot of the first jumper. This latter form is used where there is limited space or where large numbers must be handled.

C. COMBATIVE EVENTS.

1. *Wrestling*—These combative events consist of exercises whose object it is to struggle, fight or wrestle with an opponent and force him to give up his position, or force him to release something, to give up something.

   1. Hand wrestling (give up stand).
   2. Wrist wrestling (give up stand).
   3. Wand wrestling (give up wand or cane).

2. *Pushing*—These pushing events may take place either with both feet on the ground or while hopping.

   1. *Shoulder push*, both hands against opponent's shoulders.
   2. *Wand push*, either on one, or between two wands; (a) face opponent, (b) back to opponent.
   3. *Pole push*, as 2, only have two, three or more opponents at each end.
   4. *Roll over*, sitting on ground, wand under knees and between elbows.

3. *Pulling*—These pulling events may take place either with both feet on the ground or while hopping.

   1. *Hand pull*, grasp opponent's hand or wrist.
   2. *Wand pull*, either on one or between two wands; (a) face opponent, (b) back to opponent, (c) sitting on ground.
   3. *Pole pull*, as 2, only have two, three or more opponents form a team. *Tug of war.*
   4. *Hopping Contest*—(Rooster fight).

   1. *Free hop*, both opponents are free to hop anywhere.
   2. *The siege*, one opponent stands with one foot in a circle. The other hops during his attack. This event may be made more strenuous by having two or more attackers.

D. TEAM GAMES OF LOW ORGANIZATION.

Only such games are mentioned as may be played by large groups without any special training.

1. *Tag Games*—Day or Night, Stoop-tag (pairs and teams), Rabbits.
2. *Ball Games*—Circle Dodgeball, Endball, Battleball, Hurlball, Captain Dodgeball, Progressive Dodgeball, Towerball, Circle Teacherball.
3. *Miscellaneous Games*—Passball (overhead, underneath), Potato Race, Spin the Platter, Catch the Wand.

E. HANDICAP AND COMBINATION RACES.

1. *Handicap Races—*
1. Sack Race.
2. Three-legged Race.
3. Centipede Race.
4. Knapsack Race.
5. Obstacle Race.
6. Squat Race.
7. Squat Race by team connected through hands on front shoulders.
8. Exchange Race, consisting of divesting oneself of various pieces of clothing, and, on the return trip, again putting them on, also of exchanging parts of clothing with other team members at various specified times during a race.

2. *Combination Races—*There are innumerable combinations of the events enumerated above. But all possible combinations are not usable, and many that are usable are not advisable, or they may even be dangerous for certain age-groups. A wise selection is, therefore, necessary. In the following a limited selection of good combinations are presented.

In many cases hopping may take the place of running.

(a) *Running and Throwing.*

Each team member runs a definite distance and then throws a ball. This ball throw may be for accuracy, for instance, into a basketball goal, or over a rope stretched at a definite height. In case the race is in form of a shuttle the throw also may be into the hands of the next team mate.

(b) *Running and Vaulting.*

The runner during the race vaults over a piece of apparatus before proceeding or before returning.

The apparatus may be a horse, parallel bars, horizontal bar, etc.

(c) *Running and Hurdling or Jumping.*

The runner may encounter one or more hurdles; or after running a certain distance he must perform a step-jump over a mattress lying on the floor, or a series of step-jumps over several mattresses lying in a row, etc.

(d) *Running and Climbing*.

After running a certain distance the runner must climb over a double boom placed in his path, or over a scaling wall, or up one rope and down the next, or up one side of a ladder and down on the other side, etc.

F. STUNTS.

(a) *By Individuals*.

There are numerous stunts gladly performed by the average boy or girl, as well as by adults, that lend themselves well to competitive ends. The standard events are (1) chinning; (2) hand stand against a wall, also free hand stand; (3) head stand; (4) upper arm stand; (5) walking on the hands; (6) cartwheel; (7) bending backward against a wall; (8) bend the crab; (9) wind through a stick held in hands; (10) wind through a small hoop; (11) wind through a stick held vertically, one end resting on the floor; (12) hitch-kick; (13) leap-frog; (14) raise leg forward, bend to a full squat and rise; (15) jump over a stick held in both hands, forward, backward; (16) jump up with a complete turn (this jump can be made quite difficult if the landing must be in specified areas or if the body must assume specified positions when landing; (17) jump over one leg, the foot of which you hold with the opposite hand (forward and backward); (18) jump over one leg, the foot of which is placed against a wall (this necessitates a turn about while jumping); (19) push back (from a wall); (20) lie flat on back, rise up with folded arms; (21) long reach and return to standing position (hands may touch floor only once).

(b) *By More Than One Person*.

(22) Hip swing-up on a stick held on the shoulders of two; (23) caterpillar roll forward by twos, threes or more; (24) caterpillar roll backward by twos or more; (25) stand on knees of partners; (26) stand on shoulders of partners; (27) hand stand on knees of partners; (28) hand stand on hands of partners (very difficult).

APPENDIX V.

Additional Playground Activities.

Most forms of track and field work can be used for playground activities. The size and surface of the ground, as well as the age and sex of the players, must always be taken into consideration when making a selection. Running over various distances should always be selected. Then the different kinds of jumping (standing jump, running jump, hop, step and jump, jumping over low hurdles, etc.) are useful. Vaulting over low objects appeals to girls as well as to boys, and may be indulged in as follows: Vaulting over a rope while swinging on the giant stride, vaulting over a rope by means of a pole (pole vaulting); vaulting over a low horizontal bar. Walking, running or skipping on a balance-beam (a small telegraph pole placed horizontally at one side of the playground), also vaulting over the same, are admirable exercises of skill which appeal to players of all ages. Where there is a good jumping pit filled with sand, deep jumping from a jumping tower, or a ladder, or a high box is an exercise that not only appeals to most young players, but which at the same time develops courage to a high degree.

As indicated in the preface, competition brings with it a strong inclination to participate oftener in track and field events. This competition may be in the form of reaching or surpassing a record established by a champion, or a standard set by some officials. Now, while there are championship records for all imaginable events, these, obviously, are of no service to the teacher on a playground. What is needed for playgrounds are standards set by playground workers which the average boy and girl will be able to reach. The following "Age Standards" or "Class Aims" have been in use in Philadelphia for some time, and are safe guides of what may be expected of children of certain ages:

383

CHART BASED UPON AGE, SHOWING AIMS IN TRACK AND FIELD EVENTS.

For Girls and Boys 8 to 15 Years (Inclusive) in Elementary Schools.

30-YARD DASH (In Seconds and Fifths).

Years	8	9	10	11	12	13	14	15
Girls	6.4	6.4	6.3	6.2	6.1	6.0	5.4	5.3
Boys	6.2	6.1	6.0	5.4	5.3	5.2	5.1	5.0

40-YARD DASH (In Seconds and Fifths).

Years	8	9	10	11	12	13	14	15
Girls	8.3	8.2	8.1	8.0	7.4	7.3	7.2	7.1
Boys	8.0	7.4	7.3	7.2	7.0	6.4	6.3	6.2

50-YARD DASH (In Seconds and Fifths).

Years	8	9	10	11	12	13	14	15
Girls	9.4	9.3	9.2	9.1	9.0	8.4	8.3	8.2
Boys	9.2	9.0	8.4	8.3	8.1	8.0	7.4	7.3

75-YARD DASH (In Seconds and Fifths).

Years	8	9	10	11	12	13	14	15
Girls	15.2	14.3	14.1	13.4	13.3	13.2	13.1	13.1
Boys	14.0	13.3	13.1	12.3	12.1	11.4	11.2	11.0

100-YARD DASH (In Seconds and Fifths).

Years	8	9	10	11	12	13	14	15
Girls	19.1	18.3	17.1	16.4	16.3	16.2	16.1	16.1
Boys	19.1	18.3	17.1	16.1	15.2	15.0	14.1	13.2

STANDING BROAD JUMP (In Feet and Inches).

Years	8	9	10	11	12	13	14	15
Girls	3.8	3.10	4.0	4.2	4.4	4.6	4.8	4.10
Boys	4.0	4.4	4.6	4.10	5.0	5.2	5.6	5.10

RUNNING BROAD JUMP (In Feet and Inches).

Years	8	9	10	11	12	13	14	15
Girls	5.5	5.6	5.10	6.0	6.2	6.4	6.7	6.9
Boys	6.0	6.6	7.0	8.3	9.3	10.0	10.2	10.5

TRIPLE STANDING BROAD JUMP (In Feet and Inches).

Years	8	9	10	11	12	13	14	15
Girls	10.4	10.6	11.4	11.10	12.6	12.9	12.11	15.4
Boys	12.0	12.3	13.0	13.9	14.6	15.3	16.0	16.9

RUNNING HOP, STEP AND JUMP (In Feet and Inches).

Years	8	9	10	11	12	13	14	15
Girls	9.2	11.6	13.8	14.6	15.5	15.6	16.4	16.6
Boys	10.0	13.0	16.4	18.0	18.8	19.9	21.7	23.0

RUNNING HIGH JUMP (In Feet and Inches).

Years	8	9	10	11	12	13	14	15
Girls	2.2	2.5	2.8	2.9	2.10	3.2	3.2	3.2
Boys	2.2	2.5	2.8	2.10	3.0	3.1	3.2	3.3

BASKETBALL OVERHEAD FARTHROW (Feet).

Years	8	9	10	11	12	13	14	15
Girls	15	17	19	21	23	25	27	28
Boys	17	19	21	23	25	27	30	33

BASKETBALL ROUND ARM FARTHROW (Feet).

Years	8	9	10	11	12	13	14	15
Girls	13	15	17	19	22	25	28	30
Boys	19	22	26	29	33	37	42	47

PLAYGROUND BASEBALL FARTHROW (Feet).

Years	8	9	10	11	12	13	14	15
Girls	23	26	30	35	43	48	53	54
Boys	38	47	57	67	77	88	102	108

CHINNING (Times).

Years	8	9	10	11	12	13	14	15
Boys	0	0	0	1	2	3	4	4

KNEE RAISING (Times).

Years	8	9	10	11	12	13	14	15
Girls	4	8	12	16	25	28	30	30

ROPE CLIMBING (Feet).

Years	8	9	10	11	12	13	14	15
Girls	3	3	3	3	3	4	4	5
Boys	8	10	12	13	14	15	16	17

HIGH SCHOOL BOYS.

TABLE OF PHYSICAL EFFICIENCY BASED UPON AGE, HEIGHT, WEIGHT.

F indicates fair, G good, E excellent.

Age	Ht.	Wt.	50-Yard Dash (Seconds and Fifths).			Standing Broad Jump (Feet and Inches).			Running Broad Jump (Feet and Inches).			Running High Jump (Feet and Inches).		
			F.	G.	E.	F.	G.	E.	F.	G.	E.	F.	G.	E.
	52	60	...	...	...	5.0	5.6	6.0	9.0	10.6	11.0	2.6	2.8	3.6
11......53	53	65	9.0	8.2	7.2	5.0	5.9	6.3	9.0	10.8	11.2	2.6	2.10	3.6
	54	70	...	...	...	5.0	6.0	6.6	9.0	10.10	11.4	2.6	3.0	3.6
	53	65	...	...	...	5.3	5.9	6.3	9.3	10.9	11.4	2.8	2.10	3.7
12......55	55	70	8.4	8.1	7.1	5.3	6.0	6.6	9.3	11.0	11.6	2.8	3.0	3.7
	57	75	...	...	...	5.3	6.3	6.9	.9.3	11.3	11.8	2.8	3.2	3.7
	55	70	...	...	...	5.6	6.0	6.6	9.9	11.2	11.8	2.10	3.0	3.8
13......57	57	78	8.3	8.0	7.0	5.6	6.3	6.9	9.9	11.6	12.0	2.10	3.1	3.8
	59	85	...	...	...	5.6	6.6	7.0	9.9	12.0	12.3	2.10	3.3	3.8
	60	75	...	...	...	5.8	6.3	6.9	10.0	11.6	12.0	2.10	3.1	3.9
14......61	61	88	8.2	7.4	6.4	5.8	6.6	7.0	10.0	12.0	12.6	3.0	3.2	3.9
	62	100	...	...	...	5.8	6.9	7.3	10.3	12.6	12.10	3.0	3.4	3.9
	60	88	...	...	...	5.10	6.5	7.0	10.0	11.9	12.4	3.0	3.2	3.10
15......62	62	100	8.1	7.3	6.3	5.10	6.8	7.5	10.3	12.3	12.8	3.2	3.3	3.10
	64	120	...	...	...	5.10	6.11	7.5	10.6	12.9	13.0	3.3	3.5	3.10
	62	100	...	...	...	6.0	6.6	7.3	10.6	12.0	12.8	3.2	3.3	3.10
16......64	64	115	8.0	7.2	6.2	6.0	6.10	7.5	10.6	12.6	13.0	3.3	3.4	3.11
	66	130	...	...	...	6.0	7.0	7.7	10.9	12.9	13.6	3.4	3.6	4.0
	62	105	...	...	...	6.2	6.7	7.4	11.0	12.3	13.0	3.3	3.4	4.0
17......65	65	125	7.4	7.2	6.1	6.4	7.0	7.7	11.0	12.9	13.6	3.4	3.5	4.1
	68	140	...	...	...	6.6	7.2	7.10	11.0	13.0	14.0	3.5	3.7	4.2
	63	120	...	...	...	6.4	6.9	7.6	11.6	12.6	14.0	3.4	3.5	4.1
18......66	66	135	7.3	7.1	6.0	6.6	7.2	7.9	11.6	13.0	14.6	3.5	3.6	4.2
	69	150	...	...	...	6.6	7.4	8.0	11.6	13.6	15.0	3.6	3.8	4.3
	64	123	...	...	...	6.4	6.10	7.8	12.0	13.0	14.6	3.5	3.6	4.2
19......67	67	138	7.3	7.1	6.0	6.6	7.4	7.11	12.0	13.3	14.9	3.6	3.7	4.3
	69	153	...	...	...	6.8	7.6	8.2	12.0	13.9	15.0	3.7	3.10	4.4
20......68	68	141	7.3	7.1	6.0	6.8	7.5	8.2	12.6	13.6	15.0	3.7	3.8	4.4

HIGH SCHOOL BOYS.

TABLE OF PHYSICAL EFFICIENCY BASED UPON AGE, HEIGHT, WEIGHT—Continued.

F indicates fair, G good, E excellent.

Age	Ht.	Wt.	Basketball Farthrow (feet).			Chinning (times).			Climbing Rope (feet).			Standing Vault Over Bar.
			F.	G.	E.	F.	G.	E.	F.	G.	E.	
	52	60	15	25	30	2	5	6	..	..	..	F Height of navel
11.......53		65	15	25	30	2	5	6	9	14	20	G Height of nipples
	54	70	15	25	30	2	5	6	..	..	..	E Height of shoulders
	53	65	16	26	32	2	5	7	..	..	..	F Height of navel
12.......55		70	16	26	32	2	6	7	9	15	20	G Height of nipples
	57	75	17	27	32	2	6	7	..	..	..	E Height of shoulders
	55	70	17	27	33	2	6	7	..	..	..	F Height of navel
13.......57		78	18	28	34	3	6	8	10	16	20	G Height of nipples
	59	85	18	28	34	3	6	8	..	..	..	E Height of shoulders
	60	75	19	28	35	3	6	8	..	..	..	F Height of navel
14.......61		88	20	30	38	3	7	8	11	16	20	G Height of nipples
	62	100	20	30	38	4	7	9	..	..	..	E Height of shoulders
	60	88	20	30	36	4	7	9	..	..	..	F Height of navel
15.......62		100	21	32	38	4	7	9	12	17	20	G Height of nipples
	64	120	22	34	38	5	7	9	..	..	..	E Height of shoulders
	62	100	22	32	38	5	7	9	..	..	..	F Height of navel
16.......64		115	22	34	40	5	7	9	13	18	20	G Height of nipples
	66	130	23	36	40	5	7	9	..	..	..	E Height of shoulders
	62	105	23	34	42	5	7	10	..	..	..	F Height of navel
17.......65		125	24	36	44	5	7	10	14	19	20	G Height of nipples
	68	140	25	38	46	5	7	11	..	..	..	E Height of shoulders
	63	120	25	36	48	5	7	11	..	..	..	F Height of navel
18.......66		135	25	38	49	5	7	12	15	20	20	G Height of nipples
	69	150	25	40	50	5	7	12	..	..	..	E Height of shoulders
	64	123	26	38	50	5	7	12	..	..	..	F Height of navel
19.......67		138	26	40	51	5	7	12	16	20	20	G Height of nipples
	69	153	26	42	52	5	7	12	..	..	..	E Height of shoulders
												F Height of navel
20.......68		141	27	42	52	5	7	12	16	20	20	G Height of nipples
												E Height of shoulders

HIGH SCHOOL GIRLS.

TABLE OF PHYSICAL EFFICIENCY BASED UPON AGE, HEIGHT, WEIGHT.

F indicates fair, G good, E excellent.

Age	Ht.	Wt.	50-Yard Dash (In seconds and tenths).			Indoor Baseball Farthrow (Feet and Inches).			Running Broad Jump (Feet and Inches).		
			F.	G.	E.	F.	G.	E.	F.	G.	E.
	56	79	8.1	8.4	7.2	37	40.5	46	7.8	8.6	9.4
12......	59	91	8.0	7.4	7.1	39	44.9	50	8.2	9.0	10.0
	61	101	8.0	7.4	7.2	38	42.8	48	8.4	9.0	10.5
	57	84	9.0	8.1	7.3	37	43.6	48	7.3	8.4	9.4
13......	60	97	8.4	8.2	7.4	41	49.4	63	7.5	8.2	9.7
	62	107	9.0	8.1	7.4	40	44.8	58	6.10	7.9	8.7
	58	89	9.0	8.2	7.3	37	44.9	53	6.11	7.8	8.7
14......	61	104	8.4	8.1	7.1	41	49.8	62	7.8	8.3	9.11
	63	113	9.0	8.2	7.3	45	51.9	67	7.10	8.6	10.1
	59	95	9.1	8.3	7.4	39	46.1	60	6.5	7.2	9.0
15......	62	111	9.0	8.2	7.2	47	52.4	70	7.9	8.2	9.9
	64	119	8.4	8.0	7.1	44	51.0	67	8.0	8.5	10.0
	60	102	8.4	8.0	7.1	44	50.2	63	8.2	9.1	10.2
16......	63	117	8.4	8.0	7.1	48	53.5	74	8.0	8.9	10.0
	65	123	9.0	8.1	7.2	47	52.10	71	8.1	8.10	10.1
	61	109	9.0	8.1	7.3	42	50.3	62	7.11	8.5	10.0
17......	64	121	9.0	8.4	7.2	48	53.2	71	8.0	8.8	10.3
	66	127	8.4	8.0	7.2	49	59.10	74	8.5	9.4	10.6
	62	115	8.4	8.0	7.1	45	51.5	65	8.1	8.11	10.5
18......	65	125	9.0	8.2	7.3	48	57.10	72	8.0	8.9	10.4
	67	130	8.3	8.0	7.1	41	49.2	58	8.7	9.7	10.9
	62	116	8.4	8.1	7.3	45	53.5	65	8.2	9.4	10.4
19......	65	126	8.3	8.0	7.1	46	55.1	71	8.6	9.6	10.7
	67	131	8.4	8.2	7.4	48	58.8	73	7.6	8.0	8.8
20......	66	130	8.4	8.2	7.4	44	58.8	73	7.0	7.8	8.5

EVENTS AND STANDARDS FOR ATHLETIC ABILITY TESTS

Purpose: To stimulate interest and further participation in athletics.

Eligibility: To be eligible for the tests a pupil must:

1.   Be under 14 years of age for Test I and under 17 years of age for Tests II and III.

2.   Have nearly or completely attained the standards of the test to be taken.

3.   Have passed the age aims.

TEST I.

(15-Year Standards.)

BOYS.

Standing broad jump	5 feet 10 inches.
Ball throw, overhead	33 feet.
50-yard dash	7 3-5 seconds.
Ball throw, free style	45 feet.

GIRLS.

Standing broad jump	4 feet 10 inches
Ball throw, overhead	28 feet.
50-yard dash	8 2-5 seconds.
Ball throw, free style	35 feet.

TEST II.

(17-Year Standards.)

BOYS.

Standing broad jump	6 feet 6 inches.
Ball throw, overhead	39 feet.
75-yard dash	10 2-5 seconds.
Ball throw, free style	60 feet.
Chinning	6 times.

Standing broad jump.......................... 5 feet 2 inches.
Ball throw, overhead.......................... 30 feet.
50-yard dash .... 8 seconds.
Ball throw, free style......................... 45 feet.
Chinning .... 1 time.

TEST III.

(19-Year Standards.)

BOYS.

Standing broad jump.......................... 7 feet 2 inches.
Ball throw, overhead.......................... 42 feet.
100-yard dash .... 13 seconds.
Ball throw, baseball (100 feet)................. 2 times.
Chinning .... 8 times.
Swimming, free style.........................220 yards.

GIRLS.

Standing broad jump.......................... 6 feet.
Ball throw, overhead.......................... 33 feet.
75-yard dash .... 11 seconds.
Ball throw, free style......................... 50 feet.
Chinning .... 2 times.
Swimming, free style.........................220 yards.

RULES GOVERNING THE TESTS.

1.   Two trials will be allowed in the jump, ball throw overhead and ball throw, free style.

2.   The ball throw, free style, is construed to mean any single-arm throw. To be a fair throw the contestant must not go beyond the scratch line.

3.   In the baseball throw for accuracy, the contestant must hit a circular target 6 feet in diameter, suspended so that the lowest point is 6 inches from the ground, at least twice out of five trials. The contestant must not go beyond the scratch line.

4. Only one test shall be given to a contestant in one day (swimming may be given on another day).

5. On failure to pass any one event, the contestant shall be eliminated from the test for that day.

6. Official tests will be conducted by the Division of Physical Education as follows:

Test   I.   At convenience of the supervisor.

Test II.   At convenience of the supervisor.

Test III.   In June.

AWARDS.

The Division of Physical Education will award the winners of:

Test   I.   A Bronze Seal Certificate.

Test II.   A Red Seal Certificate.

Test III.   A Blue Seal Certificate.

Upon the successful completion of Test III, the contestant is privileged to buy an especially designed gold pin attesting the fact of his athletic efficiency.

APPENDIX VI.

*Quiet Games, Experiments, Problems, Etc., for Warm Days.**

SIMON SAYS, "THUMBS UP."

The players are seated or stand in a circle. The leader says, "Simon says, 'Thumbs up' " (down, wiggle-waggle, or any movement), at the same time turning his thumbs as he says, and is followed by all the players. If, however, he omits to say, "Simon says," he may do the movement, but no one else may, only those movements preceded by the words, "Simon says," being imitated.

BIRD CATCHER.

The children sit or stand in a circle, with the "bird catcher" in the middle. Each child is given the name of some bird. The leader tells a story which occasionally brings in the name of a bird. At the mention of a bird the player assigned its name quickly raises his hands and brings them down again. When the owl is mentioned (no one is given this name) all children must place their hands behind the back and hold them there until another bird is mentioned. The catcher tries to seize a hand whenever it is moved. A player whose hand is caught or who does the wrong thing must change places with the catcher.

ARMS, LEGS AND TRUNKS.

A circle is formed, the place of each player being marked with chalk, or in any other way. One of the players, standing in the center, points to any one in the circle, saying, "Arm" (or leg, or trunk), and then counts rapidly to ten. If the player to whom he points does a movement with the part mentioned before the leader finished counting, the leader goes on and points elsewhere, until some one fails to do a movement with the part called for. This player then steps out of the circle. The leader may at any time call out "Change," when all must change places. Whoever fails to secure a place becomes the next leader.

* Most of these games can be played in classrooms as well as in playgrounds.

FLY AWAY.

The children are seated with their hands in their laps. When the leader starts the game by raising his hands and saying, "Fly away, mosquito," or "Fly away, bat," or "Fly away, robin," or "Fly away," followed by the name of any other thing that flies, the rest of the players are to raise their hands and wave them. When he says, "Fly away," followed by the name of something that does not fly, the players are not to raise their hands, although the leader raises his. Any one making a miss either by not raising the hands at the right time or by raising the hands at the wrong time is out of the game. The winner is the one who remains after all the rest are out.

BUZZ.

The participants are seated in a circle, or around the room. One person begins by saying, "One," the next "Two," the counting continuing around the circle; but, whenever the number "seven" is reached, or any multiple of seven, as fourteen, twenty-one, etc., or any number having the word seven in it, as seventeen or twenty-seven, it must not be given, but in its place the person says "Buzz," and the following number is counted by the next player. On the failure of any one to say "Buzz" at the proper time, he is dropped from the circle. Thus the game proceeds, usually commencing with "one" again each time a person misses, until but one player is left to score the victory. Some action or movement, as clapping of hands, etc., can be substituted for the speaking of the word "Buzz."

SAVE YOURSELF IF YOU CAN.

The group of players form in a semi-circle or in a straight line, and before them stands a "story-teller." The story-teller tells a story in which occur the words, "Save yourself if you can." As soon as these words are pronounced all the players repeat them, then rush to a distant goal, stamp the ground three times (knock three times, clap hands three times, or, do something else, mutually agreed on, three times), then return to the starting point. The first one to arrive becomes the next story-teller. Any player who does not perform the required act three times is shut out from the game.

TOSSING THE CAP.

The players are seated or stand in two lines facing each other, while the leader tosses up a cap so that it will alight between the lines and in sight of every one. If it alights top up, one side (as agreed upon before) laughs; if bottom up, the other side laughs. If any one laughs when he should not, he steps out of the game. Those made to step out may, later, be made to run the gauntlet, or receive some other kind of punishment.

ADVANCING STATUES.

The children stand on a line about thirty feet from the teacher or some older pupil, who acts as leader, and faces away from the players. The leader counts ten before turning. The counting may be fast or slow, regular or irregular. When the leader faces them the players are to remain as motionless as statues, but when his back is turned they may advance. By turning unexpectedly at irregular intervals the leader seeks to catch the children in motion. A child detected in motion must go back to the line and start over again. The child first crossing the line on which the teacher stands is the winner.

HOW MANY ANGLES?

Give each pupil three pea sticks (or toothpicks, matches, etc.) and let him see how many angles he can form with them. No number may be repeated—that is, if the three sticks have been laid to form two angles, the next formation must show three, the next four, the next five, etc.

As a variation, have each pupil with the three sticks form angles in as many ways as possible. As soon as an angle has been formed draw it upon a piece of paper. At the end of five minutes see who has formed the greatest number of angles. No angles less than forty-five degrees to be counted, nor variations less than five degrees.

Another variation is to see how many right angles may be laid with the same number of sticks.

FLOATING FEATHER.

Divide the players into several groups, each group forming a circle. One player in each circle starts the game by blowing a feather up into the air. The object of the game is to keep the feather up in the air within the circle.

BUTTON, BUTTON, WHO HAS THE BUTTON?

Have the players seated in a circle. One player starts a button (or some other small object) around the circle. All players move one or both hands rapidly from side to side, so that the player who is "it" finds it difficult to locate the button. The player having the button when tagged is "it."

A variation of this game is to have a long rope upon which a hammock ring (a key or some other object) has been strung. This ring is passed rapidly from right to left, the tagger trying to locate it.

WHAT AM I THINKING OF?

The leader thinking of some object, says: "What am I thinking of?" Each of the other players names some object which he surmises the leader is thinking of. After all have guessed the leader names the object which he had in mind. Each of the guessers must then tell why the object which he guessed is like the object named by the leader. If the leader thought of a book and a door had been guessed he says: "Why is a door like a book?" A good answer would be, "Because you can open and shut both of them." One who guessed a tree might answer, "Because they both have leaves." For a bell the answer might be, "Because they both attract our attention." Strained resemblances must often be made use of in order to justify guesses, but this will only add to the interest and merriment of the game. One who first guesses correctly becomes the leader for the next round. The game may be varied by guessers telling why their thought is *not* like that of the leader.

ROPE AND RING.

The pupils are arranged in a circle, standing almost shoulder to shoulder, with both hands on a rope or strong twine. One child is in the center. Somewhere on the rope is a ring. At a signal, all begin to move both hands on the rope; the ring is then on its way around, the child in the center trying to locate it. If he is successful, the one who had the ring takes his place in the center.

EARTH, AIR AND WATER.

The pupils being seated in a circle, one of the number who has a knotted handkerchief or some other suitable object, calls out "earth," and throwing the handkerchief at some one, begins to count ten. The person who receives the handkerchief must mention the name of some animal before the ten counts are concluded, or he pays a forfeit. He then throws the handkerchief to some other player, calling either earth, air or water, and the game goes on. If "air" is called, the name of a bird must be given, if "water" that of a fish.

With older players other groups of things may be added to those mentioned—
e. g., flower, signifying that the player must mention a flower, or city, when he must name a city, etc., etc.

A TALK-FEST.

On rainy or hot days playground teachers often are at their wits' end to devise means of entertainment and diversion for their pupils. A game that never fails to hold the interest of the crowd for a long time is a "talk-fest." The players are seated in a circle, or in a group.

Two pupils enter the contest, the object of which is to have one pupil out-talk the other. Neither participant is allowed to smile. Who laughs or smiles is out. Who stops talking is out. What is said need have no sense, the thing is to keep on talking until one opponent gives up or until by ludicrous remarks one player has made the other smile or laugh.

HIT OR MISS.

Place a large inflated paper bag, a paper hat, an empty flower pot, a tin can, or something of like character on a spot definitely marked as the "home." Blindfold a player who has a stick in his hand, and who is standing directly in front of the "home." Upon command this person faces away from the object and takes twelve steps forward. He then again faces about, and walks back to where he imagines the object is. He then is allowed three vertical strikes at the object (not horizontal). When played as a team game a hit counts one point and the members of the teams alternate.

CHARADES.

The players are divided into two groups. One group acts out some word like fare, swim, shoot, etc. The other group guesses what is being represented. As an aid to the guessing side it is customary at the beginning of the game to state that what group number one is going to represent rhymes with another word. For instance, if shoot were to be acted, boot would rhyme with shoot. In another case, hymn would rhyme with swim, hair with fare, etc. When a performance has been rightly guessed the other group performs.

SIMPLE EXPERIMENTS.

At Times, These Simple Experiments Will Be as Welcome to Older Pupils in Playgrounds as the "Quiet" Games Are.

One of the best ways to get pupils to think is through experiments. Children like to see things, and when they observe any physical phenomenon, they wish to know the cause, and will reason for a long time upon a simple experiment to explain "what made it do that." The following attractive and interesting experiments with air can be performed with 10 cents' worth of glass tubing and 10 cents' worth of rubber tubing. The bottles and corks pupils will gladly bring from home.

EXPERIMENT No. 1.

Matter is defined as anything that occupies space. Is air matter?

Place a cork on a pan of water; over it place an inverted tumbler and press down. The cork is seen on the surface of the water at the bottom of the pan. The water does not rise in the tumbler because the air is there. We see that air occupies space, therefore is matter.

EXPERIMENT No. 2.

Matter possesses energy. Energy is the ability to produce motion. Does air possess energy?

Into a bottle put some water. Through a tightly fitting cork make a hole with a round file. Through this run a glass tube, letting it dip into the the water. Now blow through the tube and the air will bubble through the water and be compressed in the bottle above the water. When you remove your mouth the compressed air will force the water out of the tube in a fountain, thus producing motion. To work well the bottle should be large and the tube drawn to a point by holding it in the flame of an alcohol lamp. (This lamp can be made by putting a glass tube through a cork in an ink bottle, and drawing a rag through the glass tube for a wick).

EXPERIMENT No. 3.

Has the atmosphere pressure? To answer this question, thrust a glass tube into a bottle of water. Place the finger over the upper end and lift the tube up. The atmospheric pressure holds the water up in the tube.

Experiment No. 4.

Fill a tumbler with water, place a card over it and invert it. The atmospheric pressure holds the card on and the water up in the tumbler.

The tumbler can be placed on the table and the card drawn from under it, and the tumbler will remain upside down on the table, filled with water. Then the card can be slipped under again and the tumbler of water lifted from the table.

Experiment No. 5.

Two tumblers can be placed with the tops together under water and lifted from the water and set in a quiet place. They will remain filled for a long time.

A chicken's watering cup can be made by placing a fruit jar filled with water, mouth downward, in a saucer. A thin chip can be placed under the jar to let a little water run into the saucer.

Experiment No. 6.

Thrust a pin through the center of a card one inch square and place this on a spool with the pin in the hole of the spool to hold it from slipping off. Now blow through the other end of the spool. You cannot blow the card off. Why?

Experiment No. 7.

An air-pump which will show atmospheric pressure very effectively can be made by taking a gallon bottle, nearly filled with water. Fit it with a two-holed cork. Through one hole run a glass tube to the bottom of the bottle. To the top of the glass tube fasten a rubber tube two feet long, making a siphon. Through the other hole in the cork fit a short glass tube. On the lower end fasten a small rubber balloon. Now suck on the rubber tube, and as the water flows out of the bottle the atmosphere will press in through the tube and expand the balloon.

This also shows the principle of respiration. As the intercostal muscles enlarge the chest, the air rushes into the lungs. The device can also be used for a condensing pump by reversing the action and letting water run into the large bottle.

Experiment No. 8.

Another way to exhaust air is with an inspirator, which can be made by making a small hole in the side of a piece of rubber tubing, and through this hole, forcing a glass tube and running it down the rubber tube two inches or more. Now let water run through the glass tube and on through the rubber tube. The water rushing down will suck air in through the free end of the rubber tube and take it down with the water out of the lower end of the tube.

Experiment No. 9.

A machine to make gas for the Bunsen burner can be made by half filling a bottle with gasoline and fitting it with a two-holed cork. In one hole fit a glass tube which extends into the gasoline. Into the other hole fit a tube which extends just through the cork. To the outer end attach a tube leading to the Bunsen burner. Blow in the free tube and light the gas.

Experiment No. 10

To make a Bunsen burner, fit a piece of cardboard over a piece of glass tubing that has been bent once at right angles, to make it rest on the table, and again at right angles, to make it stand up. Over this set a larger glass tube, or piece of iron pipe, four inches long and a half inch in diameter and let it rest on the cardboard. Pin-holes can be made in the cardboard to let in air from the bottom and another card slipped up and down on the tube to regulate the amount of air.

To make a complete gas plant, break a piece out of the bottom of a gallon bottle, holding the edge of the bottom in the flame of a lamp. This will crack out a small piece. Set this in a small tin pail of water and let the lower end of the tube in Experiment No. 8 run in at the bottom of the bottle through the break. Now lead a tube from the cork of the bottle to the gasoline bottle and the gas plant is ready to work.

INDEX

Ace of Diamonds (Danish Folk Dance), 119.
Additional Playground Activities, 383.
Advancing Statues, 75, 395.
Alumni Three-Step, Dance (Music, "The Dorothy"), 253.
Amaryllis (Music for the Balloon Dance), 361.
Animal Blind Man's Buff, 50.
Annie Goes to the Cabbage Field, 63, 64.
"April Smiles" (An Aesthetic Dance), 322.
Arms, Legs and Trunks, 393.
A Spanish Couple Dance (Music: "Santiago"), 156.
A Talk-Fest, 397.
Athletic Ability Tests, 389.
Athletic Events (Coaching), 365.

Baby in the Hat, 135.
Bag Board, 38.
Bag in the Ring, 38.
Bag Relay, 52, 95.
Ball Games, Easy, 25, 38, 52, 72.
Ball Relay, 94.
Balloon Dance (Music: "Amaryllis"), 361.
Base Dodgeball, 141.
Baseball as Playground Ball, 101.
Baseball Drill (Music: "Chin-Chin Fox Trot"), 354.
Baseball, Foot, 222.
Baseball, Wall, 213.
Basketball Far Throw, 129, 372.
Basket Endball, 143.
Battle Ball, 207.
Beanbag Catching, 26.
Beetle Is Out, The, 50.
Bird Catcher, 393.
Black Man, 69.
Black Nag, The (English Folk Dance), 158.
Bleking (Swedish Folk Dance), 86.
Blind Man's Buff, Animal, 50.
Block Baseball, 147.
Bluff King Hal (English May-Pole Dance), 198.
Bound Ball, 26.
Break Through, 69.
Broncho Tag, 110.

Butterflies, The, 15.
Butterfly Dance (Music: "Eros"), 153.
Button, Button, Who Has the Button? 395.
Buzz, 394.

Captainball, 171.
Captain Dodgeball, 211.
Carrousel, The (Swedish Folk Dance), 44.
Cat and Mouse, 23, 35.
Catching the Beanbag, 26.
Catch the Wand, 37, 69.
Catch Me, 38.
Change Seats, Change, 51.
Change Tag, 35.
Charades, 397.
Charts Showing Age Aims in Track and Field Events—
    For Elementary Schools, 384, 385.
    For High Schools, 386, 387, 388.
Chase Ball, 96.
Chicken Market, 74.
Children's Quickstep, Dance (Music: "The Wind"), 79, 80.
Children's Polka (German Folk Dance), 45.
Chimes of Dunkirk (French Folk Dance), 29.
Chinning, 372.
Circle Pins, 168.
Circle Relay Race, 215.
Circle Tag, 73.
Civilization, Dance, 346.
Clap Dance (Swedish Folk Dance), 87.
Coaching, Track and Field Events, 365.
Combative Events, 380.
Combination Volleyball, 216.
"Come, Let Us Be Joyful" (German Folk Dance), 121.
Come, Little Partner, 54.
"Coming Through the Rye," Dance, 353.
Competitive Mass Athletics, 377.
Cornerball, 102.
Crested Hen (Danish Folk Dance), 157.
Cupid and Butterfly (Music and Dance), 189, 194.
Czebogar (Bohemian Folk Dance), 159.

Dance of Greeting, 32.
Dance with Me, 56.

Dayball, 54.
Day or Night, 73.
Did You Ever See a Lassie, 4.
Dodgeball—
    Stand, 38.
    In a Circle, 136.
    Double, 140.
    Base, 141.
    Progressive, 164.
    In Three Fields, 167.
    Run, 167.
    Fox and Chickens, 182.
    Captain, 211.
"Dorothy, The" (Music for The Alumni Three-Step), 249.
Drills (Free Exercises, with Marching, Athletic Events, etc.), 263-315.
Drop the Handkerchief, 2.
Duckstone, 52.

Earth, Air and Water, 396.
Elf's Frolic, The, Dance (Music: "See Saw"), 82.
Endball—
    Form I, 104.
    Form II, 106.
"Entr' Acte Gavotte," Dance for Girls, 317.
"Eros" (Music for Butterfly Dance), 149.
Events and Standards for Athletic Ability Tests, 389.
Experiments, 398.

Fairies, The, Dance (Music: "Spring Song"), 60, 61.
Farmer in the Dell, The, 13.
Field Ball, 209.
Field Events, 378.
First of May, The (Swedish Song Game), 46.
Floating Feather, 395.
Fly Away, 394.
Folk Dances—
    American—
        The Needle's Eye, 6.
    Bohemian—
        Annie Goes to the Cabbage Field, 63, 64.
        Czebogar, 159.
    Danish—
        Dance of Greeting, 32.
        Shoemaker's Dance, 62.

Ace of Diamonds, 119.
Three Dance, 122.
Crested Hen, 157.
    English—
        Black Nag, 158.
        Oats, Peas, Beans and Barley, 7.
        Jolly Is the Miller, 12.
        Sweet Kate, 119.
        Gathering Peascods, 196.
        May-Pole Dance (Music: "Bluff King Hal"), 198.
        Rufty Tufty, 259.
    French—
        Chimes of Dunkirk, 29.
    German—
        Little Sister, Come with Me, 27.
        My Brother, 41.
        Children's Polka, 45.
        Come, Let Us Be Joyful, 121.
        May Day, 182.
    Hungarian—
        Ritka, 261.
    Irish—
        Irish Lilt, 200.
    Norwegian—
        Mountain March, 66.
    Scotch—
        Highland Schottische, 257.
    Swedish—
        How D'ye Do, My Partner, 5.
        Our Little Girls, 30.
        I See You, 39.
        The Carrousel, 44.
        The First of May, 46.
        Gustaf's Greeting, 64.
        Bleking, 86.
        Hop, Mother Annika, 86.
        Clap Dance, 87.
        Tantoli, 88.
        Reap the Flax, 201.
        Oxdansen, 257.
Follow the Leader, 25.
Foot and a Half, 134.
Foot Baseball, 222.
Foot in the Ring, 72.
Fox and Chickens, 53.
Fox and Chickens Dodgeball, 182.
Frolic of the Brownies—
    Form I, 239.
    Form II, 241.

Games for Children Under Nine Years, 23-26.
Gathering Peascods (English Folk Dance), 196.
Goal Ball, 220.
Goal Throw, 130.
Group Contests, 295.
Guess Who, 53.
Gustaf's Greeting (Swedish Folk Dance), 64.

Handball, 208.
Handicap and Combination Races, 381.
Hand Pulling Contest, 70.
Hand Pushing Contest, 71.
Hand Tag, 25.
Hand Tennis, 145.
Hand Wrestling, 126.
Hat Ball, 135.
Hat on Back, 135.
"Here, There and Everywhere" (Music for Free Exercise Drill), 275.
Highland Schottische (Scotch Folk Dance), 256.
"Hindustan" (Music for Athletic Drill), 310.
Hit or Miss, 397.
Hoop Toss, 36, 93.
Hop, Mother Annika (Swedish Folk Dance), 86.
Hopping Contests, 92.
Hopping Races, 49.
Hop Scotch, 131.
Hop, Step and Jump, 369.
How D'ye Do, My Partner, 5.
How Many Angles, 395.
Human Burden Race, 91.
Human Hurdle Race, 178.
Human Hurdle Circle Relay Race, 215.
Hurdling, 374.
Hurl Ball Far Throw, 129.

Indian Dance (Music: "Natoma"), 350.
Indians, The (Song for Indian Boys), 349.
"In the Arena" (Music for Free Exercise Drill), 266.
"In the Barn" (Music for Dance, The Jolly Crowd), 113.
"In Lilac Time" (Music for Free Exercise Drill), 287.
Irish Lilt, 200.

I See You (Swedish Folk Dance), 39.
Isoline (Aesthetic Dance), 358.

Jacob, Where Are You, 37.
Jolly Crowd, The, Dance (Music: "In the Barn"), 116, 117.
Jolly Is the Miller, 12.
"Jolly General, The" (Music for Free Exercise Drill), 298.
Jump—
    Standing Broad, 368.
    Running Broad, 369.
    Hop, Step and Jump, 369.
    Running High, 370.
Jumping Circle, 98.
Jumping Circle Race, 214.
Jumping Circle Relay Race, 216.
Jump Over, 37.
Jumping Rope, 24, 37, 39, 70, 94.

"Keeping Step with the Union" (Music for Free Exercise Drill), 293.
Kick Ball in a Circle, 212.
Knee Raising, 372.

Lame Goose, 69.
"Larkspur" (Music for Normal School Mazurka), 184.
Last Pair Run, 73.
Leap Frog, 70.
Let Us Chase the Squirrel, 3.
Little Sister, Come with Me, 27.

Marching Drill, 302.
"Marcia Militaire" (Music for Free Exercise Drill), 296.
"Marsovia Waltz" (Aesthetic Dance for Girls), 320.
Mass Athletics, 377-382.
Mass Exercises for Exhibitions, 377-382.
May Day (German Folk Dance), 182.
May-Pole Dance (Bluff King Hal), 198.
Medicine Ball, 96.
"Moon Winks" (Music for Free Exercise Drill), 306.
Mountain March (Norwegian Folk Dance), 66.
Muffin Man, The, 9.
My Brother (German Folk Dance), 41.

"National Emblem March" (Music for Free Exercise Drill), 271.

Needle's Eye, The, 6.

Normal School Mazurka, Dance (Music: "Larkspur"), 187.

Number Race, 111.

Nymphs, The, Aesthetic Dance (Music: "The Waltz Is Made for Love"), 324.

Oats, Peas, Beans and Barley, 7.

O'Leary, 76.

"Old Faithful" (Music for Free Exercise Drill), 263.

"Officer of the Day March" (Music for Free Exercise Drill), 279.

Off for a Ride, 14.

One by One, 10.

"Our Director March" (Music for Free Exercise Drill), 291.

Our Little Girls, 30.

Overhead Far Throw, 372.

Overtake, 127.

Oxdansen (Swedish Folk Dance), 257.

Pageant—The Revival of the Play Spirit in America—Program, 329.
    Action of the Pageant, 332.
    Characters and Properties, 337.
    Costumes, 339.
    Description of the Dances, 344.

"Parade of the Wooden Soldiers," Dance, 315.

Pass Ball, 127, 128.

Pinball, 222.

Playful Sprites, The, Dance (Music: "Parade of the Wooden Soldiers"), 315.

Playground Roundel (Music: "Summer Breezes"), 85.

Poison, 92.

Potato Race, 53, 373.

Pretty Birdie, 17.

Prisoner's Base, 163.

Progressive Dodgeball, 164.

Promotion Ball, 98.

Pulling Contests, 70, 72.

Pull Over, 72.

Punch Ball, 164.

Pursuit Relay, 367.

Pushing Contests, 71.

Puss in the Circle, 51.

Pussy Wants a Corner, 49.

Quiet Games for Warm Days, 393.

Quoits, 93.

Rabbits, 125.

Racing, 24, 37.

Reap the Flax (Swedish Folk Dance), 201.

Red Rover, 74.

Relay Races, 52, 91, 95, 128, 215, 216, 367.

Relievo, 131.

Rider Ball, 207.

Rig-a-Jig-Jig, 20.

Ring Toss, 93.

Ritka (Hungarian Folk Dance), 261.

Rob and Run, 133.

Rope and Ring, 396.

Rufty Tufty (English Folk Dance), 259.

Running Broad Jump, 369.

Run Dodgeball, 167.

Running High Jump, 370.

Running Races, 24, 49.

Running and Hopping Races, 49.

Safety Tag, 143.

"Santiago" (Music for Spanish Couple Dance), 155.

"Sari" (Music for Free Exercise Drill), 281.

Save Yourself if You Can, 394.

"See Saw" (Music for Dance, The Elf's Frolic), 81.

"Secret, The" (Aesthetic Dance), 344.

"Shepherd's Dance" (From Pageant), 352.

"Shoemaker's Dance" (Danish Folk Dance), 62.

Shoulder Pushing Contest, 71.

Shuttle Ball Relay, 181.

Shuttle Relay Race, 366.

Simon Says, "Thumbs Up," 393.

Simple Experiments, 398.

Skip Tag, 25.

Snow Frolic, 18.

Soccer Football—
    Form I, 141.
    Form II, 178.
    Form III, 234.

Song Games for Children Under Nine Years, 1-22.

Spanish Couple Dance (Music: "Santiago"), 155.

Spin the Plate, 36.

Sprinting, 365.

"Spring Song" (Music for The Fairies' Dance), 60.

Squat Tag, 25.

Stand Ball, 99.

Standing Broad Jump, 368.

Stand Dodgeball, 38.

Statues, 75, 395.

Stick-I-Spy, 126.

Stunt Drill for Boys, 311.

Stunts, 382.

"Summer Breezes" (Music for Playground Roundel), 83.

Sweet Kate (English Folk Dance), 119.

Tag, 25, 35, 49, 73, 97.

Tag Football, 216.

Talk-Fest, 397.

Tantoli (Swedish Folk Dance), 88.

Teacherball, 26.

Team Games of Low Organization, 380.

"Teddy Bears' Picnic" (Music for Free Exercise Drill), 283.

Tetherball, 172.

The Beetle Is Out, 50.

The Black Nag (English Folk Dance), 158.

The Butterflies, 15.

The Carrousel (Swedish Folk Dance), 44.

"The Dorothy" (Music for The Alumni Three-Step, Dance), 249.

The Elf's Frolic (Music: "See Saw"), 82.

The Fairies, Dance (Music: "Spring Song"), 60, 61.

The Farmer in the Dell, 13.

The First of May (Swedish Folk Dance), 46.

The Indians (Song for Indian Boys), 349.

The Jolly Crowd, Dance (Music: "In the Barn"), 116, 117.

"The Jolly General" (Music for Free Exercise Drill), 298.

The Miller, 12.

The Muffin Man, 9.

The Needle's Eye, 6.

The Nymphs, Aesthetic Dance (Music: "The Waltz Is Made for Love"), 324.

"The Parade of the Wooden Soldiers" (Music for The Playful Sprites, a Dance), 315.

"The Secret" (Aesthetic Dance), 344.

"The Thunderer" (Music for Free Exercise Drill), 302.

"The Waltz Is Made for Love" (Music for The Nymphs, a Dance), 324.

"The Wind" (Music for Children's Quickstep), 78.

Third Tag and Run, 49.

Three Broad, 111.

Three Dance, The (Danish Folk Dance), 122.

Three Deep, 97.

Three Pins, 214.

"Thunderer, The" (Music for Free Exercise Drill), 302.

Tossing the Cap, 395.

Toss Up, 72.

Tower Ball, 130.

Track Events, 377.

Track and Field Events, Coaching Suggestions, 365.

Trades, 74.

Tug of War, 373.

Two Deep, 98.

Variations of Standard Games and Events, 203.

Venus Reigen (Music and Dance), 244, 247, 248.

Virginia Reel, 160.

Volleyball—
Form I, 100.
Form II, 170.
Form III, 227.
Combination, 216.

Wall Ball, 129.

Wall Baseball, 213.

"Waltz Is Made for Love, The" (Music for The Nymphs, Aesthetic Dance), 324.

Wand Pushing Contest, 71.

Warball, 169.

Water Sprite, 54.

We All Stand Here, 1.

What Am I Thinking Of? 396.

What Are You Doing in My Garden? 23

Wicket Ball, 223.

Wild Man's Field, 110.

Will You Dance With Me? 56

"Wind, The" (Music for The Children's Quickstep), 79, 80.

Wrestle for the Wand, 70.

Wrestling Contests, 126.

Wrist Wrestling, 126.

Books on
Physical Training and Games

By

WILLIAM A. STECHER, M. P. E.

Director of Physical Education, Public Schools of Philadelphia, Pa.
Secretary, Committee on Physical Training, American Gymnastic Union
Editor of "Mind and Body"

··✦✦❉✦··

GAMES AND DANCES

A selected collection of Games, Song-Games and Dances suitable for Schools, Playgrounds, Gymnastic Associations, Boys' and Girls' Clubs, etc. Fourth edition. 8vo, Cloth. Price, net $3.00; parcel post extra.

This book presents a large collection of Games, Song-Games, and Dances arranged in nine progressive grades for different Age-groups, and suitable for use in Schools, Playgrounds, Gymnastic Associations, Boys' and Girls' Clubs, etc.

For convenience in selecting, there are arranged in appendix form the following:

1. Twenty-one Drills and Dances suitable for exhibitions, Field Days, Play Days, and Pageants.
2. "The Revival of the Play Spirit in America," a complete Pageant, with action, program, costumes and dances.
3. Suggestions for coaching athletic events.
4. Competitive Mass Athletics, with Tables of Track and Field Aims and Records.
5. Additional Playground Activities.
6. Quiet Games and Experiments for warm days.

PHYSICAL TRAINING LESSONS
Including Games, Dances, Stunts, Track and Field Work

An illustrated handbook for the Classroom Teacher. Seventy-four Half-Tone Illustrations and Five Line Drawings. 8vo, Limp Cloth. Net $2.50

Normal schools and colleges after they have trained their pupils in the art of teaching, are confronted by the problem of placing in the hands of these inexperienced teachers a usable text book on elementary physical training.

With this thought in mind, Mr. Stecher has written a book for the classroom teacher in elementary schools, rural or urban.

The minimum requirements in the essential and fundamental phases of physical education are stated clearly and concretely, so that the classroom teacher can understand them. Many illustrations add to the value of the text.

For teachers working under favorable conditions, or for teachers specially trained, supplementary material is added. All games, dances, tests, drills are described and illustrated. No other book is needed.

"Physical Training Lessons," therefore, is a book that any college or school that is training classroom teachers can safely recommend to its students and graduates.

Physical Education Normal Colleges also can safely recommend "Physical Training Lessons" to those of their graduates who must supervise or teach physical education in schools and who need a handbook.

"Physical Training Lessons" is the result of experience in solving the problems of giving to the great mass of boys and girls in the elementary schools types of muscular work that appeal to them.

Special rates will be given to boards of education, teachers' colleges, normal schools, summer schools, etc., that will adopt the book as a text.